THE ENLIGHTENED PATROLMAN

CONFLUENCIAS

Series Editors

Susie S. Porter
University of Utah

María L. O. Muñoz
Susquehanna University

Diana Montaño
Washington University in St. Louis

The Enlightened Patrolman

EARLY LAW
ENFORCEMENT IN
MEXICO CITY

Nicole von Germeten

UNIVERSITY OF NEBRASKA PRESS   LINCOLN

© 2022 by the Board of Regents of
the University of Nebraska

The poem in chapter 2 was previously published in Daniel Palma Alvarado, ed., "Los cuerpos serenos y el origen de las modernas funciones policiales en Chile (siglo xix)," *Historia* 49, no. 2 (2016): 510. English translation by Nicole von Germeten.

All rights reserved

The University of Nebraska Press is part of a land-grant institution with campuses and programs on the past, present, and future homelands of the Pawnee, Ponca, Otoe-Missouria, Omaha, Dakota, Lakota, Kaw, Cheyenne, and Arapaho Peoples, as well as those of the relocated Ho-Chunk, Sac and Fox, and Iowa Peoples.

Library of Congress Cataloging-in-Publication Data
Names: Germeten, Nicole von, author.
Title: The enlightened patrolman : early law enforcement in Mexico City / Nicole von Germeten.
Description: Lincoln : University of Nebraska Press, [2022] | Series: Confluencias | Includes bibliographical references and index.
Identifiers: LCCN 2021060193
ISBN 9781496219466 (hardback)
ISBN 9781496233073 (paperback)
ISBN 9781496233295 (epub)
ISBN 9781496233301 (pdf)
Subjects: LCSH: Law enforcement—Mexico—Mexico City—History. | Crime prevention—Mexico—Mexico City—History. | BISAC: HISTORY / Latin America / Mexico | HISTORY / Modern / 18th Century
Classification: LCC HV8161.M6 G47 2022 | DDC 363.2/3097253—dc23/eng/20220621
LC record available at https://lccn.loc.gov/2021060193

Set in Adobe Caslon by Mikala R. Kolander.
Designed by N. Putens.

CONTENTS

List of Illustrations   vii

Preface   ix

Introduction   1

1. Light   29

2. Men Walking the Beat   61

3. To Protect and Serve   93

4. Nightlife   123

5. Guards in Trouble   155

6. Guards under Attack   185

7. The Night Watchmen, the Military, and Insurgency   213

Conclusion   245

Afterword: Mexico City Law Enforcement after Independence   251

Notes   265

Bibliography   307

Index   329

ILLUSTRATIONS

1. Sketch of a Mexico City lantern   38
2. Ramo number 23   65
3. Ramo number 86   65
4. Arrests by time, recorded in *Libros de Reos*   132
5. Cuartel 1   133
6. Cuartel 4   139
7. North section of Cuartel 4 (with sections of Cuartel 7 and 1)   140
8. Central city   141
9. Neighborhood around the pulquería del Palacio   142
10. Ramo number 23   144

TABLES

1. Names of the Mexico City guardas mayores   75
2. Detained children   109
3. Reos sent to the Hospicio de Pobres in the 1790s   113
4. Group attacks on lanterns   193
5. Military men in the *Libros de Reos*   220
6. Military men in the head guard's nightly report   231

PREFACE

For over three hundred years, European monarchs maintained a complex political system in very populous regions of America, areas highly valued for producing wealth to fuel international trade and war and to support the lavish spending of Old and New World aristocrats representing both church and state. Kings ruling from across the Atlantic Ocean knew that royal laws and courts, adapted to on-the-ground circumstances, provided a powerful backbone that could sustain their empires for a much longer duration than simple brute force. At its core, imperialism demanded different legal statuses for a range of colonial settlers, including those who could claim European ancestry, the millions of descendants of Indigenous peoples who continued to live in this geographic space, and the hundreds of thousands of African-descent individuals, most of whose forebearers endured enslavement and the Middle Passage in previous centuries. The empire examined in this book established a biased court system that viewed certain colonial subjects as childlike, barbaric, and prone to vice, a poor work ethic, and extreme, life-destroying substance abuse. Fearing accelerating and diverse urban population growth, the most powerful royal officials joined forces with the capital city government to create street patrols, made up of working-class men who acted as foot soldiers in a system that incarcerated, flogged, and imposed forced work sentences on men and women who violated the European vision of civilized behavior, justifying this new form of law enforcement as protection against crimes such as murder and robbery. Maybe this sounds like the history of somewhere in the South, Northeast, or Midwest of the United States, but this description in fact sums up the context for the changes in late colonial urban law enforcement in New Spain, especially the viceregal capital of Mexico City.

Many nations in the Americas continue to experience the repercussions of centuries of colonialism and legal slavery, a history that naturalizes and reinforces differences in access to and treatment in schools, courts, and financial institutions while limiting occupational opportunities based on place of origin, language, culture, and appearance—what we sum up with the word "race," a term not widely used in the modern sense during the era examined in this book. Although historians hope that our work helps today's students clarify their understanding of the hierarchies and injustices that they inherited and how they affect their lives now, still "we are condemned to repeat the past whether we remember it or not."[1] Yet, bright and hopeful signs have emerged. In the months I spent writing a first draft of this book, popular interest emerged in examining the history behind the 2020 national crisis.[2] Even the most popular mainstream media discussed the fact that early U.S. rural policing included slave patrols.[3] This book addresses this thirst for knowledge about the history of policing within the context of an inheritance of the effects of slavery and imperialism, and with an emphasis on how this history affects class difference, race-based government policies, and street-level resistance leading to political revolution.

Over the course of the book, readers will learn about the debates surrounding illuminating the center of Mexico City, the Mexican patrolmen's basic occupational duties and routines, biographical information about them as plebeian men, how they had to adapt to the demands made by the populace, as well as the nocturnal patterns of drinking to excess by urban residents, the guards' disciplinary problems, and finally the continuous resistance they faced while on the job. My first overall hypothesis is that the implementation of urban reform, which colonial leaders envisioned as beautifying and securing the city for its property-owning residents, actually created nightly opportunities for plebeian opposition to the viceregal state. At the same time, increasing surveillance of the populace provided very little in the way of a deterrent against the lively and occasionally tragic culture of public intoxication. A close reading and detailed analysis of almost four thousand interactions between the night watchmen and those urban residents who occupied the city streets at night suggests that the patrolmen represented a target for popular complaints and even violent and destructive rage against Spanish rule. More broadly, their history can teach us a great deal about the origins of policing in the largest metropolis of the late eighteenth-century Western Hemisphere. Forgotten by many North Atlantic scholars of police history, Mexico City's night watchmen merit a place in the historiography of law enforcement in the Western world. Deriving from European street patrols, especially in France and Spain, their experience shows how very early forms of policing enforced racial hierarchies in New World colonies and in the modern nation states that emerged from these imperial outposts.

This book starts with the history of street illumination (chapter 1), then turns to who exactly were the night watchmen (chapter 2), how the populace shaped their role as proto-first responders (chapter 3), and the patterns of drinking in nocturnal Mexico City (chapter 4). It then examines instances where the guards themselves faced accusations by their superiors (chapter 5) or experienced verbal or physical attacks by plebeians and soldiers on the street (chapters 6 and 7).

I enjoyed a great deal of support from my students, colleagues, and family while researching and writing this book. The dean of the College of Liberal Arts at Oregon State University, Larry Rodgers, always encouraged me to continue my scholarship while I held an administrative position as the unit head for the School of History, Philosophy, and Religious Studies. Our office staff Suzanne Giftai and Natalia Bueno frequently stepped in to help with small and large tasks, including attempting to scan an awkward large map and create a mock-up book cover. Dean Rodgers and Dean Marion Rossi approved funding for research trips to Mexico City, and Suzanne Giftai helped with the logistics.

I am lucky for the inspiring work of history students at Oregon State University, ranging from undergraduates to advanced doctoral students. David Ford helped me extensively with data entry tasks and photographing pages of the *Libros de Reos*, the logbooks of the Mexico City night watchmen. Ismael Pardo continued this task. David, Ismael, and Aimee

Hisey all worked with me at the Archivo General de la Nación in Mexico City, providing me with many laughs and moral support. These students received funding to work at the archive from generous donors via the OSU Foundation. While advancing her own scholarship, Aimee also read all the drafted chapters, corrected errors in the footnotes, and standardized the bibliography. Picabo Fraas helped me analyze the thousands of entries in the *Libros de Reos*.

My kind and generous history colleagues Kara Ritzheimer and Marisa Chappell inspired me and edited my work over many years in our beloved writing group. I would not have completed this book without their help and guidance from the perspectives of modern United States and German history. The anthropology faculty at OSU was gracious enough to invite me to present for them in the fall of 2020. The vibrant and inquisitive audience made this a very encouraging experience.

The best possible dissertation mentor, Professor William B. Taylor, provided support, encouragement, and perceptive suggestions to improve the book. Thank you to Bridget Barry and the anonymous reader for University of Nebraska for your belief in the value of this project. Only I am to blame for any remaining errors. I am grateful to Michael Lopez for humanizing the patrolman's experience, for listening to me during my struggles, and for believing in my abilities. Finally, I dedicate this book to my friend and inspiration, my daughter Inez Ayrey. Thank you for your kindness, energy, and constant companionship.

THE ENLIGHTENED PATROLMAN

Introduction

He went to the *alcalde*'s house. Finding it locked up, he called out. Some women came out, asking him, "Who are you? What do you want?" He said he was the night watchman, and that he had four in custody. The women went back into the house and told this to the alcalde. Then the women came to the door again and passed on the order that he should take the offenders to the San Pablo bivouac. Taking this order under advisement, he made it clear to the woman that he could not carry it out because he was on duty alone and could not leave his beat.
—Corporal number 3, August 9, 1791

The events narrated above resulted in a verbal altercation between the night watchman Manuel José Bernal and a volunteer neighborhood-level judicial official with the title of *alcalde del barrio*.[1] The dispute took place at 10 p.m. the night before.[2] Imprisoned for allegedly insulting the alcalde later the same night, the next day Bernal described the incident to a senior administrator of the viceroyalty, don Bernardo Bonavía de Zapata. These brief lines hint at several of the fundamental characteristics and conflicts built into law enforcement operating at the level of city streets, including confusing and conflicting jurisdictions, insufficient coverage, and most importantly for this book, push back from the general populace.[3]

This book delves into the origins of street-level policing in the Western Hemisphere by examining the history of the first professional night watchmen corps in a large American city that served as seat of government.[4] Just under one hundred men patrolled predetermined neighborhood beats in Mexico City, then the capital of the viceroyalty of New Spain. This patrol originated in 1790, as part of an ongoing series of reforms of the justice system, and endured past the insurgency movement against Spain, which commenced in 1810. While of interest to historians in terms of understanding late colonial criminal patterns, the administration of justice reforms, and masculinity, the men known as *serenos*, or *guarda faroleros* (literally lantern guards), have not received an intensive examination as working-class men whose presence every night patrolling the urban streets influenced broader political movements in the decades preceding and during mass revolt in New Spain.[5]

This is the first book-length study concentrating on New Spain's late colonial night watchmen, starting with their connection to the establishment of publicly funded street lighting in the viceregal capital and ending with their deadly street clashes with the military during the decade-long struggle for Mexican independence. The story begins with the fragmented surviving artefacts of José Bernal's biography, his career trajectory, and his nightly routine. These glimpses into Bernal's life are situated in the Mexico City of his time and contextualized within royal reforms affecting the viceroyalty of New Spain, trans-Atlantic Spanish imperial policies, and changing patterns of policing in Spain and the North Atlantic. While Bernal's origins go back to a small Indigenous village, and his orbit probably encompassed no more than two hundred square miles, his experiences fit into a global history of modernizing law enforcement, a continuous process of trial and error in European and American nations that unfolded over at least the past three centuries.[6]

Competing Courts in Late-Eighteenth Century Mexico City

Bernal worked as a lantern guard patrolling several blocks of central Mexico City, a section of town known as *ramo* (literally meaning "branch") 23. He owed his job to the recent efforts of Juan Vicente de Güemes, the second Count of Revillagigedo, who ruled as the Viceroy of New Spain from 1789 to 1794. Viceroy Revillagigedo had just established this new guards' corps less than ten months before the altercation described in the epigraph. Along with many other duties detailed by this book in the chapters that follow, these men maintained a new grid of lanterns illuminating the dark streets of the court city.

INTRODUCTION

With only three decades remaining until New Spain transformed into an independent empire and later the Republic of Mexico, the night watchmen represented a very late addition to a complex, multilayered approach to imperial law. As always when a new royal reform came to the Americas, competition ensued with preexisting institutions. Bernal experienced this himself during the aforementioned incident, when he was dismissed by the alcalde's serving women, before being yelled at and insulted by the alcalde himself. These confusing and overlapping courts, officials, and jurisdictions represented a purposeful strategy by the kings of Spain as they juggled their massive New World territories. Along with embracing a conquest ideology in the medieval era, monarchs in different regions of the Iberian Peninsula consolidated their rule by codifying laws and courts from the thirteenth century onward. Many of the structures that arrived in the Americas with the conquistadors derived from a centuries-long process of negotiation. The situation was further confused by the existence of competition between an expanded, royally sponsored judiciary and urban citizens advocating for autonomous municipal governments. State and civic institutions clashed with the wide-ranging powers of the church and powerful aristocrats. Finally, after centuries of royal consolidation, by the sixteenth century the Spanish vision of global imperialism derived in part from an understanding of the king as the source of justice.[7]

As a result of these developments, in the final decades of the viceroyalty, the new night watchmen joined a crowded array of institutions. As hinted at in Bernal's troubles on the night of August 8, from the 1520s, Mexico's viceregal court city hosted a variety of competing municipal and royal officials. These included: a town council (*cabildo* or *ayuntamiento*) led by the *alcalde de primer voto*, who was a kind of city mayor; the *corregidor*, another leading royal official with tasks relating to the justice system; and a high court (*real audiencia*), which had a *sala de crimen* (criminal court) and functioned as a kind of supreme court, with oversight over other judicial officials throughout the viceroyalty.[8] The cabildo, manned by American-born creoles and European-born Spaniards, funded the efforts to increase the orderliness and general upkeep of the city, financed by taxes and income from city-owned properties. The corregidores and the sala de crimen handled longer, more in-depth criminal investigations and trials. Several hundred of these records survive for the late eighteenth and early nineteenth centuries.[9] Because it is outside the scope of this book, I do not go into further detail regarding the other very important local arbiters of justice, including the archbishop, who had oversight over any disputes relating to sacramental interactions with the Catholic Church, as well as loosely and sporadically surveilling Christian morals. And of course, we cannot forget the infamous Tribunal of the Holy Office of the Spanish Inquisition, whose *causas de fe* dealt with offenses against the church. Many of the above institutions also dealt with civil cases, even the Holy Office.

The establishment of the guarda faroleros extended a trend of judicial reform that began in earnest in the eighteenth century, with the rebirth of the Santa Hermandad in New Spain in 1710. With an initial focus on rural areas, this "Holy Brotherhood" was an extension of Queen Isabel's royal reform of an already ancient semivigilante volunteer municipal rural police force in the 1470s and '80s. The viceroy separated out the Santa Hermandad from the audiencia in 1719, founding the Tribunal de la Real Acordada, which gained jurisdiction over urban areas in 1756 and had its own jail in Mexico City. As in Queen Isabel's day, a key reason for establishing this court in New Spain was to remind subjects of the crown's authority.[10] Patrols, or *rondas*, made by the Acordada were voluntary and unpaid.[11] In 1782 the cabildo divided the city into thirty-two neighborhoods (*cuarteles*), each with an unpaid, unarmed, honorary alcalde del barrio to patrol his own neighborhood. Within this new system, there were eight major districts called *cuarteles mayores*, with leading judicial officials in each one (*alcaldes ordinarios*), as well as a corps of armed guards who also did rounds.[12] Along with the corregidor, the magistrates of the cuarteles mayores ran tribunals that issued rapid verbal judgments, which came to form the thousands of cases listed in an important documentary source known as the *Libros de Reos*. Viceroy Revillagigedo added a ninth municipal court and founded the new force of paid night watchmen in 1790, as well as three additional groups of guards to back them up. These reforms situate Mexico City as an important contributor to the history of the modern era of law enforcement.[13] However, we cannot forget that the serenos and the efficient courts that dealt with nightly offenses coexisted with multiple, older, overlapping judicial institutions and different patrols that simultaneously exercised their jurisdiction over the court city. As the lowest ranking and least powerful representatives of the law, the lantern guards often faced resistance both from the populace and their superiors, including alcaldes and their patrols and military men, both on and off duty.

The Police and Good Government

Since the King piously conferred on me the dignity of taking command of these dominions, one of my concerns was to examine the many defects that this capital endures in the *policía* branch [of government], and what could address [these defects], according to the honor [that this city] deserves. As a result, I have learned and observed that all [of these defects] come from never having a dependable, established method for contributing to the cleanliness and adornment of this city. . . . Although at various times, rules and dispositions have been made about this serious matter, nothing continues, perhaps because no one has organized jurisdictions relating to keeping order and policía.
—Viceroy Revillagigedo, Mexico, 1790

The shops are closed; the houses are uninhabited; the streets are full of beggars who attack whomever they encounter; bakers and butchers are under siege; all the residents endure shortages, but they are persecuted by the police emissaries [*emisarios de policía*], who search houses whenever they want under the pretext of looking for people to arrest.
—*La Gazeta de México*, 1794

Bernal testified that at 10:30 last night, he saw a streetlight blown out. He brought a ladder to reignite it. A bit later he saw a carriage approaching him. He shouted at the driver to stop it, but it crashed between the fourth and fifth rungs of the ladder. He asked the driver, "Why did you want to kill me?" A passenger in the carriage, who is a sergeant of the militia, responded insolently, calling Bernal a thief, a pimp, a drunkard, and a bastard.
—Manuel José Bernal, January 4, 1802

The first two quotes, in their two different uses of the word *policía*, encapsulate the seemingly endless debate over policing—did this institution help create and maintain civil order and a higher standard of urban living, or did it carry out state-supported repression?[14] The final quote, made to a superior judicial official when Bernal was once again involved in a verbal altercation, brought this antagonism toward law enforcement to the street level with the words of a man expressing his hatred for Bernal, in response to the fact that the patrolman had almost died for no other offense than climbing his ladder to do his job.[15] From the 1790s through to the 1820s, the lantern guards often faced these kinds of insults and attacks, which may have targeted them as individuals but also expressed a widespread dissatisfaction with the viceregal regime.

The origins of the word police, or policía, grow out of ancient Greek and Roman views regarding the proper governance of their subjects. These concepts were adapted across Europe over the next two millennia.[16] However, as noted in the second quote, in the late eighteenth century Mexicans associated "police emissaries" with unpredictable persecution, the suppression of French revolutionaries, and tyranny.[17] Spaniards and Mexicans viewed the Paris police, the longstanding leaders in surveillance, as politically influenced spies. This opinion persisted despite the fact that both the French and Spanish kings hailed from the House of Bourbon: the Bourbons ruled Spain and its empire from 1700 onward when Philip V (grandson of Louis XIV of France) ascended to the Spanish throne.[18] Under the French absolutist influence, by the end of the eighteenth century, the word "policía" started to narrow to signify maintaining order and vigilance, to foster a general sense of security and tranquility in the population at large.[19] The French Revolution escalated a feeling of urgency about policing the potentially rebellious masses in both Europe and New Spain, especially in the early 1800s with the rise of Napoleon Bonaparte. At first, Spaniards had little sympathy for the revolutionaries across the Pyrenees, but after fifteen years of constant wars, starting in 1793, these developments affected the unraveling of Spain's own overseas empire.[20]

To the ruling classes of New Spain who founded the serenos, policía still meant "good government." Although the viceregal governing committees in Mexico City included a *junta de policía* since the seventeenth century, no one referred to their own night watchmen as "police" at this time.[21] Instead, policía had a more general meaning that derives from the word "polis," or ancient Greek city-states. Those magistrates or functionaries who might help with policía equated to anyone who worked within "the existing system of civil government."²² From at least as far back as the mid-fifteenth century, the Castilian author Fernán Pérez de Guzmán— discussing the shamelessness of his own era—observed a need for what we would now call policing to create policía, in the sense of good government: "Whereby, if at the present time in Castile there is discussion of that very noteworthy and useful institution that ancient Rome used called the 'censor,' used for [ensuring] policía and civility, who had the power to examine and correct the citizens' customs, which were well deserving of a harsh punishment."²³ The pioneering linguist Sebastián de Covarrubias provided a very useful definition of policía in his 1611 *Tesoro de la lengua castellana o española*: "A term relating to citizens or courtiers. A police council that governs all of the small concerns of the city, including its adornment and cleanliness. It is a Greek word 'politeia,' [or, in Latin] *respublica*. Politically, [it refers to what is] urban and courtly . . . and the science and method of governing the city and the republic."²⁴ In the renaissance era policía generally meant urban order, from political structures to laws to street cleaning, and had a positive connotation closely relating to a concept of civility—a well-governed state that permitted a vibrant public life. Although this ideal definitely did not come to fruition in Spanish cities of the era, conquistadors, jurists, bureaucrats, clerics, and poets all shaped how the idea of policía manifested itself in the Americas. No less a figure than Bartolomé de las Casas himself expressed the need for the Spanish concept of policía to rule over the so-called *indios*, while Bernadino de Sahagún rated the Mexica leaders of late pre-contact Tenochtitlán as advanced in policía.²⁵

From the seventeenth century, Mexico City created juntas de policía, which the viceroys consolidated as part of town government in the mid-eighteenth century to further urban reform projects. As noted by Viceroy de Croix in 1769, "Since I first entered this city, I have directed my wishes toward the beautification of its streets, plazas, and canals, as its residents deserve, to give them the comfort of walking on the thoroughfares without risking stumbling, flooding, and all of the other disagreeable embarrassments to transit that worry us today."²⁶ Areas of policía interest increased in the eighteenth century and included the water supply, pipes, sewers, *pulquería* regulations, fountains, bathhouses, Indigenous sweat lodges (*temascales*), ditches, roads, markets, apartment buildings, buildings in disrepair, and even preventing hunger and disease among the populace. By the end of the century, policía extended to garbage collection, address numbering with wall tiles, regulating the bread supply, animal control, and street lighting. Overall, policía contributed to clarifying the distinction between the cultivation of a beautiful, well-ordered city and the less civilized rural space, which featured bad roads, roaming livestock, pillaging highwaymen, and darkness.[27] With the advent of publicly funded illumination and night watchmen, policía also increasingly implied "public security," especially during the Insurgency era of the 1810s. While Madrid had its first Superintendencia de Policía in 1782, New Spain waited until 1812 to organize this branch of urban government. This new more unified policía tried to foster cooperation between the various different kinds of patrols that had existed for centuries, such as the alcaldes mentioned above, the newer serenos, who focused on lighting, and urban-based military units. In a time of insurrection, the authorities hoped to concentrate on vigilance and arresting offenders, an approach not particularly different from that of French law enforcement.[28] Generally, a growing state justified its expansion by equating policía with the general well-being of its subjects.

Bernal in His Locale

Manuel Bernal, a man of Spanish descent born in Ixmiquilpan, married to María Dolores Cantabrana, Lantern Guard of district number 23, aged 34.
—Real Audiencia, 1791

Our large cities are many of them neater than Mexico, but there is an appearance of solidity in the houses, and an air of grandeur in the aspect of this place, which are wanting in the cities of the United States. With us, however, a stranger does not see that striking and disgusting contrast between the magnificence of the wealthy and the squalid penury of the poor, which constantly meets his view in Mexico.... There are at least twenty thousand inhabitants of this capital, the population which does not exceed one hundred and fifty thousand souls, who have no permanent place of abode, and no ostensible means of gaining a livelihood.
—Joel Poinsett, 1822

INTRODUCTION

Bernal's biography, summed up in the lines quoted above, epitomizes the lack of information about the men who worked as rank-and-file lantern guards.[29] His occupation existed partially in response to new ideas regarding urban poverty. For reasons we cannot specifically know, Bernal chose to work in a low-paying, physical job for the viceregal state. Perhaps he sought a dependable salary and lacked the wealth to train as a priest, the social stature for employment as a government official, or the family background and connections to succeed as a tradesman. The occupation of lantern guard prevented him from falling into the poverty-stricken masses who subsisted through unpredictable day labor, factory work, domestic service, or street vending. Although low-paying, working at night for the state provided a slightly larger, more dependable salary than his other options. Nocturnal work also allowed for taking a second job in the daytime. There were, however, disadvantages besides the low pay. Working as a lantern guard demanded brute physical strength and quick decision-making but also prevented Bernal from upward social and economic mobility. While powerful in the moment, in one-to-one interactions when he represented authority, Bernal and others in this line of work lacked a way to access a more honorable occupation offering real stature and social clout. As a group of early nineteenth-century serenos explained, "We are poor men, and we only take this job because of our poverty."[30]

The work of night watchmen and other early urban patrolmen suggests that these individuals supported the state or city government, the propertied classes, and the social hierarchies that benefited the rulers of any given jurisdiction, a common interpretation of policing to the present day.[31] This theory demands a bit of caution in the sense that more modern law enforcement corps joined a montage of preexisting institutions going back to the medieval era, created without much forethought to the longer term results. Approaches to the history of law enforcement in the United States emphasize elite manipulation of fears of the poor, especially immigrants and free people of color, a process that transformed previously accepted popular leisure activities into crimes.[32] This criminalization of poverty echoes similar attitudes in eighteenth-century Spain, where the rulers focused on "the prosperity of the state, not the happiness of the individual,

[as] the pole star."³³ Yet, while increasing surveillance makes sense as a very general inspiration for the invention of new forms of policing, the patrolmen themselves and the plebeians they encountered on their beat also influenced how law enforcement developed in New Spain. The Mexico City lantern guards earned their paltry income in an occupation that represented the policies and values of the viceroy of New Spain, but we should not forget that they were both colonial subjects themselves and actors in their own right.

Men working as Mexico City lantern guards drew from a variety of what we would now call races, but the dominant group (*españoles*) made up the majority of their ranks.³⁴ Although most of them claimed the label *español*, the serenos did not reflect the consistently European background of the elite, wealthy, and powerful men who ruled New Spain. *Castas*—plebeian men labeled *indios*, *mestizos*, *castizos*, and other common terms signifying racial difference from the European rulers—also took on this occupation. Whether labeled "español" or another term, Bernal and his peers mirrored the majority of Mexico City's population, tens of thousands of people known in this era as the *plebe*, or plebeians, the racially diverse poor working class.³⁵ In some ways, these poor urban residents formed a class that did not emphasize race distinctions but instead shared a multiethnic working-class sense of community.³⁶

Although he worked in law enforcement and even supervised men, Bernal fit into the group that Enlightenment-era royal reformers feared as a threatening and expanding mass of poor wandering into and then overpopulating the viceregal capital. From the mid-eighteenth century to the 1810s, local poverty grew due to extreme fluctuations in the cost of corn (the basic staple), bad harvests, three major smallpox outbreaks between 1761 and 1798, and another serious economic crisis from 1808 to 1810.³⁷ Inflation soared from 1770 onward. The colonial leadership correctly assessed that desperate rural migrants swelled plebeian population numbers in late viceregal Mexico City, especially in 1786, known as the "Year of Hunger."³⁸ And like so many others, Bernal migrated into the city from a rural village with a predominantly Indigenous population. His place of birth, Ixmiquilpan, lies now in the modern state of Hidalgo, eighty miles north of the viceregal palace, and it would have taken him approximately four days to reach the city. Many residents of Ixmiquilpan continue to speak Otomi to the present day, which suggests that though he claimed the label "español," this migrant mostly likely had Indigenous heritage himself.

Stepping back in time for a moment, when Tenochtitlán became Mexico City in 1521, around 150,000 people inhabited this densely populated island floating in the middle of Lake Texcoco, with approximately another 500,000 living in villages like Ixmiquilpan surrounding the lake. As of the mid-sixteenth century, only three thousand Spanish *vecinos* (property-owning men) lived in the court city.[39] Native peoples represented the majority of the population until those who called themselves españoles grew due to increasing late-colonial royal intervention and European immigration. Only after 1800 did the numbers of españoles grow to over half of the city's population. Late in the colonial era, people labeled "indio" comprised only just over one-quarter of the city residents, with another 17 percent describing themselves as casta, or racially mixed.[40] Censuses recorded just under 113,000 residents in 1790, a 14 percent jump from mid-century. By the early nineteenth century, the population had grown to approximately 140,000.[41] Most of this growth came from new residents coming in from the countryside, as Bernal did, as 43 percent of inhabitants claimed a place of birth outside of the capital city.

In some ways, Mexico City represented the cutting edge of Spanish imperial policy in terms of how the government addressed urbanization and its inherent challenges. Although the 1820s United States' minister to Mexico, Joel Poinsett, criticized the poverty of the capital, some of his commentary may have derived from a sense of U.S. inferiority.[42] In the late 1700s, Mexico City ranked as the fifth largest city in the Western world.[43] By way of contrast, New York City in 1790 had thirty-three thousand residents and did not overpass Mexico City until at least the 1820s. (At this point, Mexico City numbers grew more slowly after over a deadly decade of Independence wars). Boston's population did not surpass twenty-four thousand people in 1800; Baltimore could not even boast fifteen thousand in the late eighteenth century, while Philadelphia only edged over forty thousand at the start of the nineteenth century.⁴⁴ By 1812 Mexico City had increased in size to almost 169,000—even larger and more densely populated than the twenty-first-century state capitals of Oregon (Salem) and Mississippi (Jackson). In New Spain's court city, tens of thousands of pedestrians competed with twenty-five hundred carriages on the busy thoroughfares.⁴⁵ Given its size, it is not a surprise that Mexicans looked to European metropolises, especially Paris (population around 650,000 in the late eighteenth century) and Madrid (around 200,000 residents in this era), for ideas about how to foster order in their capital.⁴⁶

Viceroy Revillagigedo and other leaders in Mexico City justified the creation of the lantern guards as a reaction to the growing population and a perceived decrease in security. Refugees from rural starvation inspired disgust and underlying fear, motivating the ruling classes to illuminate the central city and create the street patrols, who especially targeted plebeian drinking habits (see chapter 4). Indeed, the elite interpreted Indigenous drinking habits as a vicious threat to viceregal governance and economic growth.⁴⁷ Reformers situated regulation of excessive drinking as helping the "public," a more modern concept of the state's relationship with justice than the previous emphasis on Christian morality and sin.⁴⁸ But these reforms, justified with moralizing rhetoric, actually had a practical purpose. Although both Spain and New Spain experienced moments of great prosperity in the late eighteenth century, the Spanish Crown spent exorbitantly on the royal lifestyle, and, especially in the 1790s, on wars. The Bourbons counted on their "American assets" to keep them financially afloat, extracting silver and taxes at an astounding rate.⁴⁹ Due to this desperate need for resources, industriousness became a virtue viewed as leading to national prosperity.⁵⁰ Despite famine and disease, thinkers and administrators in this era "blamed the poverty of Mexican paupers on their laziness and lack of ambition," which allegedly led them to waste the superb natural resources of their land.⁵¹

The most destitute residents of the capital city might only earn sixty pesos a year and spend three-quarters of that amount on food for themselves and their families.⁵² These people bought tiny quantities of bread, chocolate, beans, coal, butter, and candle ends each day or two from neighborhood stores, unable to gather together enough cash to buy anything more than a few ounces of food at a time.[53] Common employment options for the poor included working as domestic servants, street peddlers, artisans, small shopkeepers, porters, builders, coachmen, water carriers, and cigarette rollers in a huge new factory employing up to seven thousand men and women. Others had protoindustrial jobs in essential crafts, including as metal workers, textile workers, or leather goods producers. Descendants of the region's Indigenous peoples most often worked in labor that depended on their strength, including hauling, bricklaying, or masonry. This relegation to physical tasks also made them good candidates for employment as night watchmen.[54]

This period's oft-stated elite disgust of those who spent much of their time on the streets, including to perform basic bodily functions, suggests a growing divide between a culture of rich and poor, which the lantern guards enforced even as documentation anonymized them as part of the plebeian masses. The more "Enlightened" the rhetoric of the reformers, the more they distinguished themselves from the mass of castas, Indigenous peoples, and even poor Spaniards.[55] On the other side of the economic spectrum, Mexico City was a sophisticated court city with the requisite highly fashionable and luxurious entertainments, architecture, décor, and clothing. The highest levels of viceregal society, the rulers of church and state, migrated from Spain and, earning over 50,000 pesos annually, lived in astounding opulence, on par with their European peers. The twenty or so extended families at the top of the oligarchy blended their sources of wealth, drawing from mining, landowning, and international commerce. Beyond the heights of power, a few thousand others worked in respectable professions, earning approximately 500 pesos a year managing estates; as notaries, lawyers, doctors, priests, and business owners; and in the skilled trades, making carriages, creating fine silver items, or running large commercial bakeries. These comfortable classes represented at the very most 5 percent of the city's population.[56]

Changing attitudes toward the urban and migrant poor placed the intensification of policing as one of numerous initiatives involving the creation of new institutions and regulations in the 1760s and 1770s, in Spain and throughout its empire. A new hospital, orphanage, and government-funded pawn shop gestured toward helping the most vulnerable urban denizens. Most notably, a new Poor House tried to address the needs of the growing indigent population after a 1774 decree outlawed begging. This institution provided housing, but with disciplinary expectations regarding work, piety, and behavioral standards, which reflected the elite view of plebeians as lazy and childlike. The overall failure of the Poor House, which eventually concentrated on helping poor Spanish boys, demonstrated the weakness of New Spain's attempts at social reforms, even in what historians have viewed as an authoritarian era.[57]

Intellectual and political thought originating in Europe shaped these approaches to poverty and productivity in the second half of the eighteenth century, turning the focus away from bullion and land as the source of a nation's wealth and focusing instead on the labor potential of the country's residents. From the 1740s onward, Spanish writers encouraged the Crown to find ways "to increase Spain's manufacturers, commerce, and population . . . [pleading] for an active agricultural and industrial economy under royal direction."[58] In the next few decades, economic writings addressed the perceptions that Spaniards were "lazy" and stressed that the poor needed education in crafts, especially everyday goods that would allow people to work in their homes or villages.[59] The Crown also wavered on its approaches to the wandering poor, debating on and experimenting with punitive versus productive reactions. (For example, reformers viewed forced labor sentences as more rehabilitating than simply drafting vagrants into military service).[60]

To return to Mexico City: José Bernal lived on the Calle de Cocheras, a street centrally located in the old center of the capital. When he stepped out of his building's door, he could turn his head to the right and see the ancient Santo Domingo friary just a block to the west.[61] Today this location is a very busy urban thoroughfare of shops known as República de Colombia, although the buildings themselves still look and feel as they might have two hundred years ago. In the viceregal era, wealthy residents did not live in heavily guarded high-rise condominiums or in hushed elite enclaves but instead inhabited palaces staffed by servants and retainers that stood shoulder-to-shoulder with tenements and workshops. Bernal could walk a couple blocks to the southwest and encounter the spacious, tree-filled Alameda, a favorite place for a promenade (as well as illicit sexual encounters), decorated with five fountains.[62] Several blocks to the east, he would find the breathtaking Plaza Mayor, with the cathedral and viceregal palace built adjacent to the site of the demolished Great Temple of Tenochtitlán.[63] The orderly and planned *traza*, a grid of streets originally containing thirteen square blocks, faded out as one walked a dozen blocks in any direction away from the central plazas and monumental church and government structures.[64]

While Spanish American cities under viceregal rule did not have neighborhoods formally segregated by place of origin, the original concept for colonial government had been separation between españoles and indios, with little thought to where mestizos or African-descent subjects fit into this vision.[65] In the first decades after the Spanish invasion, Mexico City had parishes designated as *doctrinas de indios*, under the guidance of mendicant friars.[66] The city government included self-governed Indigenous sections, which retained the precolonial names (with a Christian saint added) of San Juan Tenochtitlán and Santiago Tlatelolco, where around one-quarter of the population resided.[67] A 1772 reform eliminated the "race" distinction between the city's fourteen parishes, thus possibly adding to the perception of the poor as a confusing, disordered, and highly diverse uncivilized mass.[68] Despite the original intent, then, instead of racial segregation Mexico City's social divisions revealed themselves more in vertical terms, as the poor lived on the street or in simple, low buildings while the rich occupied the top floors of substantial stone edifices.[69]

Through his work and possibly because he had some formal education, Bernal actually had a step up on the rest of the poor, but he would never be part of the *gente decente* (respectable people) or claim the honorific title of *don*. Neither would he ever fit under the umbrella of another term used to indicate a man who displayed personal dignity, an *hombre de bien*, literally "a good, worthy man," a label with many subtle implications about dress, demeanor, behavior, and profession.[70] Even his simple name indicated his low socioeconomic status.[71] Education levels reinforced it even further.

Almost all of the night watchmen, including those of Spanish descent, could not read and write. The fact that Bernal could sign his own name allowed him to move up the ranks with a rapid promotion to *cabo*, or corporal, by no later than 1795.[72] This slightly elevated job still meant working on the streets, supervising the beat patrolmen, and involving himself in verbal and physical altercations, which will come up throughout this book. Despite the promotion, Bernal retained his lower-class reputation throughout his career, probably at least partially due to his missing eye, allegedly lost in a barroom brawl during one of his frequent drinking binges. Indeed, the simple fact that he frequented low class drinking establishments prevented him from appearing anything more than a disdained plebe.[73] Although it is impossible to fully know his biography, or that of any other night watchman, archived files document his on-the-job tensions and disputes and reveal something of his personality.

Bernal's Paper Trail

> Corporal number three arrested a 17-year-old español whom he found sleeping in the entryway of a building on Mesones Street. The offender said that he had stayed out late to attend the theater, and when he returned, he found his house locked up. He was set free into the custody of his debtors.
> — *Libros de Reos*, December 31, 1798

Surviving court logbooks known as *Libros de Reos* (Books of culprits, or convicts) document the arrests made by Bernal, both in his time as patrolman number 23 and when he worked as corporal number 3.[74] These bound books record the rapid sentencing decisions made by judicial officials on a daily basis. Bernal and his peers patrolled their beats during the ten or so hours of darkness, rounding up individuals they found publicly intoxicated or involved in other offenses. They took these *reos* to the jail and provided information about what had caused the arrest to the jail deputy (*alcaide*) or scribe who maintained a log of the nightly arrests. The offending man or woman remained locked up until at least the next day, when the court scribe came to the jail and took down several key points of information in his particular *Libro de Reos*. In about three cramped lines of text, the scribe recorded the title or number of the arresting official, the time and date of the arrest, the cause of the arrest, the culprit's full name, gender, age, race label, marital status, and sometimes also the location of the incident or more details about the circumstances. The scribe then brought this report to a low-level judge, who either made a summary decision on the appropriate punishment or asked for more information. After the sentencing, the scribe returned to the jail to inform the reos of their fate. A substantial number of the offenders were given a warning and immediately set free.[75]

Bernal appears in forty-eight different entries in the *Libros de Reos*, although the notary identified him only by his number. When noting the arrests, the scribe never recorded the night watchman's name, another indication of the latter's unimportant, almost interchangeable status within this system.[76] Due to this anonymity, Bernal may or may not have made the eleven arrests for public intoxication attributed in the *Libros de Reos* to guard number 23 in 1794.[77] On the other hand, longer judicial cases involving Bernal confirm his promotion to corporal by 1795, and that he held this position until at least 1802. Very likely any mention of "cabo 3" during this period refers to him. The surviving *Libros de Reos* from 1796 and 1798 show Bernal as very active, playing a role in at least thirty-seven different incidents as a supervisor on the street. Many of these involved argumentative groups of intoxicated individuals, "scandal," violence, or misbehaving night watchmen. Bernal's typical night might involve taking one of the patrolmen into custody for intoxication, preventing a man from assaulting his wife with a dagger, returning an eleven-year-old to his parents, picking up comatose individuals from where they passed out or slept, intervening when a thief tried to steal glass panels out of the street lanterns, or even carrying out the priest-like task of sending adulterous couples back to their respective spouses.[78]

In total the *Libros de Reos* dating from 1794, 1796, and 1798 document thirty-six hundred encounters between the night watchmen and those who ventured out at night in the viceregal capital, either alone or in a group, adding up to interactions with over seven thousand reos.[79] Even this large data set does not include all arrests, because many of the record books have not survived. Nor does it accurately represent all illegal acts committed in Mexico City in those years. The scribes writing the *Libros de Reos* sought to create a specific paper trail emphasizing certain crimes and offenses, while hiding others that did not reflect well on the viceregal system. As I discuss in chapter 4, the point of this nightly diary seems to be the creation of a log of plebeian drunkenness and degradation.[80]

Bernal's tendency to volatility and argumentativeness led to questioning by his superiors in at least five different investigations. Documents survive for his workplace conflicts dating to 1791, 1795, 1796, 1800, and 1802. These multipage cases reveal much more about work as a night watchman than do the *Libros de Reos*. Typical of the voluminous detail recorded by Novohispanic scribes, they include exhaustive narratives from a variety of points of view presenting how Bernal and other guards became involved in criminal acts, whether as offenders or victims. They also capture some of the highly charged language used by both the night watchmen and the populace as they interacted in conflictive situations, revealing the perceptions that existed on both sides, as well as the ways that plebeians both took advantage of, mocked, and even killed the patrolmen. According to surviving records, Bernal faced more investigations than any other night watchman during this time, although none of his offenses rose above a verbal confrontation and he did not receive any specific punishments beyond jail time during the investigations themselves. Specifically, early in his career, Bernal engaged in the argument with the alcalde and his female servants, quoted at the start of this introduction. Then in 1795, Bernal, in his role as corporal number 3, made a statement about a guard who had helped young friars escape their convent for a night of festivities. A few months later, in early 1796, he became involved in a dispute with a baker, when his men refused to help the baker discipline one of his servants. In 1800 the corregidor questioned Bernal about an altercation involving a man who held loud after-hours parties at his residence. Lastly, he featured as the plaintiff in an incident that took place on New Year's Eve of 1802, when a carriage ran into his ladder.[81] Although Bernal seemed to attract controversy, his at least seven years working nightly as a supervisor over patrolmen meant that he frequently had to intervene in highly conflictive situations. After all, this kind of activity is inherent to the roles of street-level policing.

INTRODUCTION

An additional source exists to add to the data found in the *Libros de Reos* and the detailed longer cases. The *guarda mayor*, the "head guard" in charge of street lighting, made a daily report. Although at least eighty of these logs survive, corporals like Bernal do not feature regularly in these documents, which anonymize the night watchman even more than the *Libros de Reos*. Every morning this head guard made a list of the previous night's activities of each guard, numbering them from one to ninety-nine, and addressed the report to the viceroy or, in those that survive from 1822, the victorious military leader Agustín de Iturbide. Unlike the *Libros de Reos* scribe, the head guard did not name or detail the biographies of offenders. Unless an important event occurred, these reports are very dry lists; however, they still provide statistical information and patterns of activities. While the *Libros de Reos* inscribe a plague of public intoxication on Mexico City's plebeians and the longer court cases tried to resolve highly charged disputes, the head guard's report proffers a paper trail to the reigning head of state that makes his anonymous corps of men look rather organized and disciplined.

Both the *Libros de Reos* and the head guards' reports function to assert to higher ups that the lantern guards had a degree of organization and efficacy, and that they carried out their tasks consistently across the lighted streets of the capital city. Longer cases challenging the serenos' behavior reveal the tissue-thin reality of this paper trail. However, in the details of how they justified their arrests or presented the details of their exchanges with the populace in court, patrolmen display expertise that benefits us as historians. Over fifty years ago, R. C. Cobb observed that the Paris police of this era were "always committed historians," even expert social historians, as they immersed their daily lives and work hours in the subtleties of their own neighborhood. Cobb asks: "Might it not be the case . . . that the police knew better than we do, as they were there and we were not, that, far from trying to pull the wool over the eyes of the magistrates in order to secure the conviction of those they considered ought to be guilty, far from vindictively persecuting unfortunates because they came from a certain trade, a certain province, or a certain part of the city, they were merely trying to bring in people whom they had every reason to believe guilty?"⁸² I cite this quote not to argue that eighteenth-century night watchmen did not have biases but instead to suggest that they had to use their informed judgment and in-depth understanding of a situation to balance tolerance and retribution. After all, they had to return to their beats day after day and therefore to balance carrying out the wishes of their superiors with getting along with their neighbors.

Mexico City's Lantern Guards and Spanish Imperial Reform

The new century brought in the Bourbon dynasty, which sought to turn the tide of imperial decline by transforming its American possessions into true colonies.
—Vera Candiani, *Dreaming of Dry Land*

The Bourbon bureaucracy engineered unprecedented campaigns to extirpate the vices of the people and to inculcate in them the new virtues of hard work, sobriety, and public propriety. . . . The eyes of the king, behind the mask of the public gaze, became omnipresent in Mexico City.
—Voekel, "Peeing on the Palace"

Even at its most intrusive, the Spanish colonial state was far from being a Leviathan force in peoples' lives.
—Susan Deans-Smith, *Bureaucrats, Planters, and Workers*

No historian doubts the monumental importance of the shifts in Spanish imperial policies taking place in the second half of the eighteenth century.⁸³ The judicial reforms that created the lantern guards fit under the umbrella of a broader consolidation of royal governance known as the Bourbon Reforms, after the French-descended dynasty that took power in Spain at the end of the War of Spanish Succession (1713). This new regime expanded institutions relating to public order, security, and defense, granting a political valence to actions that previously might have fit more into a criminal or immoral category.⁸⁴ Social aspects of the Bourbon reforms included improved education and promoting ideals of civic responsibility, a strong work ethic, and even so-called civilized manners.⁸⁵ In France, even before the Bourbons took over the crown in 1589, urban regulations proliferated, and police helped maintain the numbered badges worn by city workers.⁸⁶ In emulation of these French antecedents, the Spanish Bourbon

INTRODUCTION

King Charles III (1759–1788) implemented many of these reforms, which included creating new task-focused ministries centered on war, commerce, and finance. Even before Charles's reign, in 1749 King Fernando VI introduced a new rank of French-influenced bureaucrats known as intendants, as regional governors with fiscal-focused responsibilities.[87] Bourbon rulers strove for a unified system in New Spain and the metropolis, spending most of their time on economic affairs in hopes of preventing rebellions and returning the metropolis to its former prosperity.

Colonial revenues needed to grow to fund militarization in Europe and America, in reaction to the dual threats of the British navy and popular insurrection.[88] Indeed, as Spain competed with other nations within Europe, in the Americas mass revolt threatened more immediate and dramatic repercussions. In the final years of the eighteenth century, the Haitian Revolution loomed as a terrifying catastrophe for all imperialists in the Americas. Paired with the massive and devastating Tupac Amaru rebellion in the Andes, the Spanish rulers saw portents of absolute worst-case outcomes. Despite this widespread unrest among African-descent and Indigenous populations, this was a very prosperous era in terms of exports from the Americas. Revenue from New Spain multiplied from six million pesos in 1765 to over three times that amount forty years later. Most of these new funds derived from increased silver mining production, supported by state subsidies and incentives, as well as monopolies on mercury, salt, ice, alcohol and tobacco, and heavy taxation on a growing population.[89]

As noted above, New Spanish judicial institutions and the overall concept of policía followed models in the Iberian Peninsula dating back to the medieval era, but the most relevant contextualization comes from changes in street policing in Old Spain in the second half of the eighteenth century.[90] As in the Americas, the creation of new institutions in Spain responded to urban unrest and fears of mass revolt in rapidly enlarging cities.[91] An overall increase in the presence of military patrols took place in both New and Old Spain in this era and continued into the nineteenth century, alongside efforts to increase surveillance of the population and recordkeeping.[92] After the Esquilache Riot in 1766 Madrid, the king militarized the court city and created divisions and new levels of alcaldes with broad oversight over public order, which included street lighting and cleaning, maintaining fountains, taking the poor to hospices, and placing abandoned children in service.[93] By 1769 the Spanish government spread this change across other cities in Spain, and eventually to Mexico City in 1782. As already indicated, in both Madrid and Mexico City, the reformers viewed the poor as idle and underutilized resources who could turn around the economy if properly controlled. In these cities, the alcaldes focused on drinking establishments and beggars and vagrants; in the rural areas, these concerns existed along with a focus on banditry.[94] Urban policing became even more political in Spain after the outbreak of the French Revolution, but ultimately, as was the case with most of the Bourbon reforms, these efforts proved futile by the nineteenth century, or even before.[95] For example, in Madrid, the alcaldes failed in effective patrolling, and, due to political rivalries and organizational challenges, the office of the superintendent of the police only lasted from 1782 to 1792. Madrid's policing reforms reached a crossroads in 1809, with the formation of a *departamento de Policía*, the division of the city into districts each with their own *comisarios*, and an increased role for military battalions and urban militias, as well as the dreaded French-style urban spies.[96]

While the Bourbon reforms meant a growth in state power, which expressed itself most effectively in more taxes and more efficient tax collection, the average person might not have perceived increasing state intervention in their lives. But when they did, they rioted against or forced negotiations with the individuals who they perceived as imposing unjust changes to their routines. Popular demonstrations and petitions, foreshadowing Father Miguel Hidalgo's 1810 movement, evinced traditional Catholic piety combined with what could be called modern workers' goals. For example, riots broke out in response to the 1767 royal decree expelling all Jesuits from Spain and its dominions. Almost one-quarter of the approximately six thousand men and women who rolled cigarettes in the Tobacco Monopoly factory took to the streets to protest changes in their work routine in 1794. Street vendors, mainly Indigenous women, pretended to give up their children to the authorities in a successful

INTRODUCTION

protest against a ban on selling tamales and tortillas out of their baskets or stalls.[97] The founding of the lantern guards responded to the activism of Mexico City's plebeians, circumstances not unlike the motivations for instituting other new forms of law enforcement around the Atlantic world.

Were the Lantern Guards Police?

> The new police were the first force in the world organized to prevent crime by constant patrolling instead of merely apprehending offenders after the fact.
> —Wilbur R. Miller, *Cops and Bobbies*

> There were many social actors—the middling and lower classes, as well as the elites—whose aims, needs and maneuvers were instrumental in creating the modern police.
> —David Garrioch, "The People of Paris and Their Police in the Eighteenth Century"

The first quotation, which refers to Robert Peel's 1829 reform of the Metropolitan Police in London, speaks from the common ignorance of Latin America's place in important global historical developments, such as the Enlightenment or the rise of radical republics in the nineteenth century.[98] Mexico City's lantern guards, while lacking some of the basic characteristics of a modern police force, represent a key example of a growing state's efforts to surveil the populace, prevent rebellion, and strengthen an imperial project. It is arguable that they even contributed to racializing and criminalizing a significant sector of the population.[99] Overall, the serenos fit into a timeline of the process of modernizing law enforcement.[100] While lacking a uniform, nonetheless they produced a very "visually striking display," with their lanterns and pikes. In this way, and in their assigned duties, Mexico City's lantern guards did represent "the coercive power of the state" and affected how plebeians viewed the regime. As they stood out from the people who knew them in their neighborhoods, even in the 1790s, they began to develop "a defensive solidarity with their colleagues."[101]

Although until now historians have not juxtaposed them with their brothers-in-arms to the north, the establishment of the serenos marched in step with the historical trajectories of British, French, and U.S. police.

Eighteenth-century endeavors to deal with urban population growth in New Spain's capital coincided with similar processes in London and Paris, where the growth of urban residents also aroused an ill-defined and statistically vague perception of increasing danger. Some historians have interpreted this as part of the transition to industrialization, because the new urbanites seemed "unproductive, unattached, and unemployed," a threat to the "social order" from "the rapidly multiplying poor of cities whose size had no precedent in Western history."[102] And as cities in the United States grew in the mid-nineteenth century, Boston and New York faced the same challenges that larger metropolises had experienced a few generations before.[103] Similar to the formation of different police forces across Europe and the United States, the lantern guards formed as "a political instrument of the state" in a time of "consolidation." However, another century would pass before Mexico really possessed enough centralized authority to create a modern national police force.[104]

Like other proto-police, the serenos' essential characteristics blended traditional voluntary parish or neighborhood patrols with traits that historians view as more modern, in the sense of professionalization, specialization, and bureaucratization.[105] Mexico City's leaders founded the night watchmen corps for the stated purpose of attempting to control a perceived increase in murders and robberies (see chapter 1). Nocturnal patrols theoretically prevented these crimes because culprits might fear the presence of the serenos, while victims could easily call on a guard for help.[106] There were, to be sure, differences from more modern police forces: for example, the lantern guards, unlike the mid-nineteenth-century police in the United States and England, did not patrol during the day. Also different from later "cops" and "bobbies," they did not wear military-like uniforms, although even today some law enforcement such as detectives are considered "plainclothes," and despite this, we view these individuals as highly modern. In a further difference from their modern "counterparts," the serenos intersected with and competed against at least two other basic groups, the alcaldes and military men on their rondas, so their authority faced constant challenges even within their own justice system. While this interjurisdictional competition and overlap persists to the present, severe conflicts tend to arise vertically, from the patrolman on up the judicial hierarchy to the district attorney's office, not in a parallel way as experienced by the lantern guards. For example, one would not find a sheriff's deputy regularly opposing the state police today.[107] Finally, other than patrolling to prevent crime, the lantern guards had numerous other duties, from dealing with fires to dog-catching (see chapter 3), and of course lighting and maintaining the street lanterns. Yet, despite these points of divergence from what is viewed as essential to modern law enforcement, the serenos were "police-like" in terms of other basic traits: they received salaries (unlike the contemporary Bow Street Runners, who were paid by the job, and thus preferred to work only for the rich); they could use bodily force; they answered ultimately only to their head guard, who reported to his superiors, who in turn led the city and the viceroyalty; and therefore they represented government policy, not the whims of powerful local nobles.[108]

Mexico City's night watchmen fit into an era dating from the late seventeenth century to the mid-nineteenth, which historians have often viewed as "state forming," tending toward more specialization in bureaucracies. All over the Western world, cities moved away from citizens' patrols and piecework-type pay for policing toward the creation of militarized nocturnal guards led by a "chief."[109] One scholar has expressed this change as follows: "A policed society is unique in that central power exercises potentially violent supervision over the population by bureaucratic means widely diffused throughout civil society in small and discretionary operations that are capable of rapid concentration."[110] However, police scholars in general stress that we should not overemphasize the "newness" of reformed law enforcement in the decades around 1800—the newest aspect was a governmental focus on joining together various facets of urban maintenance and paying the guards a salary.[111] Mexico City residents had had experience with different kind of patrols for centuries. Because the serenos did not wear uniforms, they did not look "new" in the way that London's bobbies did. What certainly registered as new was the publicly funded lanterns carried by these men, and thus the source of light drew the most popular rage. At the level of elite discourse, Mexico

City's lantern guards also fit with contemporary trends in Europe that justified founding a system of policing to address the perceived and actual "problems of crime, riot, and disorder."[112] On the other hand, by some analyses, this increase in professional patrols took place at a time of relative orderliness in urban life.[113]

The emphasis on state-building can tend to exaggerate the ability of these eighteenth-century rulers to actually carry out their own ambitions. Top-down approaches, including those positing that increasing law enforcement worked hand in glove with state-building and that police forces somehow "modernized" toward more effectiveness over time, neglect the constant negotiation between the police and the populace, which continues into the present day.[114] For example, eighteenth-century Parisian police, whose foundations go back to the reign of Louis XIV, are often perceived as the most centralized and intrusive institution of this kind; even they, however, experienced a give-and-take with the populace not unlike the functioning of the lantern guards in New Spain's capital. French leaders, like those of viceregal Mexico, wanted a more disciplined work force and lived in justified terror of popular revolt. Paris police included forty-eight commissaries charged with public health and urban beautification projects very similar to those entrusted to Mexico City's *ramo de policía*.[115]

Even so, the Parisian guards exercised very little effective control over the populace. As in Mexico, patrolmen could not arrest offenders if a group of people opposed them. The Parisian guards feared riots and thus acted carefully to avoid provoking them. Both cities' patrolmen responded to requests for help, which means that the urban population acted to define their own perceptions of unacceptable acts as crimes—and who fit the definition of a criminal—in response to internal norms of behavior. Among other things, Mexican and Parisian parents and spouses called on the patrolmen to discipline family members, trusting these men to have some influence over domestic issues. While both cities had well-established court systems, it required a very substantial commitment of time and money to effectively make a legal complaint and achieve a result; simply calling on a guard resulted in a rapid response and potentially an effective resolution. The Mexico City night watchmen remained a part of their own communities, living with them and not dressing in a differentiated way, maintaining an even closer connection to the community than similar men working in Paris, who also received low pay and often worked another job.[116]

Overall, one must believe in the moral dissolution of the poor in order to give credence to elite voices who justify increasing law enforcement in response to a growth in crime.[117] Over the course of time, plebeians even in rapidly growing cities maintained their own communal standards of behavior, called on patrolmen when it suited their needs, and protested when they deemed conditions unbearable. Through making it possible to call on a watchman, as opposed to a rich or powerful connection, it is even possible that this institution gradually helped break down the influence of traditional networks of patronage in cities.[118] To avoid thinking like an eighteenth- or nineteenth-century reformer, one must question "the assumption that a society without the benefit of a modern police force must of necessity have been a disorderly one."[119] Instead, early patrolmen represent an overlay, or another option, for plebeians to turn to when internal values failed to shape a troublesome member of the community.

After generations of congratulatory writings, the social and political unrest of the 1960s United States demanded new approaches to police scholarship, resulting in sociological and ethnographic accounts, which began the process of assessing how law enforcement contributed to racial conflict.[120] British scholars started to question their police forces a few years after U.S. historians did, as their most destructive twentieth-century urban street revolts took place later than ours.[121] Marxist-influenced historians critiqued police history around this time, and social history methods encouraged more analysis of the daily life of patrolmen, as opposed to just their chiefs or heroic figures.[122] In the wake of further activism and the expansion of social and cultural history, historians of gender and sexuality discussed law enforcement going back at least as far as the 1980s.[123] By the twenty-first century, commentators, whether trained as historians or not, published book-length denunciations of policing in the United States[124]

INTRODUCTION

At the same time, nuanced scholarship continues to contextualize the complexities of this story in cities around the country, often emphasizing the rise of a carceral state in the last century or more of U.S. history.[125]

As the role of systemic racism in shaping law enforcement in the United States has emerged as a well-known concept, now is the perfect moment for Mexico City's lantern guards to step out of the shadows of kitschy folklore, facile critiques of south-of-the border backwardness, and rampant ignorance of the non-Anglo history of the Americas. Living through significant changes in law enforcement over the decades of his life, Manuel Payno (1810–1894) expressed ambiguity about Mexico City's serenos in his masterwork *Los bandidos del Río Frio* (1891). Although he does not shrink from expressing their brutality and incompetence, Payno also considers them as human beings: "As it darkened, and after passing review in front of the Portal de Diputación to receive their lamp oil and to light their torches, the watchmen dispersed through the streets of the city, appearing for all the world like a swarm of eye-catching fireflies. Those who observed them hurry, resignedly taking their posts on a cold and rainy night, could not help but feel a certain sympathy."[126] The first stage in the history of the lantern guards is the highly contested establishment of public lighting in Mexico City, definitely a change imposed from on high, which required almost continuous negotiation between a range of residents of New Spain's capital. None of the so-called Enlightened reformers pushing for urban illumination could have predicted the violent popular reaction against these lanterns and the men who carried them. As "enlightened" patrolmen in the largest metropolis in the hemisphere, enacting the racialized policies of their imperialist heads of state on a diverse and poverty-stricken population, these men and their experiences underscore the very long history of our current crises and calls for reform. It behooves us to pay attention to their story.

CHAPTER 1

Light

> This sense of "extraordinary danger" evokes a night whose threats are only barely contained by the street lighting and reappear the moment it is unexpectedly extinguished.... Accounts [of lighting extinguished or darkened] acknowledged setbacks in the struggle to colonize the urban night while reminding readers of the danger of an uncolonized night.
> —Craig Koslofsky, *Evening's Empire*

> People submitted to it because it promised to guarantee stability and security. But although public lighting was welcomed as holding out the promise of security, it was also a police institution and, as such, attracted all the hostility traditionally directed at the police.
> — Wolfgang Schivelbusch, *Disenchanted Night*

During the three-decade long existence of the viceregal institution of guarda faroleros, darkness threatened to reconquer Mexico City's nights. Echoing Craig Koslofsky's analysis of the same phenomenon in European cities, street lighting in New Spain's viceregal capital formed part of a "colonization of the night," carried out as an "uneven, contested, and multi-sided" process, a frequently violent facet of what enlightened reformers viewed as part of the civilizing process of their imperial subjects.[1] Both in Europe and Mexico City, the street lighting project met with sustained resistance.[2] After prolonged debates and experimentation with a variety of implementation methods in the later decades of the eighteenth century, Mexico City residents finally proved to their leaders once and for all that they would not take the responsibility to maintain privately owned lanterns to brighten the streets outside of their homes. In response, the municipal and viceregal authorities, in line with trends in

Spain and Europe more broadly, decided to create a new force of armed guards to carry out this reform.

The new streetlights caused conflicts well into the nineteenth century. Acts of resistance included regular destructive attacks on the *faroles* (lanterns) themselves. It is important to note that all of the sources of outdoor light during this period came from individuals lighting lanterns, torches, or fires—no gas or electrical grid existed.[3] Therefore, the destruction of a single streetlight meant a personal attack on a lantern guard—a closer association with a state agent than today's enormous, anonymous grid. Despite their lowly status and mundane task, the men who earned their pay igniting the streetlights clearly represented the state. The essential human element inherent to this kind of street illumination provided an obvious target for popular opposition.[4]

This chapter sets the stage for future resistance to street lighting by focusing on the contentious discussions and many administrative steps that preceded the widespread installation of public street lighting in Mexico City. Within these drawn-out debates, officials and self-appointed experts analyzed many topics, including the minutia of different types of lanterns and their positioning, the financing structure for funding them, the competing examples provided by European cities, and an enlightened vision of the impact of urban darkness and its effect on economic and racial hierarchies. Finally, the quintessential Bourbon reformer, Viceroy Revillagigedo, eventually succeeded in establishing public lighting via viceregal *bandos*, or decrees distributed around the city.[5] Revillagigedo's mandates expressed a will to impose greater surveillance for the good of the populace and to beautify the court city to European standards. Despite the definitive tone of the printed bandos, street lighting did not ultimately succeed in the viceregal era or even beyond into much more recent decades. Enlightened beautification projects could not overcome the plebeian sense of ownership of space and their right to occupy the urban streets, which persisted as the city continued to grow.[6] Dark streets where urban nightwalkers still felt damp or dusty soil under their feet instead of paving stones hearkened back to Indigenous village life. Indeed, even into the twentieth century, some outlying barrios Mexico City appeared to be made up of hundreds of rural pueblos.[7]

LIGHT

A Brief History of Public Lighting in Mexico City

Before the lantern guards made their nightly rounds, privileged access to spectacularly bright displays of fire and light remained under the purview of the rich and powerful, in both the secular and the religious realms. Nocturnal illumination signified a monumental political or spiritual celebration, not a dependable safety measure for urbanites to enjoy. Over the centuries, the viceregal state staged events boasting hundreds of candles and fireworks for the entry of new viceroys into the court city, or other important events. These events also took over the streets, shutting them down for normal use. In his early seventeenth-century chronicles, the Indigenous chronicler don Domingo de Chimalpahin described brightly illuminated royal celebrations. For example, when he received notice of the birth of a prince in Spain, the viceroy ignited hundreds of luminaries on his palace roof, placed tallow candles in every one of his windows, and set off fireworks. Celebratory bonfires were lighted on the roofs of other government buildings and in front of the palatial residences of prominent Spaniards.[8] By the eighteenth century, prosperous craftsmen, such as members of the silversmith guild, had the funds to pay for glittering processional floats adorned with thousands of flickering candles, sparkling on hundreds of pounds of silver panels.[9] Even in the final years of the viceroyalty, the city government funded the purchase of dozens of pitch-pine torches to illuminate celebrations of royal births in the plaza outside the viceregal palace.[10] All these examples show different groups lighting up the public spaces to demonstrate their power, wealth, and stature, as well as loyalty to the state.

Outside of these special commemorations, in the day-to-day life of the populace, the church monopolized the public's experience of illumination.[11] Hundreds of candles dazzled participants' eyes during masses and funerals for those who could afford it. Attendees enjoyed the thrill of fireworks in religious street festivals, and Baroque penitential processions "de luz y sangre [of light and blood]" brought together great crowds of people from all walks of life in solemn and exciting public spectacles.[12] The introduction of public lighting made the experience of illuminated streets more commonplace, no longer reserved for special occasions. Enlightened bureaucrats' control of the Mexico City nocturnal streets via street illumination countered the Catholic Church's dominion over urban space. This element of secularization is in line with efforts by Bourbon reformers to limit ecclesiastical powers on multiple levels, from burial rituals to education.[13] In choosing which type of lighting they preferred in the streets, Bourbon administrators unsurprisingly chose the lanterns of modernity over the thousands of candles that epitomized Baroque religiosity.[14] In the process of secularizing street illumination, the guarda faroleros had an almost religious function as functionaries who now controlled light, protected licit nightwalkers, and guarded the rituals surrounding the sacred events of birth and death.[15] Because previous exuberant street celebrations had attracted crowds in "ritualized submission" and "encouraged the status quo," even as they tended to encourage boundary-stretching and even violence, government control over displays of light and nocturnal pastimes felt excessive and was resisted with increasing vehemence.[16]

While they also used light and fire to celebrate monumental moments in their calendar, before the Spanish invasion, the Indigenous peoples of central Mexico had enjoyed regular urban illumination.[17] The Colhua-Mexica lighted their breathtakingly clean and well-organized city with torches made from a resinous wood called *ocote* (*pinus montezumae*), attached to the walls of Tenochtitlán buildings near their doorways. To add to the general radiance of their city, the Mexica placed burning resin in large braziers in streets and plazas. *Copal* incense burned in similar large vessels and scented their cityscape.[18] After Tenochtitlán transformed into an imperial capital city hosting the court of the viceroyalty of New Spain, some residents most likely continued lighting their doorways with ocote torches. From 1585 the city government called for volunteer guards to patrol the city center at night, and they probably carried similar torches. In the eighteenth century, owners of corner stores were supposed to burn ocote torches of a set size in the crossroads near their stores until ten at night, according to the ordinances relating to their trade. Municipal regulations discussed the placement and size of large braziers near these businesses, also fed by ocote.[19] But the rest of the streets remained dark, providing a hospitable backdrop for rumors and fears of secret journeys, criminal plans, illicit encounters, and dangerous visits.[20]

From the king in Spain down to local church, inquisitorial, and viceregal officials, imperial eyes viewed the shadows of nocturnal American cities as redolent with "public sins," drunk and scandalous carousers, and even a devilish influence.[21] With the streets almost completely dark for hours, "respectable" inhabitants avoided going outside, or if they did, they carried their own torches, traveled safely in their carriages, and enjoyed the protection of their servants. Observers noted that the middle classes only dared to go out holding lanterns. But even with their individualized protection, when darkness reigned, *malhechores* (evildoers) controlled urban space for a significant portion of the night. The poor, who lacked the funds to pay for servants, carriages, lanterns, or even torches, suffered the most during these criminalized, obscure hours.[22]

Public Illumination and Enlightened Reformers

Guided by this vision of the night as dangerous and unconquered, by the eighteenth century the Enlightenment ideals of the Spanish Bourbon dynasty combined with a desire to "secure" city streets in both the Old and New World for respectable bourgeois activities.[23] Similar to the racialized and class-driven concepts of urban safety and security, we cannot accept that the viceregal authorities viewed street lighting as nothing more than a benefit for the general public. The rhetoric surrounding light also had an economic and political edge. Nocturnal illumination meant that certain businesses could stay open for longer hours. This included establishments such as taverns, which provided taxed income on alcohol sales for the benefit of the Crown. Well-lighted streets promised to increase the spending of the poor to benefit the powerful.[24] In addition to economic goals, Bourbon plans for street lighting drew on European ideas regarding urban beautification and an elite vision of appropriate public behavior and use of the cityscape. Historians of Mexico interpret these reforms as an effort to control the lower classes, especially in terms of perceptions of their work ethic, which presumably stood in the way of imperial prosperity. As observed by Pamela Voekel, Spanish reformers wished to "create a physical urban environment that would produce the desired behavior" in poor residents.[25] Yet, these behavior ideals contrasted with the proliferation of the government monopoly on the Indigenous drink *pulque* (see chapter 4), and the brighter streets ironically may have encouraged the nightlife that the reformers disparaged.

In New Spain, late viceregal leaders invoked the beauty of European city streets, which they hoped to imitate, and a general need for "order" and "security [*seguridad*]." The meaning of the word *seguridad* changed over time. Castilian dictionaries included a definition of the word from the late fifteenth century, equating it simply with the Latin word *securitas*; Renaissance writers used it often in political treatises, giving it a financial meaning (such as security on a loan), or referring to a sense of trust, or lastly a general feeling of safety from violence in wartime.[26] In 1788, contemporary with the development of street lighting and the institution of night watchmen in Mexico, the Spanish lexicographer Esteban Terreros y Pando discussed multiple meanings for seguridad, notably with an example sentence: "Las leyes conservan la seguridad pública [laws preserve public security]."[27] The rise in street-level law enforcement coincided with a new emphasis the word related to safety from the urban poor: in other words, armed men providing official government-sanctioned protection from an enemy within one's own society.

Mexico City's plan for urban illumination fits within a longer Iberian trajectory in the aptly named *siglo de luces*, the Spanish phrase applied to the Enlightenment, "the century of light." Efforts to brighten European cities such as Paris, Amsterdam, and London extended back to the 1660s. Amsterdam originated the most effective early modern street lighting by adopting glass-paned oil lanterns. Although continuing to use candle-fueled lanterns into the eighteenth century, Paris made a key contribution to urban development by connecting publicly funded lighting to street-level policing. Quite similar to the history of Mexico City's decades of debate and resistance, various European cities had different systems for funding street illumination, either by the nobility, neighborhood authorities, or broadly applied new taxes, which of course encountered strong opposition from urban citizens.[28]

LIGHT

On the Iberian Peninsula, Barcelona and Cádiz first organized street lighting by the mid-eighteenth century.[29] Madrid had attempted but failed to achieve this reform a few decades earlier. With the stamp of royal approval, Barcelona installed 1,680 lanterns in 1759. These had cotton wicks fed by vegetable oil. Women cleaned and prepared the lanterns at a warehouse and men lighted and maintained them, a system soon discarded for an all-male night watchmen force. After an unsuccessful era of resident-funded lighting, by 1765 Madrid finally installed over 4,400 lanterns and extended this number to almost 7,300 by the early nineteenth century. Across Spain, various cities discussed the best methods for facilitating this reform, which coincided in each locale with the foundation of the institution of the lantern guards, who further emphasized the Bourbon reformers' need to see, categorize, and "secure" the streets for respectable activities.[30]

The trial-and-error period leading up to the installation of streetlights in Mexico City lasted just under thirty years, beginning in 1763 and coming to a resolution in early 1790s. During the 1780s city authorities embarked upon a decade of negotiation with the populace, before finally deciding to organize their own lantern guards. During these debates, throughout which residents took a clear stand against street lighting, decrees demanding community-funded lighting devolved into a rhetoric of anti-plebeian fearmongering. Official proclamations emphasized lanterns as a defensive weapon against allegedly prolific robberies, violent attacks, and murders. By heightening a sense of danger in the streets, reformers promoted their own importance as lighting helped prevent these supposedly growing nocturnal threats, creating a feedback loop of more fears and more need for security from criminal elements who thrived on darkness.

Initially, the viceroys and local government officials attempted to implement a self-sustaining, resident-supported system of street illumination. This approach followed the model set by the port city of Cádiz in 1763. That same year the Novohispanic Viceroy Joaquín de Montserrat, the Marquis of Cruillas, ordered that all residents of the viceregal court city "uniformly light the streets," by installing lanterns on a centrally placed balcony or a large window of their houses. Cruillas decreed that householders must ignite these lanterns from the time of evening prayers until they heard the sound of the curfew at 10 p.m. He justified this order by explaining that "by this means, the insults, sins, and damages provoked and fed by the darkness will be avoided." Those who did not obey Cruillas's decree would be fined one peso for every violation. If they refused to follow the order three times, they risked six days in jail. Cruillas also threatened anyone who "dared to remove, steal, or break lanterns" with eight days in jail.[31]

For the next fourteen years, New Spain experienced very heavy royal intervention via the tour of the powerful Spanish inspector general José de Gálvez.[32] However, Gálvez's inspections did not help the installation of streetlights. By the late 1770s Cruillas's approach had not succeeded. The urban lighting project finally restarted under the active Bourbon reformer Viceroy Antonio María de Bucareli (1771–1779). A 204-page file discussing how to illuminate the city documents this drawn-out process. In a series of petitions and debates dating from 1773 to 1785, the town council, the high court, and the viceroy vetted what seem to be spontaneous proposals in the Spanish *arbitrista* tradition, debating several different issues relating to public lighting of the capital city. Throughout the Renaissance and beyond, self-designated experts or arbitristas sent sometimes incredibly verbose written treatises to those in power, extending to hundreds of pages. These documents regaled leaders with their advice, as the arbitristas believed that they "had something to communicate of benefit to king and commonwealth."[33] In the case of Mexico City's lighting debate, the files include administrative ruminations about how to deal with the perceived temptations and dangers of darkness. They generally convey a predictable rhetoric regarding the criminality of the masses in the obscurity of the night, in line with the Bourbon vision of the populace.

In 1776 a man named Pedro Joseph Cortés sparked the discussion on street lighting by submitting a petition to Cruillas. Inspired by his "nervous desire" to help the viceroy clean the streets and light the city at night, Cortés observed that the plans communicated in previous bandos had "paused after their circulation."[34] Cortés and the other arbitrista-like commentators and city leaders made many very specific recommendations in their petitions, such as suggesting that Mexico follow the model of

Cádiz's public lighting and providing the details for measuring the distance between each streetlight (twenty-five *varas*, or just under seventy feet).[35] Cortés included a drawing for the ideal lantern to adorn Mexico City's streets (figure 1). The description of the image is as follows: "A lantern with ornamental leaves on all of its sides. In the upper triangle are found rhombuses shaped like diamonds and flowers. In the middle, the lantern is divided into sixteen glass frames. Its base consists of a kind of flag attached to the wall. The intention is that these lanterns have the same design as those that light the street passing by the Tribunal of the Holy Inquisition."[36] Expert testimonies such as these demonstrated that Mexico City's reforming commentators had studied the history and current conditions of public illumination in Europe. They allude to Greek and Roman leaders, who "perfected" street lighting in their eras, and describe the different styles of lanterns seen in London, Germany, Holland, and Madrid. Perhaps with the goal of offering examples for New Spain, the learned contributors detail how Paris installed "a running line of lanterns up the center of the streets, hanging from a rope that crosses from house to house." In contrast, Londoners enjoyed "pure glass globes without any lead placed on knobs in the walls." In Holland and Germany, the lanterns hung from "two rows of sticks . . . triangular in shape with white iron coverings." For its part, Madrid had succeeded in installing lanterns that created a large enough radius of illumination to connect, forming a consistent chain of light.[37]

Cortés and the other petitioners did point out the numerous "deaths, robberies, and fights" hidden under the cover of darkness, but they concentrated more on the global stature of New Spain's capital. Street lighting became a competitive point of pride for Mexico City to shine "as brilliantly as the very best in Spain, because of its greater size." Another petitioner, a merchant named don Ángel María Merelo, spoke to the viceroy's vanity with the observation that "the principal goal of monarchs has been to beautify their courts and kingdoms." Merelo reassured Bucareli that the residents of the capital were definitely rich enough to fund this beautification project, and, along with Cortés, discussed the specific ways to compel the general populace to pay for this reform. While Cortés introduced

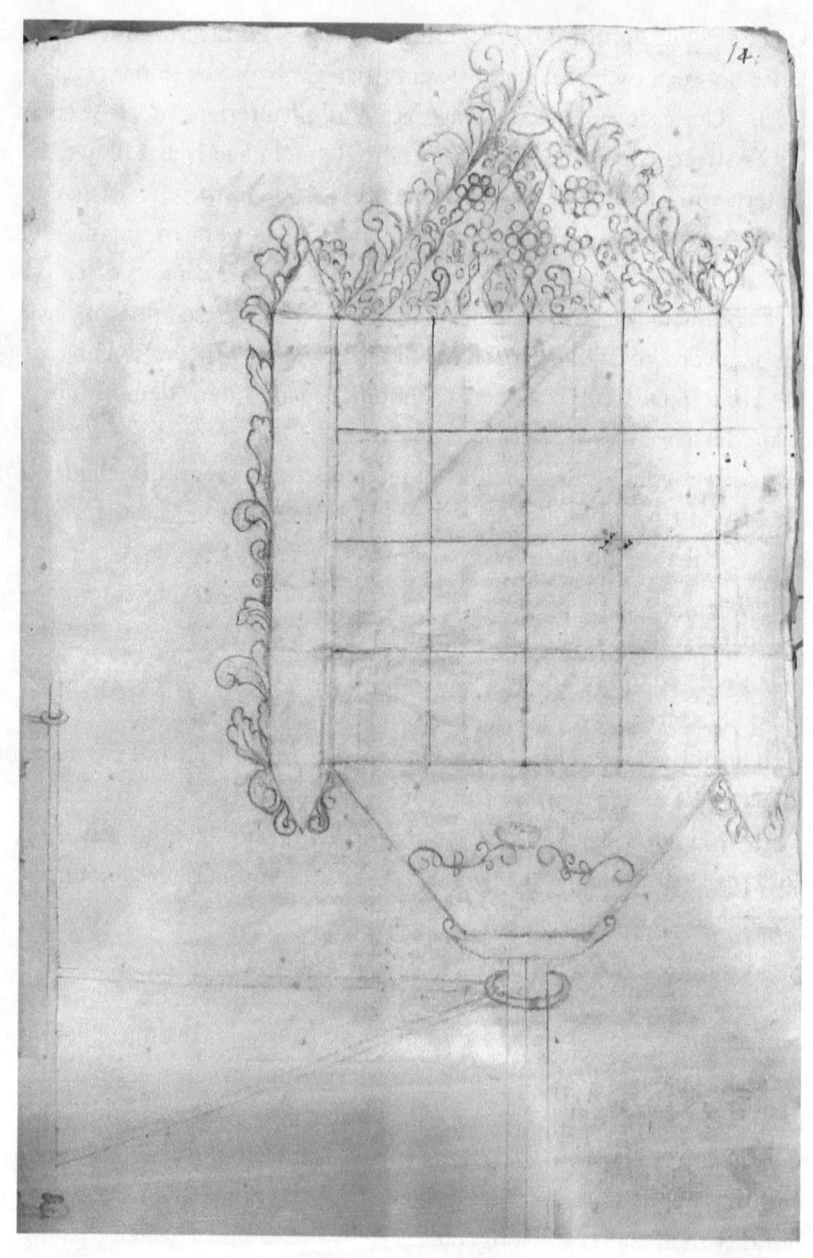

1. Sketch of a Mexico City lantern. Archivo General de la Nación, Mexico City.

the idea of a tax on flour, Merelo proposed a system whereby hundreds of small store owners (*tenderos*) would collect small amounts of money that would add up to enough income to fund the project.[38] In response, the tenderos gathered to discuss this proposal and ultimately refused to go along, along the way mocking and rejecting Merelo's proposition.[39]

Another contribution to the deliberations came from Coronel Francisco Antonio Crespo, recently returned from serving as governor in Sinaloa and Sonora. Crespo emphasized that New Spain should learn from European cities and stressed a need for more surveillance of the vice-ridden urban population:

> It should be enough to remember that in the courts and populous cities of Europe, the most energetic activity of judges and their superiors has not achieved avoiding crimes and excesses in the dark of the night, [but instead] they remedy them with the lighting of their streets, because the transgressors fear the eyes of their neighbors, those who pass them, and the magistrates. These powerful reasons [apply] everywhere, and they have greater strength in Mexico because of its multitude of inhabitants who lack a good education that would turn them away from vices, and create a fear of justice.[40]

These statements underscore how the imperial elite perceived public lighting as a way to improve the behavior and morality of a large segment of their urban subjects, even if they did not necessarily agree on how to fund it. According to Crespo, with its quickly growing population, New Spain's capital should imitate the great cities of Europe. He strongly opposed collecting money from small stores patronized by the poor, using access to light at night as a way to distinguish the rich and middle-income residents of the capital from the poor masses, who risked their lives going out in the gloom. Thus, Crespo observed that the rich avoided venturing at night. If they did, they enjoyed the safety of their carriages, perhaps guarded by servants carrying torches for them. Middling vecinos could afford to carry their own lanterns.[41]

In 1779 the reform-minded *cabildo regidor* (town councilmember) don Francisco María de Herrera joined the debate, stressing crime prevention and making the city more orderly for transit, with less focus on beautification. Herrera reminded Viceroy Bucareli that these reforms "were the principals of good government [policía], each of which have occupied, in all parts of the world, a great deal of time, thought, and expense."[42] Additionally, "Illumination is very useful, because darkness engenders enormous crimes—not only because it covers them but also because it encourages criminals to commit them. For this reason, [public lighting] has been adopted in Europe in the most organized cities. This capital has even more justification to follow this example because its population is undoubtedly very numerous, and very corrupt."[43] Herrera felt that Mexico City needed street lighting that was "useful," not perfectly "harmonious, symmetrical," or even obviously beautiful. As such, in his opinion the 1763 project of residents providing their own lights continued to serve the city best. Herrera argued that streets containing convents did not need illumination, so vecinos could focus their funds on their own neighborhoods. He believed that the poor could not afford any additional taxes; in contrast, the rich already wasted their money on "vices and entertainments," and they could afford the cost.[44]

Implementing Illumination

In response to these petitions, and incorporating some of their precise recommendations, Viceroy Bucareli proposed that each city block install eight to twelve lanterns, set up in a straight line along the streets. He further recommended a monthly salary of fifteen pesos to employ a lamp lighter who would maintain the wicks ignited all night. This pay, while small, represented 50 percent more than the income of a coachman, an occupation that probably attracted men with similar backgrounds and physical strength and endurance as the night watchmen.[45] The viceroy also suggested that the oils to feed the flames should be derived from sesame or chia seeds, turnips, or the native tree known as *manitas* (*chiranthodendron*). The city had a mill that produced this oil, located near the Arcos de Belen.[46] These ideas sound outlandish today, but other countries used olive oil or—much worse in terms of smell—a variety of fish oils, including from sardines.[47]

By 1780 wealthy Mexico City residents in select neighborhoods had already chosen to apply their personal funds to illuminating their own streets. Most likely those who volunteered to pay came from the growing class of Spanish bureaucrats caught up in European enlightened rationalism.[48] The practice of resident-paid lighting inspired a preliminary proposal for more comprehensive street lighting throughout the city. The first decree stated this goal in late 1783, on the orders of Viceroy don Matías de Gálvez, brother of the royal inspector general José de Gálvez. The idea was that the most prosperous inhabitants would not require too much governmental pressure to fund a project to beautify the city for the benefit of everyone, rich and poor. Seeking to follow other cities that had achieved resident-funded public lighting, and optimistic that affluent residents would take on the task of lighting their own neighborhoods, Gálvez called on locals' sense of pride and competition with European cities:

> In all of the great cities, the illumination of their streets has been viewed as convenient, both for the comfort of their inhabitants, as well as the prevention of disorder. These two motivations have obligated this superior government to command by decree in various occasions that this city be illuminated, with each resident installing a lantern in every house. However, experience proves, not only in Mexico, but also in various parts of Spain, that this approach is useless and unsubstantial. . . . More effective would be imitating other cities in which illumination has been established securely and beautifully, and it would be better to do the same here, by the methods of these other cities, or other equivalent ones. Many plans have been proposed to achieve this goal, but they have been met with many difficulties and delays to carrying out this beneficial and urgent idea. The quickest, simplest, and least burdensome plan for lighting is for each individual to take on the responsibility, as is the case of some streets already, where some residents now take care of it, or the neighbors of each street or block agree to give this commission to a neighbor who they trust, or the alcalde of the neighborhood who

collects a contribution. . . . I have resolved, that within four months from this date, that anyone with the wherewithal to contribute must install lanterns on their streets. Other funds will pay for the lighting in front of the Royal Palace and the offices of the Royal Treasury. All apothecaries, grocery stores, peanut-sellers, bakeries, winemakers, ham-sellers, casinos, inns, and large houses must also follow this order. All must contribute to benefit the public, proportionate to their means and status, with no exceptions for those who claim ignorance of the laws of good government, or ecclesiastical or secular privileges. . . . No resident with means is excused from such an important duty in service to God and the King, and to adorn this famous city. This does not apply to the poor, nor those who cannot obey this command without notable hardship to their families. Also, I am so resolved to facilitate this plan that I forbid any increases in the cost of lanterns or other related materials.[49]

This document presumes that the vecinos widely approved of public lighting and trusts that everyone had the same mindset as the enlightened, reforming Spanish officials. The viceroy viewed this reform as benefiting all and therefore represented it as almost a religious duty that anyone who had the means had the moral obligation to carry out. Ultimately, the most controversial element of the bando proved to be the opening it provided for individuals to claim poverty to avoid paying for lighting on their streets of residence.

Gálvez ordered the circulation of this decree widely across the city. However, less than a year after its dissemination, the reforming viceroy became ill, one of thousands of victims of the devastating epidemics suffered by inhabitants of central Mexico in this era. Two weeks before his death, Gálvez ceded his powers to the audiencia, the viceregal high court based in Mexico City (see introduction). By early 1785 the court rereleased the above bando, emphasizing that it called for "wise, timely, and very useful measures for the illumination of this city." Unfortunately, as of the date that the bando circulated, none of the measures it mandated had come to fruition.[50] Frustrated, the audiencia commanded that the installation of lanterns take place immediately as Gálvez had directed, "starting with this royal palace, where the necessary [lanterns] will be placed on the front and side [walls] to serve as an example to inspire the honest residents."[51]

As a result of this second bando, by the summer of 1785 the number of lanterns had increased significantly. As proposed, government funds did pay for lighting outside buildings relating to the Spanish empire, such as the Royal Mint.[52] The government installed six ornate and heavy iron lanterns painted green with gilded pendants (made with actual gold), firmly attached to the walls of this building. Additional costs included a receptacle for holding oil, a hand lantern for igniting the installed lanterns, and a strong ladder to facilitate this task, contributing to the total cost of 270 pesos. Even into the nineteenth century, government buildings and key locations such as the Plaza Mayor maintained their own separate accounts recording the costs to pay for lighting and guards.[53]

Outside of the blocks comprised of government buildings, residents paid for the lanterns' substantial costs themselves. By mid-1785 vecinos in select areas already funded lighting in the following streets: "San Francisco, Empedradillo, Tacuba, Donceles, Medinas, Santa Clara and its alleyway, Canoa, Esclavo, Manrique, Pila Seca, San Andrés, and Santo Domingo up to the Santa Ana parish," allegedly "without any resistance from anyone."[54] These streets, some of which retain these names to the present day, formed a rough rectangle of approximately six blocks by three blocks, located to the immediate west and ranging a bit to the northwest of the cathedral. Adjacent to the sacred center, this district hosted prestigious friaries such as San José Real, and the convents of the Belemitas and Santa Clara. Interestingly enough, not a single official pulquería did business in this neighborhood.[55] Instead, one of the most important viceregal leaders domiciled in these streets, side-by-side with more plebeian residents and businesses.

To give a sense of the costs, a typical street, such as the Calle de Vergara, might require approximately seven streetlights, with an initial investment of 177 pesos and an ongoing total monthly cost of fourteen pesos to maintain them.[56] To put this latter sum in perspective, fourteen pesos represents close to double what a poor adult male day laborer could expect to earn in a month between 1750 and 1812.[57] The basic labor cost to manufacture each lantern was also fourteen pesos, with materials (cedar, iron, glass), a ladder to install and light them, and tools which in total added up to the additional outlay of close to eighty pesos. Monthly expenses in 1785 included paying six pesos to a "*mozo* [boy]" to light the lanterns, a few reales for rags to clean them, and extra expenditures for additional candles and labor needed on especially dark nights.

To pay for the lanterns' fabrication and installation, twenty-two residents on the Calle de Vergara contributed a total of 179 pesos. The amount of each contribution depended on the wealth of each individual. The list of payments included in the relevant file demonstrates that Mexico City's different social classes truly did live together on the same street, without physical economic segregation. At the top level, two aristocrats contributed sixteen pesos each, and a noblewoman head-of-household contributed ten pesos. The donations proceeded down in quantity to parallel each resident's income, as follows: a tinsmith (six pesos), a tailor (four pesos), a barber (three pesos), a chocolatier (two pesos), a shoemaker (two pesos), and a man who rented out funeral equipment (four pesos). In terms of the monthly costs, each resident contributed between three reales for the most economically strained residents and one peso from the wealthy denizens.[58]

This particular street housed a renowned Spanish nobleman, viceregal jurist, and leader in the project to continue the drainage of Lake Texcoco: don Cosme de Mier y Trespalacios.[59] Mier, a quintessentially enlightened Bourbon reformer who advocated for the use of convict labor on Mexico City's public works projects, organized the lighting on his street and served on the ayuntamiento. He expressed no sympathy when one of his neighbors begged the town council for relief from the initial and ongoing fees due to his extreme poverty. Mier threatened this man, named Agustín Sanabria, with incarceration or confiscation of his property if he did not instantly come up with the four pesos needed to pay for his share of installing the lanterns. In his petition for relief from this unforeseen expenditure, Sanabria cited the 1783 decree, which stressed that the poor or anyone who faced hardship paying for an additional expense did not have to contribute to funding the new lights. Sanabria argued that he and his children would starve to death within two or three months if they took on a portion of the costs. Sanabria's petition ended with the time-honored polite request that Spanish officials show kindness to the unfortunates in their realms.[60]

In response, Mier sought out witnesses who knew Sanabria to ascertain the facts regarding his finances, expenditures, and his general standard of living, a common procedure in viceregal courts.[61] According to several of his acquaintances, labeled as men of African descent, Sanabria actually owned one of the more successful business on the Calle de Vergara and ranked as an officer in the *pardo* (brown, referring in New Spain to free individuals of partial African ancestry) battalion.[62] In a previous career, Sanabria had worked as the designated dogcatcher at the cathedral but left that job (passing it on to a man labeled a "free Black") to invest in the extremely lucrative business of renting funeral accoutrements. Witness statements estimated the value of Sanabria's store inventory at two thousand pesos in the form of mourning paraphernalia, coffins, and small boxes for children, of a range of quality. Because these items were rented, not purchased, Sanabria profited greatly while others suffered when an epidemic broke out in the mid-1780s.[63] To give just one example of how this business made money, the cost of renting a child's coffin for a few hours was two pesos, and he could reuse the coffin for its sad duty over and over again. With his accumulating wealth, Sanabria had managed to buy himself a commission as a sublieutenant in the free-colored militia and had been observed in an ostentatious, costly uniform, fully equipped with epaulets and costing an estimated 150 pesos.[64]

In the enlightened mindset, paying for street lighting represented the mark of a moral, intelligent man, perhaps even a new kind of religious duty. As such, Mier expressed rage at Sanabria's "haughtiness and contemptuousness" in claiming that poverty prevented his contribution to street lighting. According to Mier, any man of dignity, including clerics and soldiers, recognized the need for proper governance and public beautification brightly demonstrated by street lighting. Mier mentioned these two occupations to imply that both groups usually enjoyed other privileges that might have allowed them to avoid paying for the lanterns. Objecting to reforms that encouraged policía, which in this era still meant "good government," marked a Mexico City resident as immoral, uncivilized, or even rebellious.[65] Mier judged Sanabria with the disgust commonly expressed toward the plebeians in this era, and continuously well into the nineteenth century.[66]

Quite shocking to his listeners, supposedly Sanabria had made a comment along the lines of "que iban leyes donde querían reyes [loosely translated: kings make whatever laws they want]" to explain his refusal to pay the fees. As Mier wrote directly to the viceroy Bernardo de Gálvez (the son of the previous viceroy Matías de Gálvez, who had proposed the plan for resident-supported lighting):

> [This comment] sounds like [Sanabria] thought something was irregular or unfair about the determination of the government, even though he enjoys military privileges, as a second lieutenant of the pardo battalion. Judging from his appearance, he is one of those Blacks who have advanced from the lowest [ranks of society]. He is someone who has received important offices, and now has pride and insolence. He is not poor—his uniform, according to witnesses, is better than that of a colonel. He makes plenty of money due to the plagues that cause so many deaths in this capital. His poverty is a fantasy. He should not be poor if he has reached such a high office. . . . These kinds of people were born of bad blood. . . . All of his kind are of a presumptuous genius, dissolute, and arrogant. . . . He is the only one who has called this division of costs unjust. I do not want to tire Your Excellence with more on this, but you must fully grasp the character, and nature of this kind of people. This is wasting Your Excellency's time . . . that should be [instead spent] on graver matters.[67]

In this statement, the wealthy peninsular Spaniard Mier reduces Sanabria to an example of a bothersome rebel born of immoral bloodlines, in keeping with the increasing dismissal of poor colonial subjects in this era. In

Mier's view, Sanabria embodies precisely the kind of troublesome plebeian who needs surveillance and discipline. Sanabria's petition inscribed his resistance to civilizing urban reform. To underscore Mier's elitist message, a municipal judge reacted by observing that only "indolence" caused the poverty of those who did not contribute to the street lighting expenses. Sanabria required a "strong hand" to counter the "pernicious example" of men like him, who could destroy the ambitious plan for street lighting. The purpose of this project, after all, was to either change plebeian behavior or remove plebes from central city public spaces. Under all of this pressure, by mid-November of 1785 Sanabria had paid his share to light his street.

Public Lighting and Public Safety

Mier may have won this particular battle, but he lost the war. The audiencia returned to the issue of street lighting in early 1787, after a horrific year of drought and following a devastating typhus epidemic, which began in 1784 and resulted in thousands of deaths, including that of Bernardo de Gálvez, who succeeded his father Matías as viceroy in 1785.[68] From December of 1786 to May of 1787, New Spain again lacked a viceroy, and the high court took over. One of their actions was to issue another bando on the continuing unresolved issue of city illumination. The new decree mentioned beauty and utility as motivations to illuminate the streets, but also danger. This bando introduced the idea of safety and "common good" as a moral obligation and even began to state this duty in Christian terms.

A perception of increasing threats from new and dangerous urban residents typifies Mexico City's efforts to become "modern" in a European sense, from this time until well into the twentieth century.[69] These perceptions follow those expressed by other leaders who advocated for new and improved street-level law enforcement in growing cities around the North Atlantic world, within the bounds of a government ideology claiming to value a new concept of public safety and security. However, this concept of "safety and security" represented nothing more than an increasing criminalization of the poor and working classes and a desire to protect property and reclaim the streets for elite visions of urban space. Helping to literally enlighten the court city to fight off the dangers of the criminal poor had taken on the tone of a religious duty. The 1787 Mexican audiencia decree stated:

> We the president, regent, and *oidores* of the royal audiencia and chancellery of this New Spain, in whom resides the government:
>
> In attention to the virtue of the published decree of the order of this royal audiencia . . . that most of the principal streets of city will be illuminated, with the uniformity and beauty that is desired for this extremely useful goal. Each of the residents [should] choose a subject entrusted with the making of the lanterns, prorating their cost, distributing them one by one at proportionate distances, and to care for their cleaning and lighting, [with] everyone contributing a small monthly quantity according to their resources for this and for the oil. In spite of this good example . . . approved by royal order on February 1, 1786, many streets remain without light due to the insensibility of their residents to the common good, and their own. It can be observed that some of the first [lighted streets] are now dark again, and that the [number] of lanterns have been reduced because the residents make excuses for not continuing their contributions. . . . The idea of serving God should serve as a stimulus, as well as the obligation to attend to the common good, and prevent the thefts, deaths, and abuses encouraged by night's shadows, to facilitate the security of houses and property, and the ability to travel on lighted streets, the decree of January 15 resolved that within one month, to install lanterns on the streets that do not have them, with the residents agreeing to organize this. If they do not do so, the local authority should name a grocery owner or tavern keeper, or anyone else who can be put in charge, to determine the contribution to be made by the residents who live in the larger houses with exterior windows to organize what other streets do for the construction and maintenance of the lantern and its light.[70]

Despite years of setbacks, this new decree still maintained that residents should organize their own street lighting. Punitively, the bando ordered that anyone who resisted implementing the new orders must move out of their neighborhood within four days, because they were now a "useless and dangerous" neighbor, and another more "useful" person should occupy the house. The decree mandated the lighting of the lanterns at the sound of the curfew, until midnight, from the second day after the full moon until the sixth day of the waxing quarter moon. The high court threatened "evildoers" set on attacking the lanterns, or inducing young boys to do so, with public humiliation and a month in jail for a first offense and twenty-five lashes for a second infraction. It also stipulated that the "guardas de pito [whistle guards]," a prelude to the better-documented guarda faroleros, should pay special attention to maintaining street lighting.

The race to achieve street lighting accelerated rapidly under the reign of the Count of Revillagigedo, who entered Mexico City as viceroy in October of 1789. This viceroy ranks among the most famous in Mexican history, for his extensive reforms prohibiting throwing trash in the streets, a monumental street paving project, and efforts to control the pigs, cattle, and dogs that continued to roam around the largest city in the hemisphere. By this time local leaders had given up on resident-sustained lighting and chosen a far more expensive, tax-funded approach, in the hands of a public works or policía, still referring to "good government." A branch of the municipal government based out of the town council handled all these concerns, with oversight by the viceroy and the audiencia.[71] The high costs of these reforms and the new bureaucracy set in place underscore the great importance reformers placed on illuminating Mexico's urban streets. By spring of 1790 Revillagigedo and Mexico City corregidor Bernardo Bonavía confirmed receipt of twenty thousand pesos from the *real tribunal del consulado* (a merchant guild founded in Mexico in 1594), to pass on to "master tinsmiths" to pay them for their construction of all of the needed lanterns, which ended up numbering 1,128 in the first phase of installation.[72]

Around the same time, in April 1790, the viceroy decreed the establishment of a corps of lantern lighters, enumerating the structure of their leadership, pay, and duties in his order.[73] Highlighting that their function centered on the wise viceregal mandate to illuminate the city, the bando was titled "The Rules Made by the Most Excellent Señor Viceroy the

Count of Revilla Gigedo for the Government That Must Be Observed in the Lighting of the Streets of Mexico." This document called for the appointment of a head guard (guarda mayor), who received two thousand pesos in annual salary. His duties included "guarding in his house the oil and the wicks, administering them, and the various pieces of tin necessary to stock the lanterns when they must be lighted according to when the moon rises." Later the viceroy added a decree to organize a warehouse for the head guard to store the necessary equipment. In terms of the process for hiring men, the guarda mayor proposed his choice of lantern guards to the intendant and corregidor, who then appointed them.

This bando also explained the expectations for the guards' tasks. In a foreshadowing of the modern bureaucracy of badge numbers, the guarda faroleros had to carry a printed copy of their appointment listing the number of lanterns under their jurisdiction and the specific streets assigned to them. Each guard (ninety-nine in total) attended to no more than twelve lanterns. At dawn, they had to return to the head guard's house for oil and wicks to stock their lanterns. According to their regulations, they must clean their lanterns by no later than 9 a.m. On dark nights, they had to light their lanterns at the hour of nightly prayers. For these tasks, and others to be discussed in the next chapter, the night watchmen earned a salary of fifteen pesos per month, around double that of an unskilled day laborer, and well over double that of the mozos previously suggested to do the same basic lantern maintenance and lighting. When the head guard hired a guard, the new employee received a lantern, ladder, a container of oil, and clothes, among other objects (see chapter 2). If they needed to replace any of their equipment, or if they broke a lantern, the guards had to pay for these items out of their own salary. The guards' superiors should verbally rebuke them if their lanterns were unlighted or dirty. They risked dismissal if these infractions occurred more than once. Revillagigedo decreed harsh punishments for anyone who broke or stole a lantern from the street.[74] Even if the accused did this out of carelessness, they had to pay to replace the lantern. Those lacking money would have their pay docked at their place of employment. Revillagigedo proposed that stealing a lantern or even just planning to steal one should result in two hundred lashings in the location where the theft took place.⁷⁵ In practice, guards did not receive corporal punishment for these infractions. For example, in 1798, Marcelo Salazar, the guard in charge of patrol area number 88, spent three days locked up in the *bartolina*, or dungeon, for breaking his ladder and spilling the oil he received.⁷⁶

Six months later, in October 1790, the city government had not received royal funds needed to continue to pay for the lighting project.⁷⁷ In response, by November, Revillagigedo codified the purpose and costs of street lighting in another bando focusing on both the source of the funds and his goals for his court city.⁷⁸ The viceroy began his decree critically, observing that "having not been able to perfect completely the illumination of the streets of this populous city on dark nights," with any of the previous decrees, and that this "important and necessary" goal "will never succeed if it is tasked to the residents." As a result of population's recalcitrance, he was obligated to put this project in "one hand . . . the most Noble City [Mexico City] will take care to confirm the general lighting." In other words, with this bando, lighting became a governmental reform, not a vecinos' duty. He calculated that installing the lanterns would cost over 35,400 pesos and that their maintenance added up to 24,000 pesos annually. Together, the night watchmen's salaries tallied 16,490 pesos at a rate of 15 pesos monthly, and of course the head guard received 2,000 pesos annually. Another 6,000 pesos would go toward buying three thousand *arrobas* of oil per year. These figures highlight that the lanterns themselves consumed close to 65 percent of the budget.

Who covered these new costs? Revillagigedo levied a three-real tax on every load of flour entering the city, so anyone who consumed bread ended up paying to illuminate New Spain's capital. The viceroy observed that the city consumed 100,000 *cargos* annually, each of which made 430 loaves of bread. Three reales divided into the cost of 430 loaves increased the cost of one loaf of bread imperceptibly. Interestingly, this tax perhaps would have even less of an effect on the very poor Indigenous residents, who, as the Viceroy acknowledged, only rarely ate bread, preferring tortillas.⁷⁹ Revillagigedo predicted that a surplus of funds that might help cover any broken lantern glass or, more ambitiously, fund the extension of the lighting beyond the center of the city.

Revillagigedo then proceeded to discuss the benefits of this plan, focusing on the concept of safety for the urban property-owning classes—that the bourgeoisie needed to claim the streets at night and that only illumination could achieve this goal. In his view, established and prosperous residents possessed both the moral obligation and the wealth to improve their own city. Acknowledging Mexico City as the "first" city in the Americas, the wording of the viceroy's decree suggested that the simple fact of his capital's huge population had created more danger for its residents. The new tax most affected "the wealthy and those of middle rank," who he believed would happily pay much more for "the imponderable benefits that lighting offers, which interests everyone, because they count on it for the security of their persons and the wealth represented by their families and houses."[80] A sense of security for the residents was necessary in so worthy a city. As Revillagigedo explained: "[Street lighting] would restore the tranquility that decent men lacked. It will contain the habitual or careless delinquent, preventing evil deeds from coming to pass.... It will provide the inestimable comfort of street transit without danger. This very populous capital, with a growing number of all kinds of residents, cannot rest without establishing the good order of governance [*el buen orden de policía*], and lighting is a fundamental to everything, as it strikes at the root of the worst crimes, planned by day and executed at night."[81] In recognition of the concept of *buena policía*, the money collected in the new tax would be stored in a safe designated for the city's "policía." Continuing the theme of "defense and caution," the viceroy specified that ninety-three guards should keep watch and serve the residents in case of any accidents. These men would help prevent "the frequent robberies, assaults, homicides, and other crimes that take place in the darkness." Revillagigedo argued that "[these acts already] have declined since their establishment."[82]

The new viceroy certainly spoke with authority on this last topic, as only a week after his arrival in 1789, eleven individuals perished during a horrific murder spree in the establishment of the wealthy and powerful merchant don Joaquín Dongo. Rumors circulated that a corrupt former employee committed the homicides in order to access the thousands of pesos of cash and silver stored in Dongo's warehouse. In response to this crime, all visitors to the city were questioned, and every possible corner of the city was searched. The investigators found one of the murderers because a bystander had noticed a man with blood in his hair at a barbershop. Two weeks after the crime, Revillagigedo approved the execution of the culprits, earning himself the title of "Vindicator of Justice."[83] These incidents show how New Spain fits into the broader Atlantic world trajectory of policing: the 1811 murder of seven people in London, known as the Ratcliffe Highway murders, also resulted in calls for policing reforms.[84] Of course, murders continued in the viceregal capital, and there is no statistical way to prove if they decreased after the establishment of the night watchmen.[85]

The installation of the lanterns and carrying out their nightly lighting and maintenance fell to the newly created guarda mayor, who reported to the leading city royal official (corregidor) and the viceroy himself. Already in January 1791, corregidor Bonavía began to note some financial challenges in the *ramo de alumbrado* (literally, the illumination branch of viceregal government), which simply had not yet seen the income from the proposed flour tax.[86] Bonavía, on behalf of the first head guard José Moreno, again directly wrote to Revillagigedo in 1793 regarding providing funds to take advantage of good prices for lamp oil, and the process of constructing the lanterns, down to the details of negotiation with individual tinsmiths.[87] Conflicts over costs continued between the head guard and the leading authorities into the nineteenth century, with even the king weighing in over how the guarda mayor spent his budget.[88]

Speaking from his throne far above these petty local concerns, King Charles IV confirmed the wisdom and care that Viceroy Revillagigedo showed to his subjects by approving the street lighting reforms of November 1790, as soon as he received the information in Spain. Fourteen months after the original viceregal decree, Revillagigedo had received written royal approval for a flour tax to pay for streetlights. The king highlighted the concept of "security" in his official decree:

> To the viceroy, governor, and captain general of the provinces of New Spain. . . . In a letter dated November 27 of last year . . . [it was made clear that] the lighting in that capital would never be achieved

if left in the charge of the residents.... [The proposed solution was a charge of] three reales in each load of flour entering the city. This assessment would be so imperceptible to the public that it only resulted in a quarter of an ounce less in each loaf of bread. When [the king] examined this with a great deal of reflection, it seemed very gentle and advantageous to all of your residents.... It would allow the city to achieve the greatest security and tranquility could be offered by widespread illumination, which deserves the highest regard from the residents for such a laudable accomplishment.... Thank you for the care that you take to contribute to the security and tranquility of all of the residents.... Signed in San Lorenzo, October 17, 1791. Received by Viceroy Revilla Gigedo on January 24, 1792.[89]

Both the king and the viceroy expressed a great deal of confidence in the success of the lighting project. In 1804 Alexander von Humboldt agreed, writing that Mexico City was full of broad, clean streets, well-lighted by reflector lanterns.[90] Accounting records dating from 1798 also seem to indicate a bright future for urban illumination: while the monthly costs reported by head guard Moreno totaled four thousand pesos, and the flour tax only brought in thirty-two hundred, an enormous carry over remained of more than twenty thousand pesos.[91]

These opinions and numbers exaggerate the level of illumination in the court city of New Spain. The important guarda farolero task, covered in depth in chapter 3, of walking with priests, surgeons, midwives, doctors, and other medical experts when these professionals were called on at night in order to light their path and protect them from harm, suggests that darkness remained very pervasive even after Revillagigedo installed over eleven hundred streetlights. This key duty also reveals that Mexico City probably did not widely use "linkmen" or individuals for hire who escorted others at night carrying a lantern. Each night watchmen tended approximately twelve lanterns, adding up to close to twelve-hundred lights in the city. Their patrol area generally encompassed no more than six hundred varas, or five hundred meters of street length. That means that, by a rough calculation, the lanterns were installed only every forty or so meters (approximately every 131 feet). These lights were simply wicks in oil, providing small and isolated illumination, not spot lights radiating out several meters in all directions. True, most likely the Mexico City streets lights were reflector or *réverbère* lanterns (as Humboldt suggests), invented in Paris in 1763. This technology represented a major improvement on older models: their design included a reflector located above several wicks to project the light downward, while another reflector projected the light sideways, to prevent dissipation of illumination upward. Other technological upgrades included improvements on the candlewicks previously used in gas lanterns, and a glass cylinder to protect the flame from drafts.[92] While observers of the time perceived réverbère lanterns as extremely bright, this technology only created pools of light, absolutely no larger than several meters in diameter.[93] Thus, the lighting from these lanterns never created a connected chain of illumination to truly brighten the streets. As will be discussed in depth in chapter 6, smashing one or two of them in a block easily welcomed back darkness and all that it hid from official eyes.[94]

Darkness Returns

Soon after their installation, debates continued regarding the lanterns' efficacy. In August 1791, critics published their views in the *Gazeta de México*, the periodical that had announced the viceroy's bando regarding lighting on December 7, 1790.[95] Only eight months later, the *Gazeta* stated that the capital city would truly enjoy illumination if the number of lanterns doubled; however, it disagreed over how many outlying neighborhoods already had streetlights. Tiny alleyways and the sparsely populated outskirts of the city did not require the same investment as larger, busy thoroughfares. Commentators also noted that extinguishing the lights at midnight did not make sense in a "very populous city like Mexico, where many people transit the streets until midnight, often for honest and even necessary reasons."[96]

Not only plebeian anger destroyed the streetlights—the government itself could not carry out street illumination effectively, especially at the dawn of the nineteenth century, as civil unrest erupted in the capital.[97] The ineffective implementation of Revillagigedo's plan came to light in 1808, as major changes in Mexico City's government dominated this watershed year for New Spain.[98] The Napoleonic invasion of Spain led to reactions among viceregal leaders, about sixteen months before an insurgent priest inspired tens of thousands of peasants and miners to take up weapons against the hated *gachupines*, or European-born Spaniards. The summer of 1808 saw a complex series of events that resists a clear summary. After receiving the news of the abdication of the Spanish King Charles IV in 1808 (a few months after it took place), authorities in the Novohispanic capital attempted to push for continuity. This approach lasted only ten days before conflicts erupted between Viceroy José de Iturrigaray and the creole cabildo members. Although staffed by the landed elite, the cabildo claimed to represent the popular sentiments and strongly opposed the rule of Joseph Bonaparte. The audiencia and merchant leaders preferred to wait out the crisis. Popular sentiment veered in two directions: toward either independence or support of Fernando VII (son of Charles IV) as the legitimate ruler. Thousands of residents gathered to confirm their self-declared king, who actually languished in captivity in Spain at this time. Amid massive popular and allegedly peaceful gatherings, along with stone-throwing attacks on the wealthy, the viceroy offered to resign in early fall. Instead a coup d'état (led by wealthy merchants and militiamen, but again claiming popular inspiration) forced him out and the high court approved.[99] Beliefs in popular sovereignty, the importance of a sense of the legitimacy of the state, and a traditional contract between the king and the people undergirded the movement against Iturrigaray.[100] Merchant groups put a Spanish military leader, Pedro de Garibay, into power; he lasted in this position for less than a year. The archbishop of Mexico stepped in for another short stint as viceroy until another military man, Francisco Javier Venegas, took control, with the approval of the Spanish government. Venegas arrived in Mexico City just two days before the official start of mass insurgency in fall of 1810—a story which will continue in chapter 7.[101]

To return to the spring and summer of 1808: shortly before the political crisis that ousted the viceroy, residents, including neighborhood alcaldes, complained of complete and total darkness on certain important streets, such as the Real Calle del Rastro. These negative reports prompted Iturrigaray to investigate the work performance of the lantern guards and their superiors.[102] The following accusatory words expressed by the viceroy sparked an interrogation and a subsequent defensive reaction on the part of those entrusted with maintaining the lighting: "Despite the repeated orders that I have communicated regarding that the [bureaucracy charged with the street] lighting is maintained with the appropriate brightness, there has been no remedy for the very serious defects caused by these indolent subalterns. Therefore, their superiors, who should maintain their standards, are to be blamed." Iturrigaray worried that the darkness on certain streets showed a problem in the administration of the ramo del alumbrado and a carelessness on the part of the head guard and his lieutenants.[103]

For their part, the guards, many of whom may have lived on the beats they patrolled at night, fielded complaints from their own neighbors when the lanterns on their streets did not burn for sufficient hours. They were dismayed by the public outcry, which focused on their incompetency. In the investigation, the night watchmen and their corporals made statements that provided specifics regarding how their lanterns functioned and why they did not effectively brighten the streets. In order to remain ignited for the appropriate number of hours each night, each lantern required four ounces of oil. The guards complained that lately they had only received one ounce to supply each of their lanterns for the entire night. Sometimes, when they stopped by the warehouse that distributed their allotment of oil, they received only a half-ounce per lantern. This meant that unless the moon shone very brightly, the streets would soon return to complete darkness. Although the small distribution of oil was supposed to be enough to light the streets after the moon rose, they could not depend on moonlight for this purpose, as many nights were cloudy or drizzling. At times they did not even receive enough oil to light all of their lanterns, or they were advised to only ignite the lanterns in the most central streets of the city. Nature still provided most of the light at night, and at Mexico City's latitude and with its more tropical climate, the rainy summer months did not provide the long hours of sunny daylight enjoyed elsewhere.

Also, the guards complained about the quality of the oil. Ideally, they hoped to receive "legitimate turnip oil," but lately instead they had to make do with impure oil, poorly mixed from various varieties of oil or even with tar, or oil made out of *mamey*, also known as *sapote*, berries. This last oil burned slowly, but with an "opaque and low-quality light."[104] The lanterns had always only symbolically relieved the city from darkness as intermittent beacons illuminating isolated pools surrounded by murky shadows. If the oil quality degraded or the guards did not do their duty, it was inevitable that the city would quickly return to its previous, unenlightened state. From these statements, one judicial official concluded that the cause of darkness on Mexico's streets was "the shortage of oil, and its variations, poor quality, and mixing [the oils], and in no way due to the indolence of the guards, corporals, and even less of the performance of the head guard, who punctually performs his obligations."[105]

Not long after registering this criticism, Viceroy Iturrigaray was deposed in mid-September of 1808, after an unpopular several years in power, rife with suspicions of corruption.[106] In the months of upheaval, the street lighting situation did not improve, and issues with the guards neglecting their duties continued. The new viceroy, Pedro de Garibay, received more complaints about this concern from city officials within eleven days of taking office.[107] In spring 1809, Garibay oversaw another investigation, with a focus on the quality of the oil and the management of the head guard Dionisio Boneta.[108] In this second attempt to address the continuing darkness, higher-ranking municipal leaders expressed disappointment in the fact that such an ambitious and prestigious reform now appeared to have failed: "They are trying to ruin an establishment that is so useful and expensive . . . because of the lack of care from the person who runs it. A repeated shameful disorder was noticed last night: at 7:30 p.m. most of the city was in utter darkness."[109] Once again the blame fell on the night watchmen, although some argued that the guards did not receive their pay regularly and simply did not have the numbers to carry out the task. New hires and raises for their corporals had not helped.[110] However, the head guard at this time, Dionisio Boneta, made it very clear in his response that his men could not light their lanterns because they did not have any oil.[111]

This investigation ended with an admonishment from the viceroy to the head guard to take more care regarding the quality of oil and the work habits of his underlings. Upon his nomination for the appointment, the viceroy typically did warn the guarda mayor to take special care of the oil and the milling process, for the benefit of the city.[112] These concerns sparked a prolonged official debate and a lengthy investigation into the collection of the tax on flour, set up almost two decades earlier by Revillagigedo. It seemed that fraud was rife in bakeries, where the small additional cost should have been collected. The difficulty in monitoring the amount of flour coming into the city and gathering the reales to fund the ramo de alumbrado meant that this branch of city government had fallen into chaos. The debate surrounding this issue continued into the rule of Viceroy Francisco de Venegas, who took over just as mass insurgency began. As of 1811, after three years of discussion, the authorities had not resolved this complex problem; nor could they maintain other projects, such as collecting trash, or repairing lanterns damaged in storms.[113] Two centuries after Europeanized cities in the Atlantic world established nocturnal illumination, experts still do not agree if these efforts succeed in reducing crime or increasing the nebulous concept of security in any given urban landscape.[114] At least in this case, often interpreted as a successful Bourbon reform that dramatically increased surveillance of the populace, this paper trail of unresolved complaints instead demonstrates that publicly funded urban lighting proved unsuccessful.[115]

Even after long debate, and great expense, lanterns were frequently and erratically extinguished during angry exchanges between the populace and the night watchmen (see chapter 6). Viceroy Revillagigedo also tried to make urban denizens more visible to the viceregal regime by starting the system of numbering buildings to create addresses, another reform that faced resistance in some locales.[116] The streetlights soon dimmed in the first decade of the nineteenth century, due to the difficulty in collecting and redistributing taxes to the appropriate city maintenance budgets. The next chapter will move on to the rapid evolution of the other duties of the guards, which came to include dealing with domestic conflicts and caring for the most vulnerable and poorest Mexico City inhabitants. Even if they objected to street surveillance, extremely contentious plebeians found their own uses for the night watchmen and shaped the functions of this new institution accordingly.

CHAPTER 2

Men Walking the Beat

The long dusks of our summers and the short days of our winters are unknown in Mexico, located closer to the equator. Light and darkness divide almost equally and when at 6 p.m., the church bells announce the hour of prayer, pious Mexicans devoutly cover their heads, thus ready to assassinate anyone who does not abide by their devotion. The serenos of all the city's districts gather at the Municipal Palace, where, organized by divisions, they present a front of, at the least, one hundred lanterns, in order for their chiefs to inspect them and give their instructions. Their mission, like that of the London *watchmen*, is to call the hour, announce the good or bad weather, give the alarm in the occasion of a fire, accompany home lost strangers or those who have lost their reason due to drunkenness, and, finally, to arrest those who disturb the public peace and take them to the guard house in order to obtain more information. One cannot deny that this is a good institution and worthy of adoption in any country that lacks it. The Mexican sereno, in order to preserve that religious tone of their mission with which all Spaniards colored even their most trivial actions, preface the announcement of the time and weather with this somber statement: *praise be to God and Our Lady of Guadalupe*. Their monotonous voice resounds in the night's silence, and the philosopher can calculate the diverse effects produced by this wakeup call: if it penetrates the bedroom of an ambitious man ready to conspire against the *patria*; if it fills the heart of the eager businessman with regrets and worries about his treasures; or if it enters the room where a happy couple sleeps off their inebriated voluptuousness. An old halberd is the ostensible weapon of the Mexican serenos. They rarely need another weapon, other than a dog, faithful explorer of all of the night's dangers.
—Claudio Linati, *Trajes civiles, militares y religiosos de México (1828)*

On the night of the 29th of this month, they heard a knock on their door. . . . They asked who it was, and [heard] the reply of "open it for the guarda mayor." [Upon hearing] this voice, Brígida told her to open [the door]; and

she carried this out. A man in a cloak entered with his lantern and pike, so the witness assumed that he was a sereno.
—María Micaela Hernández, April 1, 1794

From the eighteenth and nineteenth centuries, when smashing lanterns was popular, until the present day, law enforcement always inspires strong reactions, ranging from intense loyalty to outright armed rebellion. Whether glorified as heroes or feared as robotic, sadistic, brutal weapons of state power, it seems difficult to understand police, and even their prototypical predecessors, night watchmen, as individuals with similar needs, concerns, and backgrounds to the rest of the population. However much the general population hated or used them for their own ends, the guarda faroleros were still urban working men and physical laborers, in some ways similar to other plebeians. Examining the details of their work routine, from the urban space that they patrolled to their patterns of nightly arrests, their additional repetitive tasks, as well as the variety and meaning of the basic equipment that they carried on their person during their nocturnal shifts, helps humanize them as workers. A look at their collected biographies, not just the case study of Bernal explored in the introduction, helps to understand them as men. The following chapters present more in-depth examples of controversial, violent, and even kind acts committed on the job, adding much more complex layering to their character and codes of values.

Only four years after their foundation, as observed in the second quote above, the serenos had a well-known set of identifying marks to alert the populace to their occupation, even if they lacked a uniform.[1] In terms of their internal sense of identity, the night watchmen, from their foundation to the 1820s, showed a strong occupational camaraderie that hints at primordial expressions of the famous "thin blue line," however anachronistic this phrase is for New Spain. Shortly after their formation, the Mexico City night watchmen's cooperation in emergency situations hints at a certain internal cohesion, loyalty, and esprit de corps. The lantern guards also possessed an almost clerical identity, as Claudo Linati emphasized in the leading quote, in their role as first responders in the late viceregal capital's rudimentary public health services during medical emergencies.[2] As Bourbon reforms subordinated and confined the scope of ecclesiastical justice, the night watchmen's involvement in key rites of passage, including birth and death, added a new secular element to previously sacred tasks.³ Their authority over bringing light to the dark streets suggests a kind of sacral role, explored further in the next chapter.

These working-class men did and signified much more than the igniting of twelve lanterns every night at 6 p.m.; yet they also were not "police," not by a long stretch of the imagination. Using this fairly modern term misnames them and confuses what the word *policía* meant in the eighteenth century. As defined in a 1726 dictionary, the term did not mean a group of men employed to patrol for the purposes of law enforcement. Instead it referred to something much broader: "The good order that is observed and guarded in the cities and republics, carrying out the laws and ordinances established for their best governance. [La Buena orden que se observa y guarda en las Ciudades y Repúblicas, cumpliendo las leyes u ordenanzas, establecidas para su mejor gobierno]."⁴ Common duties carried out by the 1790s guards in Mexico City included activities that absolutely do not fit into a modern idea of standard policing, including helping women in labor find a nearby midwife to come to their home and aid them in their delivery, facilitating priests to carry out the ceremony of last rites for those about to die, and the gruesome task of massacring dozens of stray dogs each night. How the watchmen dressed, what weapons and other items they carried, and how they communicated with their colleagues also differed greatly from the practices of more modern law enforcement, reflecting their role not as "police" but as men paid to help sustain policía or, in simple terms, "good government," in the previously obscure and almost lawless, stateless night.

Who Were the Night Watchmen?

To understand the lantern guards as men, as workers in Mexico City, and as subjects of the Spanish Crown, a profile of the typical individual who took on this occupation is needed. This profile also encompasses the outliers who seem unlikely candidates for the job but who nevertheless appear as employed as guarda faroleros. This analysis is a challenge, because in almost every existing archived written fragment mentioning individual night watchmen, the scribe sums up their identity as nothing more than a number between one and ninety-nine, not a name. This simplification of their humanity to a number features in both types of quantitative records used in this study, the 1790s *Libros de Reos* and the nineteenth-century ronda reports.[5]

However, the guards' numbers do not equate to either a more modern "badge" number or a number associated with a vehicle or radio communication. Instead, it refers simply to the watchmen's ramo, literally "branch," a word that makes more sense in English if translated as "beat" or "patrol area." While I have not found a map of the precise patrol areas of any of the numbered ramos, all of the existing activity reports suggest that the small geographic areas identified by any given number did not change. A guard could change his ramo and thus his identifying number, but the designated number of the space within the city streets remained constant between 1790 and 1822. For example, the arrest record of sereno number 23, identified in the early 1790s as José Manuel Bernal, shows that this number equates to an area of the city around the Callejón de Limón and the Puente de Solano (figure 2). Night watchman number 23 arrested drunk individuals at least three times on the Callejón de Limón in 1798.[6] The area called the Puente de Solano also had its fair share of offenders who interacted with number 23 (see chapter 4 for a detailed investigation of geographic drinking patterns in Mexico City's nightlife). Until 1822, the various men given the professional designation of guard number 23 remained very active in this precise area.[7] Similar patterns exist for other ramos, for example the patrol area identified as number 86, which included the streets named Chicohuatla, Reloj, and Cocheras (see figure 3).[8] In this case, the contemporary map clearly shows the beat that guard number 86, identified in the 1790s as José Morales, walked on a nightly basis, where the Calle de las Cocheras transitioned to the Calle de Chiconautla as it crossed the Calle del Reloj. As shown on the maps, streets might change names every block, or hold the same name for several blocks. The order of the numbers also mapped onto contiguous physical streets of the city. For example, guard number 87 also made many arrests on the Calles de Cocheras, Chiconautla, and the nearby Arcinas.[9] Furthermore, guards

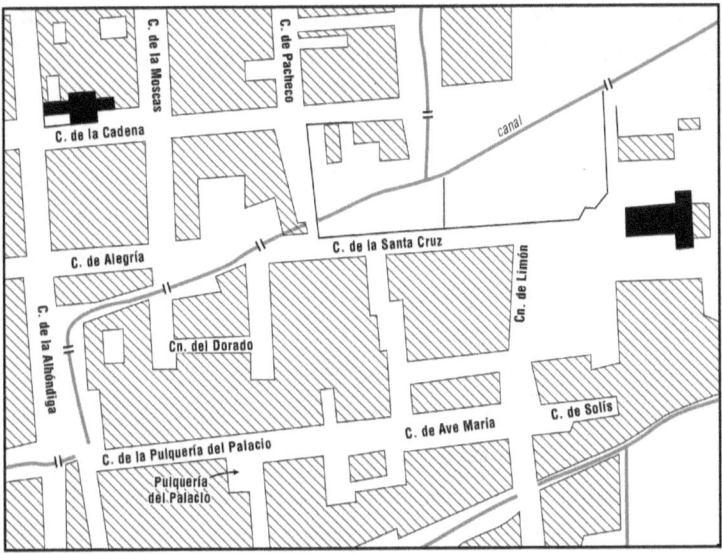

2. Ramo number 23. Created by Erin Greb.

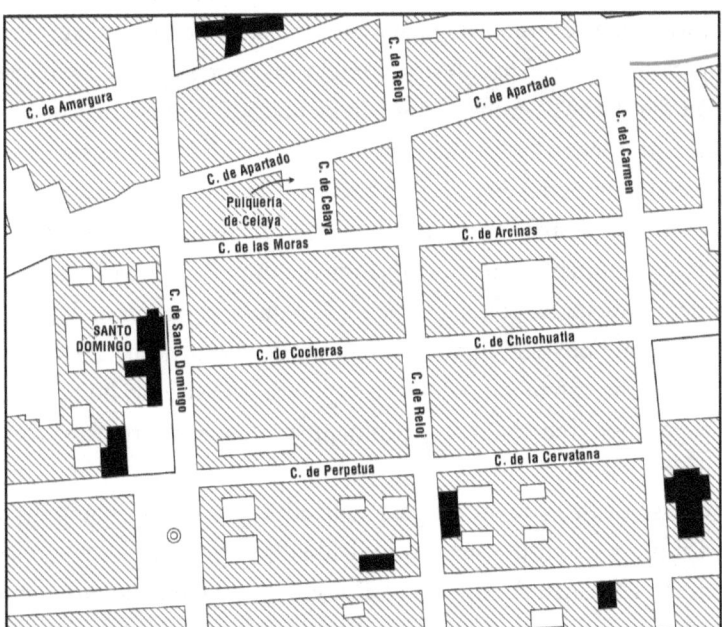

3. Ramo number 86. Created by Erin Greb.

with numbers in the twenties, fifties, and so forth, tended to work near other watchmen with similar designated numbers.

Walking their beat was a simple task that engaged a significant amount of the guards' time and energy while on their nightly shifts. More formal language referred to the ramo as their *distrito* (or district). In 1794 Viceroy Revillagigedo described a large patrol area as "no less than six hundred varas," which is equivalent to approximately five hundred meters.[10] If they stayed on the job and patrolled the same ramo, the long-term geographic proximity between these guards—especially in a nocturnal, lonely, but also conflictive and violent work setting—certainly must have contributed to a nascent camaraderie among the serenos. Their work identity, in the form of the number of their patrol area, reinforced their occupational association with a very specific small section of urban space.

As opposed to an embroidered or gilded number on their clothing or hat, or a badge affixed to their coats, the guards carried confirmation of their numbers and the streets that these numbers signified on a printed paper document. Early suggestions for how to organize Mexico City's night watchmen envisioned much more official and regal markers of their occupation. In 1777 Ángel María Merelo suggested to Viceroy Bucareli that "at night, the illuminators should be obliged to carry their titles and a shield [decorated] with the insignias of His Majesty and the coat of arms of this imperial city, so that they will be known on their patrols, and by those people who walk the street at night, [and also so they can] impose suitable penalties any individual."[11] At this early stage, this comment anticipates popular resistance to the new patrols and proposes that a stronger physical sign of identification with royal authority would help the night watchmen police the populace. The viceroy did not follow this suggestion, but the new patrolmen still became targets of regular popular resistance.

Because of this paucity of personalized identification, the only way to learn more about the serenos individually is in case files where they became defendants. A paper trail also emerges when a guard testified as a witness in an investigation. In both these circumstances, they had to make more in-depth statements, which included further biographic details. Their declarations as witnesses or defendants provide around five types of data about guards, including their names, ages, marital status, race labels, and place of birth. Another piece of information that can be found in cases involving the night watchmen is that virtually none of the street level guards knew how to sign their names. They all usually marked their witness statements with a shaky cross. Literacy was only the norm for those who ranked as corporals (*cabos*) or above. While lacking this skill limited their ability to receive a promotion, illiteracy in and of itself did not represent a source of shame for the serenos.[12]

In the several thousand arrest entries in the existing *Libros de Reos* dating from 1794 to 1798, only sixty-four guards are named in total, and all of these references come from incidents when the night watchmen were arrested themselves by their superiors for offenses such as drunkenness.[13] Many of the arrests only include their names and guard numbers, but others include all five pieces of information mentioned above. Obviously, if they were arrested, these men had very serious issues of misbehavior on the job. Perhaps guards who never faced disciplinary action had slightly different biographies. Of course, it is impossible to know anything about guards who never became involved in longer court cases, because the existing documents refer to them only by their ramo number. The second major source of guards' biographic data is the even less detailed nightly ronda reports. Existing documents of this kind cover only a few scattered dates in the late eighteenth and early nineteenth centuries, up until 1822. In these sparse lists, names never appear even for arrested individuals; instead, the head guard organized the list around the numbers of the guards and a few basic details about their routine patrols. In those rare cases where a night watchman appears in an appended further description of a nocturnal event, the head guard typically just noted his name and number. Lastly, the guards gave their bare-bones biographical information in longer criminal investigations, as mentioned above. Working with these different kinds of records, we can learn more about the biographies of a total of 101 of the guards. The next chapter discusses other aspects of their individual and unique work routine, including their patrol areas and patterns of arrests.

Drawing specifically from the arrest records in the *Libros de Reos*, the scribes recorded seventeen of the guards who committed offenses as married, and only three as single (*solteros*). While this data set is too small to have much statistical reliability, if extrapolated to the larger group, we can at least infer that the majority of the night watchmen were married. The guards identified as married ranged in age from twenty-three to forty-five, with the vast majority in their twenties, which matches with the general trends in terms of the watchmen's ages in the overall data. Over half of the married men identified their place of birth as Mexico City (nine), with the others from a variety of other nearby villages or more distant cities such as Querétaro. A plebeian claiming their status as "legitimately married" resonated strongly in this society, which had a notoriously high rate of illegitimate births.[14] A high percentage of married men conferred a certain measure of dignity to this job, because for plebeians, official marriage indicated a modest claim to honor and stability and at least some means, regardless of other markings of rank. Of course, marriage is a sacrament in the Catholic Church, which involved paying fees to a priest and gathering witnesses, all of which underscored a claim to honor and status. Because they could not claim European heritage or *limpieza de sangre* ("clean blood"), a basic qualification for claiming honor in the Spanish empire, marriage would especially add to the stature of the married serenos labeled as "castizo" (two), "mestizo" (three), or "indio" (four).[15] As explored in more depth below, the majority of the guards held the label of "español."

Although hard to trace, complications come up in terms of understanding the guards' marital status and their involvement in criminal or illicit sexual activity. For guards involved in sex-related transgressions or other questionable activities, their status as married men might cause their offenses to look worse to the modern reader. However, almost all of the married men listed as offenders in the *Libros de Reos* committed only minor acts of poor work behavior, such as sleeping or drinking on the job or abandoning their patrol area. A corporal reported only one married guard involved in a very tame but possibly sexual violation, when the cabo caught twenty-five-year-old José Aniceto Álvarez chatting with a woman of Indigenous descent around his age.[16] The couple's explanation for this conversation seems quite suspicious: that they had known each other a long time and the woman, out late at night after a fandango, asked Álvarez if she could stay at his house. Regardless, neither suspect suffered any repercussions other than a notation in the nightly logbook.

Supporting the supposition that they possessed a degree of respectability within their plebeian communities, individual lantern guards served as witnesses in church weddings. This fact offers another datum supporting the connection between marital status and the moderately elevated social stature of the night watchmen. On the other hand, only two marriage records mention a guarda farolero as a witness, and one of these had allegedly committed a violent sexual attack in his younger years. In 1807 the controversial José María Hernández, one of the most active guards in terms of number of arrests, witnessed the marriage of two young lovers claiming Spanish ancestry. The other witness was a castizo blacksmith aged fifty-nine.[17] Hernández identified himself more fully while testifying as a defendant in a 1794 rape investigation as guard number 57, a twenty-year-old of Spanish descent born in Toluca (see chapter 5).[18] Despite his admission of, at the very least, sexual improprieties with a woman thirteen years earlier, when Hernández stood in the cathedral in 1807, he still listed his occupation as a "guarda del alumbrado." The lantern guard named Manuel Toxices, a twenty-five-year-old man of Spanish descent, witnessed the wedding of another Spanish couple in 1822.[19] In this ceremony, the other witnesses included two servants of Indigenous ancestry and two Spanish-descent men who had jobs relating to petty commerce. While witnessing a wedding showed a degree of status, trust, and successful efforts to create ties within a community, the humble occupations and racial designations of the other attendees suggest that neither of these ceremonies register as above the plebeian level. However, standing at the altar signifies that individual guards did play a role in working-class social networks.

Beyond marital status, piecing together the fragmented references to the serenos also can provide a demographic sketch of this occupational group. One might presume that patrolling the nocturnal streets was a young man's job, due to the physical strength and endurance needed to stay awake, walk up and down a few blocks all night long, climb ladders, repetitively lift unconscious drunks off of the street, and restrain the belligerent. The *Libros de Reos* and other documents provide the ages of seventy-three of the night watchmen. They ranged in age from nineteen at the youngest to a shocking sixty-one at the oldest. The oldest documented guard was José Flores, a widower born in Mexico City and labeled castizo, who testified to the lack of oil available to light his lanterns in 1808.[20] The second oldest was Manuel Francisco Carvajal, a sixty-year-old español born in Tlaxcala. We know a bit about him because he appears in a disciplinary case: one night in 1796, his immediate superior found Carvajal asleep at three in the morning in his patrol area.[21] The youngest guard, José Joaquín Delgado, a married Spaniard from Mexico City, testified in a complaint about the night watchmen not responding to requests for help in 1796.[22] Even including these outliers in the analysis, just under 59 percent of the known guards were aged in their twenties. One-quarter were in their thirties, and only eleven men over forty years old still managed to work in this physically challenging occupation. The age breakdown for night watchmen, with the majority in their twenties, does not coincide with patterns in the age of the general population, according to contemporary censuses. Nor does it resemble the age ranges for the offenders that the guards took into custody. Only 37 percent of the general population and 42 percent of the arrested individuals were in their twenties in the late eighteenth century, which suggests that early young adulthood represented the ideal age range for a job patrolling the city from the authorities' point of view.[23] One could infer from this data that physical strength and endurance mattered more in this occupation than the wisdom of life experience or long military service.

Stating one's place of birth was common in legal documentation in New Spain. Of course, as mentioned in the introduction, Mexico City experienced significant in-migration in this era due to drought, famine, and epidemics, and the authorities used the burgeoning population to justify increasing a governmental presence on the streets, in the form of the new night watchmen. Different regions and eras provide examples of how law enforcement officials can do this job as locals or outsiders in relation to the groups they oversee. To assess how this played out for Mexico City, we can look at the *Libros de Reos*' entries for arrested guards and the more extensive investigations. These sources list the place of origin for sixty-two guards. Not surprisingly, given that policing often favors "locals" to patrol neighborhoods familiar to them, close to half (twenty-seven) of the night watchmen said they hailed from Mexico City.[24] This breakdown actually slightly veers away from the statistics for the individuals arrested in the general population: 60 percent were from Mexico City and 40 percent came from other locations.[25] At least in terms of the incomplete data available, offenders had a greater connection to and familiarity with the capital than did the night watchmen who provided rudimentary policing. After the capital, the second most common city of birth was Querétaro, the place of origin for four of the guards. Every other location only had one or two mentions. These included many important small and large urban settlements in New Spain, such as Toluca, Real del Monte, Cuernavaca, Pátzcuaro, Puebla, Tlaxcala, San Luis Potosí, Zempoala, Tepoztlán, San Juan de los Lagos, and Jalapa. Like so many others in this era, the majority of the serenos migrated into the city, most likely to improve their employment prospects. Some watchmen identified birth locations well within the modern urban sprawl of Mexico City, such as the Villa de Guadalupe and Tacubaya. In contrast, two of the guards journeyed from an incredible distance to patrol the streets of New Spain's capital. In an investigation of a fight that occurred in 1797 between a group of serenos and an infantry sergeant, witnesses included a guard named Antonio Rey, a forty-year-old from Santiago in the region of Galicia, Spain, and thirty-eight-year-old Antonio de Jesús Magalón, born in Manila, in the Philippines. Magalón also offers a very rare example of a guard with the ability to sign his own name. His superior education fits with trends relating to other New Spanish Filipino residents, often known as *chinos*.[26]

Although he did not have a racial designation documented, Magalón's place of origin serves as a reminder that a small group of the night watchmen could not claim Spanish ancestry.[27] Race labels in New Spain allowed for fluidity depending on the circumstances.[28] Arguably, occupation affected one's designated or chosen race label. For example, urban craftsmen were often labeled *mulatos*, and we cannot always assume that this term derived from their genetic ancestry as opposed to a stereotyping of who typically had this occupation in a given time and place.[29] The same generalizations might apply to the lantern guards. Overall, written documents record the racial designations of a total of seventy-nine serenos. Of these, over 62 percent had the label español, a much larger percentage than the 48 percent claiming this ancestry in the recent Mexico City census. Mestizo represents the next most common label, at 16 percent, which better aligns with the census data of 19 percent of the city's residents claiming it.[30] Only a handful of guards received racial designations suggesting some African ancestry: castizo (eight, or 10 percent) or mulato (three, or just under 4 percent). This low incidence of archived African-descent serenos aligns with the low occurrence of these labels in the contemporary census. These statistics make it clear that, although the guards had a low status job, it was most commonly taken on by those who could pass for españoles. Perhaps working as a sereno even helped casta men claim a more prestigious race label.

Among all of these categories, the percentage of guards labeled indio (six, or 7.5 percent), misaligns the most with census data, which reported indios as 28 percent of the urban population. Given the history of forbidding men of Indigenous descent from carrying weapons, other than with special permission for nobility, their presence as armed guards does seem surprising.[31] It is also arguable that the new patrols functioned mainly to police Indigenous drinking culture, and therefore the men hired in this role would most likely claim no Indigenous ancestry to clearly distinguish themselves from the targets of their own surveillance (see more on this topic in chapter 4). Racial designations that indicated African or Indigenous ancestry did not appear to cause any noticeable conflict in the serenos' interactions with the populace—their occupation itself inspired enough violence. While the night watchmen often suffered abuse and mockery, racial slurs did not come up in these clashes (see chapter 6). Summing up what this demographic information reveals overall, it is clear that the most common or typical sereno was an illiterate man claiming Spanish ancestry (perhaps tenuously), in his twenties, married, and born in Mexico City.

To go beyond these dry statistics requires a little creativity. Not surprisingly, historians have a much better understanding of the men who worked in Mexican law enforcement about three generations after the formation of the serenos. Of course, Mexico City experienced dramatic changes from 1800 to the last few decades of the nineteenth century, but it is not uncommon for viceregal historians to jump around across centuries. Paul Vanderwood observed that law enforcement mirrors the society that hosts it, which was true in 1790 as much as in 1890. Detailed personnel files show that later Mexican police, like the lantern guards, continued to fight with their superiors, get drunk on the job, and remained physically strong but illiterate. They also came from the poor classes of unemployed craftsmen and migrants from hungry rural regions. As in the viceregal era, later Mexican police still received a miniscule salary and had to pay for their own expenses and equipment. Few people wanted the job or stuck with it for long.[32]

The Organization of the Night Watchmen

The lantern guards did not have a complex hierarchy or ranking system. One step up from the men who maintained the lanterns and walked their designated beat, cabos directly supervised the guarda faroleros during their nightly rounds. According to Revillagigedo's instructions of April 1790, eight appointed corporals would receive twenty pesos in monthly salary. The viceroy directed that corporals should come up through the ranks of the guards on patrol, chosen from among the older guards who showed the most "zeal and punctuality." Their duties included "attending to, taking care of, and responding to precisely fulfill the obligations" assigned to the guards they supervised. The corporals carried a lantern and walked a nightly beat, but in their slightly elevated status, they also received a saber. Each morning, they had to communicate any events that had taken place in their patrol areas to the head guard, either in person or in writing.[33] Existing documents mention the cabos very frequently. However, because the files only give their numbers, most of these men remain anonymous and lost to history. Only four corporals have racial designations listed in the surviving paperwork: three labeled español and one designated a castizo. As directed in their founding documents, the job of cabo required more experience, and their ages range from thirty to fifty-nine, with six cabos in their thirties and two in their forties. All of these men could sign their name, making them outstanding exceptions among the standard younger serenos, although evidence suggests that at least four of them rose through the ranks of the night watchmen. The cabos did seem to carry out Revillagigedo's intentions for nightly tasks patterned after the typical guarda farolero, in that they appear as arresting officials in 258 incidences taking place in the 1790s, out of a total of 3,547. Oftentimes, the *Libros de Reos* refer to corporals as embroiling themselves in slightly more complex cases, for example, when they had to arrest one of the patrolling guards under their supervision for disciplinary concerns. Whenever a citizen or a bureaucrat attempted to scold the corporals in writing, their words echoed Revillagigedo's 1790 orders, which emphasized their duty to "take care of their ramos," with "punctual and appropriate care," as "honorable men and loyal servants."[34]

In contrast to their subordinates walking the nightly beat and the corporals who dealt with many nightly fracases, the guardas mayores received a high salary of two thousand pesos annually. Unlike the two lower ranks, these literate men frequently exchanged written communications directly with the most powerful bureaucrats in the viceroyalty. The head guards did not rise through the ranks of night watchmen but had elite status far above their plebian employees. Their ubiquitous use of the honorific title "don" underscores the class difference between themselves and the corporals, and patrolmen. Their status did come into question in at least one case from 1791, when a father started a court case to formally object to the marriage of his daughter to Dionisio Boneta, a Basque immigrant who later became the fourth guarda mayor.[35] Other than their key duty of providing oil needed to fuel Mexico City's street lighting, the head guards filed a nightly report directly to the viceroy, or, in 1822, Agustín de Iturbide, signing it with their names. These reports, and longer archival case files, make it possible to hypothesize a chronology of their times in service (see table 1). In terms of how they spent their time, in the 1790s the head guards appear in only eighty-seven, or around 2.5 percent, of the arrests documented in the *Libros de Reos*. At least one-third of these incidents involved serenos neglecting their duties (see chapter 5), indicating that the head guards mainly focused on supervising their underlings. They also confronted deserters from the military and intervened in attacks on the night watchmen.[36]

TABLE 1. Names of the Mexico City guardas mayores

1791 to 1799	José Moreno
1799 to 1803	Cayetano Canalejo
1803 to 1807	Ramón de la Rosa y Serrada
1807 to 1815	Dionisio Boneta
1815 to 1818	José de Quintana
1818 to 1822	Ignacio de Eguiluz y Olarte

Other than the paper trail plotting out their daily supervision of the patrolmen, and the less common documents attesting to their role in de-escalating more drawn-out conflicts, the head guards have not left a significant archival record of their lives. Their virtual anonymity suggests that they ranked as a very minor social and economic status in the viceroyalty. Don José Moreno held the job first, appointed by Revillagigedo in the founding documents for the serenos.[37] Revillagigedo highly recommended Moreno to the Marquis de Branciforte, the viceroy who succeeded him in 1794, with the following words: "In my confidential instructions, you will be informed of the comfort and public safety created by the prompt establishment of the lighting of Mexico City. This branch [of the government] is very well served due to the wise choice of don José Moreno y Pavia as head guard. I am so satisfied with his zeal, activity, and good conduct that I particularly recommend him to Your Excellency."[38] When Moreno died in 1799, the town council and viceroy Miguel José de Azanza discussed the process for appointing a successor, as well as the best candidates for the job. As Moreno's death meant the first time that the city government had to choose a new head guard, council members seemed anxious to clarify the importance of this appointment as a public servant and the qualities needed to carry it out. They specified that the guarda mayor had oversight over a budget of thirty thousand pesos, entrusted to him by the populace. With this income, he had to buy the seeds needed for growing the turnips used for their oil, outfit the lanterns with their wicks and other accoutrements, distribute oil to the guards, administer their salaries, and oversee the oil mills in the city, not to mention arrest delinquent guards and earn the respect of his subordinates.[39] The ayuntamiento put forward don Ramón de la Rosa y Serrada, who had previously served as an *alcalde del cuartel* and worked at other administrative appointments, including the drainage project. According to his supporters, Rosa y Serrada "always performed [his duties] with superb punctuality, *hombría de bien* [loosely "gentlemanliness"], and suitable economy in the use of public funds."[40] Despite this strong recommendation, Rosa y Serrada lost out to Cayetano Canalejo. Serving as head guard until his own death in 1803, Canalejo distinguished himself through his efficient use of his budget.[41]

While the appointment of the head guard belonged to the town council and the viceroy, we can only presume that the head guards hired the patrolmen directly, with the approval of the corregidor. Unfortunately, historians do not know exactly how the night watchmen applied for this job nor what qualifications they needed to gain employment with the lighting branch of the government. In other locations in the broader Atlantic world, new law enforcement corps offered the opportunity to create jobs for those loyal to a regime. In the last two centuries across the globe, increasing policing has had political implications and can bolster a particular politician or party. The political aspect of hiring the serenos emerges from fragmentary documents generated by the ayuntamiento asking the viceroy to take care to fill vacancies in order to continue to address crime in the capital.[42] When serenos did not show up for work, the head guard could draw substitutes from those who had applied for the job. The absent patrolmen had to pay for their replacement.[43] Along with the mysteries of the hiring process, no records detail any kind of training process of new serenos. Most likely they did not receive any instruction, other than from their peers and from their own experience of trial and error on the job.[44]

The Lantern Guards and the Urban Sensory Experience

We do not know how they chose this line of work or the vetting process for their hiring, but it is clear that the lantern guards had a significant role to play in the late viceregal urban landscape. They contributed to residents' nocturnal sensory experiences, especially in terms of sound. While light and the visual aspects of the occupation usually take center stage and caused the most conflicts in terms of their most basic function, the night watchmen also generated a great deal of noise. As Linati observed in the quote starting this chapter, one of their essential reasons to exist was to call out the time and the weather. A traveler to Madrid in the 1790s described the first men who patrolled the dark streets of the Spanish metropolis as follows: "Their occupation consists of shouting the time and if it is windy, rainy, or calm [*sereno*]. This word dominates over the rest, and the most frequently heard call is *sereno*, therefore these men are called serenos."[45] In contrast to the much more famous English "coppers" (named after their badge), or "bobbies" or "peelers," sobriquets deriving from the name of the 1830 reforms led by Robert Peel, Spanish speakers focused on a specific task and a noteworthy sound to identify their new night patrols, not their uniform or the name of an eminent government official. This makes sense for Mexico City, as uniforms did not exist until after Independence. Serenos in Madrid wore nothing more distinctive than a brown cape.[46] They were heard, in the dark depths of the night, much more frequently than they were seen, especially because they did not patrol during the daytime, as did the London "coppers." For these reasons, their nocturnal call resounded more with the populace than any governmental processes resonant of the heated political debate over Robert Peel's reforms four decades later.[47] Revillagigedo would have equated to Peel, in terms of their "founding father," and his name does not easily provide a slang term for his new patrols!

As in Madrid, nineteenth-century Santiago de Chile observers emphasized the sounds of the night watchmen as a familiar part of the urban nocturnal experience: "They can be heard now and then in the silent hours of the night, these fading calls of the guards, who after a loud and steady 'Ave María Purísima!' they shouted the time struck on the historic clock of the Jesuit church, and then the weather."⁴⁸ Clearly the particular evocation of the Virgin Mary in the night watchmen's repetitive shouts depended on the locale, as Linati wrote that Mexico's guards cried out in praise of the Virgin of Guadalupe. It is even possible to imagine that the serenos created a kind of poetry in their consistent, evenly spaced announcements, such as these much later poetic utterances:

> I am going to sleep now,
> Even though I am not tired.
> I am sleeping because
> It is half past four in the morning and *sereno*.
> I leave my post unoccupied:
> I go to sleep exhausted.
> Nothing is happening,
> And it is five a.m. . . . and cloudy.⁴⁹

The lantern guards share a tradition of loud, public calls with food sellers, *pregoneros* (town criers), and other street workers in the Latin American urban setting. An important difference is that they cried out not in the hectic daytime but when the streets were otherwise silent, dark, and empty. The resonance of their calls intrigued travelers even at the end of the nineteenth century.⁵⁰

The Patrolman's Tools

As they made their lonely progress through the streets, working accoutrements for the guards involved a few simple items. Although they did not always carry it around, they used a ladder to light the lanterns. They also needed wicks, containers for the turnip or other oil that fueled the lantern flames, and various small items, such as scissors for wick-trimming, to help in the lighting process. But basically, to carry out virtually all of their tasks and to deal with any emergencies, the night watchmen depended on three pieces of equipment: their handheld lantern (*farol*), a whistle (*pito*), and a pike (*chuzo*). These objects unite them with other early law enforcement corps in London and Boston, who also carried a source of light, a way to make sound (a rattle for Boston), and a rudimentary weapon.[51] Like the radios and weapons used by law enforcement in more recent decades, each of these items possessed a symbolism far beyond their physical size, with differing connotations for the guards themselves versus the general population. The lantern symbolized seeing and light, discussed in depth in chapter 1. Chapter 6 discusses lanterns in the context of disputes, crimes, and forcefully rejecting of the night watchmen and the government that they represented. Of course, the chuzo reminded the populace of the serenos' access to force to compel action and the potential violence inherent in the institution of armed guards, but its efficacy as a threat seems very questionable. Although far less controversial and inflammatory than either the lanterns or the chuzo (no one ever reported an offender breaking or stealing a guard's whistle), the whistle represented camaraderie and very quickly came to symbolize the supportive cooperation among the ranks of the patrolmen.[52]

An earlier version of the guarda faroleros existed approximately two decades before Mexico City's residents and leaders could agree on how to establish the city's public lighting and who might take on the task of maintaining it. Under the name of *guardas de pito*, from around 1770, patrolmen in the capital of New Spain imitated a similar cadre in Madrid. The Madrid guardas de pito carried a bronze whistle engraved with the coat of arms of the imperial capital.[53] The prolonged discussion of methods to light the viceregal capital included a proposal suggesting that the guardas del pito could help guard funds collected from customers at small shops, a heavily debated potential source of financing for the still-developing public illumination. Following the model of Madrid, the petitioner suggested that the job of maintaining the lanterns should connect to the "obligation to 'correr el pito [run the whistle]' all night long."[54] Ten years later, when the audiencia repeated the viceregal decree that all Mexico City residents had to maintain a lantern outside their house, the high court commanded that the guardas de pito pay special attention to this order, presumably to detain anyone (young boys were mentioned as the most likely culprits), who damaged or stole the lanterns.[55] As of May of 1790, men called *guardapitos* still coexisted with others referred to as *guarda serenos*. However, the older and less documented corps of "whistle guards" seemed to lack some of the basic structures of the soon-to-be-organized lantern guards, such as an official number indicating their patrol area.[56]

While the role and duties of the guardapitos are less delineated, Viceroy Revillagigedo very clearly explicated the function and parameters of the lantern guards' whistles in their 1790 founding documents, which state: "The whistle will not be used, other than when it is necessary *to gather them together to help each other* [emphasis added]."[57] This reads like an injunction to not make too much noise with their whistles, perhaps because the basic tasks of calling out the weather and the time already disturbed the night's quiet more than enough. Insomniacs complained of disturbances to their precious moments of rest by both the regular cries of ¡sereno! and the occasional ear-piercing whistle blast.[58] Although it annoyed sleepers, Revillagigedo's definition of the purpose of the serenos' whistle reinforces that this small object of communication achieved a great deal in terms of forging camaraderie in the newly formed lantern guard corps. From August of 1791, barely a year after their formation, allegedly the night watchmen already used their whistle to torment an unwell minor judicial official over a dispute about taking three women and a man into custody.[59] According to the accusation, along with creating a loud commotion by blowing their whistles, a group of guarda faroleros also prodded the alcalde with their pikes. However, the accused ringleader, guard number 23, the aforementioned José Manuel Bernal, told a very different story, which emphasized his affronted honor and how he depended on his fellow serenos to uphold his reputation.

Bernal explained that at 10 p.m. one evening while on duty he arrested a group of four offenders during a street brawl. Bernal led them to the nearby house of the alcalde del cuartel, don Joseph Xaraba, which he found closed up for the night. Eventually, the alcalde appeared, in a very bad mood. Xaraba brandished his stick and shouted, "¿Dónde está ese pícaro borrachón [where is that thieving drunkard]?" presumably in reference to Bernal. The guard allegedly responded calmly, denying that he was either a thief or a drunk. Xaraba then menaced Bernal with his stick, saying that he would give the night watchman a beating. Bernal responded, "go ahead," and turned his back to the official, who then began shouting about the sereno's duties and threatening to arrest him. Bernal then, in his "outrage," blew his whistle. His corporal and another patrolman showed up quickly, but unfortunately for Bernal, Xaraba convinced the corporal to transport him to jail. Judging from his adamant denials of giving any offense to Xaraba, Bernal viewed his work colleagues as available to protect both his on-the-job reputation and his honor more generally.[60] He ardently testified that he blew his whistle so that his *compañeros* (friends or associates) could bear witness to the dispute, which they could explain to the head guard, and to confirm the untruthfulness of Xaraba's accusation of drunkenness. Bernal denied that he called the other men to cause any disturbance or harm the alcalde, disputing the original accusation.

As in the case against Bernal, guards often used their whistles in a scene where they referred to each other as compañeros, which suggests a sense of group identity. This word had a complex range of meanings in Spanish language dictionaries as far back as the fifteenth century. A dictionary published in 1786 defined *compañero* in a variety of ways, including "the person who accompanies another, a friend, familiar to them, interested in the same fate," as well as "someone who has the same occupation," and even "someone who participates in the same benefits or evils."[61] While we cannot know exactly what they said while in action, this documented language seems to accurately reflect how the night watchmen actually thought of and spoke of their work colleagues.[62] The head guard also used *compañero* in his official reports of guard activities, explaining the events using phrases such as "he went to look for more compañeros" or "he found more compañeros."[63] Even the smallest jobs done as part of this occupation had a tone of teamwork, such as when guard number 9, Manuel Aguilar, a twenty-nine-year-old married castizo, neglected to appear in his patrol area at 10:30 p.m., because (he said) he was helping a compañero light his lanterns. For this infraction, Aguilar had to spend three days confined in a dungeon cell, although he probably hoped that the excuse calling on group cohesion would help his case.[64] The repetitive use of the word *compañero* increased in cases when the serenos had to defend themselves as a group, for example when a militiaman in 1790 referred to them as "thieving dogs."[65] The need for occupational camaraderie increased over the next three decades. Documented examples of serenos using their whistles to call for help from their compañeros increased during the decade of mass rebellion. Notably, when they spoke of witnessing a fatal attack, night watchmen frequently used the term as they described their reactions to the abuse of a colleague and how they tried to help their seriously injured peers.[66]

Workplace identities forge a man's gendered sense of self. This applies to late viceregal Mexico just as it does to any other time and place where masculinity revolves around providing a livelihood for one's family and dependents. Working together of course also can foster stronger personal links to one's workmates.[67] Even for Mexico City's lantern guards who lacked a uniform and lived humble lives on or near their beats, their occupation set them apart from the rest of the populace.[68] As plebeians who worked for municipal authorities, they probably found comfort in camaraderie with each other and faced suspicion from their neighbors.[69] The physicality of this particular job connects it to gender roles, to the point that patrolmen may come to embody a kind of hypermasculinity.[70] In the nineteenth century, popular police memoirs depicted authoritative actions such as quick reaction times to counter any threats and superlative fighting skills (even with minimal weapons).[71] These masculinized traits became the essence of police identity. While working in a sense as the armed and violence-prone servants of magistrates and bureaucrats, serenos such as Bernal actually behaved as typical Novohispanic plebeians, hyperalert to any insults to their honor. Patrolmen performed behavior later described as macho, earning them disdain from both their social superiors and those of their own economic group.[72]

The piercing sound of a whistle blast and the term *compañero* came to widely signify a gathering of serenos. In their testimonies, witnesses implied that hearing the watchman's whistle at night felt threatening to them. As the viceregal era ended, lantern guard number 22, Domingo González, walking his beat near the infamous pulquería del Palacio, gave a royalist soldier a light for his cigar at 10 p.m. A few moments later, González testified that he encountered another royalist having sex on the floor with a woman inside the drinking establishment, which often seemed to function as a brothel.[73] At that moment, the man with the cigar began arguing with González, "which obligated him to use his whistle to call his compañeros."[74] He received a rapid response from guard number 15, who knew this sound meant that a fellow watchmen needed help. When asked what happened that night, another witness, a twenty-two-year-old patriot (there is no explanation given for the apparently changing political loyalties of those involved in this incident), named don Perfecto de Legaspi, gave a very different story. He said that he was seated with a woman he had just met when the guard arrived and asked him, "What are you doing here with the woman?" Legaspi responded, "We are having a conversation." Legaspi went on to claim that the guard "suspected them of some evil deed, so he blew his whistle, and momentarily eight or ten of them came together, and surrounded him, trying to take him to jail, which he resisted."[75] Legaspi's testimony, however exaggerated or blatantly false, implies a preexisting rhetoric that the populace viewed the guards as sharing an excessive sense of group cohesiveness, which might appear threatening to an apparently innocent member of the public. The whistle was a small but very loud physical artefact of their solidarity, as symbolized by their use of the word *compañero*. Alone with the piercing whistle threatening a gathering of armed and united men, even just the implications of the term also could inspire fright, as in the case of a woman harassed by a sereno in her bedroom. The guard threatened "to go call other compañeros to take her to jail."[76]

In the sense of camaraderie and esprit de corps, the handheld lanterns also served as a signal, albeit at shorter range. In the aforementioned 1791 incident involving the alcalde who testified that he felt attacked by the guards, the serenos, referring to each other as compañeros, explained that they learned that guard Bernal needed help because another guard "made a sign with his lantern." This sign caused them to leave whatever task they were doing to help their colleague. When they arrived, Bernal said he saw a group of "faroles de compañeros [companions' lanterns]." Night watchmen knew when others of their occupation drew near, because they could "see the lanterns of their compañeros approaching."[77] The object that drew so much rage from the populace functioned within the corps of the watchmen to bring these men together.

The chuzo also defined the guards from the time their foundation, but to a far lesser degree than the lanterns or even the tiny pitos. This weapon was stick of about three meters in length, topped with a sharp metal end. Guards in Madrid hung their small hand lanterns on their chuzos, which greatly increased their usefulness.[78] The relative lack of importance of the chuzo is interesting considering how central weapons can be for law enforcement's symbolism broadly to the public as well as internally among themselves, and as objects that continue to add to a sense of occupational solidarity. In contrast to the dozens of examples of lantern smashing, only one recorded incident exists of an offender breaking a chuzo, in this case a Spanish woman caught in the act of having sex with a soldier on the street.[79] Although the chuzo attracted far less attention than their lanterns, when guards committed offenses while on the job, their corporals would confiscate their chuzos almost immediately.[80] The populace did not choose to destroy chuzos, perhaps because men normally had different weapons on their person at all times in this era, despite prohibitions against individuals of Indigenous ancestry carrying arms.[81] While guns appeared as deadly weapons in very few colonial homicides, people often killed others with knives (*navajas* or *cuchillos*), or even injured their victims with scissors.[82] In this era, normal daily life often called for a knife on one's person or conveniently nearby, resulting in knives as the weapon of choice in close to half of all homicides in central Mexico. Rocks, fists, clubs, swords, razors, whips, and machetes caused victims' demise in most of the other recorded homicides.[83] Gruesome murders in this era included the eleven fatalities in the 1789 Dongo case, done with machetes, and a horrific beheading of a military official in 1817, both of which ended in rapid executions of the perpetrators.[84] While Revillagigedo and other reformers intended for the lantern guards to prevent violence in Mexico City, they did not equip them with a very effective weapon.

Despite an apparent increase in urban violence during the insurgency era, the serenos' pikes had declined in importance by 1815. At this time,

Viceroy Calleja queried the leadership of Mexico City's municipal government as to why the night watchmen no longer carried them.[85] Head guard Dionisio Boneta provided a detailed answer that emphasized the contradictory duties carried out by these patrolmen, how their weapons functioned in practice, and their camaraderie as they positioned themselves against the populace.

> In 1807 I took charge of the lighting.... Many of the guards showed me how useless this weapon was, and how restrained they were with it. It was useless for their operations, particularly for [dealing with] drunks. On many occasions, [carrying] that weapon and their lantern, six guards were occupied, all six of them leaving their districts for more than one or two hours, according to the situation with the drunk. This absence defies the regulation that prevents them from leaving their districts. When don Cayetano Canalejo was the guarda mayor, an important prisoner escaped, and ... the guard was able to puncture him with the short and sharp-pointed top on the chuzo as [the prisoner] struggled to flee. The blow landed in the [prisoner's] right shoulder, and as a result he died. It was commanded that those sharp tips be removed.... I was instructed to punish the guard involved with many days in jail. Guard number 36 was punished with fifteen days [forced labor on the] public works [projects], for having a sharp chuzo.
>
> [In another incident,] guard number 97 arrived to pacify a brawl, and a woman attacked and wounded him. In response to this outrage, he raised his chuzo and broke her head, for which he suffered fifteen days of arrest by mandate of the alcalde. When the woman healed after a time in the hospital, she claimed damages, and the guard had to pay the twenty pesos demanded by the notary. As a result of these and other similar cases, the guards did not want to take out their chuzos, claiming that the weapon that they were given for their defense instead served as their punishment, so they did not want it.... They were allowed instead of the chuzo to carry a club, that they hang from their left arm. This is satisfactory to them because it does not restrain their actions.[86]

The club, or *garrote*, matched the kind of weapons that the serenos might encounter on the streets.[87] In this sense, like other patrolmen, the Mexico City guards chose to carry weapons that mirrored those of their potential adversaries, although apparently they did not use knives.

Not Man's Best Friend

As noted in the second quote at the start of this chapter, their capes, pikes, and lanterns symbolized the serenos' de facto uniform for the general populace. In contrast to popular imagery, dogs did not accompany the night watchmen, at least not as helpers. Although Linati's famous image both visually represents and verbally discusses the companionship between dogs and the Mexico City night watchmen, this portrayal contradicts historical reality. As this image can be found in Linati's collection of hand-colored lithographs, which offered readers an expensive and luxurious product, he may have chosen to take a more romantic and stylized presentation to satisfy the tastes of those who bought the book.[88] In fact, patrolling with a dog violated their work regulations.[89]

Human-dog interactions have a long and violent history in Mexico, beginning as New Spain came into existence. These brutal conflicts extend well into the twenty-first century. Since the infamous "dogs of war" of the Conquest era, European-bred canines terrorized the Indigenous peoples and other residents of the capital.[90] When epidemics ravaged the city, families could no longer manage their dogs, resulting in an increase in strays. They roamed everywhere, even in the viceregal palace, and enjoyed an abundance of food left on the streets. Stray dogs also dug up and ate the flesh of cadavers abandoned during epidemics. From the perspective of Bourbon reformers, these dogs, who might attack any decent person going about their business on the streets, offered another example of disgusting, embodied, and immoral vagrancy that Enlightenment-influenced leaders wished to eliminate.[91] Although dogs also had a positive religious connotation as symbols of loyalty and devotion, church and state united on the dog massacre project, as clerics expressed moral outrage at both the frequent scenes of canine mating on the streets and their unwelcome presence in churches.[92] Conflicts over dogs also added to the violence in the late viceregal capital city.[93]

Anti-dog legislation had a range of motivations and inspirations, from public health, to decreasing attacks on humans, to controlling this wild and vagrant population. Beginning in 1532, oft-repeated municipal decrees attempted to control and even annihilate the city's dog population.[94] Throughout the sixteenth century, the government threatened to fine owners who allowed their dogs to roam at night. In 1709 rabies sparked a public health reaction and decrees from the chief medical official (*protomedicato*) and the corregidor attempted to eliminate all city dogs who were not chained up and serving as guards.[95] Clearly this did not come to pass, as viceroys again circulated regulations regarding killing dogs found in the streets beginning in 1779, especially as an effort to prevent rabies, although complaints about violent dog attacks persisted.[96] In the same timeframe when he created the night watchmen, Viceroy Revillagigedo escalated the government's efforts to kill off all stray dogs in Mexico City. A 1790 decree spoke of the mastiffs and other "terrible dogs" common on the streets and called for a ten peso fine for any dog owner who allowed his or her dog out without a "safe bridle." The bando also threatened that all stray dogs found in the streets or plazas "of any caste [breed]" would be killed by the new guards. Over the years following this decree, the serenos had different expectations for carrying out this task. First, each corporal had to have his men kill two dogs nightly, for a total of sixteen. The individual night watchmen received a slight pay bonus of a half-real for every dog they killed. Later, minimum expectations increased and the authorities docked their pay when they did not succeed in killing the designated number.[97] Oddly, according to Payno, Viceroy Revillagigedo also decreed that shoemakers put out bowls of water in their doorways, where they worked, to help thirsty stray dogs.[98]

As in the case of street lighting, European cities with routine government-sanctioned dog killings inspired Mexico City residents as a means of promoting quieter, more salubrious streets. While summary reports claimed that Revillagidedo's 1790 decree caused the deaths of upward of thirty thousand dogs in the late eighteenth century, approximately thirty each night, observers did not notice a significant decline in their number over time. In 1779 the city authorities estimated that Mexico City contained twenty thousand dogs; forty years later, this number had increased to thirty thousand. Early nineteenth-century residents of Mexico City complained about the ubiquity of stray dogs in the capital's streets, claiming that these animals caused an "insufferable disorder" and that their barking reduced this impressive city to the ambiance of a *ranchería*. The number of hungry, vicious dogs increased in times of drought and floods, as they came in from the countryside to find food, not unlike other undesirable migrants.[99]

Therefore, existing sources suggest that urban dogs multiplied by the thousands, and at the same time also suffered seemingly continual massacres, due to orders repeated by Revillagigedo and his successors.[100] A commentator in a nineteenth-century newspaper observed that if dog owners did not put names on their pets' collars, these animals risked the gruesome fate of "perishing at the end of the lance of those entrusted with the policía."[101] Judging from the detailed evidence of nightly reports made by the head guards from 1791 to 1822, this was a very accurate prediction. Each day, the head guard himself submitted a list to the viceroy (and later Agustín de Iturbide), which detailed the activities of every individual night watchman, listed from number one to number ninety-nine. At the end of the report, the guarda mayor almost always made a very concise note of how many dogs all of the guards had killed during the previous night. The narrative of dog massacres remains simple in the head guards' logs. The vast majority of reports simply state a number and the word *perros*. Guarda mayor Ramón de la Rosa y Serrada clarified what was actually happening when he wrote "eleven dogs were killed [se mataron once perros]."[102] The longest description comes from José Moreno: "Six dead dogs were left on the streets [seis perros muertos quedaron en las calles]." This notation suggests that during the day other men passed by to pick up the carcasses, perhaps even implying that these reports were provided a work plan for the daytime streetcleaners to remove the dogs killed the night before.[103] By looking at the eighty existing nightly reports, I found 808 documented dog executions in just over thirty years, only a tiny percentage of the number presented in other sources mentioned above.[104] Of course the eighty reports cover only certain nights and skip entire years altogether. On the other hand, contrary to the summary reports discussed above, data from the eighty reports adds up to an average of ten dogs killed per night, not thirty.

This lower number seems much more likely, given the size and population of the city, the guards' other tasks, how frequently they patrolled their beats in almost complete darkness with both of their hands occupied, and the many different kinds of resistance offered by the population, including against the task of killing stray dogs. Not just dog owners resisted the *matanzas de perros*. Even the military patrols that commonly walked the city streets during the 1790s and especially the insurgency era objected to the nocturnal dog massacres. In 1794 corregidor Bernardo Bonavía and guarda mayor José Moreno countered a complaint from an infantry sergeant who observed to Viceroy Revillagigedo that at midnight on March 18, no one could find any serenos on several central city blocks. Allegedly, this meant that, on these streets, the public "lacked security and tranquility." The sergeant noted that the head guard should exercise "greater vigilance so that his subordinates carry out their obligations with more exactitude."[105] Moreno explained that around sixteen men, led by a corporal, focused on killing dogs that night from 11 p.m. to 3 a.m., following the viceroy's orders. This response must have pleased the viceroy, because as mentioned above, four months later, Revillagigedo told his successor (the Marquis de Branciforte) that Moreno had served the ramo del alumbrado very well.[106]

How to carry out the gruesome task of disposing of the dogs' bodies also caused conflict and debate. During Revillagigedo's era, a horrific pile of carcasses accumulated at the doors of the town government headquarters, the ayuntamiento building. Under the leadership of the head guard Cayetano Canelejo and encouraged by don Cosme de Mier y Tres Palacios, mentioned in chapter 1 as a neighborhood enforcer of resident-funded lighting, the serenos accelerated the massacres of dogs. But where to leave their bodies? Other leaders suggested in front of the houses of Canalejo or Cosme de Mier, and the viceroy had to rule on the debate. Wherever their bodies appeared during the night, ultimately the dogs found their final resting place in the swampy area bounded by a sixteenth-century wall, near San Lázaro, on the western outskirts of the viceregal city.[107]

The serenos did not relish killing stray dogs, a task which they had to do with their chuzos, ineffective weapons against larger or more aggressive animals. The dogs suffered a horrible and painful death, and their cries echoed through the dark streets.[108] The city also experimented with poisons.[109] After the coups d'état of 1808 (see chapter 6), the lantern guards threatened to quit their jobs in protest of the pay docking that they suffered if they did not kill the minimum number of dogs each night. This rare activism by the patrolmen succeeded in halting the massacres, at least temporarily.[110] Conflict over killing dogs continued during the era of mass insurgency. In early 1815, guard number 74 faced insults and threats from military men while hitting a dog in the head (one of twenty killed that night) at 10:30 p.m. on the Calle de la Merced.[111] Guards themselves may have had some ambivalence about carrying out this violence on a regular basis. The head guard José Quintana reported that in the spring of 1815, guard number 75 tried to hide a dog, who fled as the guard was taken to jail. Unfortunately, along with three others that night, this dog suffered the same fate as so many other canines in this era.[112] This incident gives an especial poignancy to Linati's famous image from the early national era of the sereno patrolling companionably with his dog.

Using small objects such as whistles, whose size belied their significance, Mexico City's guarda faroleros forged bonds with their plebeian peers and with each other as an identifiable group of men who met resistance from the general population. Their isolated and repetitive work routines created this esprit de corps. These men represented the state but also retained their own plebeian world views and values, as they interacted with their neighbors far more than with elite society.[113] Because they reacted as working-class men, they recognized what conflicts could be settled internally, versus who had broken unwritten community norms. Patrolmen thus helped the populace determine when to involve the state in a dispute.[114] An awareness of their connection to the masses motivated patrolmen in other large cities to reject uniforms, which made them look like outsiders and/or soldiers in the service of a tyrannical government. Robert Peel himself proposed the classic blue uniform with the intention of imitating men's standard dress styles in the late 1820s, rejecting the red and very elaborate military uniforms of his era.[115] Even without a uniform, Mexico City residents could easily identify the night watchmen and oppose them as unwelcome representatives of the viceregal state. At the same time, the guards served the city's inhabitants, in ways shaped by those who called out for their help to find solutions to their desperate nocturnal crises.

CHAPTER 3

To Protect and Serve

The very words of the streetlight regulations, made by the most excellent señor, predecessor of Your Excellency, the Count of Revillagigedo, state that the lantern guards must take care of the security of persons with a public office, such as doctors, surgeons, priests, midwives, etc. . . . and provide them with the help needed for their defense.
—Dr. don José Alejandro Jove, October 20, 1807

These men serve the public, working day and night incessantly in their ministry, almost without time to rest, and withstanding the cold, the heat, the humidity, and all the inclement weather. Every step these men take risk their lives. . . . At the very least, they harm their health for their miserable salary. They merit the compassion of the Your Excellency [Viceroy Félix Berenguer de Marquina] and all of the public, to help these wretches, which will lead to a very appreciable benefit to the city.
—Antonio de Bassoco, July 9, 1801

Patrolmen, and before them the watch, had always been involved with lost children, bewildered strangers, and the victims of accidents.
—Roger Lane, *Police Records and Recollections, or Boston by Daylight and Gaslight*

In the original founding documents of the guarda faroleros, Viceroy Revillagigedo included additional duties beyond lamp-lighting and simply walking their beats.[1] Most famously, they were to remove thousands of severely inebriated individuals from the city's public space. At the same time, while the night watchmen focused most of their time on addressing widespread public intoxication and carrying out some of the basic tasks connected to Mexico City's illumination, they also "protected and served" the urban population. As such, they acted as an extension of the paternalistic Spanish Crown, in its self-conception as the superlative God-fearing paterfamilias. This role emerges clearly from an analysis of the guards' variable interactions with Mexico City residents of different age categories, from toddlers to the very elderly, as well as their dealings with individuals with disabilities.[2] The stories of these moments show the serenos in their most favorable light, to the point of imbuing an almost heroic tinge to their occupation, a sentiment conveyed in the second quote starting this chapter.[3] This narrative of heroism is actually a more modern take on law enforcement, which contrasts dramatically with other accounts of the guards' behavior and the ongoing popular resistance against their presence.

Some of these "protect and serve" tasks were stated directly in the night watchmen's regulations; others emerged through practice, choices made on the street, and interactions with the public. This process of plebeians making use of patrolmen also took place in cities such as eighteenth-century Paris and nineteenth-century Boston.[4] The decree outlining the Mexico City lantern guards' foundation listed the following important additional obligations:

> arresting the evildoers and thieves whom they encounter, and depositing them in the nearest guard house, barracks, or jail; providing information for the head guard or his lieutenant, when he passes on his rounds; informing, when there is a fire in any house, first the house's owner, then the parish priest, the nearest military headquarters, the leading craftsmen of the city, and the other *alarifes* [builders]; without [the guards] leaving their posts, but passing the message from one [guard] to the next, when a resident asks them to locate a doctor, surgeon, or midwife, unless they are in their own distrito; but if this happens outside of it, take the name, the street name, and the house number, notify the guard in the area [where the medical professional is located] to call them. If a fire takes place after the lanterns are extinguished, return to the neighborhood where the event is occurring, and relight them, and keep them lighted until the fire has been extinguished and the residents have been calmed.[5]

The night watchmen also reported back to the head guard when the postal carriers brought the mail in or out of the capital city—and sometimes even arrested one of the "mailmen" for inebriation.[6]

The Symbolism of the Patrolman's Tasks

Most nights, at least one guard carried out a task that bears comparison to the functions of paramedics or firemen in more recent decades. In a health emergency, residents of central Mexico City could step outside their homes and look up and down their block for a night watchman, shout out for his attention, and explain their crisis to him. The guard would then either find the appropriate professional, whether a doctor, surgeon, pharmacist, midwife, or priest, or take care of the issue himself. To give an example of one of the most tragic emergencies mentioned in the records of the lantern guards, a father called on guard number 44 at 10 p.m. one evening in 1816, when a man, allegedly a stranger, sexually assaulted a six-year-old girl, who required a surgeon and a pharmacist.[7] This kind of extreme situation did not occur frequently—the most common medical emergencies dealt with by the lantern guards were the injuries or occasional fatalities that took place routinely in this city of heavy drinkers. In a general sense, the official articulation of these public-health related obligations underscored for the populace that the judiciary had both a paternalistic and punitive function. The night watchmen served on the front lines of both tasks.

While these responsibilities have a connection to basic public health, they also place the serenos adjacent to the sacred, especially in the sense of their connection to key Catholic rituals in an individual's life cycle, most notably, birth and death. In chapter 1, I mentioned that the new state control of street lighting was in line with Bourbon efforts to change public Baroque religious rituals, which commonly filled the streets with candles carried by the faithful illuminating procession routes and sacralizing urban space. Now the new guards carried lanterns and responded to urgent cries for help, similar to the pious fathers so valued in this culture. Sacred and secular mixed in the Spanish empire in so many ways, including the use of public thoroughfares and the legal rituals surrounding death, including writing one's last will and testament and organizing the legally required pious bequests. Just as they did not succeed in changing popular religious beliefs and practices, the Bourbon reforms only interjected new institutions within older, venerable traditions, which were very difficult to uproot. Similar to new public cemeteries and the expulsion of the Jesuits, the establishment of the night watchmen faced a great deal of opposition.[8]

The idea of law enforcement as having a sacred role has featured in sociological studies going back to the 1960s, especially in terms of the history of policing in Great Britain, where law enforcement drew on the traditional respect accorded to the monarch.[9] Interestingly, an example given by Michael Banton, the sociologist known for arguing that British police have a sacred status, relates to the tasks of the Mexico City night watchmen, in that it describes an incident when a policeman acted as a midwife. Stressing police officers' almost sacred role, Banton tells the story of a mother who named her baby after the officer who delivered him in an emergency.[10] More generally, Banton argues that the British police of his era, like priests, "are set apart and sacralized. . . . That they are treated as intrinsically good derives from the way they symbolize social order."[11] This rather naïve quote sounds ludicrous in light of the later history of anti-police activism in the United Kingdom; still, it offers the possibility of policing taking on a sacred status. In Mexico City, those who believed in Spanish imperialism as motivated by caring paternalism that benefited urban residents honored the efforts of the guarda faroleros. As in Great Britain, for these viceregal subjects, the guards had a strong connection "to the state, morality, and justice."[12] In contrast, those who opposed the social and political order hated the night watchmen and physically attacked them precisely because they represented the viceregal state.

Very quickly after their formation, both the viceregal leaders and the populace started to form a general vision of the guarda faroleros. The verbal and physical attacks on the guards discussed in detail later in this book make it clear that many plebeians felt negatively toward them. In contrast, some authorities in Mexico City viewed them more positively as hard-working underpaid family men with a risky, demanding job that endangered their health. Only one decade into their existence, city officials presented the night watchmen as self-sacrificing, truly almost martyrs:

> The painfulness of their work is notorious. . . . Not only do they inhabit the street all night long, exposed to all the inclemencies of the seasons, they also fuel, clean, and take care of the lanterns; they surveil the criminals, [and] they serve the residents. . . . They often risk their lives not only in the apprehension of criminals but also in their mundane duties. Cases in which they have been killed by carriages are still frequent. While on their ladders, they have been injured so [seriously] that if they did not die, they were rendered useless to [earn an income to pay for] their daily food. . . . There are few individuals of good reputation who want to serve when there are openings [for the guards], and those who do, quickly leave, because they cannot remain in [this job] without getting sick. . . . If [a guard] becomes ill due to excessive fatigue, he is unable to continue his duties. . . . [These men] are burdened with the most painful occupation. They have the unfortunate fate of endangering their lives to provide their families with a tiny livelihood of only six reales a day.[13]

These comments came from the ayuntamiento in 1801, led by the enlightened merchant Antonio de Bassoco.[14] This group petitioned Viceroy Félix Berenguer de Marquina, and later Viceroy Iturrigaray, pleading for an increase in salary for all levels of the ramo del alumbrado, from the street patrolmen to the head guard. While arguing that everyone employed in this branch of government was overworked and underpaid, the writers emphasized that only the guards walking the street often faced illness and death as a result of their nightly routine. Bassoco believed that the serenos deserved a 25 percent pay increase, raising their monthly salary to twenty pesos, but he also seemed to want a more general upgrading of their status. An important improvement would be granting them the *fuero*, judicial privileges enjoyed by all military men as well as clergymen and all levels of employees of the Holy Office of the Inquisition. Ultimately the viceroys did not approve any of these requests, and the night watchmen's work conditions declined steadily as the viceregal era came to a close.[15] While Bassoco tried to elevate the downtrodden serenos based on a description of the risks and sacrifices in their work, the last several viceroys of New Spain had neither the interest or nor the ability to spend more money on these plebeian men.

The Night Watchmen and Death

While most aspects of the transition from this life to eternal life remained the purview of the Catholic Church, the Spanish Crown and viceregal government had a long and controversial involvement in the rituals surrounding their subjects' deaths.[16] The serenos' involvement in many Mexico City residents' final moments helped priests remain essential to this ultimate rite of passage, under the physical protection of these new low-level servants of the secular state. The task of escorting priests to perform the sacrament of extreme unction was the most frequently undertaken of all the night watchmen's activities, adding a sacred inflection to the concept of "protecting and serving." It can be found in forty-five of the eighty total existing nightly reports made by the head guard. On these occasions, the serenos responded to requests from people residing in their patrol areas for a priest to come to their homes to administer their final confession and to apply the holy oil (*santo óleo*).[17] These rituals gave pious Catholics and their families a spiritual reassurance that the deceased had achieved a "good death," which helped them rest easy and boded well for their eternal fate.

Among the ninety-nine men normally on duty, typically no more than one patrolman escorted a priest to a confession on any given night. However, sometimes the death rate increased dramatically. During the atypical night of November 26, 1795, a total of four guards answered calls for priests to different addresses. On occasion, one guard responded to two different individuals making this deathbed demand in a single night, requests that indicate that two people faced their final moments within the small area marked out by only a few blocks of the watchman's beat. The requests could happen at any time during the hours of darkness, from 8 p.m. to 5 a.m. The almost nightly resort to a lantern guard walking his beat to help carry out a Catholic sacrament certainly added to the gravitas of his occupation, supporting Claudio Linati's verbiage from the mid-1820s that described the serenos' calls as sounding like a dirge. The institution of law enforcement had many very modern elements related to state formation and surveillance, but as bodyguards for priests involved in death rituals, it also helped protect a regular connection between the church and residents of Mexico City in their moments of extreme need.

However pious this service to the sacraments was, these nocturnal interactions annoyed both priests and guards. As they had done for their choice of weapons, preferring a club over the chuzo, the night watchmen attempted to define how they related with priests to suit their own preferences.[18] They imposed their own limitations on their role as messengers and servants for churchmen. Conflicts occurred with priests when the guards outright refused to accompany the clerics called to deathbeds situated *fuera del alumbrado*, or "beyond the light." Their refusal also violated the tradition of the populace in general accompanying the priest as he carried a consecrated host to a dying parishioner. At the same time, priests occasionally also resisted carrying out their own sacred duty. In 1795 head guard José Moreno reported that a particular porter for the Mercedarian friary threw "vasos inmudos" (literally "dirty glasses," but one might assume this refers to chamber pots) at the serenos who came to his door asking for help. Even when they agreed to walk with the night watchmen to the bedsides of dying residents, the priests often berated the guards as they made their way along the dark streets.[19]

In 1807 the curate stationed in the parish of Salto de Agua complained to the city judicial authorities about the night watchmen in his jurisdiction.[20] According to the priest, in their refusal to accompany him two guards cited the orders of a superior, who allegedly told them they did not have to walk with a priest when he was called to confessions in the middle of the night. He noted that this went against the founding regulations made by Viceroy Revillagigedo.[21] This particular case had subtleties, because the alleys under discussion did not have street lighting, but they were very near to the illuminated center. However, this neighborhood inspired terror for the curates who worked there, who reported that the alleyways were "extremely dangerous because they were long and murky [*lobreguez*]." Proof of the risks encountered in this locale derived from the "infinite number of cases before the royal criminal and lower courts, of numerous deaths and robberies."[22] The priests in these kinds of neighborhoods had no choice but to respond to requests for confessions, but they feared that they would be robbed, beaten, or even killed if they stepped outside their doorways at night without an armed escort. The authorities confirmed that the serenos must work to prevent these kinds of complaints in future and carry out their assigned tasks as stated in Revillagigedo's founding documents. Despite these assurances, this order does not seem to have gone into effect. In August of 1809, the curate of the San José parish complained to the viceroy that he was abandoned alone in a dangerous area when he ventured out to hear a final confession at 10:30 p.m. The priest noted that the two guards who he called on for protection only walked with him for thirty steps beyond the light of the lanterns. After that, they deserted him in the company of some "strangers" and told him, as they walked away, to "stay quiet." The priest presumed that the guards felt more fear than he did, as he continued on to carry out his duty and they avoided their own.[23]

While the normal nightly routine for the guards corps usually included one request from a resident for a priest to perform last rites, on rare occasions the serenos encountered dying individuals, or even cadavers, as they walked their beat.[24] Written reports took a serious tone when they passed on information about cadavers to the viceroy, for example on the night of September 15, 1800: "At 9:30 p.m., corporal number 8 of the alumbrado gave notice . . . that a deceased woman was found in the vicinity of the *vinatería* on the corner of Santa Catalina Martir. The doctors declared that her death had come from the excessive abuse of spirits that she had taken."[25] Similar to when conscious dying individuals or their relatives asked for priests to deliver last rites in their homes, the night watchmen attempted to organize a final confession and the application of holy oils for severely injured people whom they found in the streets, usually after a violent drunken brawl.[26] On other occasions, the serenos found cadavers with no indication of why the person had died or why their body appeared on the street. In these cases, the guard could choose to ask a doctor for help solving the mystery.[27] They might also try to question the surrounding neighbors to find out the deceased person's family, as was attempted when a lieutenant on his rounds found a man covered in blood, face down in a plaza at 8 p.m. one evening in 1805.[28] Even an indoor wake could lead to a mysterious death, with all attendees claiming ignorance as to its cause.[29] Since complete records do not exist, it is impossible to know how much death featured as part of the guards' regular tasks. However, dozens of homicide cases appear prominently in criminal court records, as well as in eighteenth-century elite commentaries arguing in favor of public lighting and street patrols.[30]

The night of April 4, 1822, might not be typical, but the report made by head guard Eguiluz y Olarte certainly suggests that the watchmen regularly encountered death, alongside more common incidences of intoxication and fighting. The drama began when guard number 24 brought a drunk man to the jail for processing at 8:30 p.m. An hour later, guard number 63 escorted a priest to a deathbed to hear a final confession. The excitement picked up at 10 p.m., when guard number 19 turned in another drunk man. Meanwhile, guard number 72 escorted an injured woman to headquarters, after a fight involving several other individuals who had fled as the watchman approached. At 10:30 p.m., guard number 24, following drops of blood near a vinatería, found a corpse on the Calle de Ave María with a fatal stab wound to his right side. Thirty minutes later, guard number 36 brought a priest to a bullfighting ring in the San Lucas *plazuela*, to hear a confession, possibly of a matador fatally injured by a bull or maybe for one of the spectators. Lastly, at one in the morning, guard number 86 heard shouts coming from a building where carriages parked. An injured man had dragged himself to the door, so guard number 87 went for a priest to give him last rites. Unfortunately, the unknown man died before he could provide any information.[31] While the night watchmen walking their beats during this particular night might have seen more action than usual, in a single night in early February of the same year, two men died in different brawls occurring between 10 p.m. and midnight.[32]

Protecting the City from Property Crimes

Along with lantern-lighting and addressing the city's persistent violence and public intoxication, Revillagigedo and other reformers hoped that the foundation of a night watchmen corps would help reduce the number of robberies, a crime they viewed as very common in this era. The surviving *Libros de Reos* from the 1790s document thirty-two cases of robberies, under 1 percent of the incidents archived in these nightly reports. While it is impossible to determine if the new street patrols discouraged robberies, the evidence suggests that the lantern guards did not have a significant effect. The 1790s incidences roughly fall into four categories: elite residents (labeled *dones* and *doñas*) complaining of thefts committed by their servants or other employees, or blaming them for their lack of care leading to theft; desperate people stealing food; drunks who claimed no memory of the crime—including leaving taverns without paying for drinks; and the theft of valuables such as horses and clothes.[33] These final offenses seem more like the acts of actual thieves, who either planned to invade and pilfer known empty houses or jumped at an opportunity that presented itself, such as an unattended horse or an open window.[34] While many of these crimes seem petty, in some cases, thieves might attack storeowners and steal all of their money and valuables for sale.[35] Even without the serenos, the owners of these stolen items probably would have reported these incidents to other judicial authorities, such as the alcalde or the corregidor. In one of the most serious cases, the robber turned himself in for stealing thirty pesos.[36] As such, it is not entirely clear that the lantern guards did much to improve the rate of theft and robbery in this decade.[37] According to the head guards' reports for the early nineteenth century, the lantern guards continued to deal with a number of thefts and robberies, including serious cases when groups of men stole hundreds of pesos in money, clothing, and other valuables, as well as the sad thefts of small amounts of food.[38] During insurgency, these offenses often involved soldiers stationed in the capital city.

To carry out their duty of preventing thefts, the serenos looked for open windows and doors while they walked their beats. Head guards' reports of these minor tasks present the night watchmen in their most benevolent but intrusive interactions with the populace. For example, on one night in September 1803, patrolmen reported two buildings at risk of theft: first, the Santa Clara convent, and secondly, a "garage" where someone stored a carriage and other items.[39] In the first case, the guards noticed a grill open at the convent and asked permission to guard the building, because they could not ask the nuns for keys in the middle of the night. For the garage (*cochera*), they had the owner carry out an inspection to see if he was missing anything. A few weeks later, guard number 46 reported a building open and asked the landlady to confirm if anyone had stolen "any of the very few pieces of furniture that she had inside."[40] On occasion, the guards came across an open building that thieves had already ravaged. One night in 1815, guard number 17 found an open door and missing bedding, clothes, and paperwork. That same night, guard number 63 received a complaint that a thief had stolen the bedding in another house. In both cases, the culprits fled into the night.[41] Lastly, neighbors called on the serenos to check out the situation when suspicious-looking men gathered around houses.[42] Overall, it seems that property owners counted on the night watchmen to keep an eye out on their buildings while they were traveling, although not necessarily to catch any thieves.[43]

Discussions among the judicial authorities in 1816 demonstrate the inefficacy of the new night watchmen as deterrents for theft.[44] At this time, the capital city's criminal court, the *real sala del crimen*, formulated a decree stressing that the guards needed to focus their attention on preventing robberies, with the help of business owners. The authorities attempted to limit the sale of goods in taverns and on the streets and encouraged merchants to keep good inventories. Lastly, business owners were directed to have clerks keep guard in their stores at night. Regulations also tried to discourage merchants from buying items from unknown persons who had likely stolen the merchandise. The decree emphasized that the serenos held the responsibility for dealing with this "continuous" worry for Mexico City residents.[45]

Eighteenth-Century First Responders

With no fire department, volunteer or otherwise, only the lantern guards officially provided a first response to fires, which must have taken place often in this large city. Viceroy Revillagigedo established a set of regulations regarding fire prevention in 1790. Some of the issues addressed included exercising more care in the placement of kitchens and ovens, avoiding stockpiles of wood in the city, keeping woodpiles away from sources of flame (such as lanterns and forges), and prohibiting fireworks, called *árboles de fuego* (trees of fire). If a fire occurred in a home, the closest church should ring its bells to call for help. Revillagigedo directed the local alcaldes to ensure that any belongings removed from a burning house should have guards to protect them from theft. In this era, the authorities called on *alarifes*, or builders, to use their expertise to determine how to extinguish the fire. The government kept pumps (*bombas*) in the palace, the mint, and the tobacco factory. Carts otherwise used in the task of cleaning the streets moved the pumps to the location of the fire.[46] Despite all of this planning, very few records exist of night watchmen carrying out their duty of responding to fires. According to the head guard's surviving logs, the only recorded fires involving the lantern guards took place in 1801 and 1822. In late December of 1801, corporal number 1 reported that one of his guards had reported smoke coming out of a residence with an absent owner. They went to the building and entered via the patio, noticing that the fire came from a pile of wood, and easily extinguished it. In early 1822 guarda mayor Eguiluz y Olarte reported a fire that started in an oven in a bakery, which he and his men extinguished rapidly, without damaging anything on the property. They called for the bomba but may have contained the fire even before the water pump arrived. Eguiluz y Olarte assigned a sereno to guard the property until morning. In April of the same year, one of the guards stopped the spread of a fire in a pulquería, but in this incident, Eguiluz y Olarte expressed no concern for any damages, noting only that he warned the management to take more care.[47]

In their role as rudimentary first medical responders, the night watchmen also escorted midwives to women in labor or with other unspecified medical complaints at all hours of the night. In the surviving nightly reports, twelve mention guarding midwives on the street. These incidents took place throughout the three plus decades of the guards' existence, with the first reference in 1795 and the last in 1822. The guardsmen walked with the midwives from 9 p.m. to after 4 a.m., with the reports carefully noting the addresses of the requests, which were presumably located on their regular beats. At times, they gathered together the personnel needed to respond to more complex birth-related emergencies, such as on the night of November 8, 1799, when guard number 26 escorted a midwife, doctor, and pharmacist to a woman's house at three in the morning. The same night, guard number 35 walked with a surgeon and a midwife to a help a woman at midnight.[48] No further details exist for any of these cases elucidating the results of the medical attention or how the situation came about. A tiny piece of evidence suggests that the population viewed even this task as a possible opportunity to take advantage of the guards for their own purposes, as opposed to simply a useful service to help women delivering babies. In late 1798 a midwife named María Marchena called on a night watchman at 10:30 p.m. to "accompany her in the streets," as was the normal practice. It turned out that she did not actually need to go out at night to assist a woman and had asked for the escort fraudulently. She received twelve lashes for the deception and was subsequently released.[49]

Taking a Paternal Role

Generally, historians view the night watchmen as carrying out the Bourbon vision of who had a right to occupy the urban streets, a combination of an effort at Enlightened authoritarianism and an attempt to "civilize" the behavior of the populace. Certainly, streets full of beggars and vulnerable people such as runaway or abandoned young people and disabled individuals did not coincide with either the reforming ideals of the era or possibly even the older Hapsburg-style paternalism. The serenos' unstated but implicit mission of "protecting and serving" can be seen in records relating to encounters with homeless children under the age of fifteen, as well as with adults who were injured, mentally challenged (described as *mentecato*), had some form of mental illness (the term used was *demente*), hearing- or sight-impaired, elderly, or panhandlers (*limosneros*).

Throughout the viceregal era, many adults—most notably the descendants of the Indigenous population—were imbued with the status of legal minors, a juridical theory and practice at the heart of this paternalistic empire. The *Libros de Reos* convey a sense of the guards' duty of caring for vulnerable children that extended also to those individuals with disabilities whom the guards encountered on the streets. In many of these cases, people passed from the guards' custody to the jail or to charitable institutions such as the poor house and hospitals.[50] As to actual children, the guards endeavored to remove those who were sleeping on the streets and return them to their families or place them in domestic or work arrangements. The idea overall was for the state to help support the family unit, if it existed, and if not, to organize a suitable substitute. An overview of the different responses across different age categories and kinds of disabilities highlights how the night watchmen carried out at the street level the Spanish Crown's paternalistic vision of protecting the vulnerable. While the guards did not ultimately decide the fate of those whom they arrested, they did control who ended up before judges. These more powerful elite men then decided the fate of people living on the street: admission to the poor house, jail, being sent back to their family, or employment. Thus, the decisions stemming from the initial encounters in the nocturnal street between the patrolman walking his beat and a person sleeping, sick, or injured shaped dozens of lives in the closing decades of the Spanish viceroyalties.

This society valued the honorable masculine ideal of fathers who carried out their duties of guarding, protecting, and caring for their dependents, a principle extending from the king down to the common man. As servants of the state, the night watchmen carried out these paternal obligations. Gender ideologies are clear not only in who served as the appropriate protectors for those perceived as weaker members of this society but also who roamed the streets unaccompanied. Almost every child recorded in the *Libros de Reos* as out in the street alone at night was a boy. The only girl listed was labeled "Spanish" and aged fifteen, arrested at 12:30 p.m.

for breaking curfew and consorting with a soldier, a description that is very likely a euphemism for sex work. Although the trend itself was not necessarily common, many teenage girls appear in the viceregal archives as involved in a variety of levels of transactional sex, from streetwalking to very lucrative personal domestic service to military officers.[51] The fact that they do not feature prominently as detained children does not mean that girls did not go out—this society did not seclude children of any gender. However, it seems that girls under fifteen generally avoided homelessness and drinking to excess, while sadly some young boys did not.

The detention of children rarely occurred: the thirty-six hundred entries in logbooks from the 1790s document only sixteen such incidents involving children fifteen and younger. These interactions had the goal of helping the minors find a safer place to live and work, because judicial traditions frowned on harsh treatment for youth.[52] The first reference of a sereno detaining a child comes from 1794, when corporal number 3 detained a "muchacho mulato" (no age given) for no other cause than being on the street.[53] Coincidentally, this particular child received a label indicating African descent, but notaries inscribed vagrant children with a wide range of race labels (see table 2).[54] The youngest example of a homeless child comes from 1798, when corporal number 2 found a two-year-old toddler with his twelve-year-old brother sleeping in a midden in San Lázaro, far to the east of the town center, at midnight. The children, labeled españoles, explained that they were orphans and had chosen to leave the house where they worked as servants. The authorities resolved the case by seeking an apprenticeship for them.[55] The next youngest child found on the street was an Indigenous boy aged eight, who told a poignant story of going out to buy tortillas for his mother, then stopping off to pray at the San Bernardo church.[56] The authorities found his parents and warned them to take better care of him. Guard number 89 helped return a nine-year-old boy of Spanish descent to his parents, after he found him sleeping at 2:30 a.m. in the infamous pulquería de Celaya, claiming that he had nowhere to sleep. Another nine-year-old found wandering the streets at 9 p.m. said that he lived with his grandmother but did not know where, so he was sent to the poor house. A ten-year-old boy found near San

Geronimo around midnight said that he had lost his mother, but the head guard was able to track down his parents.[57]

It is interesting to note that every one of these children had a story or excuse ready to tell the guards. It is possible that they consciously wanted to flee their homes or workplaces and did not appreciate the guards' involvement any more than the adults who resisted the patrolmen in other ways.[58] These sparse records do not provide any insights into the children's or the guard's emotional reactions to their encounters. No children resisted arrest, but they may not have felt great joy when the night watchmen returned them to their employers. The youngest boy sent back to his place of work was a ten-year-old labeled mestizo, apprenticed to a tailor.[59] The notations describing placement in an apprenticeship suggest that the authorities viewed this response as effective social welfare, not a punishment.[60] Although the guards took these boys into custody, most likely against their will, the meager logbook entries do at times acknowledge a respect for the personal agency of children. This comes out in the following situation, when guard number 6 found a ten-year-old boy labeled mulato on the street at two in the morning: "[The boy] said that he was lost and could not find his home. He was sent to learn a trade but the workshop was shut. His mother appeared, saying that he is inclined to learn the profession of carpenter, if he is sent to a master."[61] Another example of concern for a boy's future employment appears in the record of the arrest of a twelve-year-old indio, who said that he was an orphan but wanted to work as a tailor. The judge put him in the care of a señor Moctezuma, presumably a master tailor. As these examples and table 2 show, there does not seem to be a particular bias against boys with different race labels, in terms of sending them to a pleasant or unpleasant home or work situation. The only tendency might be toward assigning boys of Indigenous ancestry to domestic servitude.

From age eleven up, all vagrant boys detained by the serenos ended up sent to work. If they had families, the authorities told the parents to arrange work for them, probably presuming that the child needed better supervision and guidance than the family could provide, since a night watchman had found him wandering outside in the middle of the night.

TABLE 2. Detained children

RACE LABEL	AGE	RESULT
indio	8	returned to mother
español	9	poor house
español	9	returned to parents
mestizo	10	apprenticed to a tailor
mulato	10	returned to parents
mulato	10	returned to mother to find apprenticeship
mestizo	11	servant
indio	11	servant
indio	11	returned to mother to find apprenticeship
indio	12	servant
español	12	apprenticed to a silversmith
indio	13	apprenticed to a tailor
español	13	workshop or factory [*obraje*]
español	13	returned to uncle to find apprenticeship
español	13	returned to brothers
mestizo	14	apprenticed to a bakery

Employment options found for homeless boys included domestic service, working apprenticed to a silver smith, a tailor, or a baker, generally in an unnamed workshop (*oficio*), or, worst case scenario, a sentence to an obraje, proto-factories known to overwork and abuse employees, many of whom toiled there as a form of punishment.[62] Those employing children as workers were supposed to look after them in some imitation of parents and risked a scolding if the authorities found their charges wandering the streets at night. For example, corporal number 2 found a twelve-year-old Indigenous boy sleeping in the doorway of El Sagrario, the parish church attached to the cathedral, at 10:15 p.m. in early 1796. The boy explained that he had gone out on an errand for his master, a priest in the San Ildefonso College. While out and about, the boy sat down to rest and fell asleep. He was sent back to his employer, who was warned to take better care of his servant's behavior.[63] This somewhat punitive response reflects the Bourbon emphasis on creating a productive work force out of what they viewed as idle, potentially drunk, and rebellious subjects. It may also have functioned as an approach to help boys who had not yet learned how to become men who fit into their social roles.[64] Guard number 9 detained a twelve-year-old apprentice for fleeing his master, but the boy (who claimed Spanish descent), said he did not flee, because "his master had pawned his blanket," presumably to compel him to stay.[65] This accusation apparently did not ring true, and he was sent back to the workshop. Another twelve-year-old labeled a Spaniard found himself in custody because his brothers reported that he had run away for three days. The authorities brought him back to the family he had chosen to flee.[66]

In the rare situations when the night watchmen encountered boys or men of African descent who were possibly enslaved, they carried out the standard procedure returning them to their family or workplace. In a very unusual international case, at the request of the boy's father, guard number 7 arrested a fourteen-year-old called Juan Baptista Dezu, described as "a Black man from New Orleans," a *soltero* (single man, with some implication of sexually active status) who worked as a coachman.[67] The charge was "disobedience," and Dezu endured twenty-five lashes before the authorities placed him back in his father's care and possibly even endeavored to send him back to New Orleans. It is unclear whether Dezu was enslaved or free, or even where his father lived. Although odd in the sense that a sereno instigated a boy's return to another country, other parents also turned to their neighborhood patrolman to help discipline their children. In eight other cases documented in the *Libros de Reos*, mothers sought out the guards to enforce discipline on their defiant teenage daughters, to send their sons back to apprenticeships, or to report on men who had seduced their daughters.[68] Sons and daughters under age twenty who pushed their parents to seek help ranged across race labels, including Spaniards, indios, and, like Dezu, African-descent residents of Mexico City. The authorities took these requests seriously, imposing harsh punishments including lashings and even imprisonment in a dungeon for one girl who disobeyed her mother. Other than Dezu's father, one other father that we know of sought help from the guards.

In this case, the father had his son (age unknown) imprisoned for eight days to force him to go back to school.[69] Overall, the populace seemed to feel that it was appropriate to call on the night watchmen to carry out their parenting strategies.[70]

While is unknown if Dezu was enslaved or free, unlike other early law enforcement bodies in the Americas, the Mexico City guarda faroleros did not function as slave catchers in any noticeable way. An obvious explanation for this is that the population of African-descent, enslaved individuals barely existed in the viceregal capital in the late eighteenth century.[71] In fact, one example actually suggests the opposite trend—in which slaves on occasion chose to turn to the night watchmen for help. Namely, in 1794 an "enslaved Black man" asked guard number 69 for a place to sleep; the guard passed this on to his corporal and the judge, who endeavored to find his slaveholder in Valladolid (a city 170 miles to the west, now called Morelia). The only other enslaved individual mentioned in the thirty-six hundred entries for the 1790s *Libros de Reos* was also returned to his slave owner, the Marqués de Uluapa, a scion of a wealthy and politically influential family.[72]

By age fourteen, children inspired less compassion and paternalistic treatment from the low-level judiciary—henceforth, they could drift into an identity as petty wrongdoers, facing punitive reactions.[73] In nearly all cases, once a boy reached fourteen, the repercussions of arrest shifted from helping a child find a home or employment to exacting harsh punishment. For example, one spring morning in 1798, a fourteen-year-old Spanish boy broke a guard's lantern playing with a ball. He denied the offense, but his friend snitched on him, and he ended up having to pay for the lamp. A similar fate befell another fourteen-year-old with an errant ball, although he tried to make this incident political by blaming the accident on some Spanish immigrants (gachupines).[74] In contrast, a fifteen-year-old Spaniard received no punishment whatsoever for drinking aguardiente, "speaking insolently" to a guard, and even breaking his lantern. But when a boy reached the age of seventeen, "lantern smashing" led to forced labor and financial responsibility for the damage.[75] Although legal adulthood did not come until age twenty-five, at seventeen youths might face the same judicial repercussions as adults.[76] In general, from the age of sixteen on up, the record of boys arrested resembled the activities common to adult male offenders—drinking to excess, harassing women, and theft.

Patrolmen and Urban Poverty

If the guards seemed to show less compassion for youths over age fourteen, at the other distant end of the age spectrum, men sixty and above would encounter some indulgence when dealing with the night watchmen. Both men and women in this age group claimed illness when they were arrested for drinking, and a sympathetic court preferred sentencing them to extended jail time rather than forced labor.[77] While arrested drinkers aged fifty could expect serious repercussions including a month in the stocks, the authorities chose to send some sixty-year-olds and others above that age to the Hospicio de Pobres, the new Mexico City Poor House.[78] As in the examples of children under fifteen, the serenos offered the first official point of contact for those relegated to charitable and institutionalized state care.

Statistically, the individuals found by the night watchmen destined for the poor house were predominantly male, of a wide range of ages, and somewhat representative of the racial makeup of the city according to the census. The poor house did tend to cater more toward people identified as españoles as its history unfolded in this era.[79] While table 3 lists the obvious reasons why particular people might appear as needing help and destined for a state-sponsored charitable institution, small sad stories emerge from the scant records.[80] Again, in a few cases, it appears that while the guards assumed that incoherent individuals they found on the street at night suffered, like so many others, just from the effects of drinking to excess, the court later arrived at the diagnosis of "simple," presumably mentally challenged, leading to an assignment to the poor house. Like the toddler and his brother found in the garbage near San Lázaro, a sereno encountered one of the so-called simple people in a dung heap near the Alameda park.[81] One logbook entry conveys a very brief biography for an elderly mestizo man, found drunk and passed out next to the San Ramon church; he claimed to be widowed and a beggar and

TABLE 3. Reos sent to the Hospicio de Pobres in the 1790s

DATE	GENDER	RACE LABEL	AGE	STATED CAUSE OF DETAINMENT
8/21/94	female	española	?	frequent public drunk
9/25/94	male	español	?	dementia
9/26/94	male	español	?	drunk
3/4/96	male	español	21	homeless
1/2/98	male	indio	25	drunk, passed out, paralytic
1/22/98	male	español	40	drunk, passed out, beggar
1/24/98	female	española	50	drunk, passed out, epileptic
3/31/98	male	español	9	orphan
4/7/98	female	española	30	domestic abuse
5/7/98	female	india	30	beggar
5/11/98	male	mestizo	20	sick, beggar, orphan, homeless
6/14/98	male	español	59	beggar
6/23/98	male	mestizo	69	drunk, passed out, beggar
7/10/98	male	indio	?	homeless, simple
7/12/98	female	india	30	drunk, beggar
8/25/98	male	mestizo	40	drunk, passed out, deaf
9/9/98	male	indio	25	blind
9/9/98	male	español	59	drunk, passed out
10/10/98	female	india	25	drunk and/or simple
10/23/98	male	mulato	65	blind, beggar

requested to go to the poor house. A woman found wandering the streets after midnight also requested shelter at the hospicio, as she had fled her abusive husband.[82] It seems that mendicants probably chose locations that would inspire charity, as in the case of a Spanish-descent man leaning on the door of the cathedral at one in the morning, under the influence of alcohol.[83] The story of a fifty-nine-year-old español arrested as extremely drunk and comatose at 9 p.m. suggests a little bit of cunning—he claimed that he received official permission to leave the poor house and used this time to get drunk with his friends![84]

While the reformers hoped to address the issue of beggars on the street by founding this charitable institution, not all mendicants arrested by the night watchmen ended up in the poor house. Some "shame faced poor" would not dishonor themselves by publicly taking charity, a classic response to poverty in the Iberian empire, both in Spain and the Americas.[85] The illegality of begging seemed open to interpretation—one older man arrested at eleven in the morning apparently excused his alms-seeking by saying he was hungover. Like all other interactions that the serenos had with the public, their attempts to carry out this task met with resistance from the populace. Aggressive and intoxicated panhandlers responded to their arrests with profanity, one even calling a higher ranking judicial official a "carajo" when he refused to give the inebriated man a handout.[86]

Night Watchman and Healthcare

When the night watchmen took insensate or incoherent individuals into custody, usually they first presumed that these people just suffered from excessive intoxication. If the situation developed into a more complicated diagnosis than just the effects of drinking, the judicial scribe provided a confused range of speculations as to their underlying condition and its causes. Deeper investigation by the notary or judge attempted to discover the real health concern, leading to a variety of responses, from hospitalization to finding the person's family, or, frustratingly, no clear conclusion. The logbook entries mentioning the terms *demente* and *mentecato* have a tone suggesting that the authorities did not wish to persecute but instead to help, especially recognizing that remaining on the street might harm these individuals. They turned to family or the limited existing welfare institutions to address the person's issues and protect them. The first mention of this kind of scenario occurs in 1796, when guard number 74 arrested a Spanish-descent woman at 9 p.m. for drunkenness.[87] This doña refused to give any information about herself. The notary expressed frustration with her silence, not knowing if she would not speak "due to her malice or dim-wittedness [*mentecapta*]" and concluded that she was simply "loca" and needed medical care. However, after finding her husband, the authorities discovered that she was demente and had "escaped the house." We can only presume that her husband took her back into his care and confinement in her home, which would represent a satisfactory conclusion for this era.

At times, diagnoses evolved from the initial arrest for drunkenness to an observation of mental confusion or challenges and finally a conclusion that the individual in custody suffered from a long-term ailment. The common catchall term for the potential illness of such individuals was epilepsy. For example, guard number 23 arrested a very weak and sickly young woman, labeled india, just before midnight, for drinking and sleeping it off in the pulquería del Solano.[88] On further investigation, according to the judicial scribe, she seemed to fit the label mentecapta, although she had the ability to deny the accusation leading to her arrest. However, it turned out that she suffered from epilepsy, which the notary called by the eighteenth-century term *gota coral*, in reference to the idea that the sufferer had some kind of growth, or *gota*, on their heart.[89] A few weeks later, guard number 24 arrested a slightly drunk Spaniard at midnight. This man went from assumptions that he was just tipsy (*bebido*), to a diagnosis of mute, then mentecapto, and finally the conclusion that he had epilepsy.[90]

Epilepsy, or other ailments that fit under this umbrella, forced its sufferers into risky situations that led to their encounters with the guards. Those individuals labeled epileptics struggled to survive in what could be a very cruel city. Conflicts arose with authorities who did not recognize their condition or their history of dealing with it. In one sad example, after an eighteen-year-old mestizo faced arrest for repeated drunkenness, guard number 15 found he was covered in wounds as if he had suffered a severe beating. The notary wondered if this man might have epilepsy but still sentenced him to fifteen days in jail. In another case, a fifty-year-old Spanish woman self-medicated with alcohol, until guard number 90 found her passed out from extreme intoxication at 8:45 p.m. The judicial authorities sent her to the poor house for shelter.[91] Counting on their implied duties of protecting and serving, residents called the serenos when behavior interpreted as epilepsy led to dramatic and dangerous incidents.[92] In 1798 homeowners called in guard number 32 at three in the morning, because a man had jumped into their well. The guard retrieved the individual, who said he had "gone crazy due to suffering from epilepsy [gota coral]," which a doctor confirmed, and he was set free.[93] On another occasion, a drunk thirty-two-year-old Spaniard attacked the guard instead of seeking help, breaking number 70's lantern during an arrest for passed-out drunkenness.[94] Overall, these examples demonstrate the challenges faced by alleged epileptics or sufferers of other issues grouped under that name, and the lack of societal support for them. In these cases, the night watchmen strived to right a wrong—based on the idea that vulnerable people should find care within the family home—and the late viceregal judiciary took specific actions to facilitate the return to this expected norm.

The patrolmen also detained residents on the street at night who were hearing- or sight-impaired, or could not speak.[95] These individuals often ended up in the poor house, as indicated in table 3, or if possible, were returned to their families. As in the case of those arrested for extreme, passed-out intoxication, the guards and their superiors did not have a clear way to deal with those who could not communicate their names. The entries in the *Libros de Reos* stress judicial helplessness and frustration when interacting with a person who could not speak.[96] While miscommunications arose, at the same time the logbook entries hint at a community of the hearing- and sight-impaired in the viceregal capital. For example, the head guard arrested two men labeled mulato after midnight, accusing them of theft of some clothing in their possession.[97] Both men used signs to express that they were mute, had bought the clothes, and were married, so could presumably return to their wives. Usually the system seemed sympathetic to those with hearing or sight challenges and did not impose punishments. However, one man seemed to push the guards and the court to the end of their patience. This was an apparently well-known man of Indigenous ancestry named Vicente "el mudo [the mute]." Guard number 43 arrested Vicente one night at ten passed out at a pulquería, which led to eight days in the stocks. Less than two weeks later, guard number 69 again found Vicente passed out, this time in the Alameda park at 2:30 a.m. For the second offense, he found himself stuck for fifteen days in the stocks.[98]

While individuals with disabilities affecting their ability to communicate challenged the guards' capacity to react effectively, they acted more decisively with anyone found passed out and/or injured on the street. Unfortunately, this happened quite frequently—chapter 4 examines the hundreds of examples of comatose drunkenness on the street recorded in the 1790s. The jail had an in-house surgeon who dealt with some injuries that did not require hospitalization. The surgeon appears in the *Libros de Reos* in his function of officially reporting that a given prisoner was "cured" or "healthy" before he or she was released, which also emphasized that the judiciary wanted to show that they cared for these marginalized individuals. The *Libros de Reos* also document that 37 people went directly from the guards' custody to a hospital to cure their wounds. This total adds up to over 1 percent of all recorded incidents examined for this study. The only complete year of logbooks—1798—had a total of 24 hospitalizations deriving from the serenos' nocturnal patrols. The documentation of so many actions taken to help those damaged by street fights or in the course of a night out drinking certainly inscribes the night watchmen as aiding in extending the Spanish Crown's traditional paternalistic care to the subjects of New Spain, as well as a more modern kind of public health. In some of the records, the notary made it clear that the arrested individual went to the hospital as *en calidad de preso* or *en calidad de presa*, meaning that they were not free to leave the hospital and still most likely faced judicial repercussions.[99] In some cases, the docket notation shows the opposite situation: someone in the hospital reported an injured patient who should have been questioned for involvement in some kind of crime, such as public intoxication or fighting. For example, this notation occurs in the report of a twenty-six-year-old mestiza with head injuries from an unknown source, found at the Hospital de San Andrés.[100]

Excessive alcohol consumption led to physical danger and hospitalization. In March of 1798, an Indigenous woman went to the hospital after her arrest for drunkenness due to her "broken head."[101] A night watchman found a fifty-year-old mestizo man extremely drunk and passed out one night in September of 1798 at 10:30. Described as "quebrado [broken]," this man went straight to the hospital.[102] That same month, guard number

57 found a man of Spanish descent drunk and passed out, with a very serious wound to his nose. The man did not remember anything about how this injury occurred, but it required emergency attention in the Hospital de San Andrés.[103] In the final days of 1798, a forty-year-old man of Spanish ancestry went to the hospital after falling while drunk, "breaking his head, a very serious wound," in the cathedral cemetery.[104] Notaries also used the term *descalabrado* to describe severe head injuries requiring hospitalization.[105]

Other causes for a transfer to the hospital included fighting, violence in the workplace, domestic abuse, and more general unidentified illnesses. When individuals argued in the street in this era, oftentimes someone ended up needing medical care. For example, a woman standing near a fight between two men in 1799 ended up severely injured from a kick to the stomach, producing a great deal of blood.[106] Domestic altercations made their way onto the street, with the serenos arresting both combatants, even though it seemed that usually, although not always, the woman suffered injuries.[107] Women also injured each other in street brawls—not only men engaged in public violence.[108] Similar to emergency calls for midwives or priests, the guards also responded to beatings that took place indoors, working with discretion in these sometimes delicate situations.[109]

While Mexico City's nightlife always had an element of danger, fighting seemed to increase in the era of mass insurgency and just after. On a single night in February of 1822, several brawls and robberies took place. Starting at 7 p.m., the guards arrested a man who had robbed another at knifepoint. In this case, the serenos needed the help of bystanders. Only thirty minutes later, they found a mysteriously injured man, who did not remember what had happened to him. At 8:30, guard number 16 helped the military patrols escort another thief to jail. A half-hour later, three guards intervened in a scuffle involving six individuals, resulting in an injury to a woman's face done with a sword. Around this same time, guard number 90 escorted a priest to give someone last rites. The night's action only accelerated at 10 p.m., with the incarceration of a drunk man and another fracas involving several men and women. Two guards managed to catch one of the perpetrators and had to take one of the women to the hospital for a serious injury. Then at 10:30 p.m., guard number 94 heard another woman crying for help while a military officer sexually attacked her. Fortunately, the authorities managed to take the assailant into custody. Lastly, after midnight, the guards went to help out at a robbery. The next night, relatively calm, still featured more thieves, drunks, and injured people, but worst of all, a man whose wife claimed that he had attempted to murder her.[110]

First Responses to Intoxication

The *Libros de Reos*, like much Bourbon-era recordkeeping, was meant to provide a paper trail for the late viceregal regime's self-presentation as civilizers of colonial subjects, as well as inscribing these subjects as drunk and barbarous. A highlight of this collaboration between bureaucratic record keeping, new methods of surveillance, and the men who patrolled the city streets, is the record of repeat offenders. Because no catalog of recalcitrant drunks exists—no record of any kind of alphabetized names or the like—the night watchmen simply must have known their beats well enough to remember who among the thousands of drinkers in pulquerías frequently drank to excess. In 114 arrests of repeat offenders for public intoxication, an implied duty of "protecting and serving" combined with proto-policing and forays into improving the behavior of Mexico City's problematic public drinkers.

In reaction to the dozens of excessive drinkers detained by the night watchmen, the judiciary resorted to longer stays in jail, lashings, sentences to the stocks or the dungeon, all punitive responses to this perceived crisis unfolding on the urban streets. The notaries expressed frustration with additional inscriptions in the logbooks, including the descriptions of these individuals as incorrigible, scandalous, and provocative.[111] Despite these judgments, within the jail, severely drunk prisoners received treatments in hopes of saving their lives or preventing further injuries. Over the centuries, commentators and historians have interpreted the archives recording Indigenous drunkenness as proof of a declining civilization, signs of depression and ennui, or, more recently, as late viceregal accelerated racialization.[112] Despite this overall imperialistic vision of alcohol use, when questioned about their treatment of intoxicated individuals, the night watchmen and the staff in the public jail took care to present themselves as protecting the health of vulnerable and pitiful people, in line with official policies. In 1792 corregidor of Mexico City and intendant of the Province of Mexico in and around the city Bernardo Bonavía mandated that "all drunks who enter the jail should be helped with medicines and that if these are not enough to revive them, they should be turned over to the surgeon to apply the remedy that they deem appropriate."[113] The remedy viewed as most effective in dealing with severe inebriation that presented a health risk was the administration of cold-water enemas. An extended discussion of the treatment of drunks came up in 1797 when Viceroy Branciforte asked for an investigation of two or three fatalities that took place while the "patients" were in custody. The jail nurse and *alcaides* (wardens) responded with a detailed defense of the enema practice, and the viceroy also called on surgeons and the protomedicato for outside, unbiased medical perspectives.

According to this file, both employees and inmates agreed on the healthful benefits of the enemas. This technique may derive from precolonial approaches to reducing fevers, which also attempted to "cool" the body with various methods, including an enema.[114] Jail staff noted that recent fatalities occurred because those individuals were already vomiting "copious amounts of blood," and even an emergency call to the surgeon did not save them.[115] Warden Gregorio Eslava argued that enemas helped drunks stand up and remember their names, when only a few hours before they had entered the jail near death and almost unable to breathe. Three inmates also gave the following statements in favor of the effectiveness of these jailhouse enemas, based on their varying personal experiences:

> [Statement by] a fifty-year-old man arrested the night of October 8th at 9:30 by guard number 34 . . . he said that because he was not completely out of it [*perdido*], he remembers that he had two enemas administered, and that although he did not have any evacuation, he recovered and rested quietly and peacefully. When he woke up he was completely free of drunkenness and without those effects it usually produced, which are a copious thirst and tremors in the nerves.

[Statement by] a sixty-year-old man, taken into custody at 12:30 last night by guard number 89, he was drunk and passed out on the corner that is called Los Pajaritos.... As soon as he entered the jail last night, he went with four other men down to the patio, where he was given four cold water enemas. Far from causing him further damage, although he did not have any evacuation, he observed that he was refreshed from the heat produced by the brandy he had imbibed. His head cleared expeditiously and he could move naturally. He slept calmly until dawn today without suffering the discomforts of thirst, nerve tremors, drowsiness and all of the others caused by drunkenness.

[Statement by] a thirty-year-old woman, taken into custody on the night of the 10th of this month by guard number 51 for drunkenness.... About eight times she has been imprisoned in this jail for drunkenness. Each time she has received cold water enemas, but she cannot remember how many. The effects of these enemas have been copious evacuation and at dawn she felt that her head was clear and her body cooled down after the effect of the liquor.[116]

Doctors who did not have an affiliation with the jail expressed less confidence in the cold-water enemas.[117] Five doctors testified on the topic. First, Máximo Afán de Rivera argued that in the most extreme cases of drunkenness, cold-water enemas could prevent death by apoplexy, which commonly killed "these unhappy ones." Dr. Afán de Rivera described the fearful effects of spirits as deadly in their subtle expansion throughout the vascular system and into the brain. Introducing cold water to the large intestines "restored their tone" and invigorated the brain so the patient could move again and return to their senses. He believed that enemas only had a deleterious result if they were not administered in time to save the individual from apoplexy. Don Vicente Ferrer, a retired army surgeon and a department head in the San Andrés hospital, also supported their use, recommending a dosage of only one *cuartilla* of liquid at a time.

Three other doctors, however, expressed hesitancy regarding the usefulness of enemas for drunks in the jail, arguing that they could induce apoplexy. They believed, like Afán de Rivera, that cold water "condensed" the effect of liquor in the body. The key factor in determining if they would help or hinder the inmate lay in the stage of drunkenness. If an individual experienced the "enraged" or "choleric" state, enemas would help them. But if they were passed out already, "taciturn" and "fearful," they should instead receive invigorating enemas of warm salt water, while laying on their sides with their heads raised. Then the jail staff just needed to wait the typical ten or twelve hours required for the stupor to dissipate naturally.[118]

From fighting fires to escorting midwives, Mexico City's night watchmen fulfilled a number of tasks that diverged from their basic roles as lantern lighters and deterrents to crime. In the twenty-first-century United States, we entrust the police, especially the lowest ranks who walk or drive their beats in cities and towns, to carry out complex tasks relating to social welfare, duties that require training in understanding mental health, sexual assault, and domestic abuse. Commentators on this issue suggest that this mission creep is increasing, although U.S. urban law enforcement has worked on the frontlines of public health since the mid-nineteenth century.[119] This chapter demonstrates that some of the earliest patrolmen in American history also dealt with many individuals in emotional distress or struggling with a wide array of disabilities on the streets of this hemisphere's largest metropolis in the late eighteenth century. To reiterate points made in chapter 2, the serenos were impoverished and illiterate men barely one step up from day laborers. Better trained public health professionals, such as doctors, surgeons, and midwives, did not even dare to venture out in the Mexico City night without one of these guards as a chaperone. Similar to our day, although viceregal law enforcement was a far cry from modern state policing and state social welfare agencies, these patrolmen were the first contact with the authorities, expected to address violence, illness, or mental and emotional challenges in addition to their other duties. But what occupied most of their time, and filled up hundreds of pages in the judicial logbooks of the era, was apprehending literally thousands of individuals drinking to excess every night in New Spain's capital.

CHAPTER 4

Nightlife

> The pulquerías had no floor, just the flattened earth. . . . These taverns usually had only one wall in the back decorated with different scenes such as a fight, a charro [Mexican cowboy] on his horse, a bullfight, or a caricature of some historical character. At some point along the wall there was a shrine with the image of the Virgin Mary or a saint, a vase with roses and poppies and a candle. The pulque was stored in three or four large jars or barrels three to five feet high that stood five feet apart from the back wall. They had a wide bottom and a narrow top, and were painted in loud colors with their names in big letters. Close to the barrels there was a rustic shelf containing the clay cups.
> —María Aurea Toxqui Garay, "'El Recreo de los Amigos'"

In this chapter, we venture out with a few of the night watchmen to experience the most active areas of Mexico City's late viceregal nightlife, concentrating on the blocks hosting the busiest nocturnal watering holes. This stroll will take us quickly past buildings that hosted indoor and outdoor diversions such as lively theatrical productions, rowdy fandangos, scandalous *escuelas de danza* (the dance clubs of the era), occasionally co-ed bathhouses, sweat lodges (*temascales*), swimming pools, bullfighting rings, gambling dens, high-stakes elite card games held in ornate private parlors, cafes, and sophisticated *tertulias*.[1] Although all these venues drew either crowds or select groups of invited guests, most of the capital city's residents who sought out entertainment and socializing took part in a far less glamourous nocturnal activity. The plebeians made their way after work to a tavern (known as pulquerías or vinaterías, serving pulque or distilled cane liquor, respectively), drank all the pulque—which only had an alcohol content of 4 to 6 percent—or aguardiente they could afford, and then walked home, that is, if they remained steady enough on their feet. This chapter's exploration of nightlife in New Spain's capital recreates the patrols made by the night watchmen to illuminate how pulquerías, drinking, and the aftereffects of intoxication shaped both the cityscape and the labor routine of the serenos. Piecing together information from the records of 1790s arrests brings to life how the lowly patrolmen carried out elite directives against alcohol abuse, "intrud[ing] into the previously undisputed domains of the people."[2]

Before we begin to explore Mexico City's pulque-infused nightlife, remember that traversing these viceregal streets would not resemble our brightly lit electrical or gas-powered world. Darkness transforms how a city's space is experienced, obscuring attempts at surveillance, hiding activities, and changing the perception of one's surroundings.[3] It is almost impossible to imagine the mysterious, and even otherworldly, urban nights of the past, as lighting technologies unimaginable two centuries ago chase away almost all of a city's gloom.

Eighteenth-century residents of New Spain's capital occupied a very different nocturnal space than did others of their era who lived at higher northern latitudes. Other than on clear, moonlit nights, Mexico City experienced a steady eight to ten hours of full and complete darkness every day of the year. In contrast, London's nights ranged from zero hours of total obscurity from mid-May to mid-July to up to twelve hours of impenetrable murkiness in winter. London and other northern cities did not need street lighting in summer, and the colder—even snowy—weather may have discouraged some night crawlers in midwinter.[4] In contrast, New Spain's milder climate and more consistent hours of obscurity permitted routine drinking and walking around outside at night. The nocturnal population truly inhabited a different world than did those who preferred to venture out only in the sunshine.

Those who dared to go out at night risked unknown surprises in the shadowy streets, which were lit only by small pools of illumination surrounding the newly installed lanterns.[5] The guarda faroleros also carried smaller handheld lanterns. These tiny beacons made the guards themselves much more visible than their surroundings or the individuals whom they tried to surveil. The serenos' essential purpose was to enlighten the night by literally embodying the state—their physical presence outdoors at night, along with their lanterns, pikes, and whistles, symbolized that the Spanish viceroyalty and municipality now had an increased official involvement in Mexico City's nightlife. These approximately ninety-nine watchmen patrolling the streets signified the imperial government's desire to bring about a change in how the city, both its physical space and its people, functioned at night.[6] Every interaction a guard had with a nightwalker represented a claim on the plebeian-controlled darkness. But while efforts to illuminate urban gloom changed nocturnal patterns of activity by virtue of more interactions with governmental officials, the viceroys and their underlings ultimately lost their campaign to conquer the night.[7]

Enlightened Views on Mexican Drinking Culture

In their role as low-level functionaries of Spanish imperialism, the guards walked up and down their assigned blocks, carried their lanterns, maintained the public lighting, and helped in the semimedical, semisacred tasks examined in chapter 3. And, during each act of taking someone into custody, they embodied siglo de luces ideas of civilization. This task, which mainly involved arresting drunks, focused on the poor and middling individuals who ventured outside after dark seeking pulque. Through their loyal patronage of hundreds of pulquerías, this population had a significant influence on the physical landscape of Mexico City. This chapter cites the decades-long works of historians who have recognized the immutable popularity of pulquerías as well as the patterns of behavior fueled by uninhibited drinking and the resulting limitless greed for its profits. As previous historians have already done this work, I will not spend too much time on the details of proscriptive decrees against the drinking culture. No matter how many inebriates ended up in custody, historical analysis shows us that the viceregal judiciary did not have the capacity to change the colonial culture of intoxication, or even to effectively colonize the nocturnal landscape. As summed up by Michael Scardaville, "the pulquería and vinatería reforms of the late colonial period accomplished little."[8]

This failure did not come through a lack of effort. Reports and commentaries written and archived by Spanish authorities, both religious and secular, inscribed Indigenous drinking customs on the geography of Mexico City since the sixteenth century. This essentializing verbiage functioned within their documentary armory as an important weapon of Iberian imperialism. Administrative and judicial records related to patterns of alcohol consumption began in the context of the spiritual conquest of New Spain.[9] From the mid-seventeenth century, the Crown and its viceroys attempted to limit the number of pulquerías in the city and forbade more than one chair per establishment, to prevent loitering.[10] In the late seventeenth century, drinking practices became an official obsession, in terms of their alleged negative effect on workers' productivity and their assessment as non-European and even savage.[11] Energetic reformers relentlessly wrote laws and regulations relating to the urban landscape, trying to limit the locations and hours of alcohol consumption. In the nineteenth century, intellectual and political leaders continued to write and speak of plebeian drinking as barbaric, forging this tool anew as a governmental and economic concern strongly tied to visions of the Mexican nation.[12] The production of this racially charged rhetoric endured well into the twentieth century.[13]

Although highly symbolic spiritually and an important source of nutritional calories for Indigenous peoples, pulque also figured as an extremely popular beverage among plebeian Spaniards and castas in eighteenth-century Mexico City.[14] Unlike other agricultural products from Mexico, pulque does not export well beyond its place of fermentation. Pulque drinkers gathered in familiar locations, crossing over into the domestic space, even as this fermented juice of the maguey plant became a major source of income for land- and business-owner oligarchs of the eighteenth century.[15] From 1763 pulque growers and producers operated under a royal monopoly that brought in hundreds of thousands of pesos annually.[16] Outlying towns also produced cane liquor.[17] Until the era of industrialized beer production in the late nineteenth century, pulque remained the most popular drink in Mexico City. Finally, after almost a century of trying other drinks, pulquerías returned as a trend in the twenty-first century among young and middle-class urbanites.[18]

Key historiographic signposts for English-language scholarship on the topic of drinking and colonialism in Mexico include Charles Gibson's devastating final paragraph in *The Aztecs under Spanish Rule*: "What we have studied is the deterioration of a native empire and civilization.... One of the earliest and most persistent individual responses was drink. If our sources may be believed, few peoples in the whole of history were more prone to drunkenness than the Indians of the Spanish colony."[19] Fifteen years later, Gibson's student William B. Taylor complicated his mentor's conclusion by analyzing the contrasting rural versus urban drinking patterns for Indigenous Mexicans. Taylor viewed Mexico City and its pulquerías as liminal spaces that did not adhere to village traditions of alcohol use. While disagreeing with the observation that post-Conquest alcoholism rose to the level of a culturally destructive "plague" that signified "social disintegration" or widespread "depression and moral collapse," Taylor conceded that Indigenous people certainly drank more in viceregal Mexico City and in less ritualized settings than they did outside the city or before the Spanish invasion. Overall, he judges rural drinking as part of "community life" in the increasingly important "discrete landholding village."[20]

Contemporaneously to Taylor's *Drinking, Homicide, and Rebellion*, Michael Scardaville also explored drinking patterns and their regulation by Bourbon reformers in Mexico City, focusing on the data found in the *Libros de Reos*. In the 1970s Taylor and Scardaville thoroughly examined the intertwined topics of alcohol use, patterns of violence, and rhetorical stances in judicial settings. Steve Stern continued this work, looking through a gendered lens in the 1990s.[21] Despite these several decades of superb scholarship, Aaron Althouse argues that important aspects of drinking still need investigation, noting that "the ways that alcohol use functioned in individual social relations and in society 'at large' are starkly absent from the historiography."[22] The most common approach in all existing sources remains a catalogue of the frustrated efforts of high-level reformers in various eras of Mexican history to suppress or, at the very least, police and regulate, Indigenous drinking.[23]

This chapter follows Althouse's suggestion by contextualizing intoxication within the urban, plebeian space of the viceregal capital and interpreting the night watchmen as working-class men carrying out one of their key work tasks. Instead of reiterating the regulations that came from the top, it refocuses the discussion of drinking patterns to emphasize the human element in policing the night-shrouded geography of drunkenness. Even with the excellent scholarship carried out by Scardaville and Sánchez-Arcilla Bernal, historians have not thoroughly analyzed all of the information provided in the *Libros de Reos* and other archived sources created by the lantern guards and their leadership.[24] This chapter turns away from the emphasis on court processes and repercussions to focus on the street and the actual experience of drinking, examining how the paper trails map links between specific serenos, patterns of alcohol consumption, and the geography of Mexico City.

Drinkers and night watchmen moved through the urban night in certain set patterns, in a colonial choreography that informed and continued racialized notions of drinking to excess, morality, and productivity. Removing the guards as thinking, working men ignores half of the partnership in this nightly pas de deux. But carefully scrutinizing the guards' well-marked movements as they intersected with the nocturnal landscape maps intoxication onto the viceregal capital's streets. As judicial scribes wrote records to memorialize the inebriation of the people they labeled as Mexico City's indios and indias, they made it very clear that these subjects were not dancing with themselves but intertwined with men acting as Spanish government officials, even if the serenos occupied the very lowest rank within the bureaucratic hierarchy. The lantern guards at first glance might look like agents of the state, but it is worth considering that, often working alone, they determined who had so violated plebeian norms and values to deserve arrest—and who they could arrest without facing a great deal of resistance from their fellow drinkers.[25]

What was the overall political purpose for plotting thousands of archival inscriptions of Indigenous and other plebeians' intoxication on the Mexico City landscape? Bourbon reformers blamed drunkenness for a general lack of discipline within New Spanish society that weakened the working classes (especially those that they labeled indios), causing them to waste their time and money, destroy their families, and fill the streets with ragged, gross behaviors and residues.[26] The perceived hideousness and barbarity of unconscious colonial subjects on the city streets contrasted with the ambitious plans for European-style urbanity and beautification via street illumination. Viceregal authorities could not eliminate the insensate bodies just by shining a light on them, but they could hire and organize physical manpower to remove them. The installation of street lanterns, the organization of the guarda faroleros, and the carefully logged dockets of drunkenness all functioned first and foremost as evidence that the siglo de luces government had the wherewithal to surveil their subjects on a nightly basis. Much more ambitiously, this paper trail tried to demonstrate that surveillance and written notations also meant they controlled nocturnal activity more effectively than they had previously.

Judicial notaries spent hours every night documenting the viceregal battle to conquer the night and its denizens. In reference to the extensive archive of urban nightlife, Scardaville observed that the *Libros de Reos* indicate that "drink crimes represented the most commonly committed offense in Mexico City in the late colonial period."[27] The *Libros de Reos* continue the racializing process begun shortly after the fall of Tenochtitlán with careful notations of Indigenous people taken into custody for inebriation and passing out in public due to drinking, recording literally thousands of examples of this offense. This careful documentation suggests that a key purpose of creating the guards' nightly logbooks was to clearly and repetitively inscribe Indigenous degradation. Of course historians have long known that narrations of "uncivilized" drinking allowed Spaniards to differentiate themselves from their barbaric subjects,[28] but the repetitive phrasing of the *Libros de Reos* hammers home this point ad nauseum.[29] The other essential source of data on the night watchmen, the simpler set of documents labeled with the title "la parte que han dado los guardas del alumbrado de lo acaecido la noche anterior [the light guards' account of what happened the previous night]," have a different but closely related purpose. While these scantier reports of the guardas mayores do not list race labels, they effectively document the night watchmen's physical presence on the central city grid, thus mapping drunkenness and constructing a documentary repository reinforcing how hard the government worked to impose a European standard of beauty and civilization on the cityscape.

Quantifying Mexico City Drinking

Statistical evidence demonstrates that, other than monitoring urban illumination, the guards spent a great deal of their time at work physically removing drunks from the streets. Over twenty-three hundred people, or around 3 percent of the adult population, found themselves in police custody for public intoxication in 1798. According to elite Spanish observers and the venerable traveler Alexander von Humboldt, the night watchmen hauled away inebriates resembling "dead bodies" by the cartload.[30] The numbers suggest that the average Mexico City resident over age fifteen consumed close to two hundred gallons of pulque annually. Drinkers could imbibe at any of sixteen hundred legal and illegal pulquerías, which hosted an estimated sixty-two thousand customers each night. In other words, 13 percent of the adults in Mexico City could drink to intoxication every day.[31] Beyond the statistics, the gendered complexities of the pulque-fueled nightlife multiplied—venturing out in the darkness could endanger women but also provided them with important economic possibilities. Most pulquerías were unlicensed, run by women, providing food and a gender-mixed social setting where families and single people met and interacted. Hundreds of astute businesswomen exploited the lucrative but illegal business of selling pulque on the street or in makeshift stands, risking arrest and suppression.[32] Some of these entrepreneurs offered not much more than an earthenware pitcher and cups to their passing clientele. Meanwhile, the Crown and its local representatives made a significant income by gradually increasing the taxes charged on pulque entering Mexico City in the eighteenth and early nineteenth centuries. This income funded military costs, public works projects, and even helped address a late-1790s smallpox outbreak.[33] Given the money to be made, the viceregal authorities did not ban these intoxicants even though they moralized about their danger.[34]

Keeping in mind the sixteen hundred stands open for pulque consumption, let us imagine nocturnal Mexico City as experienced by a night watchman in the 1790s. He walked his nightly beat in worn leather boots, wearing a groove in the cobblestone streets that formed a grid around the churches, convents, friaries, and other religious buildings that dominated much of the space and defined particular neighborhoods. During the daytime, street activity focused around these edifices, along with government buildings, market stalls, and the substantial residences of the wealthy. Everything changed as darkness fell: government scribes and functionaries shut their courts and offices, market women selling groceries packed up, and domestic servants closed down and locked large front doors to bar the entryways of substantial private houses. As many of the active daytime population withdrew indoors, pulquerías filled with those men and women who had a few reales to spend after a hard day's work, as well as those who wanted to make some money or con a free *copa*. While they represented a social nexus for plebeians of all ages, genders, and races, pulquerías continuously flaunted city ordinances. According to viceregal decrees and municipal regulations, pulquerías were not supposed to host a crowd; yet dozens of patrons gathered at popular establishments. Some patrons sat at seats or benches, others on the ground, drinking and eating all afternoon and into the evening, possibly even sleeping in a back room for a small cost. All this took place during evening hours (see figure 4), even though ordinances decreed that pulquerías should close every night other than Saturday—any resident could find pulque for sale "anywhere in the city, at any time."[35] People enjoyed smashing the serving vessels on the ground, surrounding themselves with piles of pottery shards. Again defying urban regulations, musicians played harps and guitars to accompany dancers, a tactic that drew in more patrons and could also provide free drinks for an entrepreneurial entertainer.[36] Pulquerías even hosted an oral culture of impromptu poets, who composed hundreds of satirical verses.[37] Fights involving both men and women drinking in pulquerías often ended in death or arrests.[38]

Before all of this activity began each night, the serenos came on duty after evening prayer, as the sun receded behind the mountains on the Anáhuac horizon. First they collected their oil from the head guard, then divided up to work more or less alone. As dusk fell, the guards observed crowds of drinkers quenching their thirst at the stalls and stands selling

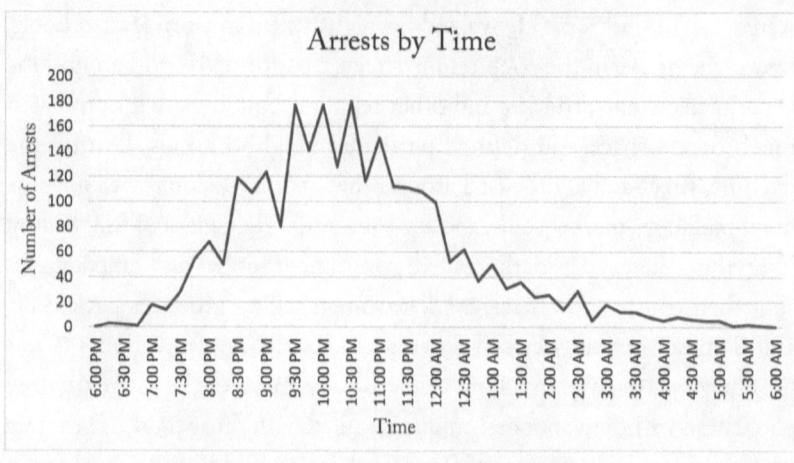

4. Arrests by time, recorded in *Libros de Reos*. Created by author.

pulque. As the streets filled with darker and more impenetrable shadows, the night watchmen climbed their ladders, filled the street lanterns with their allotment of turnip oil, and ignited the wicks. As a result, more than a thousand isolated pools of flickering light appeared, dozens of yards apart, on all of the larger city streets. As people exited from nighttime masses (some might have attended already drunk), the plazas in front of religious buildings, their narrow surrounding alleyways, and church cemeteries transformed into convenient spots where drunks fell to the ground in the course of a night, after hours of drinking in nearby taverns.[39]

In the eighteenth century, an increasing population and growing dependence on pulque revenue by the government meant that some shacks serving pulque converted into permanent buildings, while others remained more like tents or involved nothing more than a woman seller standing on the street.[40] Often located on plazas on the outskirts of the city center, pulquerías dominated the darkened space with their large size (up to one thousand square feet). Crowds of people gathered in them, sheltered by only three walls, which regulations demanded. Perhaps a canvas flap created a fourth wall for the sole purpose of evading the guards' surveillance.[41] Tempted by these prolific drinking venues, even priests and friars might soon appear drunk and disorderly on the streets.[42]

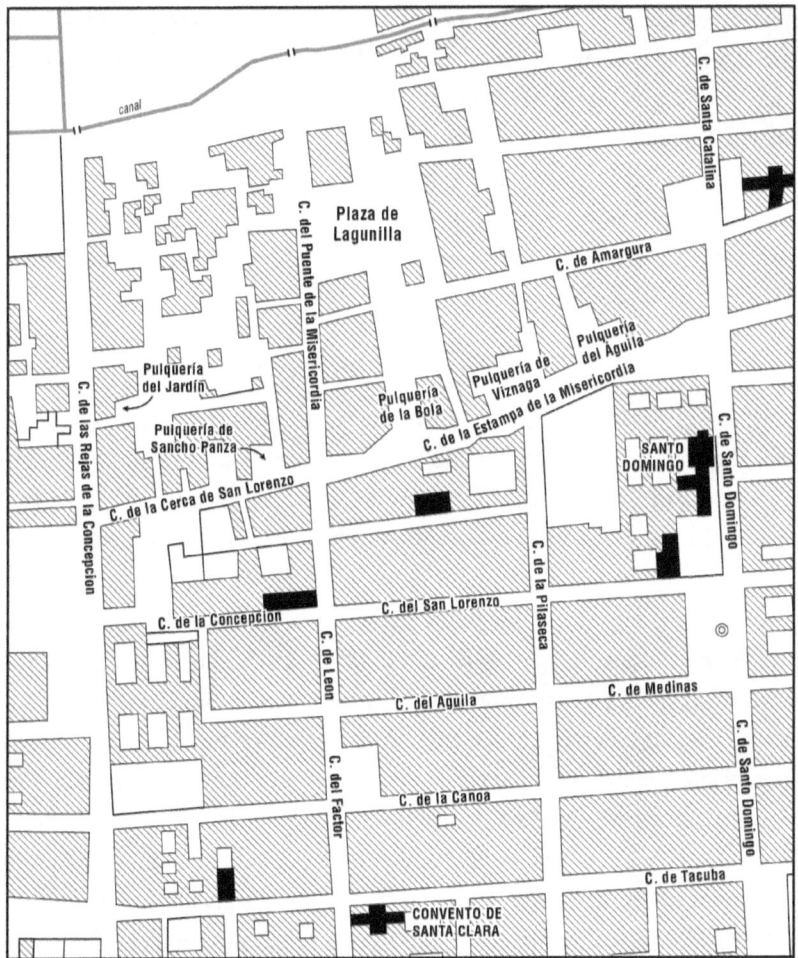

5. Cuartel 1. Created by Erin Greb.

Drinkers typically paid a half-real, one-sixteenth of a peso, in exchange for at least four drinks. In an era when the poor earned only around ten pesos a month, this might represent an individual's pay for the day.[43] Gradually, over the course of the next several hours, the patrolmen witnessed most of the drinkers stumble out toward their homes, with some remaining sleeping on the floor of the pulquerías or slumped to the ground barely past their entryways. After midnight, the thoroughfares quieted as many of the drinkers arrived at their homes or passed out on the streets and alleys before they could find shelter. The *Libros de Reos* map over eight hundred different incidents of passed out drunkenness on the viceregal streets.[44] While the purpose of this documentation was to inscribe Indigenous drinking customs on the geography of the capital as well as to record Bourbon efforts to police it, these dockets also create a geography of the diversions and conflicts ever-present in Mexico City's nights.

The Geography of Intoxication

Starting our walking tour of Mexico City's late eighteenth-century nightlife, the busiest guards patrolled around some of the most iconic and historic Catholic institutions in New Spain's capital, in what is now the historic center. Within this space converged the most significant geographic concentration of intoxication in the city, at least as can be identified by reference to one particular place name—the Santo Domingo church and friary. Pulque drinkers gathered in this neighborhood, because there were eight officially recognized buildings housing pulquerías within the boundaries of Cuartel 1, more than in any other section of Mexico City. The location may have served the poor who lived further north, where the city grid of streets faded away (see figure 5). Dominicans originally built their church in this part of the city shortly after the Spanish conquest of Tenochtitlán. The current church building, with its dramatic contrast between blood red *tezontle* and grayish stone, dates to the 1730s.[45] Figure 5 shows six friary patios that no longer exist, but a large cobblestone plaza directly to the south still captures a sense of the viceregal cityscape and the availability of open spaces where inebriated plebeians might find themselves wandering after dark. According to the notations in the *Libros de Reos*, locations identified as "Santo Domingo"—including the street, plaza, doorways, and other surrounding spaces—provided an uncomfortable resting place for dozens of comatose drunks, labeled *tirados*, in the 1790s. To give a poignant example, on a night in November 1798, these tirados included an Indigenous man who, when roused at the city jail, claimed his age as ninety-four years. The local patrolmen found him passed out in the Portal de Santo Domingo, an arched corridor opposite the Inquisition Palace. Because he was too old to work, he received a sentence of eight days in jail.[46]

Arrests recorded in the *Libros de Reos* suggest that the eight pulquerías around Santo Domingo attracted a mainly Indigenous-descent clientele, out drinking starting in the early hours of the evening or perhaps even during the day. The closest tavern to the Santo Domingo friary was the pulquería del Águila (see figure 5), known in the late viceregal and early national period as a *casilla* selling *atole* (corn stew) and other food, as well as pulque.[47] The food did not prevent the clientele's excessive intoxication. While making his rounds between 10 p.m. and 1 a.m. in the mid-1790s, guard number 43 arrested three passed-out individuals (labeled in the *Libros de Reos* as two españoles and one castizo) inside of this pulquería.[48] If patrons left the pulquería del Águila and strolled to the east or southeast, they would encounter several guards (including numbers 9, 10, 42, 43, 45), walking their beat along the long Calle de Santo Domingo, which extended six blocks from the Calle de Tacuba in the south to the Convento de Santa Clara in the north. These guards had busy work nights interacting with these drinkers. Guard number 45, whose name and other personal details are unknown, arrested twelve of his fifty total recorded arrests in the 1790s near Santo Domingo or on the street of that name. These individuals possibly collapsed after a night spent drinking in the pulquería del Águila. Drinkers may have also stumbled toward the short alleyway called the Calle de Amargura, which passed directly north of the pulquería del Águila. This was on the beat of guard numbers 88, 89, and 90. During 1798, the night watchmen took nine intoxicated individuals into custody just from this one block of urban Mexico. Drinking started early here, as was the norm throughout the city. All nine offenders had already passed out on the street between the hours of 8:45 p.m. and 11:15 p.m. Judging by the number of arrests (twenty-three recorded in all of the *Libros de Reos*) that took place in the street and plaza adjacent to Santo Domingo earlier in the evening, many of these customers drank enough to pass out well before 10 p.m. This was not a common area for Indigenous people to live, but perhaps the neighborhood drew people who worked in and around the Zócalo. Most of the drinkers claimed or received the label of indio, although there were exceptions. For example, in 1798, guard number 90, covering the Santo Domingo beat, arrested a sleeping couple labeled español and negra after three in the morning.[49]

If they walked along the Calle de la Estampa de la Misericordia to the west, drinkers could pass their time and satisfy their thirsts at four more pulquerías. Just a very small block to the southeast from the pulquería del Águila, nightwalkers could find the pulquería de Viznaga (see figure 5, also spelled Biznaga), which opened as another casilla no later than 1751. The fascinating history of this pulquería includes Jesuit ownership of the pulque-producing estates, which stocked its jars, pitchers, and cups. This lot was later confiscated by the royal government when the Jesuits were expelled. Finally, the property fell into the hands of don Pedro Romero de Terreros, the Count of Regla, a fantastically wealthy silver mine owner and global merchant, who maintained several other Mexico City pulquerías with the sap extracted from his haciendas.[50] When the count died in 1781, he bequeathed this pulquería and three others to his unmarried daughter. Along with other Novohispanic aristocrats, this family, whose members included Mexico City alcaldes, most likely disdained the plebeians who provided them with their pulque-based income.[51] Walking from the pulquería de Viznaga a small block or two to the west, a drinker would encounter the pulquería de la Bola (see figure 5, just south of the Plaza de Lagunilla). According to the *Libros de Reos*, guard number 43 and corporal 8 took a total of seven customers of la Bola into custody in a five-week period in late 1798. At least four of these offenders were either passed out or "sleeping," which might imply illicit sex acts as well as drinking to excess.[52]

Pulque drinkers could pursue more options just by crossing over a four-way juncture where the Calle de la Estampa de la Misericordia met the Calle de la Cerca de San Lorenzo. In the next block were two more pulquerías: del Jardín and Sancho Panza, the latter known in the nineteenth century for its murals depicting Miguel de Cervantes's famous character. Dating back at least to the mid-eighteenth century, the pulquería del

Jardín was originally a *jacal*, or a "room." This building structure, however basic, ignored prohibitions mandating that pulquerías have open walls on three sides.[53] At least according to the existing *Libros de Reos*, the night watchmen did not see a great deal of action in these two taverns, nor on the street just in front of them. However, many drinkers probably left the watering holes and managed to walk far enough to turn the corner and head north after a night in La Bola, Águila, or Sancho Panza. They would then stroll up the Calle del Puente de la Misericordia. This street was patrolled by guard number 66, name unknown. Between January and November of 1798, sereno number 66 arrested nine individuals for public intoxication ranging in degree from *borracho* (drunk) to *ebrísimo* (extremely inebriated) and insensate, on just a few blocks of this street.[54] As per usual for Mexico City in this era, drinking indoors in a social setting shifted to extreme inebriation and passing out on the street anytime between 8 p.m. and one in the morning. Most likely the twenty-six other arrests made in the patrol area of guard number 66 between 1794 and 1798 were also along this particular street, fueled by the nearby concentration of pulquerías. The clientele in this area varied across the viceregal social categories, with arrestees labeled indio, mulato, mestizo, castizo, and español, and ranging in age from a twenty-year-old Indigenous man to a sixty-year-old Spaniard.

Some of the drinkers arrested in the neighborhood of Santo Domingo and generally in Cuartel 1 probably walked over from Cuartel 4 (figure 6), further to the east. Moving our tour to wander into the northern reaches of Cuartel 4, we encounter a large and dense swathe of nightlife action extending to the very edge of the viceregal center. The following six guards patrolled the streets of this busy region in the 1790s: number 88, Marcelo Salazar, a married twenty-three-year-old castizo born in Mexico City; number 89, the Spanish-descent Mariano Rosales; number 90, José Castillo, a twenty-three-year-old español arrested for almost drinking himself to death on duty; number 91, of whom no further information is known; number 92, Camilo Velasco, a twenty-seven-year-old Spaniard; and number 93, no further information known.[55] Thanks to the popular pulquerías in their ramos, surviving records document that these six guards arrested in total 250 individuals in the streets shown in figures 6 and 7. Well over half of these arrestees had the race label indio, but over seventy were españoles, with another fifty-five labeled mestizos. These custodies suggest that generally this was an area where a wide range of the city's population enjoyed drinking pulque. While arrests for drinking-related offenses started only an hour or so after dusk—by 7:45 p.m. some had already drunk to excess—these six serenos continued to drag people off the street until the wee hours of the morning.

A hotspot in Cuartel 4 was the very popular pulquería de Celaya (see figure 6), one block's walk to the Calle de Santo Domingo. Celaya was a jacal dating back to before the mid-eighteenth century, torn down in later urban improvement projects. Located about six blocks north of the cathedral, in the nineteenth century the public intellectual and writer Guillermo Prieto described this tavern as a popular dirt-floored "dive" on the outskirts of the city center.[56] In 1798 alone, the guards patrolling near the pulquería de Celaya arrested twenty-four inebriated individuals in and around this establishment, passed out inside the building, just beyond its entryway, or on the ground in the small street of the same name running in front of it. Guard number 88 made two more arrests in the surrounding streets of Arcinas and Apartado, all perhaps related to excessive drinking in the Celaya tavern.[57]

The pulquería de Celaya drew a varied clientele of Spaniards, mestizos, castizas, and mulatos. Individuals of Indigenous descent represented half of those taken into custody on this block. Two very busy guards, number 88 and number 89, patrolled this area, as well as to the west into Cuartel 1. Although the two dozen arrests in the area labeled "Celaya" spread across a year, their timing at different hours of the night helps us hear the nocturnal rhythms of this one small corner of the city. As early as 8:45 p.m., guards Rosales and Salazar might find people extremely drunk inside the Celaya tavern, or even already passed out just outside the door.[58] The action did not quite pick up before 10 p.m., but still a few already had consumed a few pitchers of pulque before then, wandered out into the street, and maybe even started a slightly tipsy brawl.[59] Most of the intoxicating effects kicked in between ten and midnight, when 75

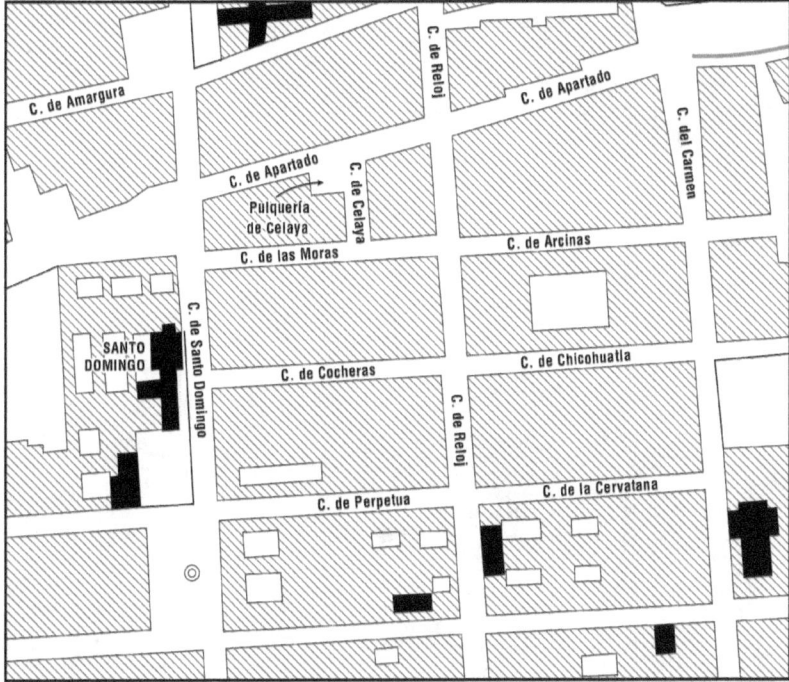

6. Cuartel 4. Created by Erin Greb.

percent of the arrests took place. By now, drinkers had reached various stages of inebriation. Some had passed out, either inside the pulquería or the street by the same name. Others were arrested as what might be called today "drunk and disorderly [*armando escandalo*]," or had severely injured themselves by this time of the night.[60] After midnight, a few last imbibers staggered home and the neighborhood quieted down, leaving the patrolmen to doze off leaning against a stone wall or in a doorway, attempting to shelter themselves from the deserted streets.[61]

Far to the north of the city center, ten blocks or more from the cathedral, an outlying district featured in dozens of arrests for public intoxication in the 1790s. In this neighborhood, three pulquerías drew a clientele from the more remote areas of San Antonio Tepito and Santiago Tlatelolco (see figure 7). These establishments went by the names of Tenespa, Granaditas, and Teposan, and occupied plazas large enough to host crowds of

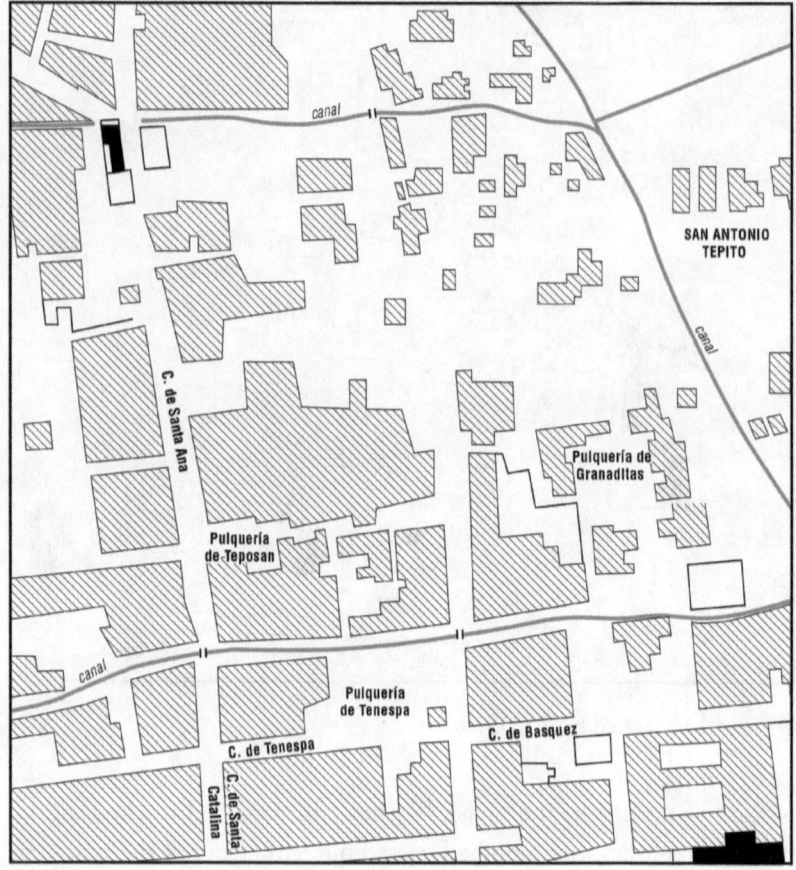

7. North section of Cuartel 4 (with sections of Cuartel 7 and 1). Created by Erin Greb.

drinkers. When not occupied by the pulquería de Celaya, guard number 89, Mariano Rosales, passed much of his time arresting intoxicated people on streets including Tenespa and Santa Catalina.[62] Most likely the area to the north of these pulquerías was fuera del alumbrado and unpatrolled by the night watchmen.

Walking south to the city center, another section of Cuartel 4 hosted an architectural concentration of structures physically demonstrating New Spain's rulers from both church and state. These blocks included

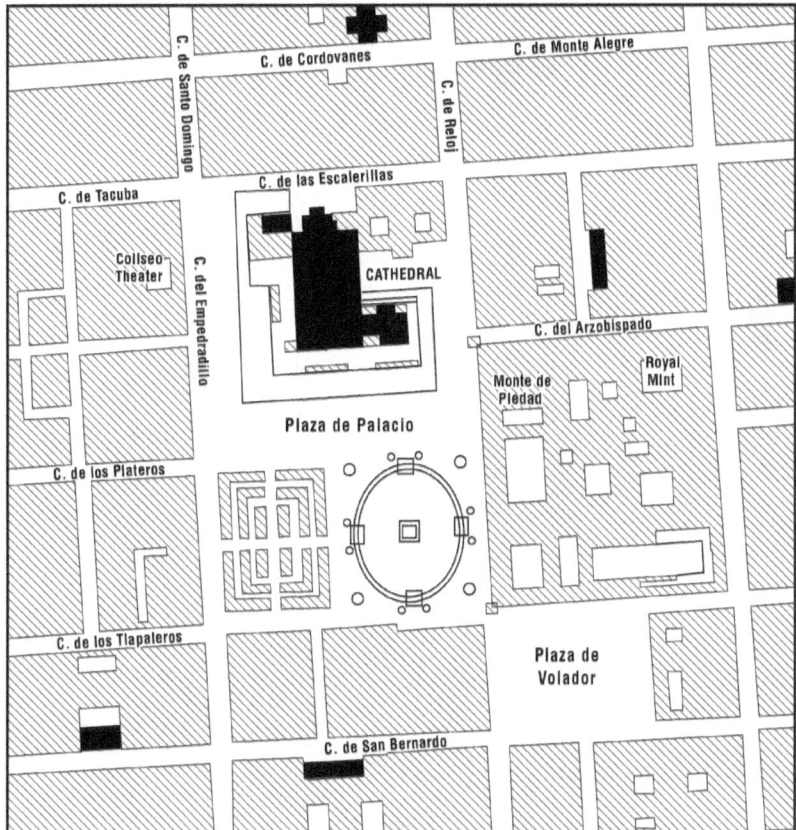

8. Central city. Created by Erin Greb.

the cathedral, the viceregal palace, the royal mint, the *monte de piedad*, the Plaza de Volador, the *coliseo* theater, and of course the large area now referred to as the Zócalo, labeled as the Plaza de Palacio (see figure 8). It does not appear that any pulquerías existed in the block or so radius right around the space of this plaza.[63] However, the night watchmen did take intoxicated individuals into custody in this area. One of the closest well-known taverns was the very exciting pulquería del Palacio (see figure 9).

While the pulquería del Palacio was not located adjacent to the viceroy's residence, a drinker could walk easily between the two buildings. If someone seeking pulque started out at the viceregal palace and turned

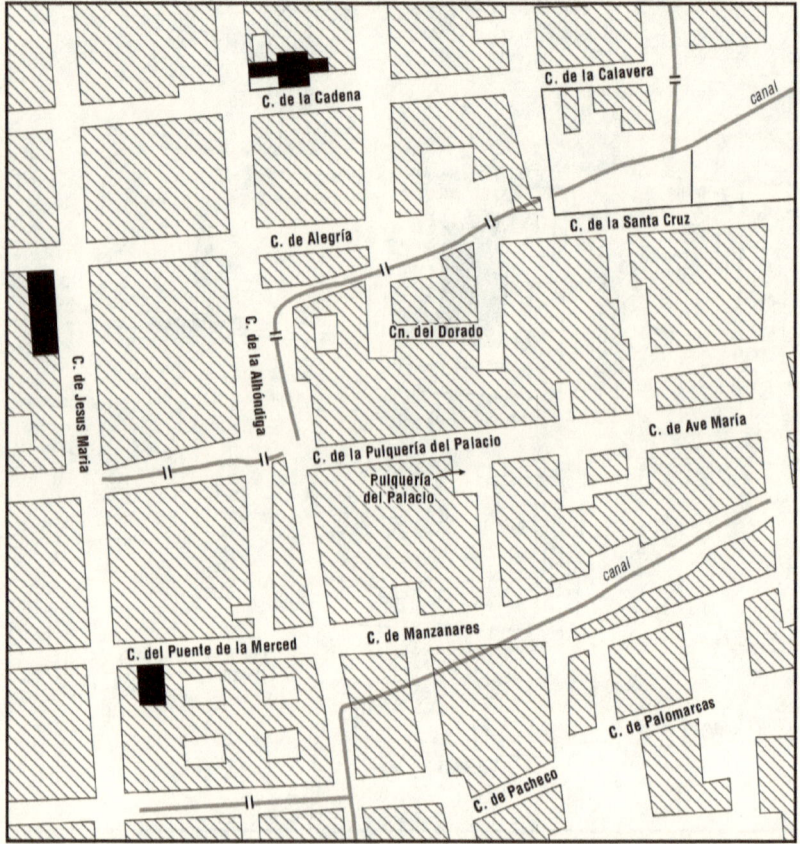

9. Neighborhood around the pulquería del Palacio. Created by Erin Greb.

left at the Plaza del Volador onto the one block Calle de Meleros, in five blocks they would encounter the Palacio establishment (see figure 9—in a location very close to one of the branches of the famous bakery, the Pastelería Ideal, today). The pulquería del Palacio existed at least since the mid-eighteenth century. Three or more taverns flourished in and around this block well into the nineteenth century.[64] Note that this famous tavern gave its name to a street, an alleyway, and (not labeled on the map) a bridge commonly referred to as "del Palacio." This establishment dominated the neighborhood, as there were no churches, convents, or friaries in the surrounding blocks. The closest parish was Soledad and Santa

Cruz, truly on the eastern edge of the urban map. Beyond this, the next religious institution to the east was San Lázaro (now the neighborhood of the national archive in the Porfirian Palacio de Lecumberri), placed well outside the center of the population. Figure 9 shows the canals that crossed near the pulquería del Palacio.

The night watchmen who worked in this part of town saw more action than any of their peers, occasionally arresting a number of intoxicated people in one night. From early in the evening until after midnight, pulque flowed freely in the Palacio watering hole. The *Libros de Reos* for 1798 document fourteen interactions with the guards inside this busy pulquería, where they found the clientele sometimes drinking themselves to the point of passing out before 8 p.m.[65] The clientele mainly drew from those residents described as indios and indias, although on any given night, one might encounter a few men labeled españoles and mestizos also imbibing pulque inside the Palacio. The guards arrested couples for having public sexual encounters here.[66] Guard number 24, a man called José Zerezo, labeled mestizo, spent his work hours in this establishment and on the closely surrounding streets of Santa Cruz, the Puente de Lena (a reference to the canal that ran through its middle), Ave María (not shown on figure 9, but directly to the west of Palacio Street), and Ave María's extension further to the west, the Calle de Solis. Over the course of his nights at work, Zerezo must have crossed paths numerous times with guard number 23, Manuel Villavivencio from Tianguistenco (an ancient settlement located thirty-five miles southwest of central Mexico City). This guard patrolled just to the north, walking a long thoroughfare that carried the names Machineuepa, Alegría, and Santa Cruz, depending on the block (see figure 10). Villavivencio holds the record for the most arrests (seventy-six) recorded in the existing *Libros de Reos*, with his companion number 24 coming in a close second, with seventy arrests.

Racialization and Mexican Drinking Culture

The written records of the viceroyalty of New Spain served to underscore the need for Spanish imperialism over Indigenous subjects, but how did this racialization function at the street level? Of course, racial bias remains

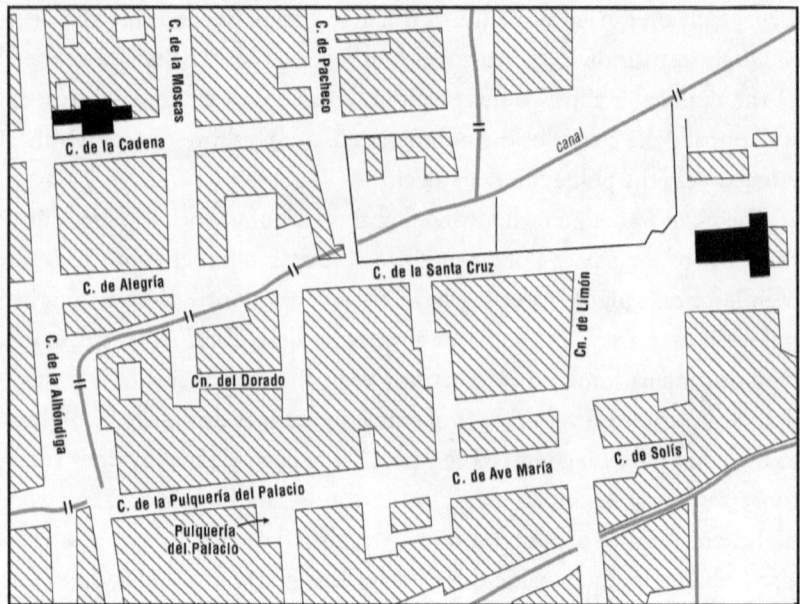

10. Ramo number 23. Created by Erin Greb.

a highly controversial and conflictive issue in law enforcement, a frequent headline in the twenty-first-century United States. This is not surprising given the slave patrol antecedents of this institution in rural areas of the U.S. south.[67] Further north, in the eighteenth century, colonial Boston's night watchmen purposely patrolled with the goal of removing African and Indigenous descent individuals from the streets.[68] The institution of lantern guards also began with a bias against residents and visitors to Mexico City labeled as *indios*, who were regarded as perpetual minors, prone to excesses and the least able within the population to hold their liquor.[69] The seventeenth-century savant Carlos de Sigüenza y Góngora was typical in his opinion that Indigenous people would spend on all their earnings on pulque and stay drunk as much as possible.[70] From the clerical perspective, which focused on acculturating Mexican native peoples to Christianity, pulque and pulque-based drinks allegedly caused "virtually all sins and social problems, including idolatry, rebellion, poverty, illness, violent crime, infidelity, and incest," to the point of inspiring churchmen to envision them in "the jaws of Hell."[71] Other commentators observed that pulquerías had both more decorations and attendees than parish churches.[72] Summed up more soberly in the words of Douglas Cope, viceregal authorities feared that "tavern socializing encouraged a systematic breakdown of social inhibitions."[73] In the context of these strong preexisting colonial assessments, arrest records in the capital of New Spain offer an illuminating example for statistical analysis of racial bias in one of the earliest corps of American law enforcement.

In New Spain offenses relating to intoxication, not theft or violence, are the most critical crime for analyzing the guards' potential biases. Scardaville observes these racial distinctions:

> As a group, Indians were particularly liable to become intoxicated, steal, and engage in interpersonal violence. Spaniards had excessive arrest rates in gambling, debt, tavern violations, sex crimes, family offenses, vagrancy, and disorderly conduct; mestizos in debt, tavern violations, informal marriages, vagrancy, and disorderly conduct; and mulattoes in theft, gambling, sex crimes, and family offenses. Indian arrest patterns were largely isolated from those of the other races. . . . In terms of patterns of criminal behavior, the division among the lower classes was not between Spaniards on the one hand, and Indians and *castas* on the other, but between Indians and *gente de razón*.[74]

Of course, the beginning of this quote mires readers in the biases of the viceregal authorities themselves, without considering that alcohol consumption became more criminal precisely in this era for the very purpose of strengthening a vision of barbarous Indigenous culture. However, the concept of Indigenous people as *gente sin razón*, that is, lacking in the intellect and sensibilities of those subjects who were more integrated into Spanish language and culture, provides a useful contextualization for this vision of embodied inebriation and barbarity.

At least four different data sets come into play when attempting to analyze if and how the night watchmen exercised racial bias on the job. First, the analysis must take into account the broader Mexico City percentages of each race label provided by census data from the era. Secondly, it is important to understand the percentage of each race label as represented in the sereno workforce. Thirdly, the very broad trends in arrest patterns can show the general bias across all of the guards as a group. Lastly, a closer look at the nightly routines and arrests made by individual guards illuminates a more nuanced understanding of how the experience of patrolling the streets intersected with colonial racialization. All these data need to be understood within the complex history of race labeling in the Iberian viceroyalties, which incorporated much more fluidity than in some other colonial settings.[75]

Race labels did affect arrest rates in Mexico City. Forty-six percent of the late eighteenth-century population of Mexico City claimed español as their racial descriptor, and only 28 percent claimed or received the label indio. As noted in chapter 2, racial designations are known for seventy-nine of the guarda faroleros, and 62 percent of them claimed the label of español. Only 7.5 percent of the night watchmen were labeled indios. Scardaville statistically analyzed the race labels applied to 4,352 arrested individuals for all offenses in the 1798 *Libros de Reos* and not surprisingly found a bias in favor of Spaniards and against indios: 41 percent of the arrests were of Spaniards, 5 percent less than their representation in the entire population according to contemporary censuses. In contrast, 38 percent of the arrests made in 1798 were of Indigenous people, 10 percent more than their overall percentage in the city.[76] Tabulating the arrests for intoxication preserved in the *Libros de Reos* reveals that 55 percent of the individuals taken into custody received or claimed the label of indio, while only 23 percent were described as españoles.[77] It must be stressed again that this statistical difference in arrest records does not prove that European-descent residents drank less than Indigenous people in Mexico City. Instead, as clarified by Taylor decades ago, this relates to the criminalization of the Mexican (and Andean) native drinking patterns, which originated in precolonial rituals. Its contrast with the traditional wine-based cultures of the Mediterranean played an important role in strengthening rhetoric around the Spanish honor code, which distinguished Iberians from all of their opponents, even within Europe itself.[78] The fact that almost double the percentage of individuals labeled indio figured in the records for public intoxication versus the general population also relates to the culture of drinking in Mexico City as well as its specific geography.[79] Indigenous people were more likely to drink pulque in public spaces, that is, the capital's hundreds of pulquerías, and later walk home. Spanish-descent residents on the whole had access to comfortable drinking at home, socializing over a much more expensive serving of imported wine. It is also possible that an individual who claimed the label mestizo to a census-taker appeared more "indio/india" to the night watchmen when he or she was taken into custody during the night and thus received this label by the judicial notary during their processing for public drunkenness.

For whatever reason, a broad prejudice stands out clearly in the overall statistics for arrests related to alcohol use. In order to assess biases of individual guards, it is most helpful to examine the most active serenos documented in the *Libros de Reos*. These dockets show that nine of the busiest guards logged a total of forty-six or more interactions with the populace in the 1790s. The watchman with the largest record of arrests was number 23, who accumulated a total of seventy-six arrests in the *Libros de Reos* dating from 1794 to 1798. However, the history of this number complicates analysis of this prolific activity in terms of viceregal race labels and biases. Early in the 1790s, a Spaniard named José Manuel Bernal (see introduction) patrolled ramo number 23, but he soon received a promotion to corporal. Later another guard, whose race is unknown, occupied this post. Both of these men definitely patrolled the neighborhood designated as number 23, and the second man, Manuel Villavivencio, may have had Indigenous ancestry. Between the two guards working beat number 23, forty Indigenous people and twenty Spaniards were arrested. Other guards seem to show a clearer bias. For example, guard number 60, Francisco Antonio Huerta, a young Spaniard born in Mexico City, clearly spent most of his time taking Indigenous people into custody for drinking to excess. While on the job, Huerta arrested forty-one indios and only fourteen españoles. Guard number 89, Mariano Rosales, an older español, had a similar pattern, arresting thirty-four indios and thirteen españoles. The logged arrests of other guards labeled españoles mimicked these statistics, with anywhere from twice as many to four times as many indios arrested for intoxication versus Spaniards. These arrest numbers indicate that these men viewed their function as eradicating the physical signs of Indigenous inebriation from the cityscape, which fits both with how Novohispanic leaders discussed their subjects for centuries and the general civilizing tone of the Bourbon social reforms. A sense of carrying out the vision of the leaders may have motivated the night watchmen, combined with the makeup of the pulquería clientele in their patrol areas. It is possible that the people who drank pulque on any given beat also shaped all of the serenos' arrest records.

In contrast to the patterns seen in the records of guard 60 and 89, three anomalies exist in the top nine guards in terms of quantity of arrests. First, the nefarious guard number 57, an español from Toluca named José Antonio Hernández, whose brutal sex crimes are detailed in chapter 5, did not seem to focus his work hours on policing Indigenous drinking. Hernández arrested twenty-one españoles for this offense, along with twenty-seven indios, a much smaller difference in quantity than the other serenos. Possibly his beat included areas where Spaniards congregated to drink pulque. Then there are the incongruities in the arrest patterns of the two very active serenos who did not carry the label español: an indio named José Leonardo Arenas and a castizo born in Mexico City, José Morales. The latter arrested an equal number of españoles and indios (seventeen each) for intoxication. He also took six mestizos and three mulatos into custody for the same crime, but no one with his own label. And what about Arenas, the lone Indigenous man in this group of highly active guards and one of the most hard-working of all of the night watchmen, with a total of fifty-eight recorded arrests? Arenas actually tended to focus on offenders labeled indios, arresting forty-two with this designation and only ten Spaniards (as well as five mestizos and four mulatos). No other guard of any race label arrested as many people with the label indio as did Arenas. It is possible that he felt uncomfortable arresting anyone who seemed to be español, given that the reo might identify him as of Indigenous ancestry and therefore challenge his authority. Still, it must be repeated that the attacks on guards examined in chapters 6 and

7 do not seem to have any noticeable anti-Indigenous racial motivation whatsoever, and certainly do not demonstrate any particular respect for Spanish guards. In contrast, somehow Morales, who claimed castizo status, had the gravitas to take into custody more Spaniards than almost any other guard on record. These patterns need contextualization in terms of their geographic location, the popular drinking establishments near the ramo in question, and their typical clientele, but generally they reflect the overall emphasis on policing and regulating Indigenous use of alcohol across the centuries of Spanish rule, and especially in these decades of siglo de luces reform.

Levels of Intoxication

When discussing individuals taken into custody for public intoxication, the scribes who wrote the *Libros de Reos* repeat four terms to signify drunkenness: *bebido, borracho, ebrio,* and *ebrísimo*. As defined in a dictionary published in 1787, ebrio, bebido, and borracho were virtual synonyms, with no different levels of intoxication implied.[80] One way to differentiate between these four terms is to analyze the punishments applied to offenders accused of each of them.[81] Using this method, Sánchez-Arcilla Bernal found that bebido/bebida definitely ranked as the least intoxicated and most lightly punished. In contrast, those arrested for the offenses summed up as borracho, ebrio, and ebrísimo inspired fairly consistent sentences of three days' labor on public works projects for men, and three days in jail for women and very elderly men. The use of the superlative ebrísimo did not lead to a harsher punishment. However, repeat offending or causing scandal did increase the sentence handed down.

Beyond Sánchez-Arcilla Bernal's focus on court-mandated punishments, can these four terms reveal more about actual patterns of alcohol use and the experiences of the night watchmen? Shifting away from legal history approaches to the nightlife of Mexico City clarifies the different levels of intoxication implied. The focus here remains on how the guards, the city space, and the populace interacted in routine and repeated ways at the street level. The *Libros de Reos* provide four pieces of information that contextualize the arrest scenario and the severity of any given case of public intoxication, along with the standard biographical details of the arrests. These details increase according to the seriousness of the effects of alcohol in each encounter. In the sparsest examples, the scribe wrote down no additional context other than a word referring to drunkenness. The notation simply testifies that the sereno arrested an individual described as ebrio, borracho, bebido, or ebrísimo. The second level of detail is a reference to the location where the person was arrested, sometimes with no information beyond that the inebriate was found "en su ramo [in his patrol area]."[82] Hundreds of other examples name a specific street, plaza, or pulquería. A third level of detail is the additional the phrase "tirado en [location]," for example, "tirado en su ramo [passed out on his beat]." This phrase indicates that the night watchman literally picked up the individual passed out either outside on a street, alley, or plaza, or inside a pulquería. Lastly, in only two cases reported in the existing *Libros de Reos* for the 1790s, the offender drank himself to death, or, more specifically in one case, "this arrested individual drowned himself with the concoction that made him drunk [Este reo falleció ahogado con el brebaje con que se embriago]."[83] In the other case, at 11:45 pm one night in 1798, "the warden reported that a man was conducted to jail so extremely drunk that he could not say his name, [and] he died."[84] During the insurgency era, guard number 65 encountered a man who had "drowned himself with aguardiente."[85] Official reports claimed that the general populace regularly drank so much that people drowned weekly falling into canals or from alcohol poisoning, although surviving documents do not back up this assessment of the degree of over-indulgence.[86]

Judicial scribes used the term *tirado* (falling-down drunk) to describe the condition of some individuals taken into custody. This term appears in close to one thousand examples in the *Libros de Reos* dating from 1794 to 1798, in just under one-third of all arrests documented for this period. It is interesting to note that Viceroy Branciforte invoked the ongoing problems with tirados in a 1796 decree sanctioning new longer sentences for public intoxication. With a clear tone of disgust, the viceroy mentioned men "found passed out on the *suelo* [floor or ground]," and "women who have forgotten the natural modesty of their sex" due to their extreme intoxication. Branciforte decreed that these individuals deserved eight days forced labor or in jail for their first offense, five more days than the previous norm.[87]

As mentioned above, the scribe made the notation "tirado" as an additional description in an arrest for drunkenness, so every mention of "tirado" also includes another word indicating the offense of intoxication.[88] The choice of words suggests a ranking of Spanish words for drunk, from "tipsy" to what we might call "plastered." Of the 920 individuals taken into to custody as tirados, in almost 85 percent (780), the scribe ranked the offender in the category of "ebrio" (553) or "ebrísimo" (227). This suggests that describing an individual as ebrio or its superlative ebrísimo indicated the most severe level of intoxication, although, as found by Sánchez-Arcilla Bernal, there is no clear archived difference in the usage of the two forms of the word. Both ebrios and ebrísimos statistically received the same punishments. A much smaller number (131, of just over 14 percent) of the tirados were merely borrachos, suggesting this word meant just "drunk" as opposed to "completely wasted." Only a handful (five) of the tirados were bebidos, which seems to signify just "tipsy." The night watchmen found far more men (80 percent) than women passed out drunk in Mexico City's public spaces. Not surprisingly, given the biases outlined above, over 58 percent of the tirados had the label of indio or india, with Spaniards second in line for this condition (23 percent), and mestizos third (11 percent). Drinking to a stupor occurred in all age groups, from fourteen to ninety-four, but just under half of the tirados (451) were in their twenties. Thus, overall, most of the people sleeping off their drinking on the street were young men of Indigenous ancestry, while most of the serenos were similarly aged men of Spanish descent.

Analysis of the records using the term *tirado* also give a sense of the nightly chronology of Mexico City drinking habits. Pulque has a low alcohol content, so drinking enough to pass out would offer quite a challenge for a person accustomed to it from childhood. Pulquerías did serve food, but pulque itself could replace a meal and speed up the process of intoxication. The fact that the guards found just over half of all of the tirados between nine and eleven at night underscores the rapid drinking that must have taken place at the end of the work day. Almost 23 percent of those found passed out in public managed to drink heavily enough to achieve this state before 9 p.m. After midnight, the night watchmen barely arrested any tirados, which might have to do with their own fatigue in those hours, as well as the curfew imposed on public drinking establishments. By the wee hours of the morning, many people were sleeping on the street, but an accusation of tirado should not be confused with the offense of vagrancy, homelessness, or sleeping.[89] Like any adult does now, the night watchmen must have known the difference between someone lacking an indoor spot to rest one's head and a passed out drunk. They patrolled their own neighborhoods, so they may have known most of the tirados at least by appearance. Location and timing probably helped distinguish between those sleeping in the rough and passing out. Furthermore, actual sleepers often provided a coherent explanation for their situation. In the forty-seven cases when the guards arrested people simply because they found them asleep on the street, the relevant entries in the *Libros de Reos* do not include any further information suggesting that these individuals were drunk.[90] Instead, the offense of "sleeping" relates to perhaps an illicit sexual act or, even more likely, homelessness.

Along with tirados, the guards also occasionally arrested drunks *en cueros*, literally "in their skin," referring to a noteworthy degree of nudity. Since pulquerías or other businesses selling alcoholic beverages often offered a pawning service, people might lose their clothes to buy their drinks.[91] Although public nudity or exposing oneself in scanty rags has featured as an important topic in the historiography, removing naked individuals from the street did not seem to occupy much of the serenos' energies at least as documented in the existing reports dating from the 1790s to the 1820s. The *Libros de Reos* mention only five incidents of "en cueros," all recorded in 1798. One of these involved a young homeless man sleeping in a suspicious location.[92] The other four involved two men and two women. The scribe described both of the women (one aged thirty, the other fifty) arrested as en cueros and ebrísima, tirada (extremely drunk and passed out), and "indecent." As such, they both received harsh sentences of eight days in jail plus twenty-five lashings. Both of the women had reached this stage of intoxication before 9 p.m. The older woman also tried to fight the other offenders, including attempting to drown a pregnant woman in the jail.[93] One of the other tirados en cueros also experienced a very bad night, before ending up in jail. After passing out ebrísimo in an alley before 9 p.m. this twenty-five-year-old Indigenous man severely wounded his face and required treatment in a hospital. The last person arrested en cueros was a drunk Spaniard, age forty-eight, found in this state at 8 p.m. in a small store.[94]

If the night watchman did not find them tirado, intoxicated individuals might protest, resist, or fight the guards, as explored in the next chapter. Drunkenness is a subjective "crime," in the sense that the effects proving the infraction wear off over time. Street patrolmen who worked on foot, lightly armed, and were not welcomed by a city's residents probably needed even more time to convince any borrachos or ebrios to willingly walk with them to jail. To this day, defendants frequently contest legal charges of intoxication, whether public or while driving. In nineteenth-century England, publicans defined drunkenness as prostrate on the ground, unable to speak or move. Before that state, a drinker might be nothing more than "merry, and quite jolly."[95] Of course now law enforcement uses body cameras and scientifically based standards of testing such as blood alcohol content and field sobriety tests to determine levels of intoxication and impairment. Even with these methods, defense lawyers often challenge the charges. In 1790s Mexico City, accusations of public drunkenness depended entirely on the observations made by the patrolmen as they interacted with people on the street. In almost all cases, the nightly logbooks record that arrested individuals confessed to their drunken state and were sentenced accordingly without any opposition to this accusation. However, in 2 percent (a total of sixty) of the entries, the offenders denied their drunkenness. This tactic never worked to lessen their punishments because the scribe called on a second opinion from the nocturnal jail warden, to support the observations made by the patrolmen on the street. Denials resulted in the inclusion of variations on the phrase "el alcaide asiente haber llegado borracho [the warden confirms that (the reo) arrived drunk"] in response to denials from the arrested individuals.

The paper trail mapping Mexico City's overindulgence in pulque and aguardiente suggests a city under surveillance, but the continuous need to repeat or adapt regulations reveals that Bourbon reformers faced ongoing challenges in modifying their subjects' alcohol consumption. Slight dips in consumption may have occurred now and then in response to specific ordinances, but the sour drink had not yet reached its peak in popularity. Even almost a century later, under the much more effectively repressive dictatorship of Porfirio Díaz, Deborah Toner observes that "the social exchanges and convivial atmospheres long associated with the disorderly social spaces of pulquerías and vinaterías [had not] been stamped out."[96] While these taverns certainly achieved great popularity in the late viceregal era, in fact the end of the nineteenth century became "the golden age of pulque."[97] Thousands of residents continued to spend hours of each day in pulquerías. While the archival record reveals the energy and personnel dedicated to this issue, the physical structures of the cityscape, and the interactions between the populace and the lantern guards tell a clearer and more dynamic story of how Mexico City plebeians passed their evenings.

CHAPTER 5

Guards in Trouble

Arrested by the head guard at 10 a.m., Pantaleón Mena, guard number 44, married, mestizo [born in] Mexico City, because he had abandoned his beat one night, today [it was determined that] he had been sick. [Mena received] a warning, and, with the consent of the head guard, [he was] set free.
—*Libro de Reos*, November 18, 1798

Ignacio Gómez, Spaniard from Real del Monte, guard number 36, [arrested] by the lieutenant of the head guard at midnight, who found him drinking in a *casa de pulque*. . . . [Gómez] saw a gathering of people, so he went to close [the pulquería], and [to tell] everyone to go home. To do this, he put his hand lantern down on the street, and he leaned his pike against the door. A while later, the lieutenant and the corporal came, and [Gómez] went outside. . . . [This led to the arrests, because] all of them [including Gómez] were drinking.
—*Libro de Reos*, July 4, 1796

Documentation from the roughly three decades of the viceregal guarda faroleros' existence suggests that several ranks of officials, from their cabos, guarda mayores (and their lieutenants), to the corregidores, and even the viceroys themselves, wanted to carefully record incidents of all kinds of misbehavior on the part of the nocturnal patrolmen. The 1790s logbooks note minor examples of dereliction of duty, while longer freestanding case files, passed on to other authorities, chronicle more egregious abuses and crimes. Judicial reactions to the guards' criminal acts were often inversely proportionate to the severity of the offense. Notaries carefully recorded trivial instances of drinking or sleeping on the job that resulted in relatively harsh punishments, while, in contrast, very serious offenses did not lead to severe repercussions or prolonged judicial conflicts. The documentary evidence suggests that maintaining a paper trail of routine nightly discipline outweighed creating a more in-depth archive detailing investigations of the guards' actual crimes. As with other viceregal institutions, this pattern indicates an official desire to protect the honor of this branch of the colonial bureaucracy—to show rigor in maintaining a consistent standard of discipline but to avoid dishonor by not imposing sanctions on the more extreme infractions. In other words, as plebeian men working in a strict hierarchy, if the serenos did not abide by the undocumented but expected norms of their occupation, they could expect a response from their supervisors.

The nightly logs of arrests from the 1790s document ninety-one incidents where guards were charged with crimes or dereliction of duty. Almost half of these accuse them of abandoning their post or sleeping on the job, and another 18 percent involve drinking or showing up drunk. The remaining offenses range from bribery and theft to assault, both in the form of blows and sex crimes, all of which I discuss below.[1] Historians with a twentieth- or twenty-first-century bias tend to assume, incorrectly, that crimes committed while at work did not result in any meaningful disciplinary actions for this very early law enforcement corps.[2] It is true that more guards were acquitted for their crimes and dereliction of duty than was the norm across members of the general population who came before the judiciary. According to Scardaville, the serenos walked away with no repercussions in over 36 percent of their court proceedings. This acquittal rate was higher than among defendants of Spanish descent from the general population (25.9 percent—and the majority of the guards did have this designation). Moreover, the night watchmen of all backgrounds were treated leniently compared to defendants among the general public labeled indios, who were acquitted only 16 percent of the time. However, remember that not showing up to work or sleeping on the job is not a crime, it is a discipline problem. Therefore, it is not certain that their supervisors and other judicial officials did not hold the serenos accountable for their infractions, and they may well have disciplined them in ways not captured in surviving records.

While this chapter demonstrates that the guards had a reputation for petty theft, and their records hint at a tendency toward violence, their most reprehensible acts involved sexual abuse of the women whom they encountered in their nightly patrols. Women who defied gender norms by rejecting monogamy occupied a very vulnerable position vis-à-vis law enforcement, both due to the cruelty of a few individual patrolmen and to the purposefully nebulous legality of transactional sex within this judicial system.[3] Culminating in a horrific case of sexual assault, this chapter begins with small incidents that took place regularly during the long nights of walking the beat and concludes with more detailed cases highlighting the risk of violence inherent to introducing a new low-level corps of armed, patrolling men as symbols of the values and laws of the imperial state. As the incidents narrated here increase in seriousness, a familiar pattern of behavior emerges. Together they amount to an archive of proto-macho behavior, with the lantern guards embodying early and overt representations of Mexican masculinity.[4]

Dereliction of Duty

The challenge of maintaining disciplined work routines caused most of the serenos' day-to-day personnel issues. Along with drinking and sleeping, on occasion some of the men just did not appear to patrol their beats. As indicated by the quote at the start of this chapter, these plebeians had no safety net when they fell ill or had to help with family emergencies, and many came from rural backgrounds with different rhythms for the work day and year.[5] Absenteeism among the night watchmen concerned their superiors, especially because when the lantern guards did not show up for work, entire city blocks remained dark all night long. While this situation was not uncommon in the 1790s, head guard Ignacio Eguiluz y Olarte noted the extent of the problem in the 1820s, with the following comments in three of his reports, all dating to the same two-week period:

> Last night, April 16, 1822, guards with the numbers 1, 4 (injured), 9, 11, 16, 22, 28, 31, 39, 42, 44, 49 (sick), 59, 65, 80, 82, 88, and 89 did not fulfill their obligations to me.
>
> On April 27, 1822, I was lacking [the presence on] the streets of guards with the numbers 16, 27, 33, 39, 43, 73, 82, 85, and 91.

[In his report for April 29, 1822] I have put under arrest the guards with numbers 16, 40, 44, 67, 86, and 90 for having missed [patrolling] the streets last night.[6]

These absences meant that between around 9 and 18 percent of the total number of guards might stay away from the job on certain nights. The head guard's phrasing—in Spanish he uses the term "me faltaron," or "I lacked"—suggests that this dereliction of duty felt personal to him as their boss. It also implied that the men owed him money on their salary when they did not show up for work. This serious absenteeism looks like an unraveling of the entire system of street lighting in the difficult insurgency era and the tumultuous 1820s, a topic explored further in chapter 7.

While Eguiluz y Olarte's frustrated lists of missing serenos show extreme examples of truancy, the 1790s *Libros de Reos* more clearly present the justifications and repercussions for neglecting one's patrol area. Like most judicial processes in the viceregal era, punishments for not showing up to work varied depending on circumstances. The logbooks do not provide much context for understanding why some serenos could neglect their work with little consequence while others suffered very serious repercussions. Short entries in the nightly logbooks document cases of a supervising officer taking an on-duty patrolman to the city jail. Afterward, the judicial scribe would record the incident and the punishment. In the twenty-four available examples of night watchmen abandoning their beat, the guards might experience no stated ramifications whatsoever, they might receive a warning, or they could suffer up to twenty-five lashes, a few days to a month in jail, shorter terms of imprisonment in the dungeon, a few weeks in the stocks, or termination of their employment.[7]

In a line or two of text, the scribe provided a bit of context explaining how the men justified avoiding work and how their superiors found out about this infraction. Usually the head guard had the responsibility for tracking down absentee serenos, although sometimes his assistant (called a lieutenant or *teniente*) or the alcaldes and corporals, the patrolmen's immediate superiors, reported them missing.[8] Explanations for choosing to stay away from walking their patrols included quite a range of excuses, from illness, spending time at home with a woman, drinking, or, at the virtuous end of the spectrum, helping family in trouble, or even making a short religious pilgrimage to the shrine of the Virgin of Guadalupe.[9] In one confusing example, guard number 60 lost his job because, he claimed, a little boy asked him to give him a guitar—presumably meaning that the guard left his ramo to fulfill the child's wishes.[10] Avoiding work was not always a lonely, malingering activity—a sereno might go AWOL with one of his colleagues, enjoying a sexual liaison with a woman, or partaking in some aguardiente with a group of friendly drinking companions.[11] But even work collegiality did not convince the guards' superiors that dereliction of duty should go unpunished, which guard number 9, Manuel Aguilar, learned the hard way.[12] This married castizo in his late twenties claimed that he left his patrol area simply to help a companion light his lanterns. As a result, Aguilar spent three days in prison.

The records of workplace reprimands for dereliction of duty reveal some of the usually hidden but basic expectations and patterns of this occupation, especially relating to the financial challenges faced by the serenos. When the head guard fired a night watchman for neglecting his beat, they mentioned that the former employee now had to "liquidate his account," suggesting that many of the patrolmen owed money for their equipment or back pay for the days they had missed.[13] Not settling up with the guarda mayor expeditiously could lead to much more serious charges of theft or perjury.[14] Because of the possibility of actually losing money by taking on this occupation, some men patrolled at night along with working another job during the day, which certainly explained their occasional absenteeism and sleeping while on night watch.[15] For example, guard number 81, a twenty-three-year-old Indigenous man named José Antonio Zamora, also worked as a *cigarrero* in the large proto-factory that employed thousands of urban workers in support of the profitable imperial tobacco monopoly.[16] In late September 1798, Zamora had not shown up for work for over a week, owing money on his salary. When the head guard tracked him down, Zamora had to spend eight days imprisoned in the stocks and of course settle his account with his boss. José Contreras, guard number 77, a Spanish-descent married man from

Tacubaya, also found himself owing money from his own salary to the head guard when he did not show up for work, but apparently he paid his debts and suffered no further punishment.[17]

The guards also had to take monetary responsibility for any damages to their lanterns, including when they stole them themselves.[18] This rule also meant that they had to find a way to take care of the lanterns when they took a meal break during the night. To their superiors, when their equipment was not in sight, it looked like the guarda faroleros had abandoned their beats when they instead had just tried to exercise caution to protect their equipment. Concerned with a potentially devastating cost, guard number 19, a young married man of Spanish ancestry, claimed that he had gone inside to eat supper around 11 p.m. and did not want to risk leaving his lantern outside. Accused of abandoning his ramo, he received a mild punishment of four days in jail.[19] The guards must have felt fearful of any accidents damaging the tools of their trade; for example, guard number 88, a twenty-three-year-old married man labeled castizo, endured three days imprisonment in the dungeon because the head guard must have noticed that his ramo remained dark. The guard explained that he had broken his ladder and spilled his lamp oil.[20] Still, while some of these incidents actually bring to light the abusive labor conditions endured by the poor men who took on this job, many other examples of absenteeism came as a result of what the guards were supposed to be policing: public inebriation.

Drinking on the Job

Several of the lantern guards patrolling Mexico City's streets had serious problems with drinking, including to the point of extreme and frequent intoxication while at work. Alcoholism features among the classic stereotypes applied to law enforcement, dating back to Boston's colonial night watchmen and nineteenth-century coppers in England.[21] In later eras of Mexican history, drinking continued to feature as the key issue for disciplining urban guardsmen, along with other familiar problems such as absenteeism.[22] However, the serenos' drinking habits did not seem to greatly concern the late viceregal populace. When residents of New

Spain's viceregal capital wanted to insult their serenos, they more often called them thieves (*ladrones*), than drunks.[23] In a statistical analysis of sereno offenses documented in the 1790s *Libros de Reos*, the frequency of reported incidences of theft and bribery ranks just under abandoning one's post, drinking, and sleeping. In other words, residents tended to report money-related abuses instead of infractions relating to dereliction of duty. Probably the populace in general did not care about issues relating to how the guards passed their tedious and tiring nights. They chose to focus their insults on the night watchmen's reputation as thieves, a concern that actually hurt urban residents. As described in the preceding chapter, the public drinking culture in Mexico City almost literally saturated certain nocturnal neighborhoods. Perhaps a guard who drank regularly did not register as unemployable, given the number of comatose drunks on the streets every night. Drinking also strengthened the serenos' ties to the lower classes, making it impossible for them to claim any other status but plebeian.[24] Reading the thirty reports of drunk night watchmen in the *Libros de Reos*, plus an additional handful of incidents mentioned in the head guards' reports, one wonders at the very low standards for hiring these men, as well as their surprising lack of discipline on the job.[25] Indeed, their superiors complained that they could not find candidates for the lantern guard corps. Head guard Dionisio Boneta wrote Viceroy Venegas explaining that he could hardly find any men to take this job due to the abuse the serenos experienced at the hands of the military patrols also working on the streets at night (see chapter 7).[26]

When the night watchmen's superiors rode their horses around the darkened city, supervising the lighting and intervening in conflictive situations, they kept alert to the demeanor of their subordinates, paying attention to signs of drinking on the job. The first recorded incident of a guard arrested for public intoxication took place in the fall of 1794, with an atypical punishment of six years' galley service, handed down by a higher-level criminal court, the real sala de crimen.[27] This more intense discipline faded over the first several years that the lantern guards walked their beats. Most cases of drinking on the job resulted in far less severe sentences, including three or eight days of forced labor, several days in the stocks, or oftentimes nothing more than a warning.[28] Perhaps the authorities understood that financial repercussions hurt the most, so a sereno might temporarily (for a period of eight days), suffer suspension from work. In only four cases, night watchmen permanently lost their jobs for workplace drinking.[29]

The guards' superiors kept a record of repeat offenders, who, like other plebeians found drunk on more than one occasion, experienced harsher punishments, including termination.[30] Additional offenses committed while under the influence might also lead to a stronger reaction, such as in 1797, when guard number 64 was escorted to jail for "having committed various scandalous excesses" while intoxicated.[31] However, finding men to take on this work was so challenging that their supervisors had to put up with a record of incidents of intoxication while at work. For example, José Castrejón, a Spanish-descent night watchman in his late twenties who also worked as a dyer, came to work drunk, explaining that he just had a bit of pulque. His drinking before going on duty led to nothing more than a warning. Several months later, corporal number 7 found Castrejón's ramo abandoned, allegedly because the guard engaged in a drinking session, partaking in aguardiente with a friend. For this second offense, he spent eight days in jail.[32] Another guard who also had a day job very nearly drank himself to death one night in June of 1798.[33] José Castillo, a twenty-three-year-old unmarried man of Spanish ancestry who also worked as a weaver, needed last rites when his corporal found him comatose at 10:30 p.m. Castillo recovered and endured most likely a very painful fifteen days in the stocks in punishment for his workplace inebriation. However, at least according to existing records, he held on to his job despite this behavior.

The nightly logbooks testify that a broad swathe of serenos of a range of ages and racial designations imbibed quite a bit of pulque or aguardiente during or before work. In line with the demographic patterns of the guard corps as a whole, the vast majority of those caught under the influence at work were Spaniards in their twenties. The circumstances of their arrests, timing, and excuses varied. While some guards must have passed their work hours drinking—one presumes openly at pulquería stands, as in the example quoted at the start of this chapter—others apparently arrived at work already drunk. In these cases, the head guard arrested them not long after they came on duty. Others must have spent many hours drinking, because their supervisors did not discover them in an inebriated state until the wee hours of the morning. Given the sometimes very light punishments for intoxication on the job, it even seems that their supervisors assumed that perhaps a cup or two of pulque represented a fairly common and acceptable way to prep for a chilly and shadowy night walking the cobblestones.[34] Some situations warranted a medicinal drink. After his arrest at 8:15 in the morning, Ignacio Ramos admitted that he drank aguardiente during his shift to self-medicate after receiving wounds on his face the night before. This excuse convinced his superiors to let him off with a warning.[35]

While from the elite perspective, intoxication led to fighting and conflicts, the supervisors of the serenos mainly seemed to worry about the neglect of the street lighting. They punished night watchmen with up to a month in the stocks for this offense.[36] But clearly, the head guard did not require teetotalers when vetting who to hire in this job. Because those in charge did not report many drunk guards after 1796, it is possible that the corporals and head guards ignored the problem. In general, drinking while at work or coming to work drunk aligned with the drinking culture of this time and place, which drew in men and women of all ranks in viceregal society. Without any specific regulations forbidding it, there is no reason to assume that the night watchmen would have different habits than their peers. As Paul Vanderwood rhetorically observed in regards to Mexican police a century later, "Imagine telling a *Rural* to police a fiesta without taking a drink."[37] Not surprisingly, some of the guards found it impossible to resist joining in the activities going on around them every night, hanging out in pulquerías to pass the time during their shifts.[38] Perhaps they depended on the food and drink sold in these establishments to keep them awake and semi-alert.[39] When found by their superiors in pulquerías, the watchmen proved themselves amenable to joining in the underlying violence that threatens any place where people drink to excess. One sereno even admitted that he arrested his fellow drinking companions after their fun banter turned to nasty insults.[40] Another wandered far from his beat to cause a scandal at the pulquería in the alleyway known as Picadero, an establishment that the head guard rated as frequently open late into the night, against municipal regulations.[41] Many night watchmen probably just resorted to pulque or aguardiente when they felt bored and tired, leading to the last common cause of dereliction of duty.

Sleeping on Duty

It was not uncommon for the patrolmen to partake in the trifecta of drinking, sleeping, and neglecting one's beat, all in one incident.[42] Staying awake while walking the dark and quiet streets all night sometimes seemed impossible, especially in the long hours between midnight and 3:30 in the morning. In the eloquent and simple words of a sixty-year-old guard, staying awake was a struggle. He admitted that "it is true that sleep defeated him," when his sergeant found him dozed off on his beat at three in the morning.[43] Sleeping on duty meant that the guards did not patrol their rounds and also "did not call the time, as serenos are supposed to."[44] They also ran the risk of misplacing their lantern and their pike. As will be explored in chapter 6, thieves and angry offenders often targeted the hand-held lanterns as an item of value or, much more often, a hated symbol of official authority. The pikes also offered their own liabilities. Perhaps as a tough warning to Lazaro Antonio Parral, guard number 73, the head guard took his weapon after finding him asleep at 11 p.m. Parral was released with a warning to take better care of his "obligations."[45]

Sleeping on duty often resulted in a warning, a short stint of incarceration, or forced labor. A typical case took place in 1796, when a corporal found José María Olivares, guard number 76, asleep at 1:15 a.m. As a result, Olivares spent one day in jail. Another guard, viewed as "inept," received eight days in jail for the same offense.[46] Without any apparent reason, some guards caught sleeping received nothing but a warning, even if their superiors reported that they "did not want to wake up" from sleeping while supposedly walking their rounds in the small hours of the morning.[47]

Holding a job that depended on physical strength and the power to use judicially sanctioned violence, the guards did not take kindly to reprimands. At the same time, night watchmen must have expected corporal punishment when they did not carry out their own duties. Early in 1796, a cabo found José Ignacio Zabala, guard number 24, a thirty-year-old español born in Mexico City, drunk and sleeping on duty.[48] The corporal claimed that Zabala hit him with his chuzo, which the guard denied, complaining instead that his superior hid his lantern. Zabala received three days forced labor in public works projects, as stated by the scribe, "to serve as an example to others." After that, he had to turn himself into the head guard, liquidate his accounts, and lose his job. His drunkenness probably led to his termination, as this extreme result was not common. Intoxication and sleeping on the job resulted in another guard enduring eight days in the stocks.[49] In another case of sleeping leading to violent repercussions, a cabo found José Morales, a twenty-four-year-old guard (number 86), labeled a castizo, asleep at 3:15 am. To wake him up, the sergeant started yelling and beating him. Morales defended himself, but as a result he received twenty-five lashings and eight days forced labor.[50] No excuses saved him from punishment. If he could not stay awake due to illness, a guard might still end up imprisoned for twenty-four hours in a dark dungeon cell (bartolina) because his superiors found them dozed off at work.[51] Lacking an excuse for the head guard who caught him asleep at 1:15 a.m., José María Morales (guard number 78), suffered three days in the bartolina.[52] However, while the guards probably had some degree of tolerance toward both giving and receiving blows, that does not mean that they did not lash out verbally when their superiors physically attacked them. When an alcalde caught him sleeping just after midnight, guard number 49 responded with his allegedly customary insolence, observing that "Saint Peter fell asleep, so what difference does it make if I do?" This remark not surprisingly led to the alcalde confiscating the patrolman's weapon and beating him.[53]

Sexual Misadventures

While public inebriation obsessed viceregal authorities who valued urban policía, they shied away from documenting much in the way of sex-related situations. The nightly logbooks very briefly record incidents of implied or certain sexual offenses, with the guards possibly or definitely asserting their power over women whom they encountered on their patrols. Night watchmen also might just take advantage of the sexual opportunities that materialized while they were working, such as when a corporal caught two of his men "frolicking [*retozando*]" with a couple of young women around midnight, while one of their husbands looked on.[54] The vagueness of the record of these acts suggests not that these events were uncommon, but more that this regime did not make an effort to record the frequency of sex work and the sexual misadventures of the new patrols on Mexico City's streets. Law codes of the era took a very opaque stance on prosecuting soliciting transactional sex. This system placed the burden on the night watchman to decide whom to arrest in cases that looked like solicitation on the street. Perceptions of gender and sexuality shaped the legal status of how women could physically exist on city streets in this era and female arrestees' stated offenses remained very imprecise.[55] As a result of this murkiness, the guards could exercise their petty authority to intimidate vulnerable vagrant or poor women out at night. The patrolmen determined whether or not to arrest women for simply walking or standing on the street, or sitting or standing in a door, or talking to soldiers or other men who presumably interacted with them as their paying customers. Women might suffer short-term incarceration even if the guard initiated the exchange and actually risked arrest if the head guard found them simply talking to a night watchman of their acquaintance.[56] These suspicious arrests of women possibly disguised the guards' efforts to covertly control street solicitation or to benefit from it for their own sexual desires.

However, sex-related incidents, if reported by the victims, also offered the opportunity for law enforcement to police its own functionaries for taking sexual advantage of women on the street.[57] For example, one morning at 2 a.m., a superior officer detained a sereno who left his beat to go home with a twenty-five-year-old unmarried Indigenous woman. The male culprit received fifteen days in jail, while the woman only had to return to her employers. Both claimed that he let her sleep at his house just because she had nowhere else to go.[58] A guard and a married Indigenous woman, both aged twenty-five, offered the same excuse in response to an arrest for chatting while the man was supposed to be walking his beat.[59] A third night watchman had the reputation of setting up women to sleep in a shack in the cathedral cemetery. A corporal caught José Reyes, of Spanish ancestry, hiding out with a teenage Indigenous girl at two in the morning. Reyes claimed that he knew the girl's mother, and that she had nowhere else to sleep. Despite this excuse, and having experience with this kind of suspicious rendezvous, the authorities rightly viewed cemeteries as potential sites for illicit sex acts.[60] Reyes received a sentence of eight days forced labor on public works projects.[61] Even worse, patrolmen attempted to seduce women just after separating them from other sexually aggressive men. One young night watchman faced a month of forced labor and a ten-peso fine when a mother complained that he had raped her fifteen-year-old daughter (no further details known).

The night watchmen, not unlike other law enforcement patrols to the present day, did not have the training or innate ability to address sexual assaults effectively. To give a terrifying example, a bystander complained that he had witnessed a horrific attack on a young girl on the street one night in 1809. The petitioner said that he contacted the nearest sereno and drew his own personal sword to stop the violence. However, because the assault took place just at the edge of the lighted area of the city, the guard refused to help.[62] At the other end of the spectrum, accusations of sex-related offenses may have represented an effort by an offender to distract from their own punishment, although this was a very risky tactic in an era that placed so much emphasis on the accuser's honorable reputation. Women arrested for nothing more than walking the streets or sitting in doorways at night already had to fight against assumptions about their virtue. For example, one thirty-year-old india accused a guard of seducing her when he arrested her for mild intoxication. The night watchman turned the accusation back on her and said that during her arrest, she offered to stay with him and "fornicate." The court apparently believed this story, sentencing the woman to fifteen days incarceration.[63] Although these cases show guards maliciously exploiting their petty power on the streets, they also indicate that the populace neither respected nor feared this new form of law enforcement enough to silently endure abuse in many different forms, including sexual assault, theft, or other forms of violence.[64] It is also possible that sexual aggression played a role in the new occupational identity of the night watchmen and in how they bonded with their peers.[65]

Conflicts during Arrests

Residents of Mexico City did not hold back from complaining when they felt mistreated by the night watchmen, especially when it came to denunciations of the guards for excessive force or theft of their money of personal belongings. Violence simmered below the surface or overtly exploded throughout the era of the viceregal lighting project. At its very essence this job demanded bodily exertion. The serenos' fundamental task of physically lifting intoxicated people off the street combined with the common judicial sentence of lashings, the stocks, or forced labor on urban improvement projects to highlight the constant threat of brute force applied to a range of bodies in a public way. For example, not long after the night watchmen's foundation, the most exalted criminal court in New Spain processed a criminal complaint involving a lantern guard who wounded an Indigenous man while arresting him.[66] Although the larger context does not appear in the short surviving documentation, a few words hint that some serenos had explosive tempers, ready to lash out at the slightest affront to their honor or their equipment, or injure those whom they arrested for public drinking, as in the case of an Indigenous man who convinced the judge that guard number 83 "broke his face" with his aggressive manhandling.[67] Although it did not happen frequently, cases exist of guards viciously fighting among themselves and with their superiors, using their chuzos to beat each other, risking severe repercussions for the inferior-ranked man.[68]

As mentioned in chapter 2's discussion of why they rejected carrying their chuzos by the early nineteenth century, the night watchmen could not cause injuries during arrests without potentially facing repercussions. Their superiors followed up on signs of injury to vulnerable people, such as a Spanish woman arrested for walking the streets at 10:30 p.m. who claimed that guard number 69 beat her on the head, leaving a mark, even though she begged him to stop.⁶⁹ In another example of a complaint from the very early months of the lantern guards' existence, a forty-year-old mother asked a notary to file a complaint for her regarding a guard named Ignacio Ximénez.⁷⁰ This sereno beat her and her fifteen-year-old daughter one night in 1791 as they went out to buy some bread at 9 p.m. The women (the mother described as a castiza and her daughter an española) claimed that as they innocently spoke with some neighbors at around 10 p.m., they saw Ximénez approaching. On observing this, one of the group commented, "Oh Jesus, here comes the lantern guard, and he is drunk."⁷¹ When he reached the mother and daughter, Ximénez started hitting them with his chuzo, leaving a scar on the older woman's head. The guard also wounded the daughter's arm, as she stepped in to defend her mother. As a result, a military patrol arrested Ximénez, and the two women went to jail, where a doctor treated their wounds. The guard remained incarcerated for a couple of weeks until the injuries that he had caused healed completely.

Surviving documents suggest that use of force often resulted in chastisement, as in the case when guard number 33 wounded a young Spanish-descent man while arresting him for sleeping in a door at three in the morning.⁷² The jail bailiffs sent in a surgeon to examine the prisoner's injured foot, and the judge warned the guard to exercise "more care/tact [*más tiento*]" in these circumstances. If needed, the authorities would send victims of violence by the night watchmen to the hospital, and it is safe to assume that the patrolmen had to cover any costs. In other cases, it appears that the court took the side of the guard against individuals who perhaps did not rate as believable complainants, such as a forty-four-year-old Spanish man who denied his obvious drunkenness and claimed that a guard injured his nose with his chuzo, "for no reason whatsoever."⁷³ This man received a sentence to the dungeon for his apparent lies. When larger group brawls took place on the nocturnal streets, the guards faced arrest by their supervisors along with any other plebeian caught up in the melee.⁷⁴ Even at this primordial moment for organized, street level law enforcement patrols, accusations of violent beatings of individuals in custody did inspire the serenos to protect each other, refuting claims that their peers hurt their custodies on the street and supporting their excuses.[75]

As noted in the cases above, women and arrested people of Indigenous ancestry voiced their complaints when they felt mistreated by the night watchmen. These investigations reveal both petty acts of disrespect as well as the ongoing rejection of the authority of the guards. The sereno José Benito Mora admitted that he beat a woman out with two companions "to pacify them" while trying to arrest all of them for a drunken brawl at 1:45 a.m. One of the women, described as a thirty-four-year-old india, had warned her two española companions to watch out for the night watchmen during their drinking session. When a group of drinkers fought or otherwise seemed "disorderly," some use of force seemed expected in order to "pacify" and arrest the individuals causing the disturbance, especially if the aggressiveness caused no permanent damage according to the jail surgeon. The fact of one guard facing a group might have led to this lack of repercussions for the patrolman. For example, one night just before midnight, two young men of Indigenous ancestry asked guard number 78 for the time. He told them to go buy watches, to which they responded that they had no money. The night watchmen must have perceived this response as insolent, so he beat one of them. His lieutenant intervened, and the young men were released from jail with just a warning, but the guard also suffered no consequences.[76]

Thefts and Bribery

Although rare (only sixteen documented incidents total in the 1790s *Libros de Reos* and a few other scattered incidents in the head guards' reports), accusations of theft and bribery show the guards in a terrible light. If even this small number recorded in the logbooks of thefts took place, it is no surprise that the populace derided the serenos as thieves. The short entries only hint at the details and context of these incidents, but they fit roughly into six sometimes overlapping categories: serenos who robbed businesses in their own patrol zones;[77] guards who robbed their own equipment, presumably to sell it for a profit; guards bribing an alleged offender; an effort to misdirect judicial attention from the arrested person to the arresting officer; drunk confusion; and proven accusations of unscrupulous guards taking advantage of vulnerable people who they encountered on the streets. Important incidents underscored the accuracy of viewing the night watchmen as a corps of state-supported robbers. In a dramatic but fragmentary case, head guard Quintana fired all eight of his corporals for stealing lanterns worth a total of fifty pesos (the equivalent of over three months' salary for their underlings) from the patrol areas that they supervised.[78]

By the late eighteenth century, viceregal subjects had more than two centuries of practice in bringing court cases against powerful authority figures, using smart strategies of sexual allegations and other accusations of abusive practices that tapped into imperial officials' desire to protect their personal honor and by extension the reputation of their institutions. Given this legal culture and history, it is no surprise that urban plebeians on occasion used the same litigious tactics to undermine the lowliest Spanish officials with whom they had the most face-to-face contact. Like accusations of sexual abuse, this move risked results that might be worse than the usual consequences of an arrest. When women pointed the finger at guards' alleged robberies, most of the complainants suffered the usual punishment for an unproven or mistrusted accusation—a painful twenty-five lashings. For example, one Indigenous woman, arrested with her husband before 9 p.m. for rowdy inebriation (*borrachos armando escándalo*), accused guard number 60 of stealing her new kerchief, which she said was worth two pesos. Even though he was drunk, her husband clearly did not approve of this maneuver, pointing out that this was actually an extremely old article of clothing. The couple received the familiar punishment of eight days in the stocks for the man and the same amount of time in jail for the woman, but she also had to endure an additional retribution of twenty-five lashings for her deception. Perhaps in a related incident, a half hour later, the corporal on duty arrested another intoxicated Indigenous man, who accused the same guard of the theft of "a painting of Saint Michael and a broach."[79] This man also received no sympathy from the authorities and suffered fifteen days in the stocks. Perhaps the later culprit heard the earlier shouting on the street about thieving night watchmen and hoped to take advantage. Other cases seem less clear and offer a glimpse of real abuse on the streets, especially of highly inebriated individuals. Although she had drunk too much to explain herself fully, a young Indigenous woman accused a guard of stealing five pesos and her *huipil* during her arrest for extreme intoxication. Judging by their documented reaction, the court did not take this accusation seriously, and sentenced her to twenty-five lashes.[80]

The logbook entries do not always clarify either the events surrounding the incidences or the repercussions of guards' stealing, hinting that perhaps their supervisors had an extrajudicial method of punishment, or that perhaps they filed another separate, longer investigation into the matter. For example, while the court believed that a night watchman had robbed a fifty-eight-year-old mestizo man of almost eight pesos, they still punished the arrestee with eight days in the stocks for public intoxication. Guard number 4 also allegedly demanded a silver dish from a woman, and his arrest took place at work, suggesting a more serious investigation would follow.[81]

Although the lantern guards had not existed for more than a decade in the late 1700s, residents of Mexico City seemed to already rate them as vulnerable to bribery, or at least believed that accusations of bribery had the potential kernel of truth to help their own cases as defendants. While bribery did occur, the judge must have made determinations based on his trust in the accuser and the guard in question. For example, guard number 50 asserted that a drunk, fifty-year-old Spanish-descent woman had walked around all night without wearing any shoes or stockings, by the time that he arrested her after one in the morning.[82] For her part, she claimed she offered these items to him, along with two reales, to tempt him to take her home. Instead she served a month in jail, a very long sentence, and then finally went back to her husband. Probably her European descent prevented her from receiving the typical lashings for this apparently false accusation.

Age did not deter the courts from prescribing corporal punishment for bribery-related incidents, a hard lesson learned by a seventy-five-year-old widow labeled castizo, who somehow found herself taking part in a rather wild night out on the town with a sixty-five-year-old mestizo visiting from Tula.[83] This married man came to the capital to buy sugar and brought a bag containing the hefty sum of twenty pesos tied up in his waistband for this purpose. When guard number 88 found him passed out on the street outside the pulquería de Celaya, with his tipsy female companion nearby, the night watchmen picked him up to take him to the jail, and sixteen pesos fell out of his shirt. The flush visitor already had spent a full peso on alcohol (possibly buying a total of sixteen drinks for that sum), and the widow claimed that she had used four pesos to bribe the guard not to take them to jail. This sum represented an entire week's pay for the serenos. While the man was sent back to Tula, the woman received the typical twenty-five lashes and a sentence to "serve in an honorable house."

The guards' reputation as thieves may have derived incidents in which they seized items from intoxicated individuals during the physical struggle of an arrest, but the serenos also justified that label by attempting to rob from their employer. Streetlights had a value and tempted a number of guards to steal these essentials of their own occupation. Guard number 66 did so in October of 1811, providing his ladder to help a military sergeant so the latter could climb a wall and steal one of the streetlights.[84] While the night watchman suffered immediate arrest, none of the superior-ranking officials could track down the actual thief. Of course the burden of replacing the lantern fell on the guard.

Helping Civilians Commit Offenses

While Revillagigedo and other reformers envisioned the presence of night watchmen on Mexico City's nocturnal streets as a deterrent to criminal activity, the serenos could also help facilitate crime. In logging these types of incidents, the head guard would describe the infraction as "haber abusado de su oficio [having abused their occupation]." The serenos' ladder represented a very useful tool for wrongdoers, as seen above in the minor case of stealing a streetlight. In 1795 guard number 28, Mariano Pantaleón Álvarez, risked a major church scandal when he loaned his ladder to help several novice friars escape their college to attend a fandango.[85]

The location the young men wanted to escape was the Portaceli Colegio, a Dominican friary built in 1606, located adjacent to the busy Plaza del Volador, which was directly south of the viceregal palace.

The nocturnal activities taking place around this square unfolded as follows, according to an investigation done by Corregidor Bonavía: Corporal number 1 testified that at 11:45 p.m. on the night of July 26, while on duty near the Palacio Bridge, he made his rounds to check up on the night watchmen under his supervision. At this time, a cleric approached him and reported that one of the guards had placed his ladder against one of Portaceli's walls. When corporal number 3, the very active José Manuel Bernal (see introduction), came to investigate the complaint, Pantaleón Álvarez responded to his questions, saying that nothing at all of interest took place on his beat that night.[86] As a side note, the investigation into Pantaleón Álvarez included his military records, which described him physically, as well as mentioning that he was from the capital and was a married man. He had worked as a weaver and enlisted in the provincial infantry as a militiaman in 1783 at age twenty-seven. He had black hair, "honey-colored" eyes, a large nose, "olive-complected [*trigueño*]" skin, black brows, a large, scarred forehead, and no beard.[87]

Another man named José Zúñiga, a sixty-year-old not affiliated with the ramo del alumbrado, also stood guard in this neighborhood. That night, Pantaleón Álvarez allegedly had requested that Zúñiga stay out of his part of the beat. Zúñiga agreed to the request because the younger guard bribed him with a cigar. Not long after, Zúñiga saw two friars hiding under the plaza arches, their habits bunched around their waists, white wrappings over their face. Zúñiga and the men had an exchange:

> FRIARS: By God, be quiet!
> ZÚÑIGA REPLIED: I am not a sereno, I just guard these doors from the thieves.
> FRIARS: We already have help from the sereno, but take these four reales.
> ZÚÑIGA: No, keep them. Go with God.

Zúñiga then ran off to tell the corporal Antonio Garcia about the exchange.[88]

Meanwhile, corporal Garcia asked the other guard in the area why he saw a ladder leaning against the friary wall. Guard number 12, Francisco Luna, stated that he had no idea. His superior officers told him to stand by it, not to move it, and to prevent anyone from climbing it if they emerged out of the darkness. Luna carried out these orders. A few hours later, at 3:30 a.m., Luna said that several men pushed him aside and insisted on climbing the ladder, even though Luna tried to prevent them. When the last man reached the top, they untied the ladder from the window, where it had been attached.[89] By 4:30 a.m., Pantaleón Álvarez found himself in jail for facilitating the escape of seven friars, even though he claimed he knew nothing about the ladder.[90] This case became ever murkier as the investigation progressed. Pantaleón Álvarez claimed the fuero, or exemption from criminal prosecution, as a militiaman (see chapter 7) and begged the viceroy for leniency and mercy for his impoverished family. He also received help from the Dominican leadership. The rector of the friars' college confirmed to the viceroy that three "seculars" accompanied four friars (not seven clerics, as originally reported), most likely helping escort them to a fandango or a dance. In the rector's opinion, a young boy had stolen one of the night watchmen's ladders, and the head guard should not punish any of his subordinates. Lastly, the friars also had judicial immunity due to their clerical status.[91] As in the majority of viceregal court cases, each group involved worked to protect their privileges and effectively maintained the status quo, smoothing over an inappropriate action.

Night Watchmen on Trial—the Case of Brígida Gómez

Although some of these cases indicate that the authorities started a criminal trial against guards who committed more serious infractions, the existing documents do not show a clear link between the very short investigations cited throughout this chapter and the longer trials that may have unfolded as a result. Only a handful of more detailed freestanding prosecutions of guards have survived. These files are not connected to any of the existing terse entries in the *Libros de Reos* and head guards' reports, although they would have also been annotated in those more routine daily logs. The longest of these files is a fifty-eight-page investigation of the violent sexual assault and abuse of authority endured by a woman named Brígida Gómez. This dossier reveals the worst kinds of exploitation carried out by the night watchmen. Gómez's experience juxtaposes the inherent contradictions built into state-sanctioned violence as it bleeds into victim-blaming and virgin/whore gender stereotypes. Both sides attempted to shape the archival record in opposing ways, and each contradictory account reveals the complex challenges of the institution of street policing.[92]

The investigation commenced when Gómez and her fifty-year-old Indigenous servant María Micaela Hernández chose to complain to the corregidor about their experience at the hands of José Antonio Hernández, guard number 57. They filed their petition a few days after events that took place on the night of March 29, 1794. On April 1, 1794, Gómez introduced herself to the public notary as a twenty-five-year-old *coyota* born in Guadalajara and residing in an *acesoria*, a two-level set of rented rooms, on the Calle de Ortega. She reported that her husband was at the moment traveling to Toluca. A few nights before, at midnight, while Gómez slept in the company of María Micaela, she woke to knocking at the door. Upon asking "Who is it?" she heard the response, "The head guard." María Micaela opened the door and saw a sereno with his lantern. He said that he was searching the house and its outbuildings for thieves who had stolen some petticoats (*enaguas*). The guard asked Gómez about the position of the small window in her bedroom, and she replied that it opened up to the patio of the main house on the property. The guard then told her to shut up and extinguished his lantern and the candle in the room. Next, he tried to get into her bed, while telling her to move over so he could sleep. She rejected his bizarre actions, asking him, "Is this your strategy for looking for thieves?"[93] At this point he put two reales in her hand, and Gómez threw them on the ground. "Far from succumbing to his crude desires," she told her servant to relight the candle, which the older woman did. In response to Gómez's continued resistance, the guard grabbed her by the hair and the leg, but María Micaela protected her by threatening him with a stick.[94] The guard then called the servant a "whoring procuress [*puta alcahueta*]" and threatened her with his pike. Grabbing María Micaela's arms, the guard said that her genitals (*partes pudendas*) tempted him and made him as hard as a club. María Micaela retorted back that the whore who had given birth to him also tempted him. Gómez tried to give him back the money off the floor, at which point he called her a cheapskate because the reales could not be found. The guard went out, threatening to call his companions to take both women to jail.[95]

Gómez took this opportunity to seek help. She wandered the streets near her residence, remembering that other watchmen patrolled there. After a few turns around the neighborhood, she saw the man who had attacked her and started to run away from him. He called for her to stop, and after a chase, finally caught up to her near the Royal Hospital. Her attacker then asked her to go out with him for a drink of aguardiente. Gómez responded, "I am not out looking for a drink. I am seeking justice to punish you for your boldness." Gómez gave the following testimony of the brutal physical assault that followed: the guard forced her to kiss him, dragged her along the ground for several feet, put his knees on her arms, bit her hand, threatened to kill her when she cried out, and beat her on the chest with his chuzo. After suffering through the violence, in the words taken down by the notary, "fearful of her life, she condescended to his lusts [*torpeza*] and he completed the act with her."[96] During her testimony, the notary saw the marks the guard had made on her hand and chest. After the night watchmen finished assaulting her, Gómez stood up crying and looked for another patrol to arrest him. However, at that moment her abuser grabbed her arm and declared he would now take her to jail for her own drunkenness. Gómez saw a royal patrol and told them what had happened, but her assailant contradicted her, asserting that she was just inebriated. In response, Gómez breathed in the other men's faces to prove her sobriety. Her attacker then grabbed her by the sleeve, ripping it, and forced her to continue walking to the jail with him and another guard. As they were passing by the Puente Quebrada, another set of guards intervened, suggesting that, since she showed no signs of drunkenness, she should just go home and submit her complaints in the morning. They succeeded in putting this plan into action and Gómez made her report at 9 a.m. the next day. Her complaint led to the guard's imprisonment, but Gómez wished not to pursue the case further. She expressed her reasoning to the notary: "Because God forgives his sins, but if possible, could she have compensation for her ripped clothing?"[97]

María Micaela gave a similar testimony to that of her mistress. Explaining that she was living with Gómez while her husband also traveled, she corroborated the knock on the door and the claim that the caller was the head guard. Upon his entrance, the servant recognized that he was a sereno because he was in a cape and carried a lantern and a pike. María Micaela narrated their dialogue, adding that Gómez told the man that she would not have sex with him even if he offered her "many doubloons." After the servant confirmed Gómez's story, the court interrogated the other serenos present that night. A twenty-two-year-old español named José Feliciano Vidales (guard number 50) had been patrolling his beat when he saw a group of guards gathered outside of their patrol areas. This indicated to him that something had happened. When he questioned the group, guard number 57 replied "in a commanding tone" that he was taking the woman present to jail. When asked why, guard number 57 said that she was drunk, scandalous, and a brothel worker. Gómez interjected, telling Vidales that if he knew what had happened, he would not take her to jail. She explained that the guard number 57 had raped her and torn her clothes. Vidales observed her and viewed this as an accurate statement. Vidales did not think that Gómez was drunk. He decided, along with guard number 55, to take her home instead, ignoring guard number 57's arguments that she was a whore who lived with a procuress. Guard number 55, Miguel Castaneda, a twenty-three-year-old español, gave a similar statement.[98]

After María Micaela and the two guards presented their accounts, on April 11, the imprisoned guard finally made his statement. He stated his name as José Antonio Hernández, claimed European ancestry, and described himself as a single man born in Toluca. He said that he believed his imprisonment derived from a complaint made by a drunk man whom he had harassed on the same night discussed by Gómez. The notary then instructed him as follows: "Brígida Gómez accused him of entering her house, pretending to be the head guard, trying to have carnal access with her, which he had not achieved. Then she went out to the street to find help, and he eventually satisfied his lustful goals."[99] Hernández denied everything and told a very different story. He said that on his 1 a.m. patrol, he saw Gómez sitting outside her doorway at this "irregular hour." Hernández called other guards to take her to jail, but as they approached, Gómez started to cry out that he had raped her. In response, one of the other guards said that he knew she was a whore, dating back to when they were acquaintances in Guadalajara before she came to Mexico City. They decided just to escort her home. Hernández said he had not harmed her physically in any way but only admitted that he tore her kerchief and sleeve in taking her into custody.[100]

Two weeks later, Gómez and Hernández took part in the classic "confrontation" in Spanish justice, the *careo*. In this practice, opposing litigants face each other in the presence of the notary and other judicial officials in an effort to force one or the other side to admit the truth of the offense. During their April 26 careo, Hernández admitted his full guilt. He said that he had lied to protect his wife (previously he had given his status as unmarried), who was living in Toluca. He readily agreed to Gómez's request for compensation for her ripped clothing.[101] However, by early June 1794, Hernández reversed his story and presented the following redacted account (presented in first person, although the scribe wrote the testimony in the third person):

> About a week before the incident in question, I was on a stroll and I saw Brígida. I called out to her and gave her the cigar that I was smoking. She asked me for a loan of two reales, which I gave her. I had seen her many times in passing, but this was our first conversation. Three days later, I went to her house and we had sex [concurrió torpemente con ella]. I paid her four reales. Nothing else happened. I did not rape her on the night in question, although I did knock on her door, and entered eager to ask her [for sex]. She answered the door, but then rejected me and went out to look for a guard, saying that I wanted to rape her. The other guard said that she was drunk and he wanted to take her to jail.[102]

The judicial official observed that even if previously he and Gómez had consensual sex, it was still a serious crime to rape her by threatening to use his weapon. Her scars proved that Hernández had used force. The fact that they were both married made this infraction even worse. The judge also expressed that he found it unlikely that Gómez would reject or even resist him after they had already had sex, especially considering that he offered to pay her. In sum, the court official expressed that Hernández violated his role as part of the judicial system, disrespecting its very name, and his duty to maintain the peace.[103]

However, at this stage, the trial shifted from prosecuting a rapist to investigating Gómez for her occupation as a "prostitute woman [*mujer prostituta*]." Elsewhere I have presented multiple examples of how no clear laws outlined this alleged offense or how the authorities should react to it. As the eighteenth century ended, the judiciary actually took a more lenient view of women and girls who sold sex, often viewing them as victims of their own parents or siblings. Especially during mass insurgency, poverty drove families to try to earn money in this way.[104] Judging from the small handful of surviving cases, to prosecute Gómez at all went against the norm for this era. Sending women to houses of female seclusion (*casas de recogidas*) and even women's jails does seem to have increased in this era, along with street level policing, but at the same time, a very strong sense of paternalism continued to dominate judicial interactions with women viewed as wayward. However, the results of investigations into sex work depended on the woman involved and how much they seemed to deserve a gesture of manly protection from the judge. Gómez was poor, had the race label of coyota, and did not seem to have any male protectors, so most likely she did not receive the fatherly pity evoked by younger, more Spanish-appearing ladies and girls who may have taken part in transactional relationships or encounters. Lastly, her complaint challenged the judicial structure itself and the reputation of a man whose occupation symbolized enlightened imperial reform. Any record of a Spanish official behaving criminally tainted the honor of the system that they represented.[105]

With the shift in the purpose of the case, the court appointed a legal advocate to defend Hernández because he was a legal minor under the age of twenty-five. This advocate proposed a set of questions that he would use to interrogate witnesses to speak against Gómez. The tone of the interrogation focused on leading questions regarding Gómez's "vulgar behavior, continuous excesses and reputation as a whore." The advocate also asked for statements regarding if "Gómez prostituted herself with all kinds of people, *paisanos* [literally, 'countrymen,' but used to refer to civilians in this era], as well as military men."[106] The respondents included more night watchmen, who demonstrated varying levels of loyalty to protect their compañero Hernández and to attack Gómez's reputation. One more mature guard, aged forty-eight, said that he had heard Gómez spoken about as a whore as he stood one day near her house washing his lantern, and also that she may drink aguardiente, but he was not sure. Another guard said that one night while he was on duty, he heard noises and found Gómez having sex with a militia sergeant on the street near the theater. He broke them up, but the militiaman went after him with his sword. A third guard testified that he knew Gómez as a public whore from the gossip that he heard from a variety of men, and the fact that he had actually seen her working in brothels, such as la casa de la Poblana in the Calle de Damas (literally, the woman from Puebla's house in the Ladies' Street). He also observed her seated in doorways, in the habit that was very common for "bad women."[107]

Moving away from the guards who were most likely eager to defend one of their own, a former neighbor testified that on the Calle de Ortega, everyone knew Gómez as a whore. They said that she lived in rooms that hosted constant fights and disturbances. The witnesses believed that a volatile relationship between Gómez and a militia sergeant sparked much of the violence. The neighbors wanted Gómez kicked out for her scandalous behavior. A neighbor woman also reported seeing Gómez drinking pulque with Hernández. Another witness, a coachman, spoke of knowing Gómez for ten years and confirmed her reputation, saying that he had seen her shut up in her room with different men and that he had transported her with her lovers in his vehicle. His friends also said that they had slept with her. Last but not least, the wife of the aforementioned militia sergeant testified and discussed how Gómez had ruined her marriage, and how the wife saw Gómez with her husband, which hurt her so much that she had tried to attack her rival with scissors.[108]

Finally, Brígida Gómez came forward to make her confession. Right away, Gómez admitted that she had lied about her marital status, in fear of Hernández. When asked if she had a sexual relationship with the aforementioned sergeant, she admitted to the "illicit friendship" but confessed she did not know that he was married. When she found out that he was, she wanted to discontinue their interactions, and this decision led to her lover beating her. When asked directly if she "prostituted herself with several men," Gómez denied the accusation, saying that her only lover was the militia sergeant, a relationship that she continued even after he abused her. Pushing this line of questioning, she was asked "if she is not a public woman, why is she seen sitting in brothels, both in Mexico and in Guadalajara, and also [soliciting] in doorways?" Gómez denied the veracity of these accounts.[109]

As the case wrapped up by the first week of 1795, Gómez's reputation and enforcing conventional gender roles and family structures seemed more important to the judge than punishing Hernández's proven violence against her. Spanish courts that dealt with issues touching on sexuality usually focused on reestablishing the status quo in terms of the power of the paterfamilias. The judicial reinforcement of paternalistic roles extended down from the king in Madrid to the most dysfunctional family in Mexico City.[110] In this case, the corregidor had a good opportunity of healing one family structure when Hernández's wife made a petition for his release after six months' incarceration, stating that she pardoned him and wanted him free from all calumny. In contrast, Gómez's advocate could not produce any witnesses in her favor. He did nothing more than make a statement to ask the court to lessen her punishment, arguing several relevant points, including that Gómez had already suffered many months in jail. Whatever Gómez's reputation, her advocate pointed out that Hernández had still raped her. He continued by noting that although Gómez denied that she was a "prostitute," and even if they had sex in the past, Hernández still committed a crime by impersonating the head guard when he knocked on her door. Their previous sexual encounters did not excuse the fact that he attacked her physically, stabbed her with his pike, ripped her shirt and head cloth, and threatened to kill her. But the corregidor did not agree with the defense on the point that Gómez had served enough time incarcerated. He sentenced her to live for four more years captive in the casa de recogidas and threated to send her to another, stricter institution if she ever solicited on the streets again. Hernández, on the other hand, received no further punishment and left the jail to rejoin his wife.[111]

Brígida Gómez's bravery stands out—even well over two hundred years later, a known sex worker might fear making an accusation of sexual assault by a law enforcement officer. Gómez follows the viceregal norm in refusing to admit to the label of mujer prostituta, regardless of witnesses' testimonies. I think it is actually unlikely that selling sex was her occupation because, by making this complaint against her attacker, she had to know that her own sex life would come under the microscope of neighborly scrutiny. Her one or two illicit, transactional relationships blew up into a scandal that her neighbors enjoyed reporting. Although the court failed to recognize her as an individual whose emotions might shape her sexual choices, her defense did crudely imagine that even a mujer prostituta should have a say in her choice of sex partners. On the other hand, speculating on the norms for this era, Gómez may represent another example of an irate plebeian who so detested the night watchman that she would risk everything if she saw an opportunity to attack one of their members. In an early illustration of the complex relationship that we still have with law enforcement, while accusing one of them of a terrible rape, she readily admitted seeking help from other guards to save her from Hernández. This kind of contradictory give-and-take between plebeians and the lantern guards runs through their entire history. Well aware of the serenos' problematic actions, Mexico City residents began attempting to tear down their authority as individuals and as an institution almost as soon as the night watchmen started patrolling the city.

CHAPTER 6

Guards under Attack

Mariano Romero, Spaniard from Teméluca [Temecula?], married, weaver, aged 29.
  Don Joaquín del Prado, Spaniard from Santa Ana Chiautempan, married, master weaver, aged 43.
  José María Rivera, Spaniard from Zacatelco, married, weaver aged 28.
  Arrested at 11:30 at night by corporal number 2 of the serenos for scandalous drunkenness and because the former [Romero] broke the lantern of guard number 23, who demanded ten reales in damages. The latter two [men] admitted that it is true that they were drinking aguardiente in a vinatería and that they were going home when the sereno stopped them. . . . The sereno wanted to take them to jail, so they fled, and for this reason he hit [Romero] on the head and broke it, which the sereno says is false, saying that [Romero] fell as he ran away and ended up hurt.
  Romero was cured in the infirmary, and paid for the guard's lantern that he broke. Prado [is sentenced to] three days in the dungeon and five in jail. Rivera [is sentenced to] eight days' [labor in] public works.
  Mariano Romero's wife admits that he is a drunk . . . and asks for more correction to amend himself, so he is condemned to eight more days in jail.
—*Libro de Reos*, August 1, 1796

Two small town weavers, out carousing one night with their boss in one of the most populous cities in the Western Hemisphere, overindulged in cane liquor and sparked a public disturbance. When a night watchman accosted them, they absolutely rejected his authority by running away, resulting in an injury with disputed causes. One of the culprits, known as a heavy drinker, reacted with destructive rage against the guard's hand-held lantern, a key symbol of the serenos' control over their bodies and their actions. This incident from 1796 sums up some of the various kinds of resistance regularly faced by the night watchmen from the general civilian population. Although this defiance often took place during drinking binges, it still had an underlying rebellious tone—a pulquería or vinatería represent the Mexican version of the Parisian wine shop, "the habitual point of departure of a riot."[1] But despite the harshly punished gestures of resistance, the viceregal justice system also responded in its classic paternalistic way, by listening and responding to the wife of the alcoholic perpetrator, attentive to her marital struggles. This incident highlights the ever-present tension between plebeians and street patrols, inherent in trying to juggle a contradictory law enforcement mission, at once punitive and "protecting and serving." The watchmen spent most of their time on duty interacting with the poor or working-class denizens of the street at night, and the serenos usually came from that class themselves. Thus, the rebellious undertone of insults and physical attacks also fit into a broader culture of simmering violence between men, although at the same time, women's resistance should not be neglected.[2]

Mexico City plebeians, both men and women, often expressed and acted on their objections to the lantern guards throughout the three decades following their formation in late 1790. This chapter analyzes approximately 120 incidents (about 3 percent of all recorded interactions with the guards in the 1790s), related to rejecting the authority of the street patrols, including insults (often phrased as *maltratando de palabras*), mockery, sarcastic comments, resisting arrest, tearing their capes and shirts, physically beating the serenos, and, most frequently, breaking the glass of the guards' lanterns. As described in chapter 1, these latter objects became a highly contested emblem of government involvement in the street life of the city. Before the establishment of the lantern guards, residents resisted paying for lighting on their streets. After Revillagigedo created these new patrols, destruction of their lanterns became a familiar, politically charged act of resistance. Other such acts included refusing to submit to arrest without the use of force. Occasional murderous acts of violence happened too, but usually in a more militarized context during the era of insurgency, which will be explored in chapter 7.

In the guards' founding documents, Viceroy Revillagigedo proposed very harsh punishments in response to attacks on the night watchmen, including extended periods (six months to a year) of forced labor while in shackles and banishment from the city and its surrounding areas. The justification for these severe measures stemmed from the belief that individuals who would commit such acts "must be extremely degenerate, and could likely hide their bad customs easily in such a populous city, inducing others to come together to commit more and more crimes."[3] This assessment of the seriousness of the infraction fits with the contemporary vision of antigovernment words or actions as treason, one of the gravest offenses possible within this particular judicial system.

Despite the potentially harsh consequences, from the 1790s through to the first decade of the 1800s, gestures of personal or small-group rebellion against the serenos persisted. Not surprisingly, the authorities did not carry out the aforementioned proposed sentences. In effect, the weakness of the punishments for attacking the lantern guards told the masses that the authorities tolerated these attacks. The viceroys and their judicial underlings would soon regret their leniency.[4] While the next chapter examines the violent military rejection of the night watchmen's authority, here I focus on civilians and subtler and persistent resistance to their authority. Both types of opposition suggest that historians should continue to question the effectiveness of Bourbon judicial reforms, including at the street level. At no moment in their thirty years of street patrolling did the viceregal night watchmen experience a compliant population. Contrary to some scholarship, this suggests that street patrols did not effectively prevent rebellions but perhaps instead offered an opportunity to help forge a culture of urban antigovernment agitation, which also included worker protests and activism based around the massive tobacco factory.[5] Although evidence is fragmentary, patterns in available documentation suggest that the resistance explored in this chapter took place consistently from the 1790s to the 1820s. And even though mass riots did not take place for the first two decades of the serenos' history, historians should question assumptions about Mexico City's "urban passivity" and "the state's ability to maintain its authority and legitimacy" in the years before popular rebellion swept New Spain.[6]

Lantern Smashing

Breaking lanterns lighted by or held in the hands of Mexico City night watchmen in the late eighteenth and early nineteenth centuries were not random acts of intoxicated fury. The frequent and small individual protests made against them suggest that the serenos' presence constituted a low-level but constantly irritating reminder of an unsatisfactory governing system. While attacks on the patrolmen demonstrated the public's objections and dissatisfaction with this new form of surveillance, a close reading of these cases also reveals the expectations that the common person on the street had for this proto-police force, as well as how quickly plebeians came to define their expectations for them, in terms of standards for their words, actions, clothing, and demeanor. This tense and violent development of a street-level definition for law enforcement often conflicted with the function of military patrols and included a desire by a wide range of individuals to call on the guards for help, as seen in chapter 3. As the populace shaped the serenos' activities and made demands on their general visual presentation, the guards themselves strengthened their own internal community by helping each other when they were under attack, whether verbally or physically.

The incident described at the start of this chapter illustrates that a decade and a half before New Spain's colonial subjects rejected the viceregal system en masse, the urban populace already aimed their resentment and aggression against the night watchmen and their equipment. In contemporary Europe, the act of "smashing lanterns" functioned as a recognized part of mass urban revolts. As of this writing, historians have not analyzed lantern smashing in Mexico in any way, much less as a political act. Of course, street lighting faced almost continuous challenges from the Mexico City populace from the initial discussion of the topic in the mid-eighteenth century through to its establishment as a publicly funded venture in the 1790s. As discussed in chapter 1, the guards' hand-held lights and the street lamps ignited by them stood for the "enlightened" reforms of the Bourbon monarchs. As rapidly as three years after the viceregal authorities finally implemented street illumination through the new "lantern guards," people began to destroy the sources of the light. In thirty-six hundred recorded interactions between the night watchmen and the public from the 1790s logbooks, seventy-three incidents took place in which individuals "broke the glass" of the hand-held lanterns as the guards passed by on their rounds or in the physical struggles that took place while the reos were taken into custody. The attacks may have targeted the mounted wall lanterns as well. The official nightly reports made by the guarda mayores confirm the continuation of this pointed destruction into the early 1820s.

In nineteenth-century Europe, commentators compared the street lanterns to a red flag waved in a bull's face, because they sparked a vicious and destructive rage in the populace. Lantern smashing became a collective plebeian gesture against the authorities—which might extend even to executing them by hanging on the iron bars that affixed lights to urban walls. Wolfgang Schivelbusch beautifully describes the aggressive joy of smashing a lantern: the shocking sound of shattering glass that rang loudly through quiet nocturnal streets, an explosive noise that satisfied an instinctive and brutal urge to destroy a symbol of civilization. Schivelbusch compares this action to the primitive impulse to urinate on a fire, which generates a similar sense of momentary and crudely exercised omnipotence. The brutality of this gesture intermixes with a modern desire to reject the state and bring back "disorder and freedom" on the streets. Lashing out in this way might even include a bit of a sexual thrill in its instantaneous and forceful potency. As noted by Schivelbusch, "every attack on a street lantern was a small act of rebellion against the order that it embodied."[7] Lantern smashing also immediately darkened the streets, extinguishing the isolated beacons of Enlightened imperial control, and turned back the clock to an era of less official surveillance of the nightly doings that had become criminal under a more modern regime. An instantly darkened street invited more rebellious and unlawful acts, under the cover of the night.[8]

The seventy-three incidents of lantern smashing recorded in the night watchmen's dockets come from the years of 1794, 1796, and 1798. It is very likely that these offenses also took place in all of the other years when the guarda faroleros patrolled the streets. Those charged with smashing, kicking, or throwing a stone at a lantern ranged across all race labels commonly used in the 1790s nightly reports, including español, mestizo, indio, mulato, and castizo. Men, women, couples, and groups of nocturnal drinkers all flouted the guards' authority in this way. Although the archive is incomplete, lantern-smashing appears to be a consistent problem over time. In 1794, the incomplete *Libros de Reos* record a total of twenty-three lantern attacks, perpetrated by twenty-nine individuals. Fragmented logbooks for 1796 document a slight decline, with twenty-six different people involved in eighteen separate incidences of lantern smashing. The year of 1798 offers the most complete records of nightly arrests. In this year, thirty incidents occurred of smashing the guards' lanterns, involving a total of thirty-six people. In all of these years, almost all lantern smashing took place between 8 p.m. and midnight, which also were both the peak drinking hours and the times when the guards made most of their arrests. Under three dozen lantern smashing incidents in one year might not seem like an important trend. However, remember that Mexico City had approximately 113,000 residents at this time. Extrapolating this statistic to a city of a million people with about three hundred acts of destruction of the most expensive piece of law enforcement equipment in existence in this era, the extent of popular outrage becomes clearer.

Because on occasion clusters of two or three perpetrators smashed lanterns in a group attack on the night watchmen, notaries in the 1790s wrote down the personal details for a total of ninety-four individuals participating in the seventy-three incidents. Just under 50 percent, or forty-six, of the perpetrators received the label of indio. According to the 1790 census, indios represented only 24.4 percent of the capital city's population.[9] The second most frequent offenders were men labeled españoles, or of European descent, with a total of twenty-three "Spanish" individuals involved in lantern smashing. About 12 percent of the incidents of lantern smashing involved mestizos, and the remaining small handful took place when the guards encountered individuals labeled castizos or mulatos. Only eleven women from across a range of racial labels took part in this destructive and symbolic rejection of the government. These included women labeled mulatas, indias, mestizas, and españolas. Women rarely committed this offense when they encountered guards alone, but they hesitated less when backed up by their male or female companions. Only two women smashed a guard's lantern outside of a group attack, coincidentally both lashing out on separate occasions in February of 1796. The scribe described these irate women as an intoxicated (ebria) mulata, charged with owing the guard three reales for the repairs, and a borracha (drunk) mestiza.[10] Less than 10 percent, or only seven lantern-smashing occurrences, do not include wording implicating the perpetrator as drunk as well as enraged at the symbol of the lantern. However, Europeanist historians' interpretations of lantern smashing argue against depoliticizing this act as just another drunken gesture on the part of savage colonials. Instead, these actions should fit into the long trajectory of small rebellions that took place almost continuously in the Spanish viceroyalties.[11]

Chapter 4 analyzed the potential for racial bias in the arrests made by guards by examining the arrest records of the most active guards whose racial designation appears in the historical record. Because I am arguing for the insurgent implications of lantern smashing, it is worth considering what possible race-based aggression might emerge from an analysis of who broke the lanterns of which guards, to speculate on whether or not this might indicate an anti-Spanish sentiment acted out in the course of nocturnal drinking binges. It is challenging to analyze this hypothesis because the notaries who wrote the nightly dockets did not provide any information about the arresting sereno beyond his number. Only seventy-nine guards have race labels documented in the *Libros de Reos* (when they faced incarceration themselves), or in other more detailed court cases when they testified as witnesses and had to provide a brief autobiography. However, even with this limited information, it is still possible to argue that lantern smashing generally did demonstrate anger directed at those who held more status in the viceregal racial and social hierarchy.

In almost every incident of lantern smashing, an individual or group attacked a guard who presented himself as higher up in the colonial pecking order, which of course ranked those who could claim European descent as socially and culturally superior to Indigenous, African-descent, and racially mixed viceregal subjects.[12] Only seven of the night watchmen subjected to these attacks on one or more occasions had a race label other than español.[13] On the contrary, guards of Spanish ancestry held the offensive lamps in over 85 percent of the occurrences of lantern smashing. This makes sense, as the majority of the night watchmen claimed Spanish ancestry. In the rare examples when a guard labeled indio experienced an attack on his lantern, the aggression usually came from other individuals also called indios.[14] Of course the night watchmen of Indigenous descent did willingly take on an occupation whose key purpose was to suppress Indigenous drinking habits, so it is no surprise that they inspired some resentment from those who carried the same racial label. In the examples of guards labeled mestizos, again, typically individuals of Indigenous ancestry smashed their lanterns. This also represents an attack on a step "up" the viceregal system.[15] In only two cases did the hostility go in the reverse direction in the colonial racial and social hierarchy, by which I mean that a person of Spanish descent attacked a sereno with the race label mestizo or indio.[16] As I have noted previously, no evidence exists that non-Spanish descent guards had any issue with racial bias standing in the way of carrying out their tasks and duties, nor did racial identities seem to inspire irate plebeians to destroy their equipment. All existing evidence suggests that those urban nightwalkers who could claim Spanish ancestry, other than soldiers, did not openly express resentment toward the policing powers of men labeled castizo, mestizo, or indio. On the other hand, lantern smashing does represent a way for the nocturnally active Indigenous population to act on their rage, directing it toward particular guards who appeared European and symbolized Spanish domination. On this point, Schivelbusch observes that oil lanterns, which designated night watchmen routinely lighted one-by-one on their predictable nightly rounds, represent a differentiated individuality far more than modern electrical or gas utility grids. Breaking a streetlight now is just hooliganism, because it does nothing to affect our centralized sources of power. In contrast, destruction of a lantern held by a specific, well-known patrolman could demonstrate an individualized and targeted fury directed against that guard in particular.[17]

Like the sound of the glass as it hit the cobblestones, the wrath of

GUARDS UNDER ATTACK

working-class Mexico City residents explodes out from the reports of lantern smashing. While a one-to-one confrontation might come from a more personal antipathy toward a particular guard or a night out drinking gone very badly, group attacks suggest a more widespread hatred for the institution of night patrols and the government that organized them. Almost one quarter of the lantern-smashing incidents involved two or three individuals versus one guard. Among the groups of people who lashed out at the handheld lamps, most comprised a number of individuals inscribed with more than one race label (see table 4).[18] The serenos targeted in group attacks also range across different colonial categories of race. It seems that in these group attacks, racial categories mattered less than the occupation of night watchman.[19]

TABLE 4. Group attacks on lanterns

DATE	RACE LABEL OF CULPRITS	# OF GUARD	GUARD'S RACE
10/18/94	Span./mulato	not given	unknown
10/22/94	indio/india	57	Spanish
11/22/94	indio/Span.	82	castizo
12/13/94	indio/mestiza	79	varies
12/16/94	indio/mestiza	79	varies
12/31/94	2 indios	Corporal 8	likely Spanish
1/7/96	2 Span./indio	Corporal 8	likely Spanish
2/4/96	2 indios	35	castizo
8/1/96	3 Span.	Corporal 2	likely Spanish
9/14/96	2 mestizos	Corporal 4	likely Spanish
9/25/96	2 indios	80	unknown
3/5/98	Span./mulato/indio	51	unknown
4/8/98	Span./mulato	29	Spanish
4/28/98	indio/castiza	92	Spanish
5/5/98	2 indios	28	indio
8/17/98	2 indios	16	unknown

In addition to their lanterns, other paraphernalia of the serenos inspired rage. Several of the brief case notes suggest that the perpetrators blamed the night watchmen's brutality for their destructive responses, especially in breaking the pikes while fighting off the guards' beatings. For example, three culprits faced off with three serenos in 1796: "At 10:45 p.m., Trinidad Antonio Esquivel, a twenty-four-year-old Spaniard, his mother María Estefanía Romero, aged forty, and Rafaela Gertrudis Rodríguez, an Indian widow from Real del Monte, aged thirty [were arrested] by corporal number 8 at 8:45 at night for drunkenness and beating guard numbers 88, 89, and 90. They broke guard number 90's lantern glass and ripped his shirt. They served three days in jail, and must pay four reales for the shirt and lantern."[20] This group represents a classic example of the mix of genders and racial categories all participating in nightly drinking and socializing. As seen in this quote, several other items besides the lights also provoked those taken into custody for lantern smashing. The objects of attack included the serenos' shirts, hats, and capes, as well as the *capote*, or cloak, of a corporal. Even a sleeve could end up destroyed in an altercation of this kind. On one occasion, even the scissors that the night watchmen used to trim their wicks were stolen in a confrontation that also resulted in the breaking of a lantern glass.[21]

The high court judges' verdicts in the cases of this kind were likely to be strongly influenced by the perpetrator's status, narrative of aggrieved self-defense, or other personal circumstances. In contrast, insurgency and revolts typically sparked a brutal and vindictive official retribution.[22] If the viceregal authorities interpreted breaking lanterns as an act of rebellion, then the offense demanded severe punishment, which would fall into line with how governments handled this infraction in Europe. For example, in Paris, lantern smashing connoted an anti-royalist sentiment, resulting in perpetrators ending up in jail. In contrast, the London judiciary did not interpret this infraction as a revolutionary act and only levied fines against the culprits.[23] Late viceregal New Spain actually combined these two forms of punishment, suggesting a displeasure with the antigovernment connotations of the act, as well as a desire to compensate the night watchmen for their monetary losses—remember that the guards themselves had to pay for damage done to their equipment. Mexico City judges did not take lantern smashing lightly and almost always demanded compensation of at least two and up to twelve reales for the damaged property, along with time spent either incarcerated (sometimes in the bartolina reserved for more serious offenses), in the stocks, or in forced labor on public works projects, as well as corporal punishment. The last two penalties often occurred for drunkenness, but the monetary compensation was added on only when the culprit had also damaged the guard's work accoutrement.[24] The following logbook entry typifies a quadruple punishment:

> Manuel Ruíz, an Indian born in Mexico [City], married, a cigar roller aged 36, and Rosalía Gertrudis Pingarron, castiza, his wife [who is] over age 30. [They were arrested] by guard number 92 at 10:45p.m. because she was scandalous and blasphemous, and they mistreated the guards with their injurious words. The man was drunk [borracho] and she was tipsy [bebida]. They confessed to their drunkenness, and broke the glass of the guard's lantern. The man [received a sentence of] eight days in the stocks and the woman eight days in jail with both [also punished with] 25 lashes. They also must pay for the damage.[25]

This couple not only damaged guard number 92's lantern but also may very well have spoken in ways that directly challenged the authority of the viceregal state and municipal government. Their very slight level of intoxication suggests that they knew what they said and spoke coherently if aggressively. No surprise that the judge chose to punish them harshly.

Although the available documents are even more sporadic than those for the 1790s, lantern smashing still took place at times even up to 1822. As explained in the introduction, in the surviving nineteenth-century nightly reports the head guard focused less on the details of the race, age, and marital status of the perpetrators and more on the guards' work routine and nocturnal activities. In the latter reports, almost no information is given about the attacks or their punishments for committing this offense. These nightly chronicles document only eight incidents of lantern smashing, suggesting that it declined during the years of actual insurgency (1810 to 1821), although it is impossible to know with certainty without more documentation.[26] While the later incidences continue to involve drunk perpetrators like those in the 1790s, they are much more obviously politically charged and relate to the ongoing insurgency movement. Chapter 7 examines these and other kinds of very violent and even fatal attacks on the night watchmen that took place during the Wars of Independence. For now, however, I turn to other routine expressions of resistance against the patrolmen.

Mockery and Insults

The nightly logbooks dating from 1794, 1796, and 1798 provide very brief documentation for twenty-six incidents of verbal attacks on the night watchmen, labeled in Spanish as *palabras injuriosas* (harmful words), *provocando*, or *maltrata de palabras* (verbal mistreatment), or simply "insults." Additionally, a few longer investigations exist that provide more context. Almost 90 percent of the cases recording insults of any kind occurred during an arrest for drunkenness. Some also involved destruction of the guards' clothing or equipment. On rare occasions, the brief log entries specify exactly what the arrested individuals wanted to communicate to the guards, filling a few sparse details of the popular complaints that plebeians directed toward the serenos. Adding these incidents of targeted spoken objections to cases of smashing lanterns, ripping the night watchmen's clothes, damaging the other items that they carried, and more general resistance suggests that the street patrols on average faced some kind of verbal or physical challenge every week of their existence in the viceregal era.

In this historical time and place, certain "fighting words" directly signified challenges to a sereno's masculine honor.[27] People spoke these specific insults purposefully to spark a violent reaction—an honorable man could not walk away from such words without responding, or he would risk his reputation. While the night watchmen typified the kind of working-class man claiming Spanish descent who might react strongly to public verbal attacks on his honor, the serenos knew they might face repercussions from their superiors, and even have to pay for health care and damages, if they physically assaulted their custodies. Their status differed from that of alcaldes, who had more direct judicial authority. These volunteers had a much more elevated social status and possessed a stronger grasp on the classic markers of honor, including demonstrable wealth, Christian lineage without the "taint" of African or Indigenous ancestry (limpieza de sangre), and service to the Crown. Given their occupation, the serenos could not respond appropriately according to the high emotional and reputational stakes inherent to plebeian understandings of honor. One night watchman did pursue a case, suggesting that these men did feel the expected sense of dishonor in common with other men of their class under these circumstances. Guard number 23, Manuel Villavicencio, requested the arrest of a man described as a *pardo libre*, aged forty-five, and a mestiza woman aged twenty-five, because these two called Villavicencio's mother and sisters *putas*. The guard said these insults happened because he had killed two neighborhood dogs the previous night. During their arrest, the woman denied saying these words, but the man resisted. The judge apparently sympathized with Villavicencio's accusation and sentenced the man to eight days in the stocks and the mestiza to twenty-five lashes.[28]

The surviving dockets record additional details regarding the words exchanged in only seven other examples of maltratando de palabras. From these cases, it is possible to learn something about why certain individuals hated about the night watchmen and the context of the verbal attacks. The dominant complaint voiced against the serenos was that they were thieves, a common and very serious insult under all circumstances.[29] For example, early in 1798, a drunk (borracho) fifty-year-old man labeled *morisco* and his "bebida" twenty-five-year-old india companion had an encounter with guard number 83, who most likely regarded himself as of Spanish descent, at 9:30 p.m. The woman called the guard a thief.[30] A Spaniard made the same accusation to guard number 48, also probably a putative Spaniard, in September of 1796.[31] Two 1798 cases of insulting the guards involved perpetrators labeled as indios. One twenty-three-year-old Indigenous man told a corporal that a night watchman stole his *burros*.³² Later in the year, some dogs attacked guard number 30, resulting in words and blows exchanged with another young man labeled indio.³³ As seen above with the dishonorable slander directed at the female relatives of guard number 23, the "dog catching" role seemed among the duties causing serious dissatisfaction among Mexico City residents.³⁴ Not surprisingly, the court that prosecuted arrests made during the nocturnal patrols did not appreciate these public insults. The punishment meted out to a fifty-year-old Indigenous carpenter, who was taken into custody at midnight in June of 1796, for "scandalous intoxication and scandalizing his neighbors" demonstrates that the justice system took insults seriously. Although he claimed the scandal was nothing more than a fight with his wife, this individual received a sentence of six days' forced labor, a longer punishment than typical, probably motivated by the fact that he called the night watchman "thieves."³⁵

The scribes took the time to record detailed profane insults in two cases, which clearly demonstrate the disdain that some Mexico City residents had for the serenos. In one of the longest descriptions written down in a nightly logbook, the notary in charge of recording nocturnal arrests by the serenos used up three pages describing an exchange of insults with two women labeled as españolas.³⁶ Fully debunking the myth of enclosed and guarded Spanish femininity, the scribe observed that the younger woman, a "doncella [girl or woman with a reputation for sexual chastity]" aged seventeen, "even went so far as to utter obscene words," directed at corporal number three and guards 27 and 29. These night watchmen found Catarina Gutiérrez and her thirty-eight-year-old companion, a widow named Rosa Flórez, loitering on the Calle de la Joya at two in the morning. During her arrest, Gutiérrez tore the corporal's cloak. After the guards removed her from the streets, she continued resisting by agitating the other women held in the jail that night. She admitted that she had drunk a very small amount of pulque while offering a toast to a priest, but her companion Flórez denied drinking at all, saying that she was sick and taking medicine. Gutiérrez denied that she had ripped the corporal's cloak or agitated the other women prisoners but did admit that "hecho carajos en esta cárcel contra los guardas." This insult could mean that the guards turned them into "dicks" in the jail, or that they "damned" them by taking them to jail. As a result of this exchange, the authorities "examined each women's life," a common paternalistic statement in these records, and then set them free with no further consequences other than a warning. A final example of specific insulting words archived in a maltratando de palabras incident took place just after midnight in June 1798, when one of the patrols arrested a Spanish woman and a mestizo man in their twenties while they were gambling and drinking in a vinatería. When the arresting official referred to the corregidor, the vinatero said that he should go to hell and later insulted the scribe who logged the arrests as a "fucking thief and a gambler."[37]

It is worth noting the racial labels used to describe these women—all of the perpetrators appeared as of Spanish descent and fluent in Castilian curses. While only a handful of cases provide specifics regarding how precisely plebeians insulted the guards or the context of the lashing out, almost all of the examples of maltrando de palabras provide a race label for those who delivered the insults. Similar to breaking the guards' lanterns, some of these verbal attacks involved couples, resulting in a total of thirty-two different people, including nine women, documented as insulting the night watchmen, in twenty-six separate incidents. Also similar to the lantern-smashing events, about a quarter of the culprits claimed the race label español or española. Only twelve, or 37.5 percent, were inscribed in the logbooks as indios. At least in terms of the total record for these infractions, this evidence suggests that individuals of Indigenous ancestry leaned more toward lantern smashing than name calling. It is worth speculating that perhaps the guards did not understand if they were being insulted in Nahuatl or other Indigenous languages spoken in Mexico City. The remaining offenders were described in the logbooks as mestizos or mestizas. The use of Spanish words as weapons against the serenos and the regime that they represented makes sense as an offense committed by those with fluency in the language and culture, while smashing the guards' equipment perhaps expresses a much deeper rage that transcended verbalization. As far as can be determined for verbal attacks on the guards, it seems that all of the targets were Spaniards, so again, palabras injuriosas signify a more general rejection of the guards as authority figures, not an opportunity to disparage individual watchmen with Indigenous or African heritage.

A special class of mild verbal affronts, which could escalate dramatically, fits under the category of *chanceando* or *mofando*, loosely meaning mocking, teasing, and the like, between men. As noted by Lipsett-Rivera, this kind of manly joking commonly contributed to men's social bonding in the eighteenth century but could very quickly result in unfunny insults or even violence.[38] In the seven recorded incidents of *hacer chanzas* with the night watchmen, the men who used this excuse often put the blame on someone else. Despite this feeble effort at self-defense, the perpetrators almost always faced repercussions of eight days' forced labor on public works projects, or time spent locked in the stocks.[39] *Chanceadores* usually had the race label indio, or another designation indicating that they were not viewed as of full European ancestry. Youth and intoxication typically created the conditions leading to these men lashing out at the night watchmen. For example, an Indigenous man, borracho and aged twenty-three, admitted to "teasing" guard number 23 but blamed his wife for the alleged act of throwing the patrolman's whistle. The judge did not find this excuse compelling and sentenced him to eight days' forced labor.[40] Another case of chanceando involved a similar culprit who received the same rather harsh punishment. In this case, the mockery involved grabbing guard number 28's lantern and running away. The perpetrator described the incident as just a joke played on a friend.[41] The same exact excuse came up when two young men, labeled mestizo and indio, joked with guard number 89 as he tried to light his lantern, causing him to fall off his ladder.[42] Chanceando might turn into a full-blown brawl, as a young man labeled morisco found out when he started mocking guard number 2, which led to a fight. Before the head guard showed up, several other guards (the exact number is not given) joined in on beating up the man. Despite the physical attack, as per usual, this alleged culprit received a sentence of eight days in the stocks.[43] In only one incident did the judge decide to just release the chanceadores with a warning, and in this case a woman was involved. The perpetrators, labeled as mestizos in their early twenties, claimed "that they were only fooling around and did not mistreat the guard."[44] Surprisingly, this time the excuse worked.

As the potential for political revolt increased, incidents continued where the populace boldly mocked and rejected the institution of the guarda faroleros. On occasion, the insults went far enough to warrant a more thorough investigation. In this era, the authorities' statements started to have a whining tone that conveys a sense of hopelessness regarding the effectiveness of the serenos. After an episode that took place on the night of October 20, 1806, the Mariscal of Castilla pleaded with Viceroy Iturigarray with the following words: "Through this petition, I hope that it pleases Your Excellency to proceed in such a way that rewards the miserable night watchmen, so that from now on they will not suffer injuries, and they will be able to carry out their duties."[45] Guard number 56, a fifty-three-year-old single man named José Carranco, explained the events that led up to this official request. While standing at his post on the Calle de Polilla (very close to his own abode), he observed two women and a boy leave a dance after 4 a.m. The boy screamed out, mocking the night watchmen's mantra, "11:30 and all is calm [sereno]!" Carranco became enraged and struck the boy with his weapon. The word used in this investigation was *garrote*, although the guards' weapon was usually referred to as a chuzo. In this case, a garrote was identified within the pages of this file as the weapon that the guards used to kill dogs. In response to Carranco's violence, the women started shouting and grabbing Carranco's sleeves, causing a struggle that attracted the attention of don Antonio Martínez, an ensign in the Querétaro dragoons, one of the provincial militias. Martínez saw the conflict from the balcony of the dance hall, exited, and began beating Carranco, wrenching away his weapon and finally grabbing him by the hair and dragging him to the nearby headquarters of another infantry regiment. Martínez shouted the favorite accusation against men of his occupation, "you little thieving sereno, why would you want to steal these women's kerchiefs?" As they passed by a woman known by the nickname La Chispas (possibly a reference to a blanket that she wore, or translatable as "sassy," as well as the modern word for chocolate chips), she began slapping and insulting Carranco.[46]

Of course the three witness who spoke, including Martínez, La Chispas, and the two women, presented the incident very differently, although they agreed that a child had mocked the classic cry of the time and sereno. All of them alleged that they interpreted Carranco's violence as the actions of a thief trying to steal the women's headscarves. La Chispas said she even heard the victim cry out "He is killing me for my kerchief!" When asked, "Why did you not realize that this man was a sereno, when it was obvious from the halberd that they always carry, and their lantern?" all the witness responded that Carranco carried no symbols of his occupation whatsoever, even though they had previously said that he had beaten the boy with his garrote or pike. In his testimony, Martínez stated his anger clearly: "Because [Carranco] was one of the watchmen known as serenos, this attack should be punished with more determination than if another person had committed it."[47] The account went on to say: "In terms of young boys, as innocents of minor age, [the guards] do not have the right to punish them more than their own parents or judges."[48] However, in this case, Viceroy Iturrigarray agreed that all the witnesses knew that Carranco served as a night watchmen, and they also knew that he did not intend to steal from them but just reacted to the boy's mockery. As a result, the complainants had to pay all court costs, including five pesos for Carranco's damages.

This case sums up what the public saw in the patrolmen. While they did not wear clothing that looked like a uniform, everyone could recognize them based on their chuzo and lantern; they had limitations on acting forcibly, especially with minors; and they should not receive any kind of favoritism from higher levels of the judicial infrastructure. On the negative side, the serenos quickly became subjects of children's mockery, while military officials viewed themselves as superior to the men who earned their meager pay by standing on the barely lighted streets all night long. This case of taunting a night watchman with a rude version of his classic call might also fit into an offense more loosely labeled as *provocando*, or provoking the guards, recorded eight times in the *Libros de Reos*.

A case of provocation from 1803 adds more information about widely held negative perceptions of the guards. At 7 p.m. on a mid-October evening, José Manuel García stood passing the time smoking with his immediate superior, Sergeant José Apolinario Guevara, on guard at the Palace Bridge (Puente de Palacio).[49] García heard the cry "Sereno!" and saw a "decent-looking man wrapped up in a cape," with another man in his custody. The man with the cape, later identified as don Gabriel Miñón, ordered García to take his captive to the nearest jail. García responded, "On whose orders?" Miñón responded, "My orders." García continued the debate, answering, "And who are you to give me orders?" To this, Miñón said, "Your Grace should know who I am . . . if you did, you would stop talking to me with that cigar in your mouth." Miñón then asked García what his number was, and García said, "My sergeant is right here, ask him." At this, Miñón had enough, and called the guard a *pícaro* (rogue) and struck him with enough force to cause his cigar to fly out of his mouth.[50]

Miñón offered a slightly different take on the conflict, presenting himself grandly as a second lieutenant in the Crown infantry, very willing to show his official insignia, and, on the night in question, only trying to save an abused woman. Miñón said he witnessed a man beating a woman passed out on the ground, so he grabbed the man and looked for the nearest guard to escort him to jail. Miñón claimed that García told the culprit, "Don't worry about this, I will set you free." Miñón also said he did not trust the patrolman or his sergeant, so he felt obliged to walk with them to the jail. When questioned as to why he hit García, Miñón explained that the insolent conversation specifically goaded his anger. He also opined that smoking looked very slack for a night watchman on duty.[51]

In closing out this investigation, the authorities pronounced that both sides could not possibly exercise an unbiased perspective in their accounts. It was true that the guard knew the arrested man for many years—after all García policed his own neighborhood. On the other hand, Miñón did lash out excessively. However, both García and his sergeant had spoken rudely to a gentleman. The title "don" indicates that Miñón was their social superior. The judicial official investigating the case took the opportunity to deride and chastise all of the night watchmen in his final summary:

The corregidor should try to determine a proper way for [night watchmen] to behave on all occasions, without using rude words or expressions, and precisely following their regulations. The truth is that among this kind of people, such conversations are very frequent, along with other crude and arrogant expressions. All of the lantern guards should receive instruction on how to behave, because, due to their lack of prudence and disrespect to the people with whom they deal, they cause many disagreements. The sergeant and the guard, and others in their class, should behave at all times with courtesy, attentiveness, and good manners, without using rude words or expressions, exactly according to their particular regulations.[52]

Here again, traditional class hierarchies continued to outweigh the effectiveness of street patrols staffed by nonelite men. If working as a lantern guard offered some hope of moving beyond plebeian social status, both the serenos' behavior and the official reaction to it certainly proved this to be an impossible ambition. The night watchmen stood out from the poor residents whom they took into custody but also failed to fit in with any socially superior group due to their low pay, general appearance, and the physical tasks inherent to their occupation.[53] Adding to the confusion, the founding documents for the guarda faroleros do not offer a code of conduct. As discussed in the first three chapters of this book, their stated duties focused on maintaining the lanterns, and removing "evildoers/criminals [malhechores]" from the streets.[54] No formal regulations addressed their demeanor in public. As noted above, suppressing any reaction whatsoever to personal and aggressive insults contradicted basic societal expectations for how an honorable working-class man should publicly defend his reputation. The idea that any policing corps needed to maintain a much higher standard of behavior than their fellow plebeians and lifelong neighbors, for instance by restraining themselves from swearing or other standard practices in casual speech, continued to cause conflicts well into the twentieth century. The very presence of an unwelcome new patrol inspired the populace to watch out for the guards, noting their every annoying habit. A few decades later, in London, people grew angry and complained at minor points of behavior etiquette such as bobbies walking together and blocking the sidewalk or speaking loudly to each other.[55] Confusing, informal, but strict behavior expectations also conflicted with internal approaches to communal bonding.

Resisting Arrest

Throughout their three decades on the street, the night watchmen never had an easy time making arrests. Keep in mind that, on average, each sereno in a sense had jurisdiction over, at the very least, one thousand people (under one hundred guards, for a city with well over one hundred thousand residents), although of course they focused their patrols on the central city. This ratio signifies far less surveillance than any large city in the nineteenth century. London had at least three times as many bobbies per person.[56] In other late eighteenth-century cities such as Paris, whose militarized law enforcement had a much longer history than Mexico and was reputed as the most invasive in the Atlantic world at this time, guards always had to remember that their every act might provoke a riot amongst the masses who surrounded them. Parisian guardsmen faced a recalcitrant population who felt no obligation to obey their commands. In this sense, patrolmen had to take care to arrest only those whose neighbors wanted them arrested; otherwise, they would face violent resistance.[57]

As noted in chapter 2, the fact that they had to carry a lantern and a halberd or pike, which occupied both of their hands, prevented them from effectively walking back to their headquarters while restraining an individual in their custody. The guards took it upon themselves to reject the chuzo as a useless weapon. No records suggest that they carried guns or had access to firearms, although the militarization of the city meant that nearby militia and cavalry patrols often helped during conflicts with their own guns and even cannons. In the viceregal era, many plebeians carried knives and daggers, but almost never guns, so the civilian patrols did not appear to see a need for firearms either. No records confirm that they had their personal knives on their person while at work, a common habit of men of this era. The serenos' limited use of weapons and lack of guns fit with the history of policing in the United States, where the police began carrying their personal pistols after this became a normal practice across the citizenry, decades after the era described in this book. In locations such as Philadelphia and Baltimore, mid-nineteenth-century police bought guns on their own, at their chief's orders, because of fatalities caused by civilians' guns. In Chicago, New York, and Boston, patrolmen carried their personal guns as shooting became more common while they attempted arrests.[58]

Judging by many examples, Mexico City plebeians were not inclined to comply with the guards' authority when they attempted an arrest. Numerous examples prove this attitude. In this section I concentrate on actions that show either a symbolic rejection of the judicial system more broadly or a personal dispute with one particular guard. These conflicts add to the tally of widespread resistance, alongside the previously discussed acts of lantern-smashing and public insults. Not including the lantern-smashing incidents, the *Libros de Reos* record twenty-three examples of destroying the guards' equipment or clothes and at least twenty more examples of resisting arrest by physical attacks on the serenos.[59]

A wide range of Mexico City residents resisted arrest and faced different consequences depending on their race, occupation, and the circumstances of their encounter with the night watchmen. The first recorded example of the specific infraction of resisting arrest took place in 1794, when a drunk Spanish soldier fought back against the head guard and guard number 75.[60] Most likely this individual could retreat behind his military judicial privileges, a common tactic used by soldiers. Other men also avoided harsh punishments because of their privileged status, as seen in the case of a forty-five-year-old Spaniard who resisted guard number 86, who took him into custody for loitering on the street at three in the morning.[61] The man protested that he had just returned from his work as a barber and found his door locked. The court examined his "life and habits," and finding him blameless, set him free with a warning.

The outcome of this incident contrasts with another which took place the very same week. Two twenty-five-year-old women, labeled a castiza and an india, allegedly insulted and threw rocks at the guards who arrested one of their husbands for public defecation (*ensuciandose*). The women only admitted to requesting that the guards not drag them by their hair or beat them, but still they received twenty-five lashes for their insubordination.[62] This was eight times less than the mandated number of lashes according to the founding documents and regulations for the guarda faroleros, which stated that anyone who took up arms against the guards could be given two hundred lashes.[63] The proposed punishments were modified in the case of Spanish culprits or minors under twenty-five. Both kinds of perpetrators should serve three years of forced labor at the fortifications of San Juan de Ulúa. Of course, women could not receive this last punishment, even though—because they commonly earned their income by working at various street-based occupations—women numbered among the most likely to oppose the new street patrols.

Plebeian women often resisted arrest and otherwise demonstrated their disdain for the night watchmen and the judicial system. Women tended to fight against the serenos when they faced arrest in a group. Rarely can we know their motivations, but an example from 1798 specified that one thirty-year-old Indigenous woman resisted arrest "because she had small children."[64] She and her companion, a younger man labeled indio, received the harsh punishment of twenty-five lashes, far beyond the norm for a simple public intoxication offense (they were described as borrachos). After serving eight days in jail, the judge ordered her to serve in "an honorable house," a classic paternalistic punishment in this era. A similar sentence applied to a twenty-year-old Indigenous woman was released into the custody of her husband, a man given the honorary title of "don," when she slapped guard number 64 and loudly resisted going to the jail.[65]

Some plebeian men and women acted in a way that possibly suggests a more general rejection of the viceregal system for punishing petty crimes. When guard number 54 tried to arrest four drunk people labeled indios, partying along with one Spaniard, and all ranging from age eighteen to forty, one of them attempted to free the others.[66] This resistance resulted in his confinement in shackles, even though normally it seems that the night watchmen did not use any restraints during arrests. A twenty-year-old Indigenous woman received twelve lashes for disturbing a group of men sentenced to forced labor, in this case sweeping.[67] With the help of this woman, the shackled men released themselves and went out to drink pulque with her. Another general melee with the guards took place when four Indigenous men and a man labeled mulato started a fight with a sereno, which may have had some connection to refusing to take off their hats for a passing military patrol, or may have just resulted from a domestic conflict. The very same night, an Indigenous woman received a beating from a guard because she tried to prevent him from arresting her eighteen-year-old sister for "scandalous insolence."[68] Lastly, two Indigenous women, aged twenty-five, attempted to release a man from the stocks, resulting in them both receiving twenty-five lashes, and no further access to the jail or the area near the stocks.[69] Two decades later, groups continued to resist arrest, as seen in a brawl that took place in a café at 10:15 one night in 1815. The owner of the café insulted a corporal and the guards, causing three more serenos to show up to defend their own.[70] Three people left the café that night with injuries. All these incidents suggest a general "us versus them" attitude between individuals labeled indios and the night watchmen.

The *Libros de Reos* testify to the struggles involved in taking an individual into custody. Women acting in a group or alone on occasion physically attacked the night watchmen. For example, an Indigenous woman punched an unnamed guard one night while she was out drinking with two male friends.[71] In early 1796 guard number 76 became embroiled in a family conflict with three women attacking him as he intervened in a domestic dispute.[72] At ten in the evening, José Mariano Vanegas, a forty-year-old coachman labeled mulato, left a vinatería near his house. Vanegas often drank to excess, and the court authorities knew him as a repeat offender. Before he arrived home, he shouted at his wife, they began arguing in the street, and she called for the sereno. His teenage daughter and niece came out to take part in the dispute. When guard number 76 confronted the group, arresting Vanegas for public drunkenness, all of four members of the family beat up the patrolman and tore his shirt, resulting in damages of two reales. Perhaps sympathetic to the issues of a drunk family patriarch, the judge set all the women (who could claim descriptions marking them as decent, sheltered women: a wife and two *doncellas*) free, but sentenced Vanegas to six days' forced labor.

When resisting arrest occurred in a group setting, the underlying popular sentiments against the night watchmen simmer just below the surface, as can be seen in a rather mysterious conflict that took place at 8:30 p.m. in 1795.[73] Unfortunately, only a few pages testify to what happened this evening, but in essence guard number 76, a twenty-six-year-old married man of Spanish descent named José María Pastrana Martínez, accused a Castilian Spaniard, Francisco Barras, of preventing the sereno from taking an intoxicated Indigenous man into his custody. The conflict took place in the doorway of a tienda/vinatería, a store that also sold hard liquor, in the Plaza del Volador, just south of the viceregal palace. Two other night watchmen came to aid Martínez as the arrested man resisted. Guard number 75, don Antonio Jurado (the only sereno with this honorific on record), testified that he had to hold the lanterns of the other two while they attempted to control the inebriated man, supporting their assertion that they had too much in their hands to effectively control anyone on the street. Barras, the owner of the vinatería, grabbed the arrestee out of the guards' custody, allegedly something he made a habit of doing. The accused vinatero told a very different story, claiming that an unknown priest had come inside the tavern, protesting the arrest, and told the guards that the man in custody was not drunk. Barras explained that he just wanted everyone out of his establishment, which led to his own arrest. As the investigation continued, it seemed that a crowd of people had tried to free the prisoner, then this group had run away, and no one could figure out what had happened. With the competing statements, and the lack of confirmed information on who helped the arrested man resist, this case was rapidly dismissed.

Judicial scribes recorded other kinds of physical confrontations experienced by the night watchmen when they met with resistance.[74] These could range from biting to stone-throwing, although the most common term used was "dar un bofetón [to give a slap]."[75] The guards risked bites, blows, pitchers broken on their heads, and stones when they inserted themselves in domestic disputes involving husbands, wives, and children.[76]

Men not surprisingly objected to guards grabbing their wives and often explained away their shouting matches with their wives as nothing more than spousal conflicts, implying this activity should not involve the patrolmen. With a lack of other weapons on hand, individuals in custody did resort to biting or whatever other way they could cause some pain. One inebriated woman caused a scandal during her arrest but did not harm anyone until she reached the door of the jail, when she bit the porter.[77] One of the most fascinating physical attacks on the night watchmen involved a mule used by a twenty-five-year-old Indigenous man who sold coal. Allegedly, this young man caused his mule to spill his load of coal onto a nearby guard who was sitting on the street cleaning his lantern. The accused perpetrator denied blame, saying that the animal had just experienced a scare. The guard actually suffered injuries that required medical attention.[78]

So far this chapter has discussed incidents of lantern-smashing and examples from the *Libros de Reos* that mention a clear act of resistance or use a form of the verb *resistir*. Another twenty-three incidents stand apart from these—clashes in which the intoxicated perpetrator specifically damaged an article of the guards' clothing, weapons, or equipment. All these examples include destructive acts, but not a broken lantern or glass. Adding together the two kinds of property damage (lantern smashing plus harm done to other objects/clothes) results in a total of ninety-six incidents from three scattered years of records, which supports the theory that the night watchmen experienced ongoing, low-level rejection of their authority. It is possible to speculate on change-over-time in terms of these attacks. While the most examples of lantern smashing peak at thirty-two in 1798, that year, the only one with somewhat complete surviving nightly dockets, only records five examples of other property damage.[79] This suggests that over time, perpetrators chose a form of resistance, smashing lanterns, that had the more dramatic effect of extinguishing the serenos' ability to surveil the streets. Over one-third of the destruction of property targeted the night watchmen's capes, probably just because this article of clothing was the easiest-to-grab item on the guards' bodies.[80] Another easily accessible and easily damaged item was the serenos' shirts. Both the chuzo and the ladders carried in order to access streetlights did not inspire much destructive rage, with only a handful of incidents on record of attacks on these items. It is worth emphasizing that over twenty-four times as many confrontations led to broken glass and lanterns, versus damage to the guards' only weapon. This could derive from the basic satisfaction of smashing glass on the cobblestones, the ease of breaking a lantern versus a heavy pike, or the fact that destroying the serenos' lantern actually made him unable to do his job at all. Like lantern-smashing, perpetrators labeled indio committed around half of the attacks on the guards' clothes and other equipment. As per usual, twenty of the acts of property damage took place in the context of a drinking binge. Some of the incidents involved intoxication described as "scandalous," which in this context appears to mean causing a public disturbance, not a sexually illicit tone. Unusual for this era of Mexican history, two of the perpetrators were labeled *negro* or "Black."

This chapter has narrated different kinds of attacks on the lantern guards, suggesting that both guards and plebeians lived through a highly charged, contested, and violent status quo on the streets of the viceregal capital in the last thirty years of New Spain's existence. Injuries and even fatalities continued as the night watchmen and the military men based in Mexico City fought each other on the urban streets. While none of these incidents necessarily blew up into the kinds of street riots seen in contemporary Europe, they do signify ongoing resistance to a new form of law enforcement.

CHAPTER 7

The Night Watchmen, the Military, and Insurgency

> At 10:30 p.m., guard number 49 berated a man [whom he encountered] sitting in a doorway, acting a bit drunk. When told to go home, the man stood up, and insulted the guard with insolent words. He then slapped the guard, causing the guard's hat to fall off, and it was irretrievably lost. A military patrol [passed by the jail after] this man was taken there and the sergeant said [that the arrested man] was in the militia, so he was transferred into their custody.
> —Ramón de la Rosa y Serrada, November 10, 1799

The serenos outlasted the viceregal era, but they faced persistent violent resistance, which accelerated in the 1810s during a decade of widespread violent revolt. Ranking as the lowest-level agents in the unsuccessful viceregal conquest over urban darkness, we have seen how the Mexico City night watchmen often lost their nocturnal skirmishes with city denizens who viewed themselves as free to enjoy the night however they wished.[1] As well as these civilian carousers, another group of armed men also practiced government-sanctioned violence and presented a very dangerous foe for serenos: military patrols and soldiers off duty and roaming the city streets at night, even well before the mass independence movement began in 1810.[2] In every one of these clashes, the soldiers clearly viewed the lantern guards as their inferiors and rejected the serenos' authority over them with sometimes fatal violence. This final chapter examines three decades of conflict between the night watchmen and the military, closing out the story of the viceregal lantern guards in the waning years of the viceroyalty of New Spain and beyond, into the first year of Agustín de Iturbide's brief reign as a homegrown emperor.[3] Although Mexico

City did not experience the battles seen in other regions of New Spain, clashes with both civilians and soldiers complicate how the capital city both reacted to and participated in the insurgent struggle.[4]

From the first moments after Tenochtitlán's defeat and throughout the centuries of colonial rule, military, church, and administrative personnel converged in Mexico City. When the populace did threaten to riot, these leaders temporarily forgot their differences and quickly reacted to any disturbances or even rumors of conspiracies, most notably in 1608–1612 and 1692.[5] Despite the food shortages and epidemics of the eighteenth century, food-based riots did not take place after 1700 in the capital, which maintained its status as a stable, wealthy, growing metropolis, with a global influence due to New Spain's massive silver exports.[6] It is therefore no surprise that the popular, armed phase of insurgency concentrated not in the court city of the viceroy but in other regions, such as the Bajío, where Father Miguel de Hidalgo y Costilla gathered his mass following. Still, discontent percolated within the city, and the night watchmen, with their connection to the viceregal state, came to represent easy targets for antigovernment sentiments. The first clashes between the serenos and the soldiers who they encountered on their nightly rounds began in the 1790s and heightened steadily, in small, anecdotal ways. These conflicts contributed to the lasting fissures that ultimately brought down New Spain. While always highly charged and brutal, only very late in the independence struggle did these quarrels between the night watchman and the military escalate to murder.

These disputes between the two different groups of armed men happened as direct consequences of efforts to expand the number of troops in New Spain, as well as an increase in military judicial privileges enjoyed by soldiers. Motivated by defeats during the Seven Years' War, Spanish rulers strove to militarize their American empire, which had previously largely depended on poorly disciplined local militias, other than in important ports. Viceroys in the mid-eighteenth century viewed the New Spanish militias as hopelessly undertrained, virtually unequipped, and utterly lacking in structure and financial support. To address these shortcomings, the Army of New Spain increased from around three thousand regulars in 1758 to close to thirty thousand militiamen and professional soldiers in 1810.[7] Over one-third of these men were stationed on the coasts or far to the north. Numerous towns, including Puebla and Veracruz, had their own regiments or battalions. These provincial militiamen also spent time in Mexico City and appear in altercations with the lantern guards. Several different categories of professional soldiers also caused legal problems in the capital. These included infantrymen, cavalry, and *dragones* (dragoons), who combined using horses with fighting on foot. Another regiment known as "del comercio [of commerce]" existed in Mexico City, supported by guilds and staffed by local tradesmen.[8]

As militarization increased, the armed forces became ever more problematic for the city's basic street-level law enforcement. From the 1790s to the end of the viceregal era, judicial and governmental authorities wrote in a pleading, almost pathetic way when they urged military leaders to compel their troops to respect the guarda faroleros. The problem derived from a fundamental policy that caused much judicial disruption in this era: as the number of soldiers increased, the military received more royally supported benefits. Most importantly, if they had an interaction with the night watchmen, soldiers avoided judicial repercussions because of their fuero militar, their privilege to judgment by a military court, a classic ancien régime perk also enjoyed by the clergy and at least two dozen other protected occupational groups. Some historians have posited that the fuero might have attracted individuals who anticipated that they would face conflicts with the judiciary and wanted to ensure their own impunity.[9] Thus, the fuero helped recruitment and fed into ideas of military honor whereby one man's prosecution for any given offense dishonored their entire regiment or battalion. Soldiers, with a communal sense that they constituted "a class apart," took full advantage of the situation, leading to a total disregard for civil and criminal law, undermining local authorities from the street patrolmen on up the ranks, even to the level of disregarding the "very foundations of royal authority." While military men viewed their fuero as absolute, or applicable in all cases, in fact they lost their fuero if they violated municipal regulations or disrespected civil magistrates. However, no one in the judiciary could enforce this technicality. And while the serenos could arrest a militiaman, they had to turn him over to a military officer and make an official report of the case within one day. The soldiers' scofflaw attitudes, supported by their superiors, led to many expressions of intense frustration from the serenos and their leadership.[10]

Ironically, this antagonism escalated even though night watchmen themselves often had a military background and, albeit unwillingly, shared the task of state-building from the ground level up.[11] But in other important ways, the two types of armed men differed greatly. For example, police (even in the rudimentary form of the serenos) live permanently where they patrol, while soldiers often have temporary assignments in a locale. In this case, the night watchmen lived near their beats and thus it behooved them to watch out for their own reputations.[12]

Initial Incidents—the 1790s

Relations between soldiers and the new patrols started off very badly, going back to May 1790, when Viceroy Revillagigedo had yet to codify the link between the guards' lantern-lighting and law enforcement duties. At this time, the night watchmen did not yet have preassigned numbered patrol areas. Instead of referring to them by number, documentation dating to this time refers to them as either guardaserenos or guardapitos ("whistle guards," relating to their role in Old Castilian cities, as described in chapter 1). A case file was opened that year when Viceroy Revillagigedo demanded an investigation of the events leading to the incarceration of an infantryman affiliated with a provincial militia regiment based in Mexico City.[13] This militiaman, named Rafael Vargas, ended up in jail and suffering from wounds inflicted by a man referred to as the guardasereno Miguel Rubio. According to another guard, named Vicente Isidoro Cristal, the violence began when he encountered some *paisanos* (a term defined as "laborers, villagers" in this era, but perhaps with other slang connotations in the capital city)[14] fighting at 10:30 p.m. Approaching the brawl, he saw Vargas beat a man only known as "El Tinoso" to the ground with a blow to the mouth. Cristal signaled for two other guards to help him, and they started leading Vargas and "El Tinoso" to jail. As they crossed the Puente de Jesús, Cristal testified that Vargas fell to the ground, appearing dead from the beating given by a sereno. Other guards who testified explained that the militiaman resisted arrest, struggled with the night watchmen, and called them "thieving dogs," eventually escaping and running into a group of men and women passing by on horseback. The serenos then managed to force Vargas to the ground with their lances. The guards began to fight among themselves, leading to intervention by a military sergeant and four more soldiers, who broke up the conflict with their bayonets.[15]

Of course, statements made by witnesses from the military presented a different series of events, emphasizing the night watchmen as threatening and violent. Shortly after Vargas fell, a rampant rumor circulated through the night that "a guardasereno had killed a man."[16] One of the sergeants from the injured man's regiment conjured up an image of the night watchmen as an angry group of "many lanterns," who grabbed Vargas by his braided ponytail and shoved him around before throwing him to the ground by hooking a lance around his neck. This treatment qualified as a serious assault. While the wounds Vargas suffered on his hands and head healed well, the neck wound festered for three weeks after the attack. Vargas himself confirmed these details, adding an account of the conversation that took place before his beating. According to his statement, Vargas and a few friends (the aforementioned El Tinoso and another man known only as "El Chillo") were fighting, when a patrolman approached and asked:

> "What's this?"
> Vargas replied, "Nothing sir."
> To this, the sereno said: "I didn't ask you, shut your mouth."
> Vargas responded, "Then why are you here, do you want to calm or escalate this fight?"[17]

After this exchange, the guard took Vargas prisoner and attacked him with his lance. Vargas denied that he had insulted the guards by calling them thieves and dogs, although he did believe that one of them stole both his hat and sleeve, which had fallen off during the fight.[18] From this very early moment in the prehistory of the lantern guards in Mexico City, higher authorities did nothing to resolve already-existing tensions and easily inflamed violence. Six weeks after Vargas suffered his beating, all involved parties were released with nothing more than a warning to avoid behavior of this kind in future. The incident relationship between new efforts at law enforcement and military patrols had begun on a very unstable footing.

Less than a year later, another conflict with a militiaman erupted, and the inquiry into the events came before the corregidor Bernardo Bonavía.[19] Revillagigedo had instituted the lantern guards officially by this time, but the guard involved in this case, Juan García Solalinde, still worked as a cigarette roller during the daytime. Not surprisingly, he walked his beat feeling a great deal of fatigue. Perhaps in an effort to address this challenge, Solalinde patrolled on the night in question with his younger brother, a sixteen-year-old boy. Just after midnight, the younger Solalinde noticed a fight in progress in the Tepechichilco plazuela, instigated by a very drunk man named José Reumaldo Hernández. This man struggled as the brothers attempted to take him into custody. As they walked him past the busy pulquería de Viznaga, another man ran out to set the offender free, leading to a fight involving the guard's chuzo and a bystander's *belduque*, a long sharp knife, which caused minor injuries to the combatants. Although willing to admit his intoxication, Hernández denied the escape attempts and asserted that he served in the free pardo militia. The authorities confirmed this status with paperwork from his battalion. Due to this fact, Hernández enjoyed the fuero (even though allowing men of African descent this privilege had caused some debate as the militia expanded a few decades earlier). Ultimately, Hernández, despite his racial designation, did not have to face any consequences other than those imposed by his military superiors.[20]

These scattered cases testify to the tensions in the first years of the lantern guards' existence. Soon, frequent and highly charged nocturnal altercations documented the ongoing disruption caused by soldiers in Mexico City. Interactions with soldiers appear in twenty-nine, or just under 1 percent of the entries in the existing 1790s *Libros de Reos* entries. Frequently, the serenos clashed with military men over sex-related offenses, but fighting, drinking to excess, and other public disturbances also caused tensions between the two groups (see table 5).[21] The surviving dockets document a total of nine incidents involving soldiers in 1794, five in 1796, and fifteen in the much more complete records for 1798. Although this suggests a worsening situation, 1798 represents by far the most complete set of arrest records, meaning that it is entirely possible that the level of tension remained consistent throughout and may have been higher than the records from 1794 and 1796 suggest. Due to their fuero, the *Libros de Reos* never refer to the soldiers by name, in a notarial gesture to protect their honor and that of their regiment. As noted in table 5, all of these offenders left the custody of the lantern guards and went back to their military superiors to face punishment, other than in the case of the recidivist public drunk.

The protection of the fuero does not fully explain why so many of the entries mentioning anonymous soldiers in the *Libros de Reos* involve women. This repeated situation hints at how gender roles intersected with the legal system and the reforming tendencies of the era. Removing certain women from the streets, most likely for soliciting sex in public, did play a small but significant part in the general project of beautifying Mexico City's streets and efforts to impose what the Enlightened elite viewed as the correct social order.[22] While certainly the cases in table 5 suggest a bias toward criminalizing female sex workers, oftentimes the judgment involved a paternalistic attempt to integrate the younger women whom the serenos had found on the street into family structures. Due to the scribes' careful choice of wording, the alleged offense remains murky. However, it is clear that the judiciary viewed women or girls simply talking to a soldier as a suspicious situation deserving action.

While the 1790s *Libros de Reos* archive a range of minor street confrontations between soldiers and night watchmen, longer investigations from this decade narrate more drawn-out conflicts. These underscore that the privilege of the fuero militar gave soldiers the option of verbally and physically attacking the serenos with nearly total impunity. A 1796 incident involving a baker who was also an infantryman demonstrates this utter disregard for the night watchman's authority, as well as suggesting a vision of them as pliable personal servants. While race-related slurs

TABLE 5. Military men in the *Libros de Reos*

DATE	OFFENSE	ADDITIONAL DETAILS
8/16/1794	scandalous drunk	culprit is a blasphemer and militiaman
8/23/1794	inebriated	mulato soldier returned to his company
9/1/1794	public sex act	only the woman taken into custody
9/6/1794	inebriated	returned to his barracks
9/14/1794	inebriated	resisted arrest
9/17/1794	inebriated	insulted the guard
9/18/1794	inebriated	
11/2/1794	solicitation	only the woman taken into custody
11/6/1794	public sex act	only the woman taken into custody
1/21/1796	very drunk	"completely deprived of his senses"
2/19/1796	scandalous drunk	works as soldier and cigarette roller
7/1/1796	domestic abuse	turned into to his coronel
7/23/1796	with a fifteen-year-old girl	only the girl taken into custody
8/31/1796	drunk	turned into the militia coronel
2/17/1798	"embracing"	woman arrested only
2/27/1798	fighting in a tavern	dispute over gambling
3/4/1798	group drinking pulque	a grenadier owns the tavern
3/18/1798	"talking"	woman arrested only
4/17/1798	illicit relationship	
5/6/1798	illegal weapon/drinking	"formese causa"[1]
6/1/1798	fighting	a dispute over attacking a woman
7/27/1798	"with a woman"	only the woman taken into custody
8/15/1798	drinking	does not know the name of his regiment
10/19/1798	drunk	repeat offender, 15 days in stocks
10/25/1798	public sex act	only the woman taken into custody
11/2/1798	with a woman	only the woman taken into custody

11/12/1798	with a woman	only the woman taken into custody
11/25/1798	fighting	militiaman, not arrested
12/29/1798	talking to a woman	a group of soldiers at the bullring

1. Meaning that this case moved to a different court, which could be the *sala criminal*, or for judgment within the military courts.

did not come up in this investigation, it is worth noting that most of the guards involved described themselves as mestizos, while their attacker had a higher social rank as a Spaniard who could claim the honorific title of "don."[23] This incident also shows the rapidly developed esprit de corps of the lantern guards. They could count on their peers to defend them verbally and physically when they heard heated words exchanged with one of their compañeros. Whenever they saw a gathering of faroles, or hand lanterns, they would know that one of their own needed help and rush to fight beside them.[24]

At the instigation of Viceroy Branciforte, an interim corregidor questioned the night watchmen involved in the 1796 dispute. None of the testifying guarda faroleros knew his name, but later in the case the baker in question was identified as don José Soriano Montes de Oca, a cavalryman in the urban battalion.[25] One night in March, at nine-thirty, guard number 31, Leonardo Campos, heard shouts near the bakery on San Felipe Street. The baker, dressed in a military uniform and armed with a sword, called on Campos to help him arrest the *mayordomo* (foreman) of his bakery, an Indigenous man who had fled. The guard responded that he could not do such a thing without the order of a judge. He also pointed out that he had no idea what crime the mayordomo may have committed. The baker then began to insult Campos and threatened to run him through with his sword. Campos fought back with his chuzo. This loud altercation drew a number of other serenos to the scene, who reacted defensively when they heard that one of their own had been physically attacked. The group of night watchmen gathered and faced off with the baker who brandished his sword as if intending to injure them.

An alcalde appeared, along with Corporal Manuel José Bernal (discussed in the introduction). Bernal conferred with the baker inside his house and found out that he was enraged because the serenos would not give him the help that he demanded. After their conversation, the baker went outside again, leading to a scuffle and more insults. Words escalated to blows and calling the night watchmen thieves, the most common insult the guards received, but also serious fighting words in this era. Montes de Oca accused the serenos of steading his cape, which later they found in the possession of the fleeing mayordomo. The irate baker questioned Bernal, asking, "Who are you to arrest me?"[26] The baker's wife also entered the fray, slapping one of the guards in the face. The guards managed to impede Montes de Oca's movement and grab his sword by embracing him. Shortly after, a militia patrol came onto the scene and took the baker to their barracks. Unsurprisingly, Montes de Oca's abuse of the guards resulted in no repercussions or punishment, precisely because of his fuero militar.[27]

While these incidents sound like minor altercations between rival gangs, a conflict that took place in the fall of 1797 suggests that the antagonism between military men and the night watchmen occasionally escalated into street fights. In this case, at least six serenos fought with five soldiers, who assaulted them with both swords and guns.[28] Viceroy Branciforte urged military leadership to address the attitudes that caused this skirmish, initiating the investigation with the following words: "I notice, with displeasure, that frequent disputes take place between the [military] patrols and the lantern guards, who are carrying out duties that comply with my own authority. . . . You must inform your commanders that they must assist and protect the aforementioned guards who watch over [the city and] maintain the peace and public safety."[29] As in all of the statements made by civilian authorities cited in this chapter, the fact that the viceroy himself had to almost beg for obedience to his own law enforcing patrols, in effect to remind them who was actually in charge, did not bode well for the ultimate fate of the viceroyalty of New Spain.

This incident captures the violence simmering below the surface in a gendered society defined by traditional ideas of honor, where men went through their daily lives always poised to boil over at verbal insults.³⁰ Cases involving insulted honor frequently feature opposing and contradictory testimonies. In this altercation, the instigators emphasized different issues than the serenos and their superiors. At the same time, the military patrols involved presented another perspective. From their point of view, the course of events was straightforward. On the night of September 3, 1797, two men described as *hombres decentes* ("respectable men"—both received the honorific "don"), both around age thirty, returned home from the theater at 10 p.m. One of them worked overseeing a bakery and came to Mexico from Trias in Asturias, Spain. The other, don Úrbano Pedroso, served as a sergeant in the grenadier company affiliated with the "commerce regiment," known as such because prominent Mexico City merchants funded and staffed it. As the two men walked over the Puente de Leña toward home, two strangers approached, with their heads covered and concealed. One of the mysterious men said,

"There are some worthless men."

Don Úrbano and his friend responded, "Who do you think you are speaking to?"

Showing his weapon, the hooded man said, "Whoever we want."³¹

At this, don Úrbano hit both of the strangers with his saber, and he and his companion started to run away. At this moment, guard number 24 appeared and beat don Úrbano with his chuzo, which the sergeant then grabbed away from the sereno with the help of his friend, who threatened the guard with his sword. When more night watchmen ran up to defend their colleague, don Úrbano continued to fight them. Later on, he hid the confiscated chuzo in his house, where reportedly a group of serenos harassed him for it, pounding on the door and throwing rocks at the windows. Don Úrbano concluded his statement by urging the head guard to punish his men.³²

Don Úrbano's statement ignored several key facts that made him appear less honorable than he would have preferred. The head guard, José Moreno, stressed that don Úrbano and his friend had drunk excessively on the night in question and that Úrbano had a reputation for starting fights.³³ The five guards who witnessed the dispute reported that when guard number 24 went to retrieve his chuzo, don Úrbano again attacked the serenos with such fury, "blinded by rage," that a woman in his house tried to hold him back.[34] Additional grenadiers intervened in this dispute, leading to a dramatic escalation of the violence. Moreno said that the military men beat guard number 23, Manual Villavivencio, almost to death with the butts of their rifles. Some of the soldiers also destroyed the lantern held by guard number 24. Although no one sustained injuries as a result, the troops shot a gun during the brawl, causing the night watchmen to run and, in the case of Villavivencio, hide in an empty canoe.[35] The three grenadiers involved also testified, claiming that they came to the altercation because their superior had told them that two men died in the brawl, a false rumor. From their perspective, the initial fight was a "trifle," or a "chimera." As men of honor, they expressed their disdain for the guards who ran away.[36]

As a military superior investigated these events, it should come as no surprise that don Úrbano received the benefit of the doubt as an honorable man who enjoyed every right to defend himself by whatever means necessary. According to the file's final summary, the guards involved, however serious their injuries, should not have fled the scene and acted disrespectfully toward a military officer.[37] This case underscores that plebeian serenos did not stand a chance when violently engaging with an upper-class person. The tension and violence of these initial conflicts only escalated as the residents of Mexico City became more politicized in the years leading to mass insurgency.

Conflicts Escalate—the Early Nineteenth Century

Hostilities intensified between the night watchmen and the military in the early years of the nineteenth century. The head guards' concise nightly reports show an increasingly problematic military presence on the streets of the capital from 1799 to 1822 (see table 6).[38] More in-depth investigations also repeatedly confirm that men affiliated with the armed forces outright rejected any interference by the serenos or their leadership in their lives or property. For example, on September 9, 1800, a lieutenant of the watch named don Antonio Erescano faced strong resistance by José Villegas, a musician in the Mexico City militia, who absolutely rejected the purview of the night watchmen to intervene in his life in any way.[39] According to statements made by Erescano, two corporals, and sereno number 30, Villegas ran a vinatería on the corner of the streets called Venero and Mesones, about six blocks southwest of the viceroy's palace. Villegas kept his establishment open and active until almost midnight, selling food, pulque, and aguardiente. On the night in question, passersby could hear music from a *vihuela*, a late-medieval kind of Spanish guitar. Nightwalkers also glimpsed men costumed as dancers celebrating inside. The guards noticed these infractions for two nights in succession before they attempted to enter the tavern and eject the patrons. As the night watchmen approached the doorway, a soldier gestured for everyone inside to quiet down. Questioning the dancers about why they were in this house at such a late hour, the guards heard the simple response that they had gone there to drink some aguardiente after an outing to visit the shrine of the Virgin of Guadalupe. Erescano then sent Corporal José Manuel Bernal in to send the gathering home. As Bernal entered, Villegas came to the doorway and asserted that no one could enter his establishment, unless they were from the military. Villegas then called for his jacket, belt, and sword, which his servant brought to him. Lieutenant Erescano went into the house himself, provoking Villegas to respond with a scathing comment: "Your Grace, get out of here. No sereno will enter this house. . . . At night they exercise authority which they are not able to speak of in the daytime, when it is taken away from them. They are worthless."[40] As he put on his uniform and brandished his saber, Villegas's wife also continued to berate the night watchmen with similar disrespect, calling the lieutenant a "broken monkey, unworthy of taking her husband into custody alongside criminals."[41] The guards called for military backup the nearest bivouac in order to arrest Villegas.[42]

When the soldiers returned to the vinatería, they only found children sleeping. Villegas backed this up, and his statement repeats his disdain for the serenos:

On the night in question, [Villegas] says that he was in his house at 12:30 p.m. There he found a Black man named Fernando who plays the vihuela, and another paisano dressed as a dancer, whom the deponent knows by the nickname of "La Gaña." They were eating Villegas's wife's food, which she made for sale. Villegas had gone to play his instrument in the celebration that the tobacconists had for the Day of our Lady of Guadalupe.... As the guests went out the door, they saw a paisano on horseback, alone, without anyone accompanying him, who asked them, "Who are you?" The two paisanos gave their names and said that they had come in to have dinner and were now leaving. The man on the horse prevented it, and another guard started to enter his house. The deponent responded that no one searched his house. He warned the guard (whom he later learned was the lieutenant [in charge] of the lighting), that he was a soldier. Then the lieutenant replied, "What do I care that he was a soldier. . . . It could not be verified, and he had to prove who he was." Villegas declined in view of these insults. . . . Still ignorant of who insulted him, Villegas told him to go to the devil.[43]

The head guard who made the initial report, Cayetano Canales, focused on this incident as a serious public affront to the guards. Although Canales did not use the word *honor*, he described Villegas's words as "insolent," "scandalous," "denigrating," and "iniquitous" as he shouted his "vilifications" of the lieutenant, Corporal Bernal, and the night watchmen in general. Villegas also refused to calm down as the serenos walked him to the military headquarters.[44] On the other hand, clear in their loyalties, the soldiers who assisted the lantern guards denied that Villegas caused any scandal or resisted. As usual, this altercation resulted in nothing more than a gentle warning by higher authorities, who instructed Villegas to show "utmost respect and decorum" in dealing with functionaries who carried out "royal justice."[45] From his attitude, it seems very unlikely that Villegas took this suggestion to heart.

A similar disdain for the night watchmen comes from the testimonies of a group of military men accused of crashing into a corporal of the guards with their carriage as he lighted one of his lanterns on New Year's Eve of 1801.[46] From the perspective of forty-one-year-old Corporal Bernal, he was attacked while innocently carrying out his job relighting a lantern at around 10:30 p.m. Bernal testified that he yelled out as he saw the carriage approaching him too quickly. Because it did not stop, Bernal jumped off of his ladder, just before the carriage crashed into its middle rungs. The driver commented, "Man, I would have thrown you." Bernal proceeded to arrest him. In response, a man named Antonio Corte, a sergeant of a company of the provincial infantry regiment, started yelling at Bernal, calling him a thief, a drunk, a bastard (*cabrón*), and a panderer (*alcahuete*), common degrading insults in this era. A cashier working nearby claimed he heard someone yell out "shut-up one-eye [*tuerto*]!" Others of the party shouted something along the lines of "killing all of the guards, just because we are arguing about letting one of them kill himself."[47] This implication that the guards protected each other so much that they exaggerated how many of them suffered injuries on the job may have been a commonplace, as it also appears in a murder case described later in the chapter. Cayetano Canales summarized the events the next morning for the viceroy, expressing his anger at the incident: "Everyone was remarkably outraged and vilified in the presence of infinite people who came together to witness this scandal," another gesture toward asserting the night watchmen's fragile and contested claims to honorable status and respect.[48]

Corte and artillery sergeant Francisco Zárate, both in their midthirties and stationed in Mexico City, took a different view as they described their version of the events. They explained that the incident took place as they returned from celebrating that night in Tacuba, riding in a carriage along with their wives. Sergeants Corte, Zárate, and another infantry soldier named don José de Laso (who also owned a vinatería in the neighborhood) seemed determined to dishonor Bernal. They mocked him as drunk on the job on the night in question, as per his usual tendencies. Laso recounted that in the past, Bernal, in one of his typical outings passing time in a drunken frenzy at Laso's bar, had lost his eye. Another night while dining in the tavern, Bernal began to beat his wife. When the server begged him to stop, the sereno attacked him too. The soldiers denied that they insulted Bernal during the events under discussion, testifying that the most shameful aspect of the scene was Bernal's intoxication.[49] Typical of a conflict between the serenos and the military, this case ended indefinitely, without any known repercussions for any of the parties involved. The leadership of the night watchmen did not have the wherewithal to challenge the military establishment, who clung to their superior rights and honor. In this case, Viceroy Felix Berenguer de Marquina declined to involve himself in the dispute. The statements made by the soldiers stand in the record to memorialize the lowly status of Corporal Bernal, whom they portrayed as a brutal and crude thug.

Over the course of the early nineteenth century, a paper trail emerges of the antagonism between the military and the serenos. In a total of eighty-one reports of the guards' nightly activities, soldiers feature as offenders in thirty-five incidents (see table 6). Well over half of these conflicts took place in 1822, but as in the *Libros de Reos* for 1798, this year provides much more complete records than any other, especially for April.[50] While these reports lack many of the details found in the *Libros de Reos*, such as the name, race, age, and marital status of the offender, the head guard often filled in more context for his entries. These specifics show how soldiers brought violence, public intoxication, theft, and disruption to Mexico City's nights. The night watchmen concentrated on alcohol-related offenses in the 1790s, but by 1822, brutal attacks by soldiers and an increasing use of guns feature as new concerns. The fuero still protected these men, so much so that it became a dishonest excuse to avoid repercussions: one man caught in a group of four other thieves stealing valuable items from a house claimed that he was a soldier, although officers soon revealed his lie.[51] While the 1790s *Libros de Reos* incidents mainly involved drinking to excess or exchanges with women that were viewed as illicit and undesirable, the head guards' reports more clearly illustrate the vicious street brawls that regularly exploded between the soldiers and the night watchmen.

On a couple of eventful nights in late September of 1803, the military men involved in these melees ranged from cadets in training to soldiers destined for service in Manila. Repeating what sounds like a mantra of the era, a leader of the city council, Manuel de Cuevas Monroy, begged

Viceroy Iturrigaray to address the cadets' disrespect for the lantern guards, whom he presented as victims: "These individuals deserve the greatest care because on them rests the upkeep and tranquility of this populous court city. They are unhappily charged to serve in this poorly paid occupation, exposed to continuous attacks by criminals."[52] Monroy made this petition because, on the night of September 27, a group of cadets attacked three guards with their swords, including their corporal. One of the young men had been arrested the previous night for throwing stones at doors of different buildings, including an arch over the door of a church, "provoking people, and committing a thousand other excesses." Approaching the guards with swords in hand, one cadet said, "Here are some of them who took you in last night, but they won't arrest me tonight!" The corporal attempted to fight the cadets off with his bare hands. On the same night, a grenadier from the Crown regiment told a guard to be quiet. The guard responded, "Very well, sir," and then the soldier "broke his head" with his sword, a severe injury that required an emergency visit to the hospital surgeon.[53] All of these men enjoyed the protection of the fuero and evaded punishment from civilian law enforcement.

Similar to the 1790s, in the fragmentary existing nightly reports, of the eight reported incidents of nineteenth-century lantern smashing, three involved drunk perpetrators.[54] However, it is worth repeating that intoxication does not necessarily preclude the possibility of a political undercurrent to this destructive offense. For example, in 1804, what may have begun as an unpremeditated drunk act of personal resistance to the guards quickly escalated to a mini-riot that dramatically protested the physical cruelty of early urban law enforcement. At around 8 p.m. on April 9, guard number 1 called for assistance from the guards working at the Parián market.[55] A woman, in the company of a drunk man, had robbed a *biscochera* (a woman selling *bizcochos*, which could mean cakes, cookies, or biscuits, presumably outdoors). As the drunk man seemed to be about to throw a stone at the guard while mocking and laughing at him, guard number 1 called for help from guard number 4. One of the guards grabbed the woman by her braids, a common aggressive and degrading act in this era; simultaneously, she broke his lantern.[56] Suddenly, as if the piercing sound of broken glass called them to arms, an angry mob gathered, led by military cadets who urged them on. The crowd threw mud in the guards' faces and prodded them with their swords and sticks, encouraging the man in custody to flee. When an alcalde appeared, making his own rounds, and the guards informed them of the ongoing riot, the cadets threatened to toss the alcalde in the river, and called him a "rogue [pícaro]" for involving himself in the situation. The head guard's report also noted a conflict regarding the behavior of guard number 1 in this riot, because he insisted on leaving the scene to take the perpetrator to jail. According to official regulations, he should not have tried to go out of his patrol area without checking in with his superior. While only one long paragraph exists narrating this incident, the anecdote suggests that lantern smashing may represent an "tool" in the Mexican toolbox of urban rioting in this era, alongside acts more common in Indigenous villages, such as destroying symbols of Catholicism outside the parish church.[57]

Conflicts during the Era of Insurgency

Insurgency led to increasing militarization of Mexico City in the 1810s. As political crises occurred in the court city during the summer of 1808, droughts starved the countryside.[58] Father Miguel de Hidalgo's popular rebellion began on September 16, 1810, in the village of Dolores, over two hundred miles to the northwest of the viceregal capital. Moving even further west in the next few days, his growing masses of followers targeted the mining town of Guanajuato. When Hidalgo and his sixty thousand rebels marched toward Mexico City in October of 1810, rumors circulated that he would soon capture the seat of the viceroyalty. However, royalist troops fought off the insurgents at the Monte de las Cruces battle near Toluca, with about two thousand casualties and the flight of perhaps half of the rebels. Under threat, Viceroy Venegas did not fear Hidalgo enough to surrender the capital to him. The insurgent priest advised other rebel leaders not to further attack the metropolis, because of the likelihood of defeat by the better-trained royalist troops.[59] Not long after, Hidalgo retreated to Guadalajara and further north to Coahuila, where he was captured in March, 1811.[60] In the next few months, Hidalgo faced

TABLE 6. Military men in the head guard's nightly report

DATE	OFFENSE
11/10/1799	drunk, insulting, and beating a guard
9/26/1803	robbery, in a group of ten men, of a woman's house
9/26/1803	military cadets throwing stones at the Mercerdarian church
9/27/1803	fighting with the guard over a woman's arrest
10/20/1806	officer beating a guard[1]
10/20/1808	soldier involved in brawl, guards' clothing ripped
12/2/1813	robbing a house, beating owners
4/24/1814	beating a woman who was under arrest
10/4/1814	robbery and murder at a bathhouse
2/6/1815	drunk
3/10/1815	destroying the guard's ladder, says he should be a *patriota*
10/2/1815	drunk
10/2/1815	drunk and a deserter
10/4/1818	knocking on doors, pretending to look for deserters
10/5/1818	three soldiers with stolen goods
10/5/1818	royalists fire shots in the street
2/9/1822	drunk
2/23/1822	robbing two women of their head scarves
3/31/1822	fight involving guards and soldiers
4/1/1822	drunk
4/1/1822	theft
4/1/1822	wounded man
4/2/1822	group of soldiers knocking on doors, one is broken
4/9/1822	drunk
4/9/1822	attacking a market stand, threatening the guard with a pistol
4/10/1822	trying to enter a closed business, resulting in a shooting
4/14/1822	a group of soldiers cause a disturbance at a residence
4/15/1822	soldiers rob and beat a man
4/16/1822	two soldiers found drunk and passed out
4/19/1822	two soldiers rob and beat a man

4/19/1822	drunk
4/20/1822	a soldier found with eight women in the Alameda park
4/25/1822	two soldiers break a guard's lantern and ladder
8/26/1822	three cadets rob and almost beat a man to death
4/27/1822	fight resulting in a death

1. See ch. 6 for a discussion of this case. See AGN, Mexico, Indiferente virreinal, Caja 6411, Expediente 5, 1806, 4.

prosecution by both the Holy Office of the Spanish Inquisition and a military court, which executed him that July.

Hidalgo's movement initiated the popular phase of New Spain's insurgency, which reached its peak in 1813, leading to a variety of changes and reactions in the capital relating to law enforcement. Less than a month after the outbreak of Hidalgo's rebellion, the viceroy issued a decree implicitly acknowledging the potential for more conflict between the military in Mexico City and those entrusted with maintaining policía.[61] Venegas said that in preparing this decree, he had conferred with military leadership, making an agreement with them that in any case involving the cleanliness of the city, soldiers lost the privilege of their fuero and should face a standard trial, not the judgment of their military superiors. Venegas specified that any verbal or physical abuse of the night watchmen would lead to a court case. This decree actually adhered to the original intention of the fueros, which did not protect military men when they disobeyed municipal regulations.[62] Fifteen months later, clearly Venegas's plans had not come to fruition, as soldiers continued to insult and attack the guards without any fear of repercussions. Of course, according to viceregal reports, the patriots were the worst offenders. The rebels even went so far as setting arrested individuals free as the serenos attempted to take perpetrators into custody or walk them to the jail. In 1812 local leaders optimistically hoped that recirculating the 1810 decree would encourage military men to respect the night watchmen as they carried out their duties of "guarding the city at night, taking care of the lighting, as well as gathering up the drunkards, and apprehending violators."⁶³ Not surprisingly, this plan also failed.

Venegas's efforts culminated in the 1811 creation of the junta de policía, which united military and judicial patrols and attempted to prevent rebels from entering the capital, as well as prohibiting large gatherings in private houses, legal casinos, pulquerías, and vinaterías. Following the French model of urban law enforcement introduced to Madrid by Napoleon in 1808, this new body represented the first time that Mexican policing became truly political in its focus, although it also retained the classic policía concerns of sanitation, lighting, and street cleaning.⁶⁴ Key aspects of this reform included the naming of Pedro de la Puente as an unpaid superintendent of police who oversaw sixteen mounted lieutenants based in the different neighborhoods of the city, and emphasizing the words tranquility, security, and order in communications made about the new system.⁶⁵ After carrying out a census, Superintendent de la Puente reported that the population had swollen to almost 169,000 by 1812. This temporary increase included refugees from the countryside who fled the rebels.⁶⁶ In fear of urban sedition, the superintendent created one hundred posts for volunteer guards. This increasing surveillance led to a reported 1,631 arrests in the last four months of 1811. These arrests included desertion from the royalist forces and other offenses relating to the military.⁶⁷ The reforms were controversial from the start: a dispute ensued between Viceroy Calleja, who took office in early 1813, and the Spanish *cortes*, about the constitutionality of the junta de policía. Superintendent de la Puente resigned in 1813, fearful of assassination.⁶⁸

While Mexico City itself did not see military action during the decade-long independence movement, mass rebellion in the countryside unsurprisingly affected urban life. From the early days of insurgency, residents of the viceregal capital witnessed an influx of rebel prisoners who regularly marched in from the countryside. These imprisoned revolutionaries often received sentences of forced labor on public works projects.⁶⁹ Perhaps observing this ongoing spectacle of retribution by gachupin leaders, residents remained highly politicized and supported independence in a nonviolent way through a new election process. Mexican delegates helped create the 1812 Spanish constitution, which led to celebrations and new voting opportunities to elect leaders as town council members in the viceregal capital. Originally, the audiencia limited the suffrage to male heads of households labeled españoles, but the intendant later broadened the vote to all men, other than vagrants and the unemployed. Poll watchers claimed that many "miserable" people voted. The results indicated an almost total lack of support for peninsular Spaniards and royalists and a strong inclination toward electing cabildo members from the ranks of traditional Indigenous leaders, parish priests, and pro-insurgent candidates.[70]

As the struggle persisted throughout the 1810s, the urban military presence continued to conflict with civilian law enforcement. While important political change happened in various locations throughout New Spain, individual royalist soldiers continued to disturb the viceregal capital city. Even wealthy property owners were vulnerable to urban crimes committed by soldiers. In late 1813, for example, the night watchmen found three men, including two from the Zamora regiment, threatening a homeowner at knifepoint with an intimidating belduque, while they robbed him of his valuables, money, and clothes. The thieves fled to the roof of the house, but the guards managed to chase them down, at which point the items that they stole fell from their clothing.[71]

As the peak years of the insurgency era wound down by 1814, two accounts of lantern-smashing incidents suggest that violent and possibly even revolutionary sentiments had penetrated Mexico City. One night at 10:30 p.m. in 1814, a group of soldiers became angry when a hearing-impaired guard did not respond quickly enough to their demands, so they beat him with sticks and stole his lantern. Less than a year later, a man purposefully extinguished a lantern at three in the morning and attacked the guard as he tried to reignite it. The perpetrator yelled, "You would illuminate the jail if you were a patriot!" while also destroying the sereno's ladder. This comment implies that lighting the street was an occupation reserved for royalist lackeys.[72]

The last attempt by a Spanish viceroy to reform Mexico City policing motivated by the traditional ideology of "good government" took place in early 1814, with the circulation of a bando focusing on cleanliness and order. At this time, the government used the term *celadores* to refer to a new neighborhood watch–type group of volunteers. Similar to earlier and later decrees promulgated after independence, this document worked toward a more sanitary city in several ways: regular trash collection (proposed to take place three times a week), with strict regulations against throwing garbage in the streets and canals, a prohibition against raising livestock within the city, maintenance of the street paving, and even an attempt to abolish "terrible dogs." Defecating in the streets or plazas could lead to a jail sentence, and the bando encouraged a general vigilance on this point. Repeating earlier bandos, candy and snack sellers were forbidden from setting up their stands during Holy Week. The ten points covered in this decree included a reminder that all residents had to comply, without the protection of fueros, or risk a fine.[73]

Scattered reports from the head guard during the decade of Mexican insurgency illustrate how the serenos passed a significant amount of their time trying to rein in the armed and violent soldiers based in the capital city. In 1815 several events demonstrating a street-level rejection of the night patrols again escalated to the point of motivating the judicial authorities to desperately beg the viceroy to make some effort to enforce respect for the judiciary in all of its forms. Incidents involving soldiers persisted with no sign of deference to the authority of the night watchmen. Military officers intervened in arrests for no clear motivation other than to annoy the night watchmen, as in an incident where an artillery gunner brandished his weapon at a guard escorting a drunk to jail.[74] Another incident in 1815 also almost escalated to the point of firing gunshots. When a judicial official named don Manuel Martínez Mancilla tried to arrest several "women who live evil lives [*mujeres de mal vivir*]," the soldiers accompanying the women would not allow it, threatening the patrol with their firearms.[75] Martínez Marcilla pleaded with Viceroy Calleja to take some action so that the patrols were not ignored or disrespected and could carry out their duties. Again, this appeal did not work. Incidents of conflicts show that soldiers did not even respect the military patrols who tried to police the city alongside the night watchmen, their superiors, and the alcaldes. For example, during a robbery of a bathhouse in 1815, six soldiers faced off against another group of military men, ending in the shooting death of one of them. The night before this killing, other violent altercations took place, including an infantry sergeant starting a fight over a stolen cape, the night watchmen incarcerating a guard for drunkenness, and the capture of a deserter.[76] Another outbreak of criminal activity took place in October of 1818, when, over a period of two nights, soldiers wreaked havoc in the city in three different episodes documented by the head guard. First, a group of deserters harmlessly annoyed homeowners by knocking on their doors in the middle of the night. More seriously, the patrols caught three militiamen holding a stolen sack full of leather goods, bedding, and clothes. Worst of all, soldiers started firing their guns in the middle of a residential area.[77] Alcaldes also complained of the mockery and disrespect shown to them by soldiers.[78] Undoubtedly, the military men resisted, rejected, and mocked all efforts by the viceregal authorities to improve safety and respect for residents of Mexico City.

Murder and Mayhem in New Spain's Final Years

Unfortunately for the serenos, the danger inherent to their occupation increased in the early 1820s. As the new decade began, the continuing militarization of the city provided a backdrop for a soldier's homicidal fury against two of the night watchmen. Although the entire situation remains murky, it is possible that a murderous European assailant especially resented a particular guard of Indigenous ancestry. At 2 a.m. during the night of November 28, 1820, Eusebio Gómez, night watchman number 32, died in the San Andrés Hospital of injuries described as very deep and wide slashes, which he received while on patrol a week earlier.[79] A postmortem exam confirmed the cause of death: a wound to his left parietal bone, which exposed bone, flesh, and brains. He also suffered wounds on his right parietal bone, his left eyebrow, a fractured and separated left cheek bone, three cuts on his shoulders, and two on his scapula. Two surgeons present determined that a saber made these wounds with a top-to-bottom slash. Gómez suffered these brutal injuries just before 1 a.m. on the night of November 21 while on duty in the Calle del Rastro near the corner of San Felipe de Jesús and San José de Gracia, four blocks south of the viceroy's palace. Shortly after Gómez received these ultimately fatal blows, two other guards (numbers 2 and 20) heard the sound of a sergeant's whistle calling for help. Rushing to his aid, his companions picked Gómez up from the middle of the Calle del Rastro, and carried him to the San Andrés hospital, ten long blocks to the northwest, where he remained from 2 a.m. onward. Blood stains and chunks of his hair marked the location of his assault. In the hospital, Gómez's very serious wounds continued to hemorrhage, preventing efforts to cure him. Soon after his arrival, the surgeons called in a priest to give him last rites. Other than some incoherent and frightening groans and bellows heard by the men who came to help him as he bled out into the street, Gómez never spoke or regained consciousness after the attack. He had worked as a night watchman since approximately 1802.[80]

Near Gómez's deathbed, guard number 76, a thirty-four-year-old married Indigenous man from Real de Monte named Damasio Pérez, also suffered from several cruelly inflicted injuries. Pérez fortunately experienced more success in the slow process of healing, although for a time his head wound festered and a fever persisted.[81] From his hospital bed, he had the strength to communicate who had attacked him and Gómez, describing their assailant as a "capitán de Zaragoza." Pérez further elaborated on the assault:

> He does not know why, but when the deponent was sitting at the *esquina de brindis* [the name of a corner where the streets called Migueles, San José de Gracia, Puerto Nuevo, and Olmedo met, one block east from where Gómez's suffered his fatal wounds], at about 1:30 this morning, said captain, without speaking any words, struck a sharp blow with his saber on [Pérez's] left shoulder. [The deponent] started to run away . . . then he fell and [the captain] reached him, he stopped and stabbed him in the left side of [Pérez's] head; the captain was drunk, the two of them were not enemies, nor had any pretense of enmity, and Pérez forgives him because God forgives his sins.[82]

As an illiterate man, Pérez could not sign his statement, but his testimony helped the investigation progress. Along with the gruesome hair and gore where Gómez received his fatal blows, noticeable blood stains remained on a wall near the corner where the attack on Pérez took place.[83] A few days later, as he regained some physical strength, Pérez provided more details about the night in question. He described what he remembered of the captain's clothing, including his cape, boots, and a round hat. Pérez remembered that after he fell while fleeing the attack, he yelled for assistance from his compañero Agapito Zorilla (guard number 80). The supervising lieutenant also appeared and spoke these words to the murderer, "My captain, what is this? He says that Your Grace has injured him."[84]

An uninjured guard, number 30, Cayetano Bonilla, filled in the details leading up to the incident, providing some context for the seemingly spontaneous stabbings. Bonilla reported that he heard voices in the Calle de la Joya, and, upon investigation, he found three men and one woman fighting. One man wore a dark cape, blue pants, and a round hat, and his companions referred to him as "captain." Bonilla heard a paisano (civilian or compatriot) laughingly say, "My Captain, first you spend my money, and now you want my sister. This will not happen, because I am a man." The paisano held the saber by the hilt at this moment of conflict, and Bonilla demanded that he release it and give it back its owner. For a moment, peace seemed restored, but then the captain pushed the paisano in the chest, and the latter ran away, throwing stones. With the help of Bonilla, again the men calmed down momentarily, even hugging each other, but then continued arguing and throwing stones. The captain taunted the other man as he ran, calling out, "Come back here, Stony!" After this brawl continued for a half hour or so, Bonilla heard his sergeant's whistle and ran to see Gómez propped up on his pike and lantern, with horrific head wounds. The sergeant commented, "Look what happened to this poor man!" Bonilla responded, "That could have been me. . . . I know that a captain with a big mustache did this."[85] Bonilla feared that the attacker would continue his violence because he still held onto his sword. The watchmen were vulnerable because they did not have these weapons and might be found and attacked while seated. Bonilla encountered Pérez on the street, and the injured man had the strength to describe his attacker, who by now had been taken into custody by a military patrol. Bonilla recognized the description as of the same man whom he had seen involved in the brawl earlier. After finishing his account, the witness was asked if Pérez and Gómez were known to be argumentative or drunks. Bonilla denied this, saying that they both had calm temperaments, although he admitted that they both drank liquor, but never to the point of drunkenness.[86] Several other night watchmen confirmed that the victims were "moderate men [hombre regular]," who did not drink to excess or provoke fights.[87]

The guards' statements relating to this attack demonstrate their street camaraderie, especially in terms of fast reactions to injuries incurred by one of their own. Guard number 75, Joseph Joaquín Lara, stated that as he sat on a corner in his patrol area, his compañero Agapito Zorilla stopped to chat with him. The two of them heard the sound of fighting, and Lara said, "Hombre, it seems to me that one of our compañeros is calling for us."[88] The two of them ran toward the sounds as quickly as they could and found Pérez injured. His attacker had already fled. A nearby company of dragoons had arrived to help arrest the aggressor, and Lara remained with them and the wounded Pérez, but shortly had to return to "take care of his own beat." Lara described the attacker as "of a very light white color, with an enormous curly mustache."[89] His saber stood out to Bonilla: it was curved, with yellow decorations, carried in a leather sheath hung from a black leather belt. Lara and Zorilla chased down the fleeing assailant but needed help from the military patrols to take him into custody.

Members of the dragoon infantry regiment actually arrested the culprit, who, as a military man himself, enjoyed the judicial privileges of the fuero. Sergeant Major and Lieutenant Corporal don Joseph Mendivil led the investigation.[90] During the course of the trial, Mendivil called on the dragoons who took the alleged murderer into custody. They testified that the mustachioed man, identified as Captain Juan Power, was drunk upon his arrest, mentally distracted with bloodshot, completely red eyes but able to stand.[91] The dragoon Hermengildo Barros heard the following conversation between a lieutenant of the watch and Power:

LIEUTENANT: Good evening, my captain. Do you know me?
POWER: Yes.
LIEUTENANT: This sereno says that you hurt him.
CAPTAIN: No.
PÉREZ: Yes, sir. You have hurt me for no reason, while I was sitting here without bothering you, you hit me and knocked me down.[92]

While standing in the street in custody of the dragoons, Captain Power made some sharp comments and statements asserting his honor and his right to house arrest, heard by those around him. Upon seeing the wounded night watchman, apparently he complained, "Now they will probably accuse me of hurting other guards when I am already locked up. . . . They will probably say that I murdered all of the guards." This observation confirmed a well-known stereotype that a general sense ingroup loyalty existed among the night watchmen. Captain Power also refused to give up his saber, denying that he was actually under arrest.[93] Eventually a military superior confiscated the weapon and stored it.

Later on in the questioning, Captain Juan Power revealed more about his biography. He stated that he was a Roman Catholic born in Dublin in 1788.[94] In 1820 he still served in the Zaragoza Dragoon Infantry Regiment, on the side of the Spanish Crown, in the final months of the ten-year struggle for independence. Power had earned a reputation since 1818 as a successful royalist military leader, according to a report in the *Gaceta del Gobierno de México* written by the commander general coronel don Manuel de la Concha. In July 1818 Power and one hundred of his regiment succeeded in defeating insurgent forces in the region of Tecomate, near a mesa called Mundo Nuevo, helping to eject all the rebels in the area. With this distinguished military service record, Power carefully guarded what he viewed as symbols of his honor. He expressed a strong desire to maintain control of his saber and successfully petitioned the viceroy to allow his wife to take it back.[95]

The investigation became more complicated as various clues confused the matter of Captain Power's guilt. Apparently neither the captain nor his sword indicated any noticeable blood stains when he was in jail, which would be impossible given the brutality of the wounds he allegedly caused. On the other hand, he very suspiciously had his manservant bring him clean pants and shoes from his home shortly after his arrest.[96] Despite these damning actions on his part, Power's statement denied all involvement in the incident. He claimed that on the night in question, he did nothing more criminal than go out to a dance with a friend. He said that afterward, they passed the time drinking cane liquor at home. Power testified that he heard the patrol outside and asked, "¿Hombre, que hay? [Man, what's happening?]" and received the response that a sereno had been injured. When Power asked who hurt him, and the guard said, allegedly without even looking up, "You hurt me."[97]

Power went on to explain an ongoing enmity that he claimed he had with the guarda mayor, which in his mind explained why he was falsely accused of severely wounding one guard and killing another. Power claimed that several months before he had asked a night watchman to light his cigar with his lantern. Allegedly the guard refused in a rude way, and Power insulted him and threatened to kick him and his lantern, which drew the attention of a group of guards, including the former head guard Ignacio de Aguilar. After Power described the incident, the guarda mayor responded, "I am the only one with any authority over my serenos, and for them, there are no officers or soldiers," a clear assertion of where he stood on the tense interactions of guards and the military.[98] A group of night watchmen then surrounded Power, who hit Aguilar in order to escape. Aguilar proceeded to take a dagger from one of his men, and Power just managed to twist it out of his hand. Power received eight days' house arrest after this incident and a verbal warning not to roam the streets late at night.[99] Aguilar did not testify in response to this story, but the current head guard, Eguiluz y Olarte, responded that he did not feel malice toward Power and had even invited the Irishman, his wife, and his son over to his house, after meeting them with a friendly embrace at the Café de la Gran Sociedad. In contrast, when Eguiluz y Olarte later saw Power at either the Café de Apolo or the Café de León de Oro, the captain had threatened to kill him. The head guard expressed disgust and a desire for vindication from Power's "atrocious and ugly calumny."[100] These statements about escalating conflicts between Power and the two head guards suggest that competing claims to insulted honor may have motivated Power's alleged murder of one guard and attempted murder of another.

As is often the case in the Novohispanic judicial archives, this investigation produced no definitive results, even when the healing Pérez and Power faced off in a careo in the hospital to try to determine if the victim had ever even looked his attacker in the face.[101] Mendivil also had master sword makers examine the saber for blood and organized a walk around the streets where the incidents took place. All of these efforts to determine the truth had inconclusive results. An unsatisfactory closure of this investigation comes from the fact that Power died a few months later (most likely while still in custody), in February of 1821, with the matter still open.[102] Also that month, royalist general and future Mexican emperor Agustín de Iturbide united with the rebel and future president of Mexico Vicente Guerrero to form the Army of Three Guarantees, eventually leading to Mexico's independence from Spain.[103] By March, Mendivil decided to archive the file, leaving future historians entirely mystified as to who killed Gómez and wounded Pérez, but very clear on the level of hatred that some in the military felt toward the night watchmen in these final months of New Spain's existence, as well as the proto-police comradery inspired by this antagonism.

Conflicts between the serenos and the military continued in the months when New Spain became an independent empire led by Iturbide. The last Spanish viceroy Juan O'Donoju stepped down in September of 1821, claiming that the royalist forces had evacuated Mexico City. However, this opened up the city to a victorious entry of fifteen thousand soldiers, the largest army ever seen in the capital.[104] During the very early months of the military leadership of Iturbide, military men from both sides of the conflict continued to resist the night watchmen's authority, while at the same time keeping them very busy by causing a significant amount of criminal activity, from drunken antics to robbery and assaults.[105] The lantern smashing that started as a prelude to rebellion thirty years previously now took on a more deliberately political and brutal tone. For example, at 6:15 p.m. one spring night in 1822, two soldiers attacked night

WATCHMEN, MILITARY, INSURGENCY

watchman number 72 as he attempted to light his lanterns. The soldiers threw a piece of wood at the lantern, breaking three panes of glass, and then ran away. In April 1822, a carriage ran into the ladder of guard number 2, also while he attempted to ignite a lantern, resulting in the loss of his eye and destroying both his hand lantern and his ladder. Due to the guard's wounds and the violence of the attack, he could not provide any more information to help find the carriage. A clear sign of the tension between the guards and soldiers took place later in April 1822, when two soldiers approached guard number 78 and attacked him verbally, while also breaking his hand lantern and his ladder. These soldiers were incarcerated and fined nineteen pesos for the damages.[106] Another incident in 1822 suggests confused loyalties between the serenos and the military. At 10:30 p.m. one night, two serenos tried to arrest two men who they thought were soldiers. The men fled but then returned and started a fight with the guards, one of them threatening them with a pistol, a rarely wielded weapon in this era of daggers and sabers. While being marched to the military headquarters, one of the culprits said that he was "a soldier of New Spain," and the man brandishing the gun ended up admitting that he was guard number 43, grossly negligent of his duties guarding his beat.[107]

These insurgency-era incidents of lantern smashing and personal attacks on the guards underscore the ever-tense relationship between the night watchmen and a variety of military men stationed in Mexico City. Tensions built up from the early 1790s to the 1820s, occasionally and increasingly exploding out into ever more deadly street-level violence. The privileges of the soldiers exacerbated the ongoing conflict. As Lyle McAlister argues persuasively, the fuero militar helped undermine "the very foundations of royal authority."[108] Soldiers joined plebeians in their rejection of the serenos. This new law enforcement corps did not prevent mass rebellion in New Spain. Evidence suggests, on the contrary, that the lantern guards only further enraged poor residents of the city, providing them with a clear target for their dissatisfaction with the viceregal regime. Unfortunately, a new form of government, independent of Spain, also did not prevent escalating violence and unrest in the capital city.

Conclusion

> But when a riot is successful, it is no longer a riot, it becomes . . . a Revolution, to be suitably commemorated in papier-mâché triumphal arch and column, to be replaced, if the regime lasts long enough, by something more solid in stone and marble. Here the police records will be of little help. There are no arrests, at least among the rioters; the police, in the face of success, will discreetly disappear, leaving the terrain to the victors.
> —Cobb, *The Police and the People*

The last seven chapters have examined late viceregal Mexico City through the experiences of the capital's night watchmen, emphasizing the give-and-take between the authorities and their subjects. The history of New Spain's serenos suggests that successful law enforcement reform requires an ongoing negotiation with the general populace. The patrolmen's nightly actions must respond to concerns felt and expressed by both the government and the masses of urban residents. The people whom the guards met on the street actually had more influence on how they carried out their duties than the directives that they received from on high.

This experience parallels the broader history of the era. In their overview of the eighteenth-century Atlantic world, Allan Kuethe and Kenneth Andrien summarize the historiographic debates over the Bourbon reforms. While Novohispanic historians often veer toward presenting a coherent surveillance state, other scholars emphasize "the diverse and often contradictory aims of Madrid policy makers, who struggled haltingly and inconsistently to balance the crown's various fiscal, commercial, administrative, and military objectives." Some historians even question the rulers' overall goals, especially under the reign of Charles IV, who "lurch[ed]

CONCLUSION

from one policy to another by the mid-1790s, in a desperate search for resources needed to meet the exigencies of war."[1]

On a much smaller scale, the serenos also stumbled along, underpaid, virtually unarmed, and undersupplied with the oil that they needed to illuminate the night. They faced disdain and resistance from the populace and attacks from the military patrols. They struggled most of all to simply stay awake. For Mexico City's night watchmen, every step in their development, every step in walking their rounds, involved negotiations with the public. Decades before the establishment of these new lantern-lighting patrols, Mexico City authorities debated with residents about how to effectively install public lighting and met with resistance in carrying out their plan of individually funded lanterns. Once the city established a tax-funded system of illumination, the populace responded by smashing the lanterns held by the men who carried out the reform. Clearly, even in the eighteenth century, the urban masses in the Americas and Europe already had strong opinions regarding how law enforcement patrols should serve their needs, and not necessarily the state's.

Let's invite Bernal, the corporal of the watch whom we have followed throughout this book to guide us in summing up the experiences of the Mexico City lantern guards. Born around the late 1750s, Bernal lived through the peak era of the Bourbon reforms and witnessed the growing rebellions against them. Throughout Bernal's childhood and young adulthood, the competent King Charles III ruled over Spain and its empire. From his rural upbringing in Ixmiquilpan, Bernal experienced some of the enlightened reforms emanating from the metropolis, such as the introduction of potable drinking water during the rule of Viceroy Bucareli. However, as a child in the 1760s, most likely Bernal was not aware of the ambitious lighting projects underway at that time in Barcelona, Madrid, and Mexico City. Viceroy Cruillas's idea of resident-paid public lighting, introduced in 1763, probably did not interest a young boy growing up several days' journey north of the viceregal court. As the debate continued under Bucareli in the 1770s, Bernal may have heard of opportunities to earn a better living in the metropolis and considered emigrating to find work on one of the many public works projects undertaken during this

CONCLUSION

period. Certainly by the mid-1780s, as epidemics raged in New Spain, Bernal joined the thousands of people on the move and desperate to escape drought, starvation, and disease in the countryside. When he first entered the capital city, perhaps he strolled around the central plaza and from there walked east toward the Alameda park, observing the lanterns illuminating the streets that ran past the solid and intimidating palaces of elite residents. As the "hunger years" of the mid-1780s tapered off, Bernal would have noticed that urban beautification projects picked up, especially after King Charles IV came to power in late 1788.

One year later, the king sent over a new viceroy, the Count of Revillagigedo, whose entry inspired lavish fanfare and festivities, which surely Bernal enjoyed along with thousands of *capitalinos*. The celebrations ended quickly. On October 24, 1789, Bernal must have heard the terrible news: a shocking home invasion and massacre of one of city's wealthiest men, don Joaquín Dongo, along with ten of his employees. The thieves and killers stole Dongo's carriage and disappeared into the night. Approximately twenty thousand pesos disappeared from Dongo's warehouse that night, more money than the majority of the city residents' would earn in their entire lives. This atrocity exacerbated the elite perception of a city descending into unchecked criminality. The day after the murder at the Dongo establishment, the authorities begged for help from the "whistle guards," military men on the streets at night, and the traditional neighborhood justices, the alcaldes. But none of these men could provide many details, as darkness hid the perpetrators speeding away from the bloody scene. This horrendous crime inspired Revillagigedo to accelerate the project for illuminating the city and institutionalizing a new, more systematic night patrol to prevent such acts occurring in the future.

These night patrols created new employment opportunities for uneducated, nonelite men with limited career options. As a man seeking to establish himself as a permanent resident of the hemisphere's largest city at this time, Bernal must have perked up his ears when he heard of Viceroy Revillagigedo's ideas for organizing a corps of lantern guards. Perhaps the horrors of the Dongo killings inflamed his desire for vengeance to atone for the invasion of an honorable man's house, or maybe he just needed a steady income. How he took on the occupation of sereno is unknown, but by August of 1791, Bernal patrolled beat number 23 and already had a reputation as a heavy drinker, like so many other men of his social class. He also worked hard and formed strong ties with his compañeros, which may have helped him achieve his promotion to corporal in the next few years. Although he was a bit older than most serenos, Bernal patrolled with many men like himself: migrants from smaller villages and towns who perhaps only tenuously claimed Spanish ancestry and who depended on their physical strength to carry out their assigned tasks. On the job, these men maintained their plebeian worldview and values, even as they worked for the authorities. They still drank to intoxication at pulquerías, reacted angrily to personal insults to their honor, and struggled to feed their families on their small wages. Of course, this era also saw heavy recruitment by the military—which offered the privileges of legal protection by the fuero militar—but working as a sereno may have offered more attractions for men like Bernal, with wives and families settled in Mexico City. Even if the intentions of Revillagigedo to Europeanize the city and its population remained impossible to achieve, the job offered an opportunity for a small step up the social ranks for men like Bernal.

Despite his argumentative personality and tendency to drink heavily at pulquerías, Bernal must have excelled as a watchman in order to earn his promotion to corporal. He had to effectively and quickly respond to cries for help in his patrol area, including bringing midwives to women in labor and escorting priests to deathbeds in the darkest hours of the night. He knew the people on his beat who dealt with physical, mental, and emotional challenges, as well as many cases of spousal abuse, disciplinary problems with children, and unfaithful partners. As a corporal, he took on additional tasks. He now chastised, verbally or physically, serenos who did not show up to work, fell asleep on duty, stole from people they arrested, or sparked altercations during the night. Most notably, Bernal mixed work and pleasure—he both participated in and policed the raucous drinking culture of New Spain's capital. Bernal's disreputable behavior at pulquerías gave the military men who fought with him a weapon in their anti-sereno arsenal, but on the other hand, it may have connected Bernal more closely with the plebeians he dealt with on his rounds.

With uneducated, rural men like Bernal on patrol, the reformers set themselves up for failure in their ambitious plans to regulate the consumption of pulque or prevent theft, beatings, murders, and large and small acts of rebellion. The presence of the serenos only exacerbated the tensions between different groups residing in or visiting the capital. Most likely all of these offenses actually increased in the early nineteenth century, and many of the crimes were committed by soldiers who hated the night watchmen. All of the documented conflicts between Bernal and residents of Mexico City involved soldiers, highlighting the fault lines so prevalent in the final years of the viceroyalty of New Spain, as the empire as a whole became more militarized. For Indigenous people, the new street lighting provided an opportunity to destroy a symbol of Spanish rule with slight consequences, other than a loud noise. These attacks became ever more political during mass insurgency. Files that have been lost in the last two hundred years might document high stress arguments between Bernal and lantern-smashing plebeians who viewed him as representing a detested regime. Poor and powerless, other than in the brief moments when they successfully made arrests, an act that also required support from passersby, Bernal and the other serenos failed to prevent insurrection, as well as the disruptions caused by the expansion of the military and its privileges.

This conclusion began with a quote depicting how the role of law enforcement changes when a revolution takes place. In hindsight, history portrays destructive acts of rebellion leading to a successful revolution as heroism, not criminal activity. As a result, when a revolution succeeds, ancien régime police, such as Bernal, become reactionaries, not heroic crime fighters. Bernal is not mentioned in any surviving records during the insurgency years. His disappearance as a locus of conflictive moments and encounters preceded the declining importance of the serenos as an institution and ultimately Spain's loss of its wealthiest and most populous territory. Because historians have neglected to examine the point of view of men like Bernal and his compañeros, they instead tend to believe the story that

CONCLUSION

the Bourbon reformers told about themselves: that they were conscientious record keepers, working hard and effectively to civilize a city with a deplorable drinking culture and reprehensible animal physicality in full public view. When we consider the histories of Bernal and other serenos, as well as the actions of plebeians and the nightly exchanges between the night watchmen and the people on the streets, we must question this imperial narrative. Policing that only responds to the desires of the elite to protect their personal property and maintain what they view as order will not endure without protest, and potentially even revolution. Unfortunately, history also proves that revolutions do not succeed in effectively reforming law enforcement.

Afterword

MEXICO CITY LAW ENFORCEMENT AFTER INDEPENDENCE

> Serenos? All of you should be hanged, for pandering to thieves. If they didn't have you all watching their backs so carefully, if you weren't always drunk, or sleeping, or abandoning your posts, all of these robberies would be impossible!
> —Fernández de Lizardi, *El periquillo sarniento*

Reforms in rural and urban law enforcement continued on and off during the decades that separated the founding of the first Mexican republic in 1824 from the Mexican Revolution in the early twentieth century. As the years passed, the night watchmen became a humorous and folkloric oddity that visitors from countries to the north would comment on in their writings. These depictions originally derived from a satire of viceregal society written by a respected Mexican political and social commentator but quickly evolved into an English-language joke poking fun of Mexico's national-era backwardness.[1] In other words, Mexican literature started this trajectory, but foreigners exploited it for a broader North Atlantic readership, who had their own reasons for depicting Latin American countries as struggling nations. This trivialization of the night watchmen's history meant that, for decades, historians ignored the guarda faroleros as they narrated the history of law enforcement in the Americas and in the Western world more broadly. Although short and sparsely documented, the lantern guards' historical chapter, combined with persistent popular objections to their existence, adds to the larger story of Latin American democracies in the nineteenth century. These new nations were more radical experiments in modernity than seen in nineteenth-century Europe or the United States.[2] Before ending this book with a sampling of literary depictions of the night watchmen, an overview of the crucial decade after independence shows the declining importance of this particular Bourbon reform.

Night Watchmen Reform

The 1820s saw increased unrest in Mexico City, as the poor and working-class residents faced off with a new system of government and the ongoing presence of both wealthy Spaniards and the military. Viceregal leaders had made desperate attempts to reform urban law enforcement in the era of mass insurgency, trying their best to tamp down military abuses. But in the decade after Mexicans achieved independence from Spain, a rapid succession of governments took advantage of soldiers and their weapons to counter ongoing mass protests.[3] From the first months after New Spain dissolved as a political entity, tensions persisted between urban rioters and the political victors of the Wars of Independence. Although the populace supported him because they perceived him as representing anti-Spanish sentiments, the victorious former royalist general Iturbide expressed displeasure with the raucous mobs in the city. Over the course of the 1820s, plebeians increased their protests against the Spanish presence. This unrest eventually led to violent consequences and political decentralization during the post-insurgency era.

After the final Spanish viceroy fled and Iturbide became the emperor of Mexico in May 1822, the lantern guards did not experience changes in their duties. The first small indication of a change in the concept of urban policing came with the re-release, in July 1822, of an 1813 decree that discussed the duties of eight *fieles celadores* (faithful guards). The tasks of these volunteer guards seemed to mainly focus on enforcing regulations for businesses.[4] That same summer, the provisional government junta created a new urban militia in an attempt to control the military men who continued to cause so many disturbances.[5] Later that year, Iturbide faced rumors of mass rebellion and looting, along with vigilante organization in his capital and military revolt in the provinces. Iturbide abdicated and the first Mexican Empire fell in 1823. This first attempt at self-rule faced opposition by conservative "Bourbonists" who wanted a European prince to rule Mexico as a constitutional monarchy with limited suffrage.

AFTERWORD

Iturbide himself also had a Bourbon vision of Mexico, centralized as it had been for centuries in Mexico City.[6] As the first Mexican Empire disintegrated, the legislature imposed curfews and bans on gatherings, inspired once again by the persistent violence between city residents and the military. A few months later, on the thirteenth anniversary of Father Hidalgo's call to arms, the moment that started the era of violent popular insurgency, a rumor circulated about destroying the tomb of Hernán Cortés.[7] Although they now lived in an independent state, anti-Spanish sentiments still motivated the populace to act against the authorities.

Popular demonstrations and rioting multiplied even as major political reforms took place. Most importantly for the territory of the former Spanish viceroyalty, the Constitution of 1824 ushered in the Estados Unidos Mexicanos, governed as a federal republic, a system which lasted until 1835.[8] This foundational document created the Federal District of Mexico City, which extended two leagues (or about six miles) in all directions from the Zócalo. The new constitution emphasized the organization of high-level national and regional courts but did not discuss the details of street-level policing.[9] More significant reforms to law enforcement began in early 1825 and continued sporadically for the next one hundred years, as Mexican governments faced the French invasion, and the Second Empire, and the country passed from the era of the Reforma into the Porfirian dictatorship and finally into the Mexican Revolution.[10]

Under the government of the first president of the Mexican Republic, Guadalupe Victoria, the 1825 decree known as the Bando de Policía y Buen Gobierno focused on maintaining the sanitary conditions and general upkeep of the city.[11] The decree thereby interpreted policía in the older definition, as opposed to in the modern sense of a corps of armed law enforcement. This bando sounded very much like a checklist of Bourbon beautification aspirational projects aimed at civilizing barbaric plebeians. Regulations included the following: littering would result in a fine, as would throwing dirty water out a window or into a canal; residents should not block the streets with their carriages, washing their horses, dishes, or clothes; coachmen should not park their empty carriages in a line; throwing fireworks was absolutely forbidden due to the serious harm that this act always caused; windows should not display vases or other containers that could fall into the street; trash collection was to occur between six and eight in the morning on Mondays, Wednesdays, and Saturdays; businesses such as butchers should not throw animal parts or feathers into the street; taverns should have clean benches outside of their establishments; water carriers had to clean the fountains that they used to prevent spreading disease from the filthy water; dead animals had to be moved quickly out of the streets by their owners; and parents had to prevent their children from urinating or defecating in public, or risk paying the fine charged to adults for the same offense. In an appeal to the teachers and grammarians, even putting up a sign containing a spelling error risked a fine.

The next year (1826) saw the foundation of a more military-like municipal police force, overseen by the federal district government. With this reform, Mexican law enforcement moved toward a narrower definition of policing and encountered some of the same conflicts that changes of this kind typically caused with urbanites in other cities around the Atlantic basin. From the late 1820s to the 1840s, in cities such as Baltimore and London, reformers feared popular reactions to uniforms and increased armaments, since this visual movement away from the familiar neighborhood volunteer night watchmen clearly signified an increase in governmental militarization and surveillance.[12]

For the first time in Mexican history, militarized patrolmen wore uniforms, in imitation of long-established traditions in France. These outfits included white pants and blue jackets with red accents. They also carried guns, a far cry from the viceregal lantern guards, who oftentimes had little more than ropes to literally haul people into custody. Divided into infantrymen (armed with rifles) and cavalry (mounted and equipped with a sword and a pair of pistols), each of these new policemen wore a badge labeling them as public employees charged with enforcing public security.[13] All of this represented a clear effort by the state to militarize law enforcement.[14] In contrast, the civilian alcaldes and other volunteer neighborhood watchmen still could not carry guns as they went about enforcing sanitary regulations or even arresting criminals and the disorderly public, including the military men exercising their fuero. This new policing corps did not improve urban law enforcement, instead making it, by some accounts, even more threatening and corrupt.[15]

Indeed, a more militarized police force did little to prevent public unrest in Mexico City, by this point divided into followers of the Masonic lodges known as Yorkinos and Escoceses, even as city officials expanded its reach.[16] In 1828 the authorities most feared vagrants and robberies, stating that protecting property was a government's most important duty. They consolidated the public security corps to include the lantern guards, the military-like guards described above, as well as the urban militia, with nightly military patrols on horseback. This reform promised more oversight over the serenos.[17] Yet these reforms did nothing to prevent the most significant rebellion in the capital city since 1692. After losing the presidential election of September 1828, the insurgent hero Vicente Guerrero (referred to mockingly by his opponents as *el negro*) dedicated the next few months to successfully opposing the election of Manuel Gómez Pedraza. Guerrero's faction took part in a late November revolt centered on the Acordada compound, a fortified jail that symbolized Spanish judicial reforms dating back to the early 1700s. In addition to showing that popular rebellion still thrived both in the city and the countryside, this revolt also focused on a widespread desire to expel all Spaniards from the new nation.[18] A few days after the Acordada revolt, Guerrero himself allegedly urged the plebeian mob to sack the Parián market, buildings that housed market stalls in the Zócalo, steps from the cathedral. Associated with elite Spanish international merchants, this market sold luxurious goods, such as silk and porcelain, imported on the Manila Galleons from the Philippines and China. Rioters also had attacked the Parián market in 1692 and even burned the nearby viceregal palace.

Very few documents exist describing the 1828 riot, and those that have survived distort the events to fit two contemporary and opposing political stances. Although conservative writers may have exaggerated, the attack on the Parián market did result in casualties (figures range anywhere from two to eight hundred fatalities), and millions of pesos in damages.[19] Military leaders claimed that they stopped the looting after only a few hours by firing cannons into the crowd, but other eyewitnesses remember a city that raged out of control for weeks. One fact is not disputed: no civilian guards or any representatives from the new public security force even attempted to quell the riot. On the contrary, observers noted that the corrupt police officers both intimidated the merchants and sold the stolen goods that they confiscated from looters. The strongest message that emerges from historical sources discussing these events is the blatant disgust that some commentators felt toward the rioters. This sentiment echoes the opinions of Bourbon reformers described throughout this book.[20] The Parián riot also demonstrates that Mexico City plebeians understood that violence and destruction of property could help expel the last remaining Spaniards who inspired so much popular hatred. Various decrees achieved this goal in 1829.[21]

Unfortunately the violence of late 1828 extinguished the optimism of the early Mexican republic, led to restrictions in what had been almost universal male suffrage, and ultimately encouraged the elite to retract their political engagement with the Mexico City poor for the next eighty years.[22] Plebeian protests, starting small with lantern smashing in the 1790s, finally burnt out in the late 1820s, during the peak radical moment under President Guerrero, the insurgent hero who was deposed from office in late 1829.[23]

The Lantern Guards in Literature

Witnesses to the Parián riot, whose statements are recorded in both government documents and in historical memoirs, did not give civilian law enforcement any credit for preventing or ending this disturbance. Nor did contemporary fiction writers bestow praise on the serenos. Instead, they became either a subject of disdain or a romantic holdover emblematic of a city that English-language writers depicted as premodern. Over the course of the nineteenth century, the lantern guards came to signify not a dynamic reform made to beautify and encourage safety in an important American metropolis but rather Mexico's lack of modernity, a nostalgic remnant of another time.[24]

The first important literary source describing the serenos spans the viceregal and national eras. One of Spanish America's first great novels, *El periquillo sarniento*, written in 1816 and published in 1831, portrays Mexico City's guards realistically at work. The revealing anecdote takes place during a robbery, quoted at the beginning of this afterword. The author of this picaresque novel was the renowned journalist José Joaquín Fernández de Lizardi (1776–1827). Known by to his pen name, "The Mexican Thinker," Lizardi wrote a fifty-two-chapter epic critique of viceregal society from the perspective of its final years.[25] Lizardi's account of an interaction between a lantern guard and the book's narrator echoes archival court cases written by judicial notaries, of the kind cited in the last seven chapters. Even two centuries later, writers still depend on Lizardi for their fictionalized depictions of the night watchmen.[26]

Lizardi breathes life into a night on Mexico City's late eighteenth-century streets, redolent with the problems that beset the insurgency-era viceroyalty. The scene starts as the protagonist Periquillo, the so-called Itching Parrot, easily hides himself in a doorway at 10:30 p.m., because "the streets had almost no lighting."[27] Lizardi's readers would recognize this passing observation as a direct criticism of their city's infrastructure and failed beautification plans. Periquillo then proceeds to initiate a friendly exchange with the sereno he found sitting on the corner, another implied criticism of the guards' reputed laziness. In an incident ripped directly from the judicial archives, the two share a courteous conversation along with some *cigarros*, lighting them with the night watchman's handheld lantern. When a girl, the victim of a robbery, screams for the serenos from a balcony window, the guard tries to call for help from his colleagues by "whistling as well as he could" and "making some benedictions with his lantern at the crossroads." In simpler terms, he waved around his light to indicate his location. As the thieves ran away, the guard called out to stop them. No one arrived to help him. The empty streets suggest a lack of other alert patrolmen in the neighborhood. Finally, a group gathers, including a military sergeant, soldiers, and other night watchmen, an accurate summation of the different types of patrols that would have roamed the streets in this era. The guards effectively respond to the victims' calls for a doctor and a priest to attend to them. In response to the accusations quoted above regarding his drunkenness and that he served as a lookout for the thieves, the sereno quickly swears that he had not been asleep or negligent, but the sergeant ignores his denials. Lizardi continues this incident with a hilarious description of Periquillo's processing at the jail, again accurately depicting everything that historians read in the *Libros de Reos*, but with much more humor in his account of "a million" prisoners who he found incarcerated with him, and, in classic Cervantian style, a reference to a bribe paid to the jailer (the alcaide) as a fee to enroll in a religious brotherhood (*cofradía*). The next several chapters describe life in jail and the grossly corrupt criminal courts.

Lacking Lizardi's biting insider critiques, for the next century, travelers from other countries portrayed the night watchmen as Mexican folk characters, embracing the classic stereotypes that northern Europeans applied to Spaniards over the centuries. In 1828 the most famous of these *costumbristas*, Claudio Linati, described the serenos as inherently Catholic—almost priestly.[28] Just over two decades later, Lady Emmeline Stuart-Wortley, an English poet and memorialist, wrote of starting a journey at around four in the morning. She mentioned that the sereno would soon leave his nightly work, as she "plunged into the half lamp-lit darkness." While in the port city of Veracruz, Lady Emmeline observed the "astonishing and alarming" "bawling" and "howling" of the guards, "who seem to be in the habit of perpetually frightening people to death, to assure them that they are safe." She attributes the constant refrain, in her words "the terrible hollabulloo," to the fact that the weather never changes—it is always "cloudlessly fine."[29] In the decades leading to when Stuart-Wortley made her observations, the number of lanterns in Mexico City steadily increased to number over fifteen hundred. Not long after, the capital gradually started using other sources of fuel to illuminate the streets, including turpentine, and city leaders even began considering gas lighting.[30]

Perhaps drawing from Lizardi's realistic depictions, in the mid-nineteenth century, the French adventurer and writer Gabriel Ferry, who spent several years living in Mexico, narrated an anecdote that reads like a day in the eventful life of patrolman and later corporal Manuel José Bernal, whom I first mentioned in the introduction:

Startled by the noise of the carriages, a refractory horse struck violently against a ladder, on the top of which a *sereno* (watchman) was lighting a lamp suspended from the walls of the barrack of La Acordada [the hated viceregal jail]. The sereno fell from a height of fifteen feet and lay motionless on the pavement. . . . I could not help envying for an instant the fate of the sereno, insensible at least to the rude hustling of the crowd, who mercilessly trod him underfoot. . . . In compliance with the magistrate's orders, the still inanimate body of the sereno was placed on a *tapastle* (a kind of litter), always kept at the barracks for similar incidents.[31]

Ferry's descriptions of Mexico City inspired reviewers of his book to comment on the lawlessness of Mexico City in this era, in contrast to their own metropolises, which they perceived as more civilized and organized. According to an 1856 issue of the *London Quarterly Review*, if someone chose to go with their night policemen to "the haunts of the most depraved and desperate," nothing more than a lift of the copper's finger would guarantee safety. In contrast, no authority figure dared to enter similar neighborhoods in Mexico City, but instead the patrolman "shuffles humbly along," "mutters a prayer," or makes the sign of the cross.[32] Although Mexico City had a regulated and salaried corps of urban night watchmen before London, the former viceregal capital had become a backward and chaotic place by the mid-nineteenth century, at least according to the Londoner's point of view. This was a matter of perspective. From the point of view of a New York City police chief, nineteenth-century London bobbies appeared as humorously unprofessional in contrast to "the police force of New York City . . . without a doubt the finest of its kind in the world."[33] It seems that law enforcement institutions in this era offered an opportunity for observers and leaders to brag about their level of progress over urban crime and disorder. Northerners' portrayal of Mexico City as lacking respectable and effective policing contributed in a small way to the former viceregal capital losing its status as an important city in the broader nineteenth-century Atlantic world.

By the late 1860s, although it had not grown as quickly as metropolises such as New York, London, and Paris, Mexico City proudly installed a gas grid for street lighting.[34] Only the poorest neighborhoods continued to use turpentine-fueled lanterns or Tenochtitlán-style ocote torches.[35] As Mexico's capital strove for wealthy, European-style modernity in the last decades of the nineteenth century, travelers now perceived the serenos as gentle reminders of a romantic past. In contrast to the comments above, in the 1880s, a visitor judged the city as very safe:

> Look along the streets. Every fifty feet there is a lantern set in the middle of the carriage way. Every lantern counts a policeman. Every policeman bears a sword, a carbine, and a revolver. With the hood of his coat drawn over his head, the Mexican policeman (sereno) looks like a monk: but he is a good fellow and will pass the stranger along the lines safely to the hotel. . . . Our home police could learn something from these Mexicans. During the night the hours are heralded by the serenos by a whistle of the most doleful note. It is a sort of a cross between a whip-poor-will and a tree-toad.[36]

Late nineteenth-century visitors continued to interpret Mexico City's night patrolmen as "cavaliers of old." In 1897 traveling writers even reported hearing them make the same call of "sereno" that they would have sounded more than a century before.[37]

To briefly expand the discussion to the broader topic of literature and policing in this era, these discussions formed part of the rapidly expanding genres of crime fiction, police memoirs, and criticism of law enforcement, which continues to grow to the present day. For the last two centuries, policemen and their predecessors (such as the Bow Street Runners) have inspired cultural production from academic historical studies to classic epic novels, beloved detective stories, wildly popular television series, and movies. Crime fiction actually began at least as long ago as Song China, with still-popular examples of Judge Di stories dating back to the eighteenth century. So much of our cultural production and consumption contributes to a narrative of lifesaving crime solvers in our most popular books, shows, and movies across decades.[38] While polarized literary interpretations of men in law enforcement have existed since the mid-nineteenth

AFTERWORD

century, the contrast between the police officer as villain and hero seems to become more inflammatory with every passing day. Perhaps no other occupation, even the clergy, inspires so many extreme opinions expressed in writing and popular culture. This book has attempted to position the serenos as very early characters in this two-hundred-year-old obsession.

Since only the scantiest literary references exist discussing the guarda faroleros, we have to turn to other sources to fill in detail about how they might have felt about this occupation. The nineteenth century saw a boom in memoirs, novels, and stories that focused on the newly created professional street patrols, their leadership, their competitors, and their adversaries. English language works help us understand what it might have felt like to do this job, even in distant Mexico City. Published around the same time as *El periquillo sarniento*, fast-paced adventure stories about the London Bow Street Runners spin daring tales of their bravery and ingenuity. In these, the hero explains that he joined the group because wearing the basic uniform of a blue coat and a red waistcoat was "not quite so bad and low as a livery"—he wanted a routine life, but also adventure, and he abhorred servitude or sitting in an office. He found the other men who took on this employment to be lively, friendly, and eager to share their exploits.[39] Unfortunately, Mexico did not produce tales of this kind, narrated from the point of view of the patrolmen.

Underscoring the lack of a Mexican contribution to this burgeoning literature, leaders of Mexican law enforcement also did not portray themselves as the heroes of their own autobiographies. In contrast, by the late nineteenth century, police chiefs in the United States involved in mid-nineteenth-century departmental reforms started to write their memoirs. Their biased chronicles offered congratulatory and uncritical views of what they viewed as progress in law enforcement during their eras.[40] The most accessible of these somewhat romantic, self-aggrandizing accounts come from Boston's Edward Savage and New York's George Walling.[41] An emphasis on "great men" as well as proud histories of the success of nineteenth- and twentieth-century departments dominated the history of law enforcement for the next several decades, although fiction writers already had started a robust tradition of criticizing the police.

AFTERWORD

Literary sources from outside Mexico also offer a growing critique of policing. From the era of the Bow Street Runners, writers noted that "everybody has a dislike and horror at the very sight of an officer."[42] Mid-century European literary classics filled in the specifics with hundreds of pages lamenting the injustices of policing.[43] Starting in the mid-nineteenth century, beloved private detective series focused on educated and elite writers' attitudes of high snobbery toward bumbling or crude coppers, a common portrayal that persists strongly to the present day in many cinematic and television interpretations. Summed up, tales of amateur investigators exist to critique the police for their lower-class status, their captivity within a slow government bureaucracy, their stupidity, their ignorance of scientific methods, and their boring lack of innovative methods or even the most basic imagination and reasoning skills. Although extremely popular among the public, these stories encapsulate the views of the educated bourgeoisie who looked down on professional law enforcement and rejected the involvement of police in their own lives.[44] Along with this hugely popular mocking and critical genre, police officers who themselves had a literary bent helped create a literature that enthralled readers with tales of incredible acts of competence, quick-wittedness, heroism, and courage. In fact, in some ways, both memoirs and fiction construct policemen as representing masculine ideals, even when a few human flaws enter the story.[45] This heroic presentation also persists to the current day in the almost superhero-like representation of law enforcement in some fictional and true crime accounts. It is interesting to note that all of the above, whether apparently for or against the police, all support goals of solving crimes, and in a sense, fighting evil within society with both personalities and institutions that valued surveillance and order.

In the same decades when outsiders to Mexico City imagined the old-fashioned lantern guards almost as knights errant trapped in amber, internally, dramatic change was taking place. To combat rampant banditry all over the countryside, Benito Juárez created a national rural police force in 1861.[46] The *rurales* dressed not in military-style uniforms but in imitation of the infamous and highly successful bandits, wearing huge felt sombreros and *charro* outfits. This choice of outfit indicates the intention for them to fit in with the bandits, as opposed to the military, although this corps of men came from both groups. The rurales directly supported presidential goals aiming for at least a patina of peace in the countryside, manifesting an aura of law and order to appease the fears of foreign investors. The plan worked, as visitors started to view Mexico as less dangerous, patrolled by a tough and rugged epitome of an idealized Mexican man.[47] Meanwhile, urban elites favored a greater police presence in what they viewed as the capital's highly modern central business district, brightly lighted blocks hosting luxury shopping.[48] While the Mexican rurales helped forge a new set of national mythologies about both law enforcement and manliness, residents of the city and in the countryside clearly demonstrated a long-term distrust of both the police and the judicial system more broadly, which persists to the present day.[49]

NOTES

All Spanish to English translations are the author's unless otherwise noted.

PREFACE

1. Alameddine, *Unecessary Woman*, 194.
2. Todd May and George Yancy, "Policing Is Doing What It Was Meant to Do. That's the Problem," *New York Times*, June 21, 2020, https://www.nytimes.com/2020/06/21/opinion/police-violence-racism-reform.html, with a reference to the work of Sally Hadden, *Slave Patrols*.
3. See for example, Mary Elliott and Jazmine Hughes, "Four Hundred Years after Enslaved Africans Were First Brought to Virginia, Most Americans Still Don't Know the Full Story of Slavery," part of the *New York Times*' 1619 project, accessed July 16, 2020, https://www.nytimes.com/interactive/2019/08/19/magazine/history-slavery-smithsonian.html.

INTRODUCTION

1. Lozano Armendares, *La criminalidad*, 24–25.
2. Mexico, Archivo General de la Nación (hereafter AGN), Real Audiencia, Criminal 37, Contenedor 170, vol. 340, Exp. 12, 1791, 249. See chapter 2 for more details on what happened next during this incident.
3. For an overview of the alcaldes and law enforcement reform in the century before 1822, see Yáñez Romero, *Policía mexicana*, 74–115. The Spanish Crown purposefully confused jurisdictions and made official jurisdictions overlapping as part of their ruling strategies. See Lynch, *Bourbon Spain*, 103.
4. As noted below, Anglo–North American cities such as New York and Boston did not approach Mexico City's size until at least 1820, when the Mexican capital decreased in size, with growth slowed down after the decade of insurgency. Citizen and military watches existed in urban centers such as Boston, New York, Philadelphia, and Charleston going back to the 1600s. Paid night watchmen appeared, sometimes temporarily, in the eighteenth century. While their equipment resembled that of Mexico City's guarda faroleros, in contrast to the latter they patrolled tiny cities in small numbers. See Wadman and Allison,

To Protect and Serve. A police chief in New York City from the mid-nineteenth century described the night watchmen in his city as rudimentary and subject to well-deserved derision well into the 1800s. See Walling, *Recollections of a New York Chief of Police*, 29–32.

5. Lipsett-Rivera, *Origins of Macho*, 81, 146; Sanchez-Archilla Bernal, *Jueces, criminalidad y control social*; Scardaville, "Crime and the Urban Poor"; Oberto, "Alumbrado y seguridad," 43–54; Oberto, "Policing"; Oberto, "Los alcaldes de barrio," 49–59.

6. While older police historiography, written by police chiefs and other officers themselves, emphasized reforms that improved law enforcement, this is no longer an accepted approach: "Reform, as is now well established, did not represent a Whiggish progression of legislative milestones on the inevitable route to modern, professional police forces." Jennings, "Policing Public Houses in Victorian England," 52–75, quote on 53.

7. MacLachlan, *Spain's Empire in the New World*, 140n13; O'Callaghan, *History of Medieval Spain*, 57–67.

8. The Crown of Castile appointed corregidores with oversight over specific towns in the early fourteenth century. The first audiencias, with civil and criminal jurisdiction in different *salas*, began in the late fourteenth century and instituted criminal prosecutions in Mexico City in 1554. See MacLachlan, *Criminal Justice in Eighteenth-Century Mexico*, 9–12; Lozano Armendares, *La criminalidad*, 155–58.

9. Authors including Lipsett-Rivera and Lozano Armendares have deeply mined the detailed information these files provide on the general population in their excellent books on crime, gender, and masculinity. See Lozano Armendares, *La criminalidad*; Lipsett-Rivera, *Gender and the Negotiation of Daily Life*.

10. Vanderwood, *Disorder and Progress*, 18–19.

11. MacLachlan, *Criminal Justice*, 10–11; Lozano Armendares, *La criminalidad*, 160–62; Martínez Ruíz, *Policía y proscritos*, 24–25.

12. Lozano Armendares, *La criminalidad*, 18–26.

13. Scardaville, "(Hapsburg) Law and (Bourbon) Order," 510–11.

14. Nacif Mina, *La policía en la historia*, 24; Pulido Esteva, "Policía del buen gobierno," 1612.

15. AGN, Mexico, Real Audiencia, vol. 17, Exp. 15, 1801–1802, 209.

16. Emsley, *Theories and Origins of the Modern Police*, xiv–xv.

17. Eighteenth-century England also viewed police as French and repressive. See Dodsworth, "The Idea of Police," 583–604.

18. Lynch, *Bourbon Spain*, 23–45.

19. Yáñez Romero, *Policía mexicana*, 40–47, 52–54.

20. For the French Revolution's effect on Spain, see Herr, *Eighteenth-Century Revolution*, 239–315; Lynch, *Bourbon Spain*, 380–421.
21. However, I do not think it is worth critical nitpicking if historians use this term, as Scardaville does throughout "Crime and the Urban Poor," iv, v, ix.
22. Dodsworth, "The Idea of Police," 589.
23. Lechner, "El concepto de 'policía,'" 401.
24. Lechner, "El concepto de 'policía,'" 398; Pulido Esteva, "Policía: Del buen gobierno," 1598.
25. Lechner, "El concepto de 'policía,'" 407; Pulido Esteva, "Policía: Del buen gobierno," 1599.
26. Nacif Mina, *La policía en la historia*, 20.
27. Pulido Esteva, "Policía: Del buen gobierno," 1600–1605.
28. Pulido Esteva, "Policía: Del buen gobierno," 1596, 1611–16.
29. Mexico, AGN, Real Audienca, Criminal 37, Contenedor 170, vol. 340, Exp. 12, 1791, 242.
30. Ávila González, "Voces y ladridos," 92.
31. See May and Yancy, "Policing Is Doing What It Was Meant to Do." To this day, sworn officers vow to uphold the laws of the state that employs them, so, as noted by the philosophers May and Yancy, we must understand the values of the government and the society that they work for:

    "That is the question that we should be asking of the police. Not why do they regularly fail to perform their duties correctly and thus need reform, but rather, what duties are they succeeding at? Once we ask that question, the answer is entirely clear. They succeed in keeping people in their place. They succeed in keeping middle-class and especially upper-class white people safe, so long as they don't get out of line. They succeed in keeping people of color in their place so that they don't challenge the social order that privileges middle- and upper-class white people."
32. Malka, *The Men of Mobtown*, 55–64. For a detailed analysis of both police history in the United States and theories about policing, see Williams, *Our Enemies in Blue*.
33. Herr, *Eighteenth-Century Revolution*, 151.
34. For statistics on police officers in the United States, see "Data USA: Police Officers," accessed July 21, 2020, https://datausa.io/profile/soc/police-officers.
35. Cope, *Limits of Racial Domination*, 15, 22–23.
36. Arrom, *Containing the Poor*, 17; Cope, *Limits of Racial Domination*, 6, 22. The term *léperos* gained popularity in the nineteenth century and is not commonly seen in records directly generated by the night watchmen and their supervisors. Poinsett, *Notes on Mexico*, 67.

37. Lozano Armendares, *La criminalidad*, 35.
38. Arrom, *Containing the Poor*, 7, 25.
39. Mundy, *The Death of Aztec Tenochtitlan*, 1, 76.
40. Scardaville, "Crime and the Urban Poor," 1; Warren, *Vagrants and Citizens*, 9–10.
41. Lozano Armendares, *La criminalidad*, 43.
42. Poinsett, *Notes on Mexico*, 66.
43. Arrom, *Containing the Poor*, 17.
44. Toner, "Everything in Its Right Place?," 28; Warren, *Vagrants and Citizens*, 9; Scardaville, "Alcohol Abuse and Tavern Reform," 644; Lozano Armdendares, *La criminalidad*, 43; Chesnais, "Population, Urbanization, and Migration," 191; Klein, *A Population History of the United States*, 92–93; Risjord, *Chesapeake Politics*, 16–17; LeMay, "Mushrooming Cities," 56.
45. Lozano Armendares, *La criminalidad*, 15, 38.
46. London dominated European cities in terms of size (around a million people in 1800) but did not modernize law enforcement until 1830. See Turrado Vidal, *La policía*, 35; Arrom, *Containing the Poor*, 18. It is interesting to note the relationship between population growth in the eighteenth and nineteenth centuries, and the increase in professional police. Some small cities established these forces before massive metropolises. See Bayley, "Police and Political Development in Europe," 70–71.
47. Scardaville, "Alcohol Abuse and Tavern Reform," 644, 654.
48. Voekel, "Peeing on the Palace," 183–84.
49. As noted by John Lynch, "they gained a revenue and lost an empire." See Lynch, *Bourbon Spain*, 18–21, quote on 21.
50. Dodsworth, "The Idea of Police," 598.
51. Arrom, *Containing the Poor*, 20.
52. Lozano Armendares, *La criminalidad*, 121–23.
53. AGN, Mexico, Ayuntamiento, vol. 107, Exp. 1, 1777, 29. This description of shopping habits was given to argue against having small stores collect money from the populace to pay for installing street lights. See chapter 1 for more details.
54. Scardaville, "Crime and the Urban Poor," 4, 21, 49–53; Tutino, *Mexico City, 1808*, 41–43, 75–94.
55. Voekel, "Peeing on the Palace," 186–92.
56. Tutino, *Mexico City, 1808*, 41–43, 59; Lozano Armendares, *La criminalidad*, 122.
57. Arrom, *Containing the Poor*, 1–33, 66–69, 100. Spain created similar institutions in the same era. Herr, *Eighteenth-Century Revolution*, 33–34.
58. Herr, *Eighteenth-Century Revolution*, 48.
59. Herr, *Eighteenth-Century Revolution*, 50, 54–55. Herr discusses broader economic reforms relating to international trade, labor regulations, and factories, on 120–53. These reforms succeeded in increasing prosperity in Spain by the 1780s.

60. Lynch, *Bourbon Spain*, 239.
61. AGN, Mexico, Real Audiencia, vol. 17, Exp. 15, 1801–1802, 209.
62. Lipsett-Rivera, *Origins of Macho*, 67, 127–28.
63. Lozano Armendares, *La criminalidad*, 14–17.
64. For urban space hierarchies, see Lipsett-Rivera, *Gender and Negotiation*, 44–58.
65. Cope, *Limits of Racial Domination*, 9–10.
66. Cope, *Limits of Racial Domination*, 16, 20.
67. Tutino, *Mexico City, 1808*, 91–93; Lozano Armendares, *La criminalidad*, 13, 21–23.
68. Lozano Armendares, *La criminalidad*, 23; Walsh, *Virtuous Waters*, 34–35.
69. Cope, *Limits of Racial Domination*, 32.
70. Fernández de Lizardi, *The Mangy Parrot*, xxxiv–xxxv.
71. Stevens, *Mexico in the Time of Cholera*, 42–44.
72. Cope, *Limits of Racial Domination*, 108, observes that most master craftsmen in Mexico City were literate, while the opposite was the case for journeymen. Bernal's signature appears on AGN, Real Audiencia, Criminal 37, Contenedor 170, vol. 340, Exp. 12, 1791, 250.
73. AGN, Mexico, Real Audiencia, vol. 17, Exp. 15, 1801–1802, 216. Toner, "Everything in Its Right Place?," 30.
74. The *Libros de Reos* also heavily inform the scholarship of Michael Scardaville and José Sánchez-Arcilla Bernal. While I cite their pioneering work throughout, this book does not focus on what these scholars have already conveyed regarding the poor in Mexico City, the history of crime, or more generally, the judicial system. A fundamental aspect of writing archive-based history is to take advantage of well-known sources to provide new interpretations based on recent activism, or new theories and interpretive lenses; original work can still come from a document that other scholars have studied before, especially if previous scholarship comes from a very different era. Both historians made and continue to offer superb contributions, but Scardaville published his work mainly in the 1980s, and thus far Sánchez-Arcilla Bernal writes only in Spanish, and with a very erudite legal history approach. As with many other topics in Mexican history, we still have much to learn from the substantial documentary repositories created under Spanish rule.
75. Scardaville, "Justice by Paperwork," 984–85.
76. Patrolling alcaldes had their names noted, as did the lieutenants of the head guard. These men were always dons, men of honor, never plebeians. Martínez Ruíz, *Policía y proscritos*, 68.
77. AGN, Mexico, *Libros de Reos*, Caja 73, Exp. 45, August 21, August 31, September 14, October 22, October 24, November 4, December 10, December 13, December 25, 1794. On two nights, number 23 made two arrests. His custodies reflect a

normal breakdown in terms of race labels in the *Libros de Reos*. Over half of the culprits have the label indio, and all but one are men.

78. Mexico, AGN, *Libros de Reos*, Caja 73, Exp. 46, September 12, 1796; Exp. 50, June 1, September 24, October 18, November 8, 1798.

79. My focus is not on the background or punishments meted out to arrested individuals, so I did not count each person as a separate data point; instead I work from a count of each interaction with the lantern guards, whether it involved one or ten people. In his dissertation and articles, Scardaville counted and analyzed all the existing arrest records from the late colonial era, resulting in an in-depth study of 7,067 recorded crimes from 1794 to 1807. More recently Sánchez-Arcilla Bernal tabulated the records found in the existing books dating from 1794 to 1798, the same ones that I refer to in this book. Sánchez-Arcilla Bernal found a total of 7,029 arrests. Sanchez-Arcilla Bernal gives this total in "La delincuencia femenina," his article dealing with crimes committed by women, although he is also familiar with the later *Libros de Reos*, some of which have disappeared. He explains in detail why he and Scardaville have different totals and the basic statistics of each *Libro de Reos* in "Fondos del Archivo General," 162–68.

80. Germeten, *Profit and Passion*, chapter 5.

81. AGN, Mexico, Criminal 37, Contenedor 170, vol. 340, Exp. 12; Ramo de Policía y Empedrados, Caja 4536, Exp. 13, 1795; Criminal, Caja 1150, Exp. 10, 1796; Indiferente Virreinal, Caja 4536; Exp. 16, 1800; Real Audiencia, vol. 17, Exp. 15, 1801–1802.

82. Cobb, *Police and the People*, 14, 18–19, 44, quote on 73.

83. Candiani, *Dreaming of Dry Land*, 154.

84. Voekel, "Peeing on the Palace," 183, 186.

85. Martínez Ruíz, *Policía y proscritos*, 28–34, 46; Arrom, *Containing the Poor*, 15.

86. Cobb, *Police and the People*, 24–25.

87. Herr, *Eighteenth-Century Revolution*, 12; Lynch, *Bourbon Spain*, 102–6, 170, goes over the complex expansion and retraction of the various responsibilities of intendants.

88. Barbier, "Culmination of the Bourbon Reforms," 52–55.

89. Deans-Smith, *Bureaucrats, Planters, and Workers*, 6–7; Barbier, "Culmination of the Bourbon Reforms," 58, 62; Brading, "Bourbon Spain and Its American Empire," 392–95; Klein, *American Finances of the Spanish Empire*, 81–95. Factories opened by the government dated back to the early eighteenth century in Spain. See Herr, *Eighteenth-Century Revolution*, 123.

90. The Portuguese king also founded a force to both provide lighting and royal security via nocturnal patrols in the fourteenth century. Fiães Fernandes, "Early Centuries of the Portuguese Police System," 448–59. These *quadrilheiros* even

carried a pike-like weapon but operated as a volunteer force. In the second half of the eighteenth century, Portugal created an intendancy overseeing national policing.

91. Martínez Ruíz, *Policía y proscritos*, 18.
92. Turrado Vidal, *La policía*, 28–41; Martínez Ruíz, *Policía y proscritos*, 52, 153–54.
93. Lynch, *Bourbon Spain*, 262–68.
94. Arrom, *Containing the Poor*, 16.
95. Deans-Smith, *Bureaucrats, Planters, and Workers*, xiv.
96. Martínez Ruíz, *Policía y proscritos*, 64–71, 514–18, 76–90; Turrado Vidal, *La policía*, 46–50; Yáñez Romero, *Policía mexicana*, 60–67.
97. Deans-Smith, *Bureaucrats, Planters, and Workers*, xvi–xvii, 236–47; Rodríguez O., "We Are Now the True Spaniards," 31; Tutino, *Making a New World*, 242–52; Scardaville, "Crime and the Urban Poor," 235.
98. Cañizares-Esguerra, *Puritan Conquistadors*, 215–33, provides an excellent historiographic essay on this issue. Cañizares-Esguerra points out that, in terms of religious ideology, political innovation, scientific research, literary production, the history of ideas, and "cultural and racial hybridization of global proportions . . . the Iberian empires . . . first set into motion the processes . . . that typify our modern world." The quote comes from 219. For radical republics in the nineteenth century, see Sanders, *Vanguard of the Atlantic World*. Even within the United Kingdom itself, this attitude is disputed, as Glasgow and Edinburgh had more professional policing from around 1800. Emsley, *Theories and Origins*, xiii.
99. Garrioch, "The People of Paris and Their Police," 511.
100. Miller, *Cops and Bobbies*, 2. Other cities in the British Isles also claim early professional law enforcement. See Garnham, "Police and Public Order in Eighteenth-Century Dublin," 81–91.
101. Loftus, Goold, and Mac Giollabhui, "From a Visible Spectacle to an Invisible Presence," 629–45. Quotes on 629, 632.
102. Emsley, *Theories and Origins*, xii. See also Silver, "Demand for Order," 25–26.
103. Savage, *Police Records and Recollections*.
104. Vanderwood, *Disorder and Progress*, 47–49, 60.
105. Emsley, *Theories and Origins*, xvi.
106. Dodsworth, "The Idea of Police," 593.
107. Reiss and Bordua, "Environment and Organization," 32–34.
108. These contrasts and comparisons derive from a summation of what "modern" policing is in Williams, *Our Enemies in Blue*, chapter 2. See also Emsley, *Theories and Origins*, xx; Reith, "Preventive Principle of Police," 4.
109. Denys, "The Development of Police Forces," 332–44.
110. Silver, "Demand for Order," 30.

111. Dodsworth, "The Idea of Police," 593.
112. Styles, "The Emergence of the Police," 17–20.
113. Bayley, "The Police and Political Development," 71–79; Paley, "'An Imperfect, Inadequate and Wretched System'?," 414. This article sums up the London situation in a way that applies very well as a contrast/comparison to Mexico City and the serenos.
114. For an overview of older historiography, see Robinson, "Ideology as History," 7–21.
115. Emsley, *Theories and Origins*, xvii.
116. Garrioch, "The People of Paris," 512, 515.
117. Sociologists more than historians have discussed concepts of perceptions of criminality, especially toward new, different, and expanding groups within a local population, as well as how the presence of a preventative as well as reactive patrolling corps affects the general implementation of legal processes within a society. See Reiss and Bordua, "Environment and Organization"; Silver, "The Demand for Order," 1–24.
118. Garrioch, "People of Paris," 512, 514–23, 528–30.
119. Paley, "Imperfect, Inadequate, and Wretched System," 415.
120. Manning and Van Maanen, *Policing*.
121. Emsley, *Theories and Origins*, xii–xiii.
122. Johnson, *Policing the Urban Underworld*; Von Hoffman, "An Officer of the Neighborhood," 309–30.
123. Rey, "Police and Sodomy in Eighteenth-Century Paris," 129–46; Merrick, "Sodomites and Police in Paris," 103–28; Kushner, *Erotic Exchanges*.
124. Williams, *Our Enemies in Blue*.
125. Raspa, *Bloody Bay*. For the rise of the carceral state, see Christie, *Crime Control as Industry*; Gilmore, *Golden Gulag*; Gottschalk, *Caught*.
126. Payno, *Bandits of Río Frio*, 69–70.

1. LIGHT

1. Koslofsky, *Evening's Empire*, 158–63, quote on 173.
2. Schivelbusch, *Disenchanted Night*, 97.
3. Schivelbusch, *Disenchanted Night*, 76, 112. Street-light smashing done one by one does not have the same resonance when a huge grid maintains tens of thousands of lights.
4. Cordovil Cordeiro, "De-electrifying the History of Street Lighting," 37.
5. I use the English convention of Revillagigedo as one word, other than when directly citing original documents, which divided the viceroy's name as Revilla Gigedo.

6. A parallel and even greater challenge to urban control came from plebeian drinking habits, which has generated a huge historiography. I cover some aspects of this topic in chapter 4.
7. Johns, *City of Mexico in the Age of Díaz*, 35–49; Schivelbusch, *Disenchanted Night*, 85, 106. Most of the Ramo de Policía y Empedrados files in the AGN in Mexico City deal with the massive Bourbon street-paving project. See Glasco, *Constructing Mexico City*, 142–52.
8. Muñón Chimalpahin Quauhtlehuanitzin, *Annals of His Time*, 79, 87, 161.
9. Curcio-Nagy, *Great Festivals*, 68–69, 97–99, 104.
10. AGN, Mexico, Ramo de Policía y Empedrados, Caja 6494, Exp. 1, 1803.
11. Leonard, *Baroque Times in Old Mexico*, 5, 14, 122, 129; Schivelbusch, *Disenchanted Night*, 6–7.
12. See Germeten, *Black Blood Brothers*; Larkin, *The Very Nature of God*, 39–44.
13. Voekel, *Alone before God*.
14. Curcio-Nagy, *Great Festivals*, 108–12, 116–24, discusses Bourbon attempts to control traditionally boisterous religious festivals, arguing that urban reforms offered another way to strengthen urban imperial community.
15. See chapters 2 and 3 for more on the guards as semireligious figures.
16. Curcio-Nagy, *Great Festivals*, 146–53.
17. For the New Fire Ceremony, see Clendinnen, *Aztecs*, 237–40; Sigal, *Flower and the Scorpion*, 143–51.
18. Carranza-Castellanos, *Crónica del alumbrado*, 15.
19. AGN, Mexico, Ayuntamiento, vol. 107, Exp. 1, 1777, 33, 47.
20. Senosiain, *La noche develada*, 49–51.
21. For example, see the famous nighttime wakes and even witches' Sabbaths described in mid-seventeenth century Cartagena de Indias, in the New Kingdom of Granada (now Colombia). Germeten, *Violent Delights, Violent Ends*, 141.
22. AGN, Mexico, Ayuntamiento, vol. 107, Exp. 1, 1777, 54. See also Binder, "Introduction," 15.
23. Bru and Vicente, "¿Qué produce miedo en la ciudad?," 23–24. While the assumption for Mexico would be bourgeois occupation vs. plebeian, in Paris, lighting also illuminated corrupt aristocratic diversions. See Schivelbusch, *Disenchanted Night*, 103–4n49.
24. Pottharst and Wukovitz, "The Economics of Night-Time Illumination," 204–6.
25. Voekel, "Peeing on the Palace," 189–91, quote on 196. See also Juárez Flores, "Alumbrado público," 13.
26. Valdés, *Diálogo de Mercurio y Carón*; Nebrija, *Vocabulario español-latino*, 177.
27. Terreros y Pando, *Diccionario castellano con las voces de ciencias y artes*, 3:456.

28. Koslofsky, *Evening's Empire*, 130–45; Schivelbusch, *Disenchanted Night*, 86. Paris's 1667 street lighting was a response to the Fronde revolt.
29. Fernández-Paradas, *La industria de gas de Cádiz*, section 1.2.
30. Font, "El miedo a la ciudad oscura," 74–78. Other terms for understanding Enlightenment-era "seeing" include transparency, clarity, and curiosity. Cicchini, "A New 'Inquisition'?," 615.
31. AGN, Mexico, Gobierno Virreinal, Bandos, vol. 5, Exp. 76, 1763; a shorter version of this document can be found in Bandos, Caja 3506, Exp. 9, 1763.
32. See Priestley, *José de Gálvez*.
33. Elliott, *Spain and Its World*, 243–46.
34. AGN, Mexico, Ayuntamiento, vol. 107, Exp. 1, 1777, 1.
35. AGN, Mexico, Ayuntamiento, vol. 107, Exp. 1, 1777, 7.
36. AGN, Mexico, Instituciones Coloniales, Mapas, Planos e Ilustraciones 280, April 8, 1777.
37. AGN, Mexico, Ayuntamiento, vol. 107, Exp. 1, 1777, 132–34.
38. AGN, Mexico, Ayuntamiento, vol. 107, Exp. 1, 1777, 9, 15, 17–18. This document is summarized (with a drawing of figure 1) in Carranza-Castellanos, *Crónica del alumbrado*, 17–20.
39. AGN, Mexico, Ayuntamiento, vol. 107, Exp. 1, 1777, 65–90.
40. AGN, Mexico, Ayuntamiento, vol. 107, Exp. 1, 1777, 52.
41. AGN, Mexico, Ayuntamiento, vol. 107, Exp. 1, 1777, 53–54.
42. AGN, Mexico, Ayuntamiento, vol. 107, Exp. 1, 1777, 6.
43. AGN, Mexico, Ayuntamiento, vol. 107, Exp. 1, 1777, 45.
44. AGN, Mexico, Ayuntamiento, vol. 107, Exp. 1, 1777, 38–51.
45. AGN, Mexico, Ayuntamiento, vol. 107, Exp. 1, 1777, 31.
46. Carranza Castellanos, *Crónica del alumbrado*, 17–18, 21.
47. Cordovil Cordeiro, "De-electrifying the History of Street Lighting," 49n30.
48. Voekel, *Alone before God*, 8, 43.
49. AGN, Mexico, Instituciones Coloniales, Bando, vol. 12, Exp. 67, November 6, 1783.
50. AGN, Mexico, Instituciones Coloniales, Bandos, vol. 13, Exp. 61, January 29, 1785.
51. AGN, Mexico, Instituciones Coloniales, Bandos, vol. 13, Exp. 61, January 29, 1785.
52. AGN, Mexico, Real Hacienda, Casa de Moneda, vol. 190, Exp. 10, 1785. This document enumerates the various costs relating to these expensive lights, and the labor required to make and install them.
53. AGN, Mexico, Ramo de Policía y Empedrados, Caja 6494, Exp. 1, 1803; Casa de Moneda, vol. 501, Exp. 48, 1813 discusses repairs needed in the Casa de Moneda's lanterns.
54. AGN, Mexico, Instituciones Coloniales, Ayuntamiento, vol. 194, 1785.

55. See chapter 4 for more on this topic.
56. AGN, Mexico, Instituciones Coloniales, Ayuntamiento, vol. 194, 1785, 7.
57. See Challú and Gómez-Galvarriato, "Mexico's Real Wages," 83–122. Interestingly, this amount was also what the lantern guards eventually received as their monthly wage.
58. The most common currency used on a daily basis—eight reales equaled one peso, as is implied in the English phrase "pieces of eight." The peso de ocho reales was a basic unit of currency like the dollar, but the one real piece was the most common coin in circulation.
59. Candiani, *Dreaming of Dry Land*, 252–97; Tutino, *Mexico City, 1808*, 44–45.
60. AGN, Mexico, Instituciones Coloniales, Ayuntamiento, vol. 194, 1785, 1.
61. Germeten, *Profit and Passion*, 65.
62. For more on men like Sanabria, see Vinson, *Bearing Arms for His Majesty*.
63. For more on funeral rentals as a way for African-descent individuals to earn a good income, see Russell Wood, "Black and Mulatto Brotherhoods in Colonial Brazil," 567–602.
64. AGN, Mexico, Instituciones Coloniales, Ayuntamiento, vol. 194, 1785, 3–6. See chapter 7 for more on the increase in military recruitment in the late eighteenth century.
65. See the introduction for more on the history of the word *policía*.
66. Arrom, "Politics in Mexico City," 245–68.
67. AGN, Mexico, Instituciones Coloniales, Ayuntamiento, vol. 194, 1785, no pagination.
68. Cooper, *Epidemic Disease in Mexico City*, 70–85.
69. For a long trajectory of anti-plebeian rhetoric and judicial policies, see Campos, *Home Grown*.
70. AGN, Mexico, Indiferente Virreinal, Bandos, Caja 658, Exp. 5, February 13, 1787.
71. Anna, *The Fall of the Royal Government in Mexico City*, 32–33, 122–23.
72. AGN, Mexico, Instituciones Coloniales, Ayuntamiento, vol. 219, 106–7, March 10, 1790. For the history of the *consulado*, see Smith, "A Research Report on Consulado History," 41–52.
73. AGN, Mexico, Instituciones Coloniales, Bandos, vol. 1, Exp. 60. See also Carranza-Castellanos, *Crónica del alumbrado*, 21.
74. Sánchez-Arcilla Bernal, "La administración de justicia inferior," 355; Sánchez-Arcilla Bernal, "La delicuencia femininina," 116.
75. AGN, Mexico, Instituciones Coloniales, Bandos, vol. 1, Exp. 60.
76. AGN, Mexico, *Libros de Reos*, Exp. 50, February 2, 1798. See chapter 5 for more on disciplining the lantern guards.
77. AGN, Mexico, Real Hacienda, Caja 2225, Exp. 28, 1790.

78. AGN, Mexico, Instituciones Coloniales, Bandos, vol. 15, Exp. 94, 1790.
79. Pilcher, *¡Que Vivan los Tamales!*
80. AGN, Mexico, Instituciones Coloniales, Bandos, vol. 15, Exp. 94, 1790.
81. AGN, Mexico, Instituciones Coloniales, Bandos, vol. 15, Exp. 94, 1790.
82. AGN, Mexico, Instituciones Coloniales, Bandos, vol. 15, Exp. 94.
83. Calderón de la Barca, *Life in Mexico*, 325–28.
84. See Critchley and James, *The Maul and the Pear Tree*.
85. See Lozano Armendares, *La criminalidad*, for detailed analysis of homicides and other common Mexico City crimes in the early nineteenth century.
86. AGN, Mexico, Real Hacienda, Caja 4304, Exp. 41, 1791.
87. AGN, Mexico, Policía y Empedrados, Caja 4536, Exp. 1, 1793.
88. AGN, Mexico, Reales Cedulas Originales y Duplicados, vol. 190, Exp. 79, 1803.
89. AGN, Mexico, Reales Cedulas Originales y Duplicados, vol. 150, Exp. 15, 1791.
90. Carranza Castellanos, *Crónica del alumbrado*, 26.
91. AGN, Mexico, Ramo de Policía y Empedrados, Caja 5282, Exp. 60.
92. Curto and Landi, "Gas-Light in Italy," 1–4.
93. Schivelbusch, *Disenchanted Night*, 40–42, discusses the difference with gas lighting—much brighter, more uniform, and easier to regulate and control.
94. Schivelbusch, *Disenchanted Night*, 89–96.
95. Valdés, *Gacetas de México*, 221–22. For a summary of the history of the *Gazeta de México*, see Jaffary, *Reproduction and Its Discontents*, 143–44.
96. Carranza Castellanos, *Crónica del alumbrado*, 26–28.
97. Grumblings from the viceroy about poor performance of their duties by the guards went back a bit further, although with less detail. See AGN, Mexico, Indiferente Virreinal, Caja 5625, Exp. 13, 1806.
98. Tutino, *Mexico City, 1808*, 3–16; Warren, *Vagrants and Citizens*, 23–74; Anna, *Forging Mexico*, 49–50.
99. Tutino, *Mexico City, 1808*, 171–228; Curcio-Nagy, *Great Festivals*, 136–37.
100. Van Young, *The Other Rebellion*, 461.
101. Tutino, *Mexico City, 1808*, 241, 244.
102. AGN, Mexico, Indiferente Virreinal, Caja 4201, Exp. 22, 1808. European lamplighters faced similar challenges and accusations. In Amsterdam, they struggled to keep the lamps clean, and in London and Paris, complaints included the following: the lamps went out early due to neglect, the lamps used cheap whale oil, the glass was too murky, and the lights left most of the streets still in darkness. See Brox, "Out of the Dark," 16–17.
103. AGN, Mexico, Indiferente Virreinal, Caja, 4201, Exp. 22, 1808, 12–15.
104. AGN, Mexico, Indiferente Virreinal, Caja 4201, Exp. 22, 1808, 15–20.
105. AGN, Mexico, Indiferente Virreinal, Caja 4201, Exp. 22, 1808, 21.

106. Noll, *Life and Times of Miguel Hidalgo y Costilla*, 49–63.
107. AGN, Mexico, Indiferente Virreinal, Caja 2772, Exp. 4, 1809, 2–13.
108. AGN, Mexico, Indiferente Virreinal, Caja 2772, Exp. 4, 1809, 15–17.
109. AGN, Mexico, Policía y empedrados, Caja 2611, Exp. 2, 1809, 2.
110. AGN, Mexico, Indiferente Virreinal, Caja 6268, Exp. 56, 1809, 2.
111. AGN, Mexico, Ramo de Policía y Empedrados, Caja 2611, Exp. 2, 1809, 2.
112. AGN, Mexico, Ayuntamiento, vol. 107, Exp. 2, 1799, 6.
113. AGN, Mexico, Indiferente Virreinal, Caja 2772, Exp. 4, 1809, 29–78; Ramo de Policía y Empedrados, Caja 5220, Exp. 51, 1811.
114. It should be noted that other cities in New Spain followed Mexico's model, with similar justifications and implementation processes for their own street lighting. Regional centers also depended on turnip oil for their lanterns. As the nineteenth century progressed and urbanization increased in some areas, the intensive and continuing use of resin from pine and ocote trees caused an environmental crisis. Juárez Flores, "Alumbrado público."
115. Pottharst and Wukovitsch, "Economics of Night-Time Illumination," 218. In fact, brighter streets might even encourage crime. See Brox, "Out of the Dark," 18.
116. Cicchini, "A New 'Inquisition,'" 621–23.

2. MEN WALKING THE BEAT

Epigraph: "One hundred lanterns" is perhaps a poetic estimate, larger than what really happened on any given night. Original in English.

1. AGN, Mexico, Corregidores Procesos Civiles, 16, Exp. 105, 1794.
2. Linati, *Trajes civiles, militares y religiosos de México*, 95. The original publication was in French; this is my translation of the Spanish text. The word *sereno* appeared in Spanish in the French original. Claudio Linati was a lithographer from Parma who derived the inspiration for this description of the sereno, and a number of other familiar *costumbrista* images, from a trip he made to Mexico in 1825 and 1826, when he also helped found a political journal that ran to forty issues. Fernández, "Introducción," *Trajes civiles*, 20.
3. Taylor, *Magistrates of the Sacred*.
4. Gortari Rabiela, "La ciudad de México," 115–35, quote on 116.
5. These two types of documents are explained in the introduction.
6. AGN, Mexico, *Libros de Reos*, Caja 73, Exp. 50, February 5, March 12, and May 13, 1798.
7. AGN, Mexico, Gobernación sin Sección, Caja 61, Exp. 13, 1822, 96.
8. AGN, Mexico, *Libros de Reos*, Caja 73, Exp. 50, February 5 and July 24, 1798; Gobernación sin Sección, Caja 61, Exp. 13, 1822, 54, 68, 202.

9. AGN, Mexico, *Libros de Reos*, Caja 73, Exp. 50, August 8, October 1, October 14, November 2, November 6, November 15, 1798.
10. AGN, Mexico, Ramo de Policía y Empedrados, vol. 4536, Exp. 11, 1794, 9.
11. AGN, Mexico, Ayuntamiento, vol. 107, Exp. 1, 1777, 20. These debates were covered in depth in chapter 1.
12. Lipsett-Rivera, *Origins of Macho*, 34.
13. This information comes from AGN, Mexico, *Libros de Reos*, Caja 73, Exps. 45–50, 1794 to 1798.
14. Boyer, "Honor among Plebeians," 152–78.
15. Lipsett-Rivera, "Scandal at the Church," 216–23; Seed, *To Love, Honor, and Obey*, 24–25; Arrom, *Women of Mexico City*, 111–21.
16. AGN, Mexico, *Libros de Reos*, Caja 73, Exp. 50, October 10, 1798.
17. Both of the spouses were described as solteros, or sexually active. Interestingly, they were also related "in the second degree of consanguinity." See AGN, Mexico, Matrimonios, vol. 9, Exp. 26, 1807, 381–85.
18. AGN, Mexico, Corregidores Procesos Civiles 16, Exp. 105, 1794.
19. AGN, Mexico, Matrimonios, 69, vol. 97, Exp. 50, 1822, 310–14.
20. AGN, Mexico, Indiferente Virreinal, Caja 4201, Exp. 22, 1808, 14.
21. AGN, Mexico, *Libros de Reos*, Caja 73, Exp. 46, September 26, 1796.
22. AGN, Mexico, Criminal, Caja 1150, Exp. 10, 1796, 6.
23. Scardaville, "Crime and the Urban Poor," 41.
24. Johnson, *Policing the Urban Underworld*, 122–46; von Hoffman, "An Officer of the Neighborhood," 309–30.
25. Scardaville, "Crime and the Urban Poor," 44.
26. AGN, Mexico, Indiferente de Guerra, Caja 2992, Exp. 38, 1797, 15–16. See Seijas, *Asian Slaves in Colonial Mexico*, 115–16.
27. In this time and place, a range of social and economic markers summed up as *calidad* meant much more than phenotype when it came to colonial racial categorizing. High status occupations tended to "whiten" an individual. See Büschges, "Don Manuel Valdivieso y Carrion Protests," 224–35.
28. This discussion goes back at least as far as the 1970s. Sources include, among many others, Valdés, "The Decline"; Vinson, "Free Colored Voices," 170–82; Schwaller, *Géneros de Gente*.
29. Germeten, *Black Blood Brothers*, 104–58.
30. For why this label became less common in the Spanish viceroyalties, see Rappaport, *Disappearing Mestizo*.
31. Lipsett-Rivera, *Gender and Negotiation*, 197; Borah, *Justice by Insurance*, 111.
32. Vanderwood, *Disorder and Progress*, 101–2, 112–17.
33. AGN, Mexico, Bandos, vol. 15, Exp. 60, 1790, 161.

34. AGN, Mexico, Indiferente Virreinal, Caja 2772, Exp. 4, 1808, 16; Real Hacienda, Caja 3748, Exp. 5, 1811, 3; and Ramo de Policía y Empedrados, 87, Contenedor 10, vol. 28, Exp. 10, 1807, 333.
35. AGN, Mexico, Corregidores Procesos Civiles, vol. 13, Exp. 43, 1791. This late colonial legal process is explored in depth by Seed, *To Love, Honor, and Obey*.
36. AGN, Mexico, *Libros de Reos*, Caja 73, Exp. 50, October 15 and November 27, 1798.
37. Fonseca and Urrutia, *Historia General*, 5:431–32.
38. AGN, Mexico, Ramo de Policía y Empedrados, Caja 4536, Exp. 11, 1794.
39. AGN, Mexico, Ayuntamiento, vol. 107, Exp. 2, 1799, 5–7.
40. AGN, Mexico, Ayuntamiento, vol. 107, Exp. 2, 1799, 2–3.
41. AGN, Mexico, Ramo de Policía y Empedrados, vol. 27–28, 225; Ayuntamientos, 2833, Exp. 23, 1803.
42. AGN, Mexico, Propios y Arbitrios, Caja 3382, Exp. 44, 1815.
43. Ávila González, "Voces y ladridos," 88.
44. Johnson, *Policing the Urban Underworld*, 143–43.
45. Palma Alvarado, "Los cuerpos de serenos," 514.
46. Simón Palmer, "Los serenos," 62–66.
47. See Gash, *Sir Robert Peel*; Reynolds, *Before the Bobbies*; and Evans, *Sir Robert Peele*.
48. In an article about the history of law enforcement in Chile, Daniel Palma Alvarado gathered a handful of evocative and beautiful quotes from the eighteenth through the twentieth centuries, which add to the costumbrista tone of Linati's description. See Palma Alvarado, "Los cuerpos de serenos," 511.
49. Palma Alvarado, "Los cuerpos de serenos," 510. "Ya me voy a mi retiro a dormir sin tener sueño. Me retiro porque son las cuatro y media y sereno. Ya dejo mi punto solo; me retiro fatigado. No he tenido novedades y son las cinco . . . y nublado."
50. See the conclusion for more on this topic.
51. McCormack, "'A Species of Civil Soldier,'" 60; Savage, *Police Records*, 133.
52. An early Boston police chief noted, "I heard the sharp crack of the rattle . . . and I well knew that some of my boys were in trouble." Savage, *Police Records*, 144.
53. Alvarado Palma, "Los cuerpos de serenos," 514; Simón Palmer, "Los serenos, faroleros," 62–66.
54. AGN, Mexico, Ayuntamiento, vol. 107, Exp. 1, 1777, 19–20.
55. AGN, Mexico, Bandos, Caja 727, Exp. 25, 1787.
56. AGN, Mexico, Criminal, 547, 2ª parte, Exp. 14, 1790, 469–506.
57. AGN, Mexico, Bandos, vol. 15, Exp. 60, 1790, 159.
58. Palma Alvarado, "Los cuerpos de serenos," 521.

59. AGN, Mexico, Criminal, vol. 340, Contenedor 170, Exp. 12, 1791, 234, 236–43, 246–56.
60. AGN, Mexico, Criminal, vol. 340, Contenedor 170, Exp. 12, 1791, 249–50.
61. Terreros y Pando, *Diccionario castellano*, 2:471, column 2.
62. AGN, Mexico, Criminal, Caja 1150, Exp. 10, 1796, 4–12; and Criminal, vol. 340, Contenedor 170, Exp. 12, 1791, 250–52. "Compañero" is used numerous times on these pages.
63. AGN, Mexico, Indiferente de Guerra, Caja 2992, Exp. 38, 1797, 6, 9–11.
64. AGN, Mexico, *Libros de Reos*, Caja 73, Exp. 50, February 2, 1798.
65. AGN, Mexico, Criminal, 547, 2ª parte, Exp. 14, 1790, 477.
66. AGN, Mexico, Criminal, Caja 924, Exp. 11, 1820, see pages 11, 25, 54, 58. See Johnson, *Policing the Urban Underworld*, 144, for early police bonding over fatalities in New York City.
67. Lipsett-Rivera, *Origins of Macho*, 79–105, explores Mexican men and their work identities in depth.
68. Some nineteenth-century patrolmen resisted wearing a uniform, so they did not stand out so much. Johnson, *Policing the Urban Underworld*, 136.
69. Van Maanen, "Working the Street," 85, 102–3: "When a policeman dons his uniform, he enters a distinct subculture" (85). See also Lipsett-Rivera, *Origins of Macho*, 152.
70. Barrie and Broomhall, "Introduction," 2–3, 10–13.
71. Savage, *Police Records*, 132–33.
72. Dodsworth, "Men on a Mission," 128–29; Shpayer-Makov, "Shedding the Uniform and Acquiring a New Masculine Image," 142–43; Lipsett-Rivera, *Origins of Macho*, 178–79.
73. For discussion of these establishments and transactional sex, see Germeten, *Profit and Passion*, chapter 5.
74. AGN, Mexico, Criminal, 37, Contenedor 245, vol. 531, Exp. 9, 1821, 137.
75. AGN, Mexico, Criminal, 37, Contenedor 245, vol. 531, Exp. 9, 1821, 142.
76. AGN, Mexico, Corregidores procesos civiles, 16, Exp. 105, 1794, 4, 7.
77. AGN, Mexico, Criminal, vol. 340, Contenedor 170, Exp. 12, 1791, 250, 253.
78. Simón Palmer, "Los serenos, faroleros," 65.
79. AGN, Mexico, *Libros de Reos*, Caja 73, Exp. 45, September 1, 1794.
80. AGN, Mexico, Ramo de Policía y Empedrados, Caja 4536, Exp. 13, 1795, 11, 27; Criminal, Caja 547, 2ª parte, Exp. 14, 1790, 497. When the guarda mayor accused guard number 73 of sleeping on the job and losing his farol and chuzo, 73 responded by claiming that his cabo took his weapon from him. See *Libros de Reos*, Caja 73, Exp. 46, September 11, 1796.
81. Lipsett-Rivera, *Origins of Macho*, 176.

82. Lozano Armendares, *La criminalidad*, 62, 67, 77, 101–2.
83. Taylor, *Drinking, Homicide and Rebellion*, 80–81.
84. Lozano Armendares, *La criminalidad*, 347–49.
85. AGN, Mexico, Ramo de Policía y Empedrados, 12, vol. 34, Exp. 18, 1815.
86. AGN, Mexico, Ramo de Policía y Empedrados, 12, vol. 34, Exp. 18, 1815, 302–3.
87. Examples of attacks by garrotes include AGN, Mexico, *Libros de Reos*, Caja 73, Exp. 50, September 22, 1798; Ramo de Policía y Empedrados, Caja 5478, Exp. 9, 1815, 2; Gobernación sin Sección, Caja 61, Exp. Exp. 13, 1822, 22.
88. Peter Betjemann, Personal Communication, February 24, 2021.
89. For an in-depth study of the branch of city government archived as "Matanzas de Perros [Dog Massacres]," see Ávila González, "Voces y ladridos." Ávila González calls Linati's image "idyllic" (90).
90. Ávila González, "Voces y ladridos," 21–28.
91. Oberto, "Perros asesinos," 103–4.
92. Ávila González, "Voces y ladridos," 53–58.
93. Lipsett-Rivera, *Origins of Macho*, 138.
94. Ávila González, "Voces y ladridos," 30.
95. Ávila González, "Voces y ladridos," 46–47.
96. Glasco, "A City in Disarray," 92, 141–42; Oberto, "Perros asesinos," 100–101, 105; Ávila González, "Voces y ladridos," 72–74.
97. Oberto, "Perros asesinos," 95–97, 99–100, 107; Ávila González, "Voces y ladridos," 75, 93.
98. Payno, *Bandits from Río Frío*, 69. A century after the night watchmen began this brutal and bloody task, Payno wrote about the horrors of the guards ganging up on dogs, the cruelty of the regime that mandated the massacres, and the brutality of the thousands of canine deaths.
99. Pulido Esteva, "Policía: Del buen gobierno," 1605–1606, 1631, citing statements published in *La Gazeta de México* in 1805. See also Ávila González, "Voces y ladridos," 135.
100. Ávila González, "Voces y ladridos," 62–63.
101. Pulido Esteva, "Policía: Del buen gobierno," 1605–6, 1631; Oberto, "Perros asesinos," 106–7.
102. AGN Mexico, Ramo de Policía y Empedrados, Caja 5325, Exp. 105, December 22, 1806.
103. AGN Mexico, Ramo de Policía y Empedrados, vol. 20, Exp. 8, May 6, 1795.
104. Over eighty reports on nightly patrolmen's rounds can be found in the AGN, Mexico, in the following files: Ramo de Policía y Empedrados, Caja 3339, Exp. 8, 1793; idem, vol. 20, Exp. 8, 1794–1795; Indiferente Virreinal, Caja 2645, 1797; idem, Caja 2992, Exp. 38, 1797; idem, Caja 6031, Exp. 50, 1797; Ayuntamiento,

caja 6031, Exp. 53, 1797; Ramo de Policía y Empedrados, 2645, Exp. 41, 1798; idem, Caja 5960, Exp. 53, 1799; Indiferente Virreinal, Caja 3292, Exp. 8, 1803; Criminal, Caja 164, Exp. 48, 1804; Ramo de Policía y Empedrados, Caja 3323, Exp. 34, 1805; idem, Caja 5492, Exp. 38, 1805; idem, Caja 5325, Exp. 105, 1806; Indiferente Virreinal, Caja 689, Exp. 9, 1806; idem, Caja 3968, Exp. 21, 1807; Ramo de Policía y Empedrados, Caja 3677, Exp. 23, 1808; Indiferente Virreinal, Caja 1325, Exp. 10, 1813; Indiferente Virreinal, Caja 4729, Exp. 8, 1813; Indiferente de Guerra, Caja 3458, Exp. 10, 1815; Ayuntamientos, Caja 1414, Exp. 9, 1815; Indiferente Virreinal, Caja 6603, Exp. 13, 1815; Ramo de Policía y Empedrados, Caja 5478, Exp. 9, 1815; idem, Caja 5115, Exp. 44, 1815; idem, Caja 4198, Exp. 4, 1818; idem, Caja 2733, Exp. 26, 1821; and Mexico Independiente, Gobernación sin Sección, Caja 61, Exp. 13, 1822.

105. AGN, Mexico, Ramo de Policía y Empedrados, 4536, Exp. 11, 1794, 6.
106. AGN, Mexico, Ramo de Policía y Empedrados, 4536, Exp. 11, 1794, 9.
107. Ávila González, "Voces y ladridos," 80–85, 156.
108. Payno, *Bandits from Río Frío*, 70.
109. Ávila González, "Voces y ladridos," 139–46.
110. Ávila González, "Voces y ladridos," 97–100.
111. AGN, Mexico, Ramo de Policía y Empedrados, Caja 5478, Exp. 9, February 25, 1815.
112. AGN, Mexico, Ramo de Policía y Empedrados, Caja 5478, Exp. 9, April 25, 1815.
113. Von Hoffman, "An Officer of the Neighborhood," 309.
114. Garrioch, "People of Paris," 514, 522.
115. Miller, *Cops and Bobbies*, 33–35.

3. TO PROTECT AND SERVE

1. AGN, Mexico, Ramo de Policía y Empedrados, 87, Contenedor 12, vol. 34, 1807, 145.
2. Lane, "Introduction," x.
3. AGN, Mexico, Ramo de Policía y Empedrados, vol. 27–28, 1801, 205.
4. Garrioch, "People of Paris," 527–28; Von Hoffman, "An Officer of the Neighborhood," 312.
5. AGN, Mexico, Bandos, vol. 1, Exp. 60, 1790.
6. AGN, Mexico, *Libros de Reos*, Caja 73, Exp. 45, September 12, 1794. For documentation of guards meeting the mail carriers as they entered or left the city, see Indiferente Virreinal, Caja 6031, Exp. 50, November 26, 1797, 1; Ramo de Policía y Empedrados, vol. 20, Exp. 8, December 17, 1795, 182; Indiferente de Guerra, Caja 3292, Exp. 8, September 7, 1803, 9; Criminal, Caja 164, Exp. 48, March 1, 1804, 8; Ramo de Policía y Empedrados, Caja 5478, Exp. 9, April 25,

1815, 24; Gobernación sin Sección, Caja 61, Exp. 13, February 7, 14, and 21, April 26, 1822, 18, 31, 45–46, 106.
7. AGN, Mexico, Indiferente Virreinal, Caja 5777, Exp. 43, October 2, 1816.
8. Voekel, *Alone before God*, 108.
9. Manning and Butler, "Perceptions of Police Authority," 333.
10. Banton, *Policeman in the Community*, 238–39.
11. Banton, *Policeman in the Community*, 237.
12. Manning, "Policing," 28.
13. AGN, Mexico, Ramo de Policía y Empedrados, vol. 27–28, 1801, 199, 212–13.
14. Torales Pacheco, "Ilustrados en la Nueva España," 168–69.
15. AGN, Mexico, Ramo de Policía y Empedrados, vol. 27–28, 1801, 231–32.
16. Voekel, *Alone before God*; Eire, *From Madrid to Purgatory*. Church and state also allied in the legal requirement of preparing a last will and testament.
17. In order to understand the typical public health–related duties carried out by the night watchmen on a regular basis, I draw from the same eighty nightly logs discussed in the last chapter in relation to controlling the stray population. These tasks are mentioned in AGN, Mexico, Ramo de Policía y Empedrados, vol. 20, 1795, 182, 193, 197, 198, 199, 202; Indiferente Virreinal, Caja 6031, Exp. 50, 1797, 1–2; Ramo de Policía y Empedrados, Caja 5960, Exp. 53, 1799, 3; Indiferente de Guerra, Caja 3292, 1803, 7–9; Criminal, Caja 164, Exp. 48, 1804, 8; Ramo de Policía y Empedrados, Caja 3323, Exp. 34, 1805; idem, Caja 5325, Exp. 105, 1806, 4–5; Indiferente de Guerra, Caja 3968, Exp. 21, 1807, 1; Ramo de Policía y Empedrados, Caja 2611, Exp. 2, 1809, 3; Indiferente Virreinal, Caja 6603, Exp. 13, 1815, 6; Ramo de Policía y Empedrados, Caja 3326, Exp. 53, 1815; idem, Caja 5478, Exp. 9; Ayuntamientos, Caja 1414, Exp. 9, 1; Ramo de Policía y Empedrados, Caja 4198, Exp. 4, 1818, 2, 4, 7; idem, Caja 2733, Exp. 26, 1821, 4; and Gobernación sin Sección, Caja 0061, Exp. 13, 1822, 5, 8, 11, 14, 20, 25, 32, 37, 45, 51, 57, 59, 62, 64, 68, 70, 74, 78, 84, 92, 94, 96, 100, 104, 108, 112.
18. See chapter 2 for this discussion.
19. AGN, Mexico, Ramo de Policía y Empedrados, vol. 20, Exp. 8, 1795, 198.
20. AGN, Mexico, Ramo de Policía y Empedrados, vol. 87, Contenedor 12, vol. 34, 1807.
21. AGN, Mexico, Ramo de Policía y Empedrados, 87, Contenedor 12, vol. 34, 1807, 144–45.
22. AGN, Mexico, Ramo de Policía y Empedrados, 87, Contenedor 12, vol. 34, 1807, 146.
23. AGN, Mexico, Ramo de Policía y Empedrados, vol. 28, Exp. 10, 1809, 329.
24. An example from after the era of this book can be found in Mexico, AGN, Independiente Justicia, vol. 129, Exp. 18, 1830.

25. AGN, Mexico, Indiferente Virreinal, Caja 6008, Exp. 26, 1800.
26. AGN, Mexico, Indiferente Virreinal, Caja 4729, Exp. 8, 1813, 3.
27. AGN, Mexico, Policía y Empedrados, Caja 5632, Exp. 22, 1804.
28. AGN, Mexico, Policía y Empedrados, Caja 3892, Exp. 31, 1805.
29. AGN, Mexico, Gobernación sin Sección, Caja 61, Exp. 13, February 4, 1822, 8.
30. Lozano Armendares, *La criminalidad*.
31. AGN, Mexico, Gobernación sin Sección, Caja 61, Exp. 13, 1822.
32. AGN, Mexico, Gobernación sin Sección, Caja 61, Exp. 13, 1822, 16.
33. AGN, Mexico, *Libros de Reos*, Caja 73, Exp. 50, September 23, 1798; Ramo de Policía y Empedrados, Caja 5325, Exp. 105, December 22, 1806, 2. *Libros de Reos*, Caja 73, Exp. 45, October 7, 1794, records a theft of some cheese at the bullfight. See also *Libros de Reos*, Caja 73, Exp. 46, March 13, 1796.
34. AGN, Mexico, *Libros de Reos*, Caja 73, Exp. 50, February 3 and November 6, 1798.
35. AGN, Mexico, Ramo de Policía y Empedrados, Caja 5478, Exp. 9, March 7, 1815, 11.
36. AGN, Mexico, *Libros de Reos*, Caja 73, Exp. 50, July 19, 1798.
37. Lozano Armendares, *La criminalidad*, 46–47, documents 170 trials for robbery from 1800 to 1812.
38. AGN, Mexico, Ramo de Policía y Empedrados, Caja 5478, Exp. 9, March 10, 1815, 14; Gobernación sin Sección, Caja 61, Exp. 13, February 14 and 18, 1822, 31, 39.
39. AGN, Mexico, Indiferente de Guerra, Caja 3292, Exp. 8, September 27, 1803, 9.
40. AGN, Mexico, Real Audiencia, vol. 694, Exp. 4, October 14, 1803, 46.
41. AGN, Mexico, Policía y Empedrados, Caja 5492, Exp. 38, September 14, 1815, 13.
42. AGN, Mexico, Gobernación sin Sección, Caja 61, Exp. 13, February 1, 1822, 2.
43. AGN, Mexico, Gobernación sin Sección, Caja 61, Exp. 13, February 5 and 7, 1822, 11–14.
44. AGN, Correspondencia de Diversas Autoridades, Caja 2027, Exp. 10, 1816.
45. AGN, Correspondencia de Diversas Autoridades, Caja 2027, Exp. 10, 1816, 5.
46. Yáñez Romero, *La policía mexicana*, 24–28.
47. AGN, Mexico, Gobernación sin Sección, Caja 61, Exp. 13, 1822, 14–15, 110.
48. See references to *parteras* in the following files: AGN, Mexico, Ramo de Policía y Empedrados, Caja 4536, Exp. 13, 1795, 3; Ayuntamiento, Caja 6031, Exp. 53, 1797, 2; Ramo de Policía y Empedrados, Caja 5960, Exp. 53, 1799, 3: Cárceles y Presidios, Caja 2418, Exp. 10, 1814, 1; Ramo de Policía y Empedrados, Caja 5478, Exp. 9, 1815, 2, 20; idem, Caja 4198, Exp. 4, 1818, 2, 7; idem, Caja 2733, Exp. 26, 1821, 12; and Gobernación sin Sección, Caja 61, Exp. 13, 1822, 42, 80.
49. AGN, Mexico, *Libros de Reos*, Caja 50, Exp. 73, October 30, 1798.
50. Arrom, *Containing the Poor*, 15–16.
51. AGN, Mexico, *Libros de Reos*, Caja 73, Exp. 46, July 23, 1796. See Germeten, *Profit and Passion*, chapters 5, 6, and 7 for more information on girls selling sex on the

street in the late viceregal era, streetwalkers' interactions with soldiers and the night watchmen, and efforts to reorganize and reunite families who depended on their own daughters' income from sex work.

52. Cope, *Limits of Racial Domination*, 104.
53. AGN, Mexico, *Libros de Reos*, Caja 73, Exp. 45, August 26, 1794.
54. AGN, Mexico, *Libros de Reos*, Caja 73, Exps. 45, 46, 50.
55. AGN, Mexico, *Libros de Reos*, Caja 73, Exp. 50, May 1, 1798.
56. AGN, Mexico, *Libros de Reos*, Caja 73, Exp. 46, August 20, 1796.
57. AGN, Mexico, *Libros de Reos*, Caja 73, Exp. 50, December 2, 1798.
58. AGN, Mexico, *Libros de Reos*, Caja 73, Exp. 45, December 18, 1794, a child described as español found on the street at 10 p.m.
59. AGN, Mexico, *Libros de Reos*, Caja 73, Exp. 50, October 10, 1798; Lipsett-Rivera, *Origins of Macho*, 33.
60. Cope, *Limits of Racial Domination*, 104; Arrom, *Containing the Poor*, 24, 30–31, 95–65.
61. AGN, Mexico, *Libros de Reos*, Caja 73, Exp. 46, February 20, 1796; June 5, 1796; August 14, 1796; Exp. 50, July 24, 1798; July 29, 1798; September 21, 1798; October 4, 1798; October 11, 1798; October 18, 1798; December 26, 1798.
62. AGN, Mexico, *Libros de Reos*, Caja 73, Exp. 50, October 10, 1798.
63. AGN, Mexico, *Libros de Reos*, Caja 73, Exp. 46, January 19, 1796.
64. Lipsett-Rivera, *Origins of Macho*, 40–41.
65. AGN, Mexico, *Libros de Reos*, Caja 73, Exp. 50, October 11, 1798.
66. AGN, Mexico, *Libros de Reos*, Caja 73, Exp. 50, October 26, 1798.
67. AGN, Mexico, *Libros de Reos*, Caja 73, Exp. 50, June 15, 1798.
68. AGN, Mexico, *Libros de Reos*, Caja 73, Exp. 50, March 6, March 8, May 28, May 30, June 18, July 15, October 26, and December 13, 1798.
69. AGN, Mexico, *Libros de Reos*, Caja 73, Exp. 46, July 18, 1796.
70. Von Hoffman, "An Officer of the Neighborhood," 315, 319.
71. See Proctor, *Damned Notions of Liberty*.
72. AGN, Mexico, *Libros de Reos*, Caja 73, Exp. 45, September 26 and October 31, 1794. See Stein and Stein, *Crisis in an Atlantic Empire*, 237, 268, 272, 289, 318.
73. In this era, boys became men without an official acknowledgment of adolescence as a legal status or part of their development; however, in late colonial ecclesiastical court cases, accused men were eligible for free legal counsel if they had not reached their twenty-fourth birthday. Lipsett-Rivera, *Origins of Macho*, 21–22.
74. AGN, Mexico, *Libros de Reos*, Caja 73, Exp. 50, April 9 and August 20, 1798.
75. AGN, Mexico, *Libros de Reos*, Caja 73, Exp. 50, April 28 and July 4, 1798.
76. Cope, *Limits of Racial Domination*, 104; Arrom, *Women of Mexico City*, 57.

77. AGN, Mexico, *Libros de Reos*, Caja 73, Exp. 46, February 28, March 2, and August 1, 1796; Exp. 50, March 4, March 14, July 14, October 27, and November 17, 1798.
78. Arrom, *Containing the Poor*, 76–119.
79. Arrom, *Containing the Poor*, 134–41.
80. AGN, Mexico, *Libros de Reos*, Caja 73, Exps. 45, 46, 50.
81. AGN, Mexico, *Libros de Reos*, Caja 73, Exp. 50, July 10 and October 10, 1798.
82. AGN, Mexico, *Libros de Reos*, Caja 73, Exp. 50, April 7 and June 23, 1798.
83. AGN, Mexico, *Libros de Reos*, Caja 73, Exp. 45, September 26, 1794.
84. AGN, Mexico, *Libros de Reos*, Caja 73, Exp. 50, September 9, 1798.
85. AGN, Mexico, *Libros de Reos*, Caja 73, Exp. 50, September 14, 1798.
86. AGN, Mexico, *Libros de Reos*, Caja 73, Exp. 50, February 15 and October 28, 1798.
87. AGN, Mexico, *Libros de Reos*, Caja 73, Exp. 46, April 11, 1796.
88. AGN, Mexico, *Libros de Reos*, Caja 73, Exp. 46, May 8, 1796.
89. For historical terms for epilepsy in Spanish, see Apice, "Epilepsia: Mito o realidad, breve historia de epilepsia," accessed April 20, 2020, https://www.apiceepilepsia.org/epilepsia-y-sociedad/breve-historia-de-la-epilepsia/.
90. AGN, Mexico, *Libros de Reos*, Caja 73, Exp. 46, *Libros de Reos*, June 20, 1796.
91. AGN, Mexico, *Libros de Reos*, Caja 73, Exp. 50, *Libros de Reos*, January 24, 1798.
92. AGN, Mexico, *Libros de Reos*, August 15, 1796.
93. AGN, Mexico, *Libros de Reos*, Caja 73, Exp. 50, April 25, 1798.
94. AGN, Mexico, *Libros de Reos*, Caja 73, Exp. 50, March 18, 1798.
95. AGN, Mexico, *Libros de Reos*, Caja 73, Exp. 45, August 27, 1794, and Exp. 50, July 1, 1798.
96. AGN, Mexico, *Libros de Reos*, Caja 73, Exp. 46, February 6, 1796.
97. AGN, Mexico, *Libros de Reos*, Caja 73, Exp. 50, February 17, 1798.
98. AGN, Mexico, *Libros de Reos*, Caja 73, Exp. 50, November 19 and December 1, 1798.
99. AGN, Mexico, *Libros de Reos*, March 11 and July 6, 1798.
100. AGN, Mexico, *Libros de Reos*, August 29, 1798.
101. AGN, Mexico, *Libros de Reos*, Caja 73, Exp. 50, March 10, 1798.
102. AGN, Mexico, *Libros de Reos*, Caja 73, Exp. 50, September 2, 1798.
103. AGN, Mexico, *Libros de Reos*, Caja 73, Exp. 50, September 29, 1798.
104. AGN, Mexico, *Libros de Reos*, Caja 73, Exp. 50, December 29, 1798.
105. AGN, Mexico, *Libros de Reos*, Caja 73, Exp. 45, 1794, August 4, November 1, November 8.
106. AGN, Mexico, Ramo de Policía y Empedrados, Caja 5960, Exp. 53, November 10, 1799, 4.
107. AGN, Mexico, Real Audiencia, vol. 694, Exp. 4, October 14, 1803, 46; Indiferente de Guerra, Caja 3968, Exp. 21, February 11, 1807; Ramo de Policía y Empedrados, Caja 5478, Exp. 9, March 10, 1815, 14.
108. AGN, Mexico, Cárceles y Presidios, Caja 2418, Exp. 10, November 2, 1814, 4.

109. AGN, Mexico, Ramo de Policía y Empedrados, vol. 20, Exp 8, October 2, 1795, 198–202.
110. AGN, Gobernación sin Sección, Caja 61, Exp. 13, February 14 and 15, 1822, 31–34.
111. AGN, Mexico, *Libros de Reos*, Caja 73, Exp. 45, October 23, 1794; Exp. 46, January 20 and April 15, 1796.
112. Chapter 4 covers this topic in greater depth.
113. AGN, Mexico, Real Audiencia, Criminal, vol. 444, Exp. 10, 1797, 215.
114. Schendel, Álvarez Amézquita, and Bustamante, *Medicine in Mexico*, 67.
115. AGN, Mexico, Real Audiencia, Criminal, vol. 444, Exp. 10, 1797, 216.
116. AGN, Mexico, Real Audiencia, Criminal, vol. 444, Exp. 10, 1797, 218–19.
117. AGN, Mexico, Real Audiencia, Criminal, vol. 444, Exp. 10, 1797, 221–29.
118. AGN, Mexico, Real Audiencia, Criminal, vol. 444, Exp. 10, 1797, 228–29.
119. Savage, *Police Records and Recollections*, 263–73. Although a source that romanticizes and creates heroes out of its writer and other police officers, Savage's account of the gruesome and high-conflict tasks of dealing with a cholera epidemic in 1854 ring true.

4. NIGHTLIFE

1. Viqueira Albán, *Propriety and Permissiveness*, 27–51; Walsh, *Virtuous Waters*, 39–46, presents both the social options for swimming and bathing and Bourbon reforms to regulate these activities. For the elite pursuits, including socializing with women in private salons and casinos, see Germeten, *Profit and Passion*, 50–87. For both rich and poor, gambling could be a serious addiction. See Lozano Armendares, *La criminalidad*, 146–48. For *temascales* and card games, see Lipsett-Rivera, *Origins of Macho*, 68–69, 131–33.
2. Johnson, *Policing the Urban Underworld*, 126, 129, 133, quote on 129.
3. Lipsett-Rivera, *Origins of Macho*, 70, 126.
4. Schivelbusch, *Disenchanted Night*, 89–91.
5. Schivelbusch, *Disenchanted Night*, 81–82, on darkness and fear.
6. The understudied paving project is another obvious and dramatic undertaking meant to reshape space and civilize people. See AGN, Mexico, Ramo de Policía y Empedrados. For more on the use of space to impose behavior ideals, see Toner, "Everything in Its Right Place?," 26–48.
7. Koslofsky, *Evening's Empire*. See also chapters 6 and 7 for resistance against nocturnal illumination.
8. Scardaville, "Alcohol Abuse and Tavern Reform," 668.
9. Bernadino de Sahagún relates a myth of drunkenness and the origins of pulque. See Bruman, *Alcohol in Ancient Mexico*, 63–64. See also Burkhart, *Slippery Earth*, 160; Jackson, *Conflict and Conversion*, 22–23, 95–98.

10. Toxqui Garay, "El Recreo," 62–65.
11. Scardaville, "Alcohol Abuse and Tavern Reform," 643–71. This vision continued into the twentieth century. See Campos, *Home Grown*.
12. Toner, "Everything in Its Right Place?," 26–48.
13. Pierce, "Parades, Epistles and Prohibitive Legislation," 151–80.
14. For a vision of pulque in the 1930s, see Bruman, *Alcohol in Ancient Mexico*, 61–82.
15. Tutino, *Mexico City, 1808*, 48; Taylor, *Drinking, Homicide, and Rebellion*, 28–60.
16. Bobb, *Viceregency of Antonio María Bucareli*, 241–44.
17. Scardaville, "Alcohol Abuse and Tavern Reform," 651.
18. The *New York Times* announced the return of Mexico City's pulquerías in 2009. See Alexis Okeowo, "Pulquerias in Mexico City," *New York Times*, January 23, 2009, https://www.nytimes.com/2009/01/25/travel/25bites.html. See also Tamang et al., "Editorial," 97–99.
19. Gibson, *The Aztecs under Spanish Rule*, 409.
20. Taylor, *Drinking, Homicide, and Rebellion*, 45, 66, 72.
21. Stern, *The Secret History of Gender*, 50–51.
22. Althouse, "Drunkenness and Interpersonal Violence in Colonial Michoacán," 68.
23. One of the most innovative works on this topic is Brandes's *Staying Sober in Mexico City*. This is also a trend in studying crime in the national era. See Piccato, *A History of Infamy*, 263–69.
24. See introduction for an overview of these scholars' work.
25. Von Hoffman, "An Officer of the Neighborhood," 319.
26. Taylor, *Drinking, Homicide, and Rebellion*, 64–65, 94–97, 104–5; Hamman, "Eyeing Alameda Park," 149–50, 184–94; Voekel, "Peeing on the Palace"; Toxqui Garay, "El Recreo," 63–64. In Madrid, the authorities also equated drinking to increasing urban crime, so this stereotype encompassed the urbanized poor in general. See Meijide Pardo, "Mendicidad, vagancia y prostitución," 576–78, 591. The huge number of plebeian men incarcerated for drunkenness provided an important forced labor pool for the viceregal authorities. This may have actually cleaned up the city significantly. Haslip-Viera, *Crime and Punishment*, 98–99, 102–3, 116. For forced labor sentences to improve the plebeian work ethic, see Arrom, *Containing the Poor*, 3, 20–21, 24.
27. Scardaville, "Crime and the Urban Poor," 208.
28. Taylor, *Drinking, Homicide, and Rebellion*, 41–43.
29. It is interesting to note that the viceregal authorities demonstrate, through their nightly logs, that Indigenous and other casta drunkenness was very important to document and archive, but the "public sins" of streetwalking were hidden in similar sources. See Germeten, *Profit and Passion*, 88–108.
30. Toxqui Garay, "El Recreo," 76.

31. Scardaville, "Alcohol Abuse and Tavern Reform," 645–46, 645n7; Scardaville, "Crime and the Urban Poor," 209.
32. Scardaville, "Crime and the Urban Poor," 211, 227–28, 249–50.
33. Scardaville, "Alcohol Abuse and Tavern Reform," 669–70.
34. Viqueira Albán, *Propriety and Permissiveness*, 132–57, describes the contradictory attempts to reform and simultaneously tax pulquerías.
35. Scardaville, "Alcohol Abuse and Tavern Reform," 647, 652–54, quote on 654.
36. AGN, Mexico, Ramo de Policía y Empedrados, Caja 5325, Exp. 105, December 24, 1806, 6, discusses the arrest of a guitarist who played for aguardiente and made a mockery of the arresting guard and corporal. See also Toner, "Everything in Its Right Place?," 33; Lipsett-Rivera, *Origins of Macho*, 130–31.
37. Curcio Nagy, *Great Festivals*, 123.
38. Lozano Armendares, *La criminalidad*, 34, 70, 75, 112.
39. AGN, Mexico, Ramo de Policía y Empedrados, Caja 5220, Exp. 52, 1.
40. Toxqui Garay, "El Recreo," 80.
41. Scardaville, "Alcohol Abuse and Tavern Reform," 648–49; Toxqui Garay, "El Recreo," 60–61.
42. AGN, Mexico, Ramo de Policía y Empedrados, vol. 20, Exp. 8, September 26, 1795, 188–96.
43. Scardaville, "Alcohol Abuse and Tavern Reform," 657.
44. This number differs from the analysis above because it counts each incident and where it took place, not each individual and their degree of intoxication.
45. A porous volcanic rock used in many central Mexican buildings.
46. Mexico, AGN, *Libros de Reos*, Caja 73, Exp. 50, November 17, 1798.
47. Toxqui Garay, "El Recreo," 92.
48. Mexico, AGN, *Libros de Reos*, Caja 73, Exp. 46, May 11, 1796; Exp. 50, April 21 and July 25, 1798.
49. AGN, Mexico, *Libros de Reos*, Exp. 73, Caja 50, 1798, January 25, February 7, March 5, March 15, July 31, September 11, October 3, November 1.
50. Toxqui Garay, "El Recreo," 82, 176–77; Tutino, *Mexico City, 1808*, 40, 45–47.
51. Kicza, "Pulque Trade of Late Colonial Mexico City," 193–221.
52. AGN, Mexico, *Libros de Reos*, Exp. 73, Caja 50, 1798, November 1, November 18, December 5.
53. Toxqui Garay, "El Recreo," 66, 82, 323–44. Several pulquerías by this name existed into the twentieth century.
54. AGN, Mexico, *Libros de Reos*, Exp. 73, Caja 50, January 15, February 5, February 10, February 18, October 4, October 6, October 15, November 9, and November 25, all 1798.

55. AGN, Mexico, *Libros de Reos*, Exp. 73, Caja 45, November 12, 1794; Caja 46, January 18 and September 14, 1796; and Caja 50, February 2 and June 8, 1798. A guard who previously patrolled ramo 90 also had two offenses for intoxication on duty.
56. Toxqui Garay, "El Recreo," 66, 73, 92–93, 97n203.
57. AGN, Mexico, *Libros de Reos*, Exp. 73, Caja 50, April 12, November 10, 1798.
58. AGN, Mexico, *Libros de Reos*, Caja 73, Exp. 50, April 27, August 16, 1798.
59. AGN, Mexico, *Libros de Reos*, Caja 73, Exp. 50, September 18, December 23, 1798.
60. AGN, Mexico, *Libros de Reos*, Caja 73, Exp. 50, June 13, October 2, 1798.
61. AGN, Mexico, *Libros de Reos*, Caja 73, Exp. 50, February 2, July 16, October 7, 1798.
62. A few examples: AGN, Mexico, *Libros de Reos*, Caja 73, Exp. 50, April 8, April 9, May 5, October 6, December 16, 1798.
63. Scardaville, "Alcohol Abuse and Tavern Reform," 653.
64. Toxqui Garay, "El Recreo," 80–82, 96–97, 300, 337, 340.
65. AGN, Mexico, *Libros de Reos*, Caja 73, Exp. 50, February 17, March 2, March 22, March 24, April 3, April 6, August 3, August 31, September 7, November 13, December 11, 1798.
66. AGN, Mexico, *Libros de Reos*, Caja 73, Exp. 46, August 4, 1796; Exp. 50, August 15, 1798.
67. Hadden, *Slave Patrols*.
68. Savage, *Police Records and Recollections*, 27. "The watch ordered to 'look out for disorderly Negroes and Indians.'"
69. Sellers-Garcia, "Walking while Indian, Walking while Black."
70. Toner, "Everything in Its Right Place?," 31.
71. Taylor, *Drinking, Homicide, and Rebellion*, 40.
72. Toxqui Garay, "El Recreo," 64.
73. Cope, *Limits of Racial Domination*, 35.
74. Scardaville, "Crime and the Urban Poor," 20.
75. See the classic debate regarding class, caste, and calidad, including Martínez, *Genealogical Fictions*; Twinam, *Purchasing Whiteness*.
76. Scardaville, "Crime and the Urban Poor," 45.
77. Scardaville, "Crime and the Urban Poor," 208, 258.
78. See Germeten, *Violent Delights, Violent Ends*, 72–75, for an example of Spanish disdain for inebriated Britons.
79. Scardaville, "Alcohol Abuse and Tavern Reform," 646n12.
80. Terreros y Pando, *Diccionario castellano*, vol. 2, accessed March 29, 2019, ntlle.rae.es.

81. Sánchez-Arcilla Bernal, "La administración de justicia inferior," 367–405.
82. It is assumed that if no location is given, most likely the individual was arrested in the ramo of the guard identified as the arrestor.
83. AGN, Mexico, *Libros de Reos*, Caja 73, Exp. 45, December 19, 1794. See also Sánchez-Arcilla Bernal, "La administración de justicia inferior," 390.
84. AGN, Mexico, *Libros de Reos*, Caja 73, Exp. 50, November 23, 1798.
85. AGN, Mexico, Ramo de Policía y Empedrados, Caja 5492, Exp. 38, September 15, 1815, 3.
86. Scardaville, "Alcohol Abuse and Tavern Reform," 656. Attempting to help people who drank to this degree of excess fits into an idea of these prototypical police as "protecting and serving" a vulnerable population, as discussed in chapter 3. Although these cases cited demonstrate a clear failure in this role, the new patrols did try to connect those arrested for intoxication with healthcare, a topic also discussed in chapter 3.
87. Sánchez-Arcilla Bernal, "La administración de justicia inferior," 375–76.
88. Although "tirado" appears in arrests of two or more individuals in around twenty different times in the existing *Libros de Reos*, to avoid confusion of parsing out separate cases perhaps coincidentally linked in one notation, my analysis here will just look at examples of when this word was used to describe one person arrested in one single incident.
89. There may be disagreement on this point. Sánchez-Arcilla Bernal, "La administración de justicia inferior," 376.
90. Of course many of those sleeping on the street at night were night watchmen, or minors, as noted in chapter 3.
91. Toxqui Garay, "El Recreo," 63.
92. AGN, Mexico, *Libros de Reos*, Caja 73, Exp. 50, August 14, 1798.
93. AGN, Mexico, *Libros de Reos*, Caja 73, Exp. 50, July 8 and July 12, 1798.
94. AGN, Mexico, *Libros de Reos*, Caja 73, Exp. 50, September 24 and November 27, 1798.
95. Jennings, "Policing Public Houses," 64–65.
96. Toner, "Everything in Its Right Place?," 43.
97. For attempts to regulate pulque around 1900, see Garza, *Imagined Underworld*, 23–29. Quote on 23.

5. GUARDS IN TROUBLE

1. Scardaville, "Crime and the Urban Poor," 270.
2. Scardaville, "Crime and the Urban Poor," 248, presents the guards generally as incompetent and undisciplined.

3. See Germeten, *Profit and Passion*, which analyzes viceregal streetwalkers, mistresses, and courtesans from the perspective of the last fifty years of sex worker activism.
4. An observation also made for both the United Kingdom and the United States. See Barrie and Broomhall, "Introduction," *History of Police and Masculinities*, 12–13. Lipsett-Rivera posits this precise era as foundational to the concept of machismo. Lipsett-Rivera, *Origins of Macho*, 173–79.
5. Deans-Smith, *Bureaucrats, Planters, and Workers*, 174–215, details both the challenges and incorrect assumptions about labor in late eighteenth-century Mexico City. See the introduction and chapter 2 for more on the serenos' origins.
6. AGN, Mexico, Gobernación sin Sección, Caja 61, Exp. 13, 1822, 90, 110, 114–15.
7. AGN, Mexico, *Libros de Reos*, Caja 73, Exp. 45, August 8, October 19, 1794; Exp. 50, January 8, March 13, July 25, and November 24, 1798.
8. AGN, Mexico, *Libros de Reos*, Caja 73, Exp. 46, March 17, 1796; Exp. 50, October 9, 1798.
9. AGN, Mexico, *Libros de Reos*, Caja 73, Exp. 46, January 18, 1796; Exp. 50, January 2, 1798.
10. AGN, Mexico, *Libros de Reos*, Caja 73, Exp. 46, May 11, 1796.
11. AGN, Mexico, *Libros de Reos*, Caja 73, Exp. 45, December 12, 1794. Exp. 50, January 15, and March 19, 1798.
12. AGN, Mexico, *Libros de Reos*, Caja 73, Exp. 50, February 2, 1798.
13. AGN, Mexico, *Libros de Reos*, Caja 73, Exp. 50, November 17, 1798.
14. AGN, Mexico, *Libros de Reos*, Caja 73, Exp. 45, December 7, 1794; Exp. 50, July 15, 1798.
15. Unfortunately, only the sparsest information can be found about work patterns of this kind among the serenos. I cite every available incident but do not have enough to make many observations about them.
16. AGN, Mexico, *Libros de Reos*, Caja 73, Exp. 50, September 30, 1798; Deans-Smith, *Bureaucrats, Planters, and Workers*.
17. AGN, Mexico, *Libros de Reos*, Caja 73, Exp. 50, October 21, 1798.
18. AGN, Mexico, Ayuntamientos, Caja 3352, Exp. 1, 1815.
19. AGN, Mexico, *Libros de Reos*, Caja 73, Exp. 50, January 8, 1798.
20. AGN, Mexico, *Libros de Reos*, Caja 73, Exp. 50, February 2, 1798.
21. Johnson, *Policing the Urban Underworld*, 135; Jennings, "Policing Public Houses," 55.
22. Neufeld, "Behaving Badly in Mexico City," 90–99.
23. See below and chapter 6 for more detail on these accusations.
24. For a parallel example from a century later, see Neufeld, "Behaving Badly in Mexico City," 90–99.
25. Scardaville, "Crime and the Urban Poor," 248.

26. AGN, Mexico, Real Audiencia, Caja 790, Exp. 24, 1811.
27. AGN, Mexico, *Libros de Reos*, Caja 73, Exp. 45, September 7, 1794.
28. AGN, Mexico, *Libros de Reos*, Caja 73, Exp. 45, October 18, October 19, November 12, 1794; Exp. 50, June 16, 1798.
29. AGN, Mexico, *Libros de Reos*, Caja 73, Exp. 45, October 18, 1794; Exp. 46, February 29, 1796.
30. AGN, Mexico, *Libros de Reos*, Caja 73, Exp. 45, October 10, 1794.
31. AGN, Mexico, Policía y Empedrados, Caja 2645, Exp. 41, 1797.
32. AGN, Mexico, *Libros de Reos*, Caja 73, Exp. 50, January 15, 1798.
33. AGN, Mexico, *Libros de Reos*, Caja 73, Exp. 50, June 8, 1798.
34. AGN, Mexico, *Libros de Reos*, Caja 73, Exp. 46, March 27, July 4, September 14, and October 1, 1796; Exp. 50, December 24, 1798.
35. AGN, Mexico, *Libros de Reos*, Caja 73, Exp. 46, August 15, 1796.
36. AGN, Mexico, *Libros de Reos*, Caja 73, Exp. 50, June 3 and August 27, 1798.
37. Vanderwood, *Disorder and Progress*, 96–97, 117. The Rurales were toasted annually at a banquet in their honor: "For them no wine is made, but only reddish pulque."
38. Also an issue in nineteenth-century England, although the publican faced more serious charges than the constable. See Jennings, "Policing Public Houses," 62.
39. AGN, Mexico, *Libros de Reos*, Caja 73, Exp. 50, April 5 and September 24, 1798.
40. AGN, Mexico, *Libros de Reos*, Caja 73, Exp. 50, January 23, 1798.
41. AGN, Mexico, Gobernación sin Sección, Caja 61, Exp. 13, April 29, 1822, 114–15.
42. AGN, Mexico, *Libros de Reos*, Caja 73, Exp. 45, December 8 and December 22, 1794.
43. AGN, Mexico, *Libros de Reos*, Caja 73, Exp. 46, September 26, 1796. He only received a warning for his punishment.
44. AGN, Mexico, *Libros de Reos*, Caja 73, Exp. 46, August 1, 1796. In this case, a guard named José Antonio Bonilla (labeled indio) was taken into custody by order of the corregidor at 9:45 p.m. Bonilla incurred no punishment other than surrendering to his sergeant.
45. AGN, Mexico, *Libros de Reos*, Caja 73, Exp. 46, September 11, 1796.
46. AGN, Mexico, *Libros de Reos*, Caja 73, Exp. 46, March 1, 1796; see also Exp. 50, October 9, 1798.
47. AGN, Mexico, *Libros de Reos*, Caja 73, Exp. 50, August 27, 1798.
48. AGN, Mexico, *Libros de Reos*, Caja 73, Exp. 46, January 6, 1796.
49. AGN, Mexico, *Libros de Reos*, Caja 73, Exp. 50, September 2, 1798. José Faustina Montoya received just three days of forced labor for sleeping at work; see also September 23, 1798.
50. AGN, Mexico, *Libros de Reos*, Caja 73, Exp. 50, February 20, 1798.

51. AGN, Mexico, *Libros de Reos*, Caja 73, Exp. 50, July 31, 1798. Ignacio Ramos, from Queretaro, a mestizo and guard number 96. See also October 21, 1798, and October 26, 1798.
52. AGN, Mexico, *Libros de Reos*, Caja 73, Exp. 50, August 8, 1798.
53. AGN, Mexico, Ramo de Policía y Empedrados, Caja 5443, Exp. 27, 1819.
54. AGN, Mexico, *Libros de Reos*, Caja 73, Exp. 50, January 22, 1798.
55. See Germeten, *Profit and Passion*, 88–108; Germeten, "Police Voyeurism in Enlightenment Mexico City," 248–63.
56. AGN, Mexico, *Libros de Reos*, Caja 73, Exp. 50, January 11, 1798.
57. Scardaville, "Crime and the Urban Poor," 248, 263n174, 270–71.
58. AGN, Mexico, *Libros de Reos*, Caja 73, Exp. 46, January 18, 1796.
59. AGN, Mexico, *Libros de Reos*, Caja 73, Exp. 50, October 10, 1798.
60. Lipsett-Rivera, *Origins of Macho*, 71.
61. AGN, Mexico, *Libros de Reos*, Caja 73, Exp. 46, May 11, 1796. See also vol. 73, Exp. 47, May 5, 1795, and vol. 73, Exp. 50, for the tale of a young widow from Puebla who received a sentence of eight days in jail for "diverting herself" with two married men in the San Sebastian cemetery.
62. AGN, Mexico, Ramo de Policía y Empedrados, vol. 87, Contenedor 10, vol. 28, Exp. 10, 1809.
63. AGN, Mexico, *Libros de Reos*, Caja 73, Exp. 50, January 7, 1798.
64. AGN, Mexico, *Libros de Reos*, Caja 73, Exp. 46, February 26 and June 8, 1796; Exp. 50, May 30, 1798.
65. Neufeld, "Behaving Badly in Mexico City," 90–99.
66. AGN, Mexico, Real Audiencia, Criminal, Contenedor 170, vol. 340, Exp. 11, 1791.
67. AGN, Mexico, *Libros de Reos*, Caja 73, Exp. 50, December 2, 1798.
68. AGN, Mexico, *Libros de Reos*, Caja 73, Exp. 45, August 14 and August 29, 1794; Exp. 46, August 17, 1796.
69. AGN, Mexico, *Libros de Reos*, Caja 73, Exp. 45, July 16, 1794; Exp. 46, July 23, 1796.
70. AGN, Mexico, Corregidores, Caja 196, Exp. 6586, 1791.
71. AGN, Mexico, Corregidores, Caja 196, Exp. 6586, 1791, 1. My translation of "Hay Jesús llego el guarda faroles que estaba ebrio."
72. AGN, Mexico, *Libros de Reos*, Caja 73, Exp. 45, July 16, 1794; Exp. 46, July 23, 1796.
73. AGN, Mexico, *Libros de Reos*, Caja 73, Exp. 50, June 23, 1798.
74. AGN, Mexico, *Libros de Reos*, Caja 73, Exp. 45, September 22, 1794; Exp. 46, August 29, 1796.
75. AGN, Mexico, *Libros de Reos*, Caja 73, Exp. 46, August 31, 1796.
76. AGN, Mexico, *Libros de Reos*, Caja 73, Exp. 50, April 15, October 13, October 27, November 18, 1798.

77. An official accused guard number 56 of robbing a chocolate shop. AGN, Mexico, Ramo de Policía y Empedrados, Caja 5801, Exp. 5, 1812.
78. AGN, Mexico, Indiferente de Guerra, Caja 5084, Exp. 22, 1814.
79. AGN, Mexico, *Libros de Reos*, Caja 73, Exp. 50, September 16, 1798.
80. AGN, Mexico, *Libros de Reos*, Caja 73, Exp. 46, June 8, 1796.
81. AGN, Mexico, *Libros de Reos*, Caja 73, Exp. 50, January 6 and December 25, 1798. See also *Libros de Reos*, Caja 73, Exp. 46, March 28, 1796, for a confusing example of guards "showing" some indios seven pesos, related to an incident of defecating on the street. Definitely some corruption took place here, but the entry is not clear.
82. AGN, Mexico, *Libros de Reos*, Caja 73, Exp. 50, August 20, 1798.
83. AGN, Mexico, *Libros de Reos*, Caja 73, Exp. 50, March 21, 1798.
84. AGN, Mexico, Ramo de Policía y Empedrados, Caja 741, Exp. 16, 1811.
85. AGN, Mexico, Ramo de Policía y Empedrados, Caja 4536, Exp. 13, 1795.
86. AGN, Mexico, Ramo de Policía y Empedrados, Caja 4536, Exp. 13, 1795, 10–12.
87. AGN, Mexico, Ramo de Policía y Empedrados, Caja 4536, Exp. 13, 1795, 15.
88. AGN, Mexico, Ramo de Policía y Empedrados, Caja 4536, Exp. 13, 1795, 13–14.
89. AGN, Mexico, Ramo de Policía y Empedrados, Caja 4536, Exp. 13, 1795, 12.
90. AGN, Mexico, Ramo de Policía y Empedrados, Caja 4536, Exp. 13, 1795, 4, 14.
91. AGN, Mexico, Ramo de Policía y Empedrados, Caja 4536, Exp. 13, 1795, 7, 27.
92. AGN, Mexico, Corregidores, Procesos Civiles, 16, Exp. 105, 1794.
93. AGN, Mexico, Corregidores, Procesos Civiles, 16, Exp. 105, 1794, 3.
94. Lipsett-Rivera, *Gender and Negotiation*, 233–46, discusses the socially insulting and sexually demeaning implications of hair-pulling in Mexico at this time, which may have had a particular resonance for Indigenous people.
95. AGN, Mexico, Corregidores, Procesos Civiles, 16, Exp. 105, 1794, 2–3.
96. AGN, Mexico, Corregidores, Procesos Civiles, 16, Exp. 105, 1794, 4.
97. AGN, Mexico, Corregidores, Procesos Civiles, 16, Exp. 105, 1794, 4–5.
98. AGN, Mexico, Corregidores, Procesos Civiles, 16, Exp. 105, 1794, 5–9.
99. AGN, Mexico, Corregidores, Procesos Civiles, 16, Exp. 105, 1794, 15.
100. AGN, Mexico, Corregidores, Procesos Civiles, 16, Exp. 105, 1794, 15–16.
101. AGN, Mexico, Corregidores, Procesos Civiles, 16, Exp. 105, 1794, 17–18.
102. AGN, Mexico, Corregidores, Procesos Civiles, 16, Exp. 105, 1794, 21.
103. AGN, Mexico, Corregidores, Procesos Civiles, 16, Exp. 105, 1794, 21–23.
104. Germeten, *Profit and Passion*, chapter 7.
105. Burkholder, "Honor and Honors in Colonial Spanish America," 18–44.
106. AGN, Mexico, Corregidores, Procesos Civiles, 16, Exp. 105, 1794, 27–28.
107. AGN, Mexico, Corregidores, Procesos Civiles, 16, Exp. 105, 1794, 29–33.

108. AGN, Mexico, Corregidores, Procesos Civiles, 16, Exp. 105, 1794, 33–37.
109. AGN, Mexico, Corregidores, Procesos Civiles, 16, Exp. 105, 1794, 44–45.
110. Germeten, *Profit and Passion*, 130–51.
111. AGN, Mexico, Corregidores, Procesos Civiles, 16, Exp. 105, 1794, 55–58.

6. GUARDS UNDER ATTACK

1. Cobb, *Police and the People*, 20.
2. Lipsett-Rivera, *Origins of Macho*, 173–79.
3. AGN, Mexico, Bandos, vol. 15, Exp. 60, 160.
4. Cobb, *Police and the People*, 91.
5. Deans-Smith, *Bureaucrats, Planters, and Workers*, 230–47, discusses contemporary labor agitation at the tobacco factory, which was appeased through more typical viceregal paternalistic concessions.
6. Scardaville, "(Hapsburg) Law and (Bourbon) Order," 501–2.
7. Schivelbusch, *Disenchanted Night*, 98, 105.
8. Schivelbusch, *Disenchanted Night*, 100–109.
9. Carrera, *Imagining Identity in New Spain*, 39. These statistics somewhat relate to those for a sampling of insurgents arrested in the 1810s: 55 percent labeled indio, 25 percent labeled español, and 20 percent casta. See Van Young, *The Other Rebellion*, 46.
10. AGN, Mexico, *Libros de Reos*, February 2 and February 29, 1796.
11. See Taylor, *Drinking, Homicide, and Rebellion*.
12. It is very possible that some individual serenos claimed Spanish ancestry although they may have had Indigenous or African ancestors. Unfortunately, I do not have enough data about them, such as information about their parents, to speculate on this issue.
13. These include number 17, Montoya (indio); number 28, Arenas (indio); number 35, Rodríguez (castizo); number 50, Albera (mestizo); number 58, Mirando (indio); number 60, Mendez (mestizo); and number 82, Gonzales (mestizo). These seven men were attacked a total of ten times by reos who smashed their lanterns.
14. AGN, Mexico, *Libros de Reos*, Caja 73, Exp. 50, May 5 and May 16, 1798.
15. See Rappaport, *Disappearing Mestizo*.
16. AGN, Mexico, *Libros de Reos*, December 18, 1794; August 8, 1798.
17. Schivelbusch, *Disenchanted Night*, 112.
18. AGN, Mexico, *Libros de Reos*, Caja 73, Exps. 45, 46, and 50.
19. The scanty information inscribed in the records of group attacks involving Indigenous perpetrators does not provide any additional context for their acts of lantern smashing, other than that these incidences typically occurred early

in the evening and the perpetrators were young men and women under thirty years old. AGN, Mexico *Libros de Reos*, Caja 73, Exp. 45, dated October 22, 1794, involved a couple described as ebrios, with no other information provided. In the same book, on December 31, 1794, the two Indigenous men were also called ebrios. AGN, Mexico *Libros de Reos*, Caja 73, Exp. 46, dated February 4, 1796, lists two ebrios, Indigenous men, both aged twenty-five. The incident on August 17, 1798, involved a boy aged sixteen and a twenty-year-old man, borrachos at 7:30 in the evening. Only one report on an episode that took place on September 25, 1796, contains more detail: guard number 80 arrested an Indigenous man and woman, aged twenty-five and forty, at nine in the evening for "scandalous drunkenness," which we might call "drunk and disorderly." They had left a vinatería after a dispute involving a kerchief. The older woman actually broke the glass, but for an unknown injury, she ended up in the hospital. AGN, Mexico, *Libros de Reos*, September 25, 1796.

20. AGN, Mexico, *Libros de Reos*, Caja 73, Exp. 46, January 7, 1796.
21. AGN, Mexico, *Libros de Reos*, Caja 73, Exp. 45, August 4, August 23, September 14, September 21, October 18, October 22, November 22, December 21, 1794; Exp. 46, January 7, September 14, 1796; Exp. 50, April 28, May 27, 1798.
22. See Cope, *Limits of Racial Domination*, 125–57, for the most significant Novohispanic rebellion pre-1800.
23. Schivelbusch, *Disenchanted Night*, 98–99.
24. Sánchez-Arcilla Bernal, "La adminstración de justicia inferior," 420, 423, 431–34; Sánchez-Arcilla Bernal, "La delicuencia feminina," 146–47.
25. AGN, Mexico, *Libros de Reos*, Caja 73, Exp. 50, April 28, 1798. See chapter 4 for a discussion of the terms for drunkenness. This number of lashes was typical in this era for drunkenness.
26. AGN, Mexico, Ramo de Policía y Empedrados, Caja 5325, Exp. 105, 1806, 6; idem, Caja 1954, Caja 14, 1814, 5; idem, Caja 5478, Exp. 9, 14; Gobernación sin Sección, Caja 61, Exp. 13, 1822, 5, 42, 95–96, 106.
27. Germeten, *Violent Delights, Violent Ends*, chapter 3; Boyer, "Honor among Plebeians," 152–78.
28. Mexico, AGN, *Libros de Reos*, Caja 73, Exp. 50, January 22, 1798.
29. Lipsett-Rivera, *Origins of Macho*, 163–67.
30. AGN, Mexico, *Libros de Reos*, Caja 73, Exp. 50, January 24, 1798.
31. AGN, Mexico, *Libros de Reos*, Caja 73, Exp. 46, September 27, 1796.
32. AGN, Mexico, *Libros de Reos*, Caja 73, Exp. 50, January 5, 1798.
33. AGN, Mexico, *Libros de Reos*, Caja 73, Exp. 50, March 17, 1798.
34. See also Ávila González, "Voces y ladridos," 153–54.
35. AGN, Mexico, *Libros de Reos*, Caja 73, Exp. 46, June 10, 1796.

36. AGN, Mexico, *Libros de Reos*, Caja 73, Exp. 46, April 14, 1796.
37. AGN, Mexico, *Libros de Reos*, Caja 73, Exp. 48, June 20, 1798.
38. Lipsett-Rivera, *Origins of Macho*, 156–59.
39. AGN, Mexico, *Libros de Reos*, Caja 73, Exp. 50, July 5, 1798.
40. AGN, Mexico, *Libros de Reos*, Caja 73, Exp. 46, August 1, 1796.
41. AGN, Mexico, *Libros de Reos*, Caja 73, Exp. 50, February 8, 1798.
42. AGN, Mexico, *Libros de Reos*, Caja 73, Exp. 50, September 7, 1798.
43. AGN, Mexico, *Libros de Reos*, Caja 73, Exp. 50, April 8, 1798.
44. AGN, Mexico, *Libros de Reos*, Caja 73, Exp. 50, July 8, 1798.
45. AGN, Mexico, Indiferente Virreinal, Caja 6411, Expediente 5, 1806, 4.
46. AGN, Mexico, Indiferente Virreinal, Caja 6411, Expediente 5, 1806, 6.
47. AGN, Mexico, Indiferente Virreinal, Caja 6411, Expediente 5, 1806, 7–10.
48. AGN, Mexico, Indiferente Virreinal, Caja 6411, Exp. 5, 1806, 11.
49. AGN, Mexico, Real Audiencia, Criminal, vol. 694, Exp. 4, 1803, 56.
50. AGN, Mexico, Real Audiencia, Criminal, vol. 694, Exp. 4, 1803, 55–56.
51. AGN, Mexico, Real Audiencia, Criminal, vol. 694, Exp. 4, 1803, 56–57.
52. AGN, Mexico, Real Audiencia, Criminal, vol. 694, Exp. 4, 60–64.
53. For a parallel example from a century later, see Neufeld, "Behaving Badly," 90–99.
54. AGN, Mexico, Bandos, vol. 15, Exp. 60.
55. Miller, *Cops and Bobbies*, 38–39.
56. Miller, *Cops and Bobbies*, 36.
57. Garrioch, "The People of Paris," 515–17.
58. Johnson, *Policing the Urban Underworld*, 137–42.
59. On the symbolism of attacking clothes in this time and place, see Lipsett-Rivera, *Gender and Negotiation*, 227–32; *Origins of Macho*, 147. Similar to lanterns, one of the key issues with harming someone's clothes was the serious expense that this action would incur.
60. AGN, Mexico, *Libros de Reos*, Caja 73, Exp. 45, September 14, 1794.
61. AGN, Mexico, *Libros de Reos*, Caja 73, Exp. 50, February 8, 1798.
62. AGN, Mexico, *Libros de Reos*, Caja 73, Exp. 50, February 6, 1798. For more on insults relating to hair, see Lipsett-Rivera, *Gender and Negotiation*, 233–44.
63. AGN, Mexico, Bandos, vol. 15, Exp. 60, 1790, 159.
64. AGN, Mexico, *Libros de Reos*, Caja 73, Exp. 50, August 6, 1798.
65. AGN, Mexico, *Libros de Reos*, Caja 73, Exp. 50, May 7, 1798.
66. AGN, Mexico, *Libros de Reos*, Caja 73, Exp. 46, March 17, 1796.
67. AGN, Mexico, *Libros de Reos*, Caja 73, Exp. 50, May 19, 1798.
68. AGN, Mexico, *Libros de Reos*, Caja 73, Exp. 46, September 27, 1796.
69. AGN, Mexico, *Libros de Reos*, Caja 73, Exp. 50, August 6, 1798.

70. AGN, Mexico, Ramo de Policía y Empedrados, Caja 5478, Exp. 9, 1815, 24.
71. AGN, Mexico, *Libros de Reos*, Caja 73, Exp. 45, August 8, 1794.
72. AGN, Mexico, *Libros de Reos*, Caja 73, Exp. 46, February 3, 1796.
73. AGN, Mexico, Criminal, Caja 196, Exp. 6608, 1795.
74. AGN, Mexico, *Libros de Reos*, Caja 73, Exp. 45, August 11, 1794.
75. AGN, Mexico, *Libros de Reos*, Caja 73, Exp. 45, August 27, 1794; Exp. 50, March 15, April 17, and June 29, 1798.
76. AGN, Mexico, *Libros de Reos*, Caja 73, Exp. 50, September 9 and September 24, 1798.
77. AGN, Mexico, *Libros de Reos*, Caja 73, Exp. 50, June 7, 1798.
78. AGN, Mexico, *Libros de Reos*, Caja 73, Exp. 50, July 27, 1798.
79. AGN, Mexico, *Libros de Reos*, Caja 73, Exp. 50, April 4, June 5, June 9, July 2, September 2, 1798.
80. AGN, Mexico, *Libros de Reos*, Caja 73, Exp. 45, September 13, December 15, 1794; Exp. 46, January 4, February 4, March 18, April 26, July 4, July 19, 1796.

7. WATCHMEN, MILITARY, INSURGENCY

1. AGN, Mexico, Ramo de Policía y Empedrados, Caja 5960, Exp. 53, 1799, 3.
2. For a discussion of incidents causing conflicts, and the increased tension between men as militarization increased, see Lipsett-Rivera, *Origins of Macho*, 6, 120, 162–63, 176–77.
3. See Anna, *Mexican Empire of Iturbide*, 28. Anna mentions how the head guards shifted the recipient of their nightly reports from the viceroy to Iturbide.
4. For other incidents of soldiers causing unrest and complaints from residents of the capital city, see Van Young, *The Other Rebellion*, 184, 336.
5. For 1692, see Cope, *Limits of Racial Domination*. For 1608–12, see Sierra Silva, *Urban Slavery in Colonial Mexico*, 155–60.
6. Tutino, *Mexico City, 1808*, 30–31.
7. For background on the military in late viceregal Mexico City, see McAlister, "Reorganization of the Army," 28–29; Domínguez, "International War and Government Militarization," 2–3; Archer, *Army in Bourbon Mexico*, 22–23, 110–11; McAlister, *Fuero Militar*, 1–33, 93–99.
8. McAlister, *Fuero Militar*, 2, 31–32, 98.
9. I hypothesize this in a horrifically sadistic case involving a very low-ranking nonclerical official (a nuncio) of the Holy Office of the Spanish Inquisition. Germeten, *Violent Delights, Violent Ends*, 61–68.
10. McAlister, *Fuero Militar*, 6–15, 22–28, quotes on page 15.
11. Denys, "Development of Police Forces in Urban Europe," 336.
12. Vanderwood, *Disorder and Progress*, 166, 175.

13. AGN, Mexico, Criminal, Caja 547, 2ª parte, Exp 14, 1790, 469–506.
14. Terreros y Pando, *Diccionario castellano*, vol. 2, 6.
15. AGN, Mexico, Criminal, Caja 547, 2ª parte, Exp 14, 1790, 472–77.
16. AGN, Mexico, Criminal, Caja 547, 2ª parte, Exp 14, 1790, 488–89.
17. AGN, Mexico, Criminal, Caja 547, 2ª parte, Exp 14, 1790, 481.
18. AGN, Mexico, Criminal, Caja 547, 2ª parte, Exp 14, 1790, 477–82.
19. AGN, Mexico, Corregidores, Procesos criminales, Caja 196, Exp. 6596, 1791.
20. McAlister, *Fuero Militar*, 43–51, summarizes the debate regarding granting the fuero to pardo militiamen, especially in connection to their paying tribute. For more detail, see Vinson, *Bearing Arms for His Majesty*, 173–98. In the document confirming his militia affiliation, Hernández was described as "a brown man of good color, straight hair, regular features . . . a round pockmarked face, with a scar near his left eye." AGN, Mexico, Corregidores, Procesos criminales, Caja 196, Exp. 6596, 1791, 3.
21. AGN, Mexico, *Libros de Reos*, Caja 73, Exps. 45, 46, 47, 50, 1794–1798.
22. For discussion of street-level sex work, and the military, see Germeten, *Profit and Passion*, chapters 5, 6, and 7.
23. AGN, Mexico, Criminal, Caja 1150, Exp. 10, 1796, 1–17.
24. AGN, Mexico, Criminal, Caja 1150, Exp. 10, 1796, 13.
25. AGN, Mexico, Criminal, Caja 1150, Exp. 10, 1796, 14.
26. AGN, Mexico, Criminal, Caja 1150, Exp. 10, 1796, 8.
27. AGN, Mexico, Criminal, Caja 1150, Exp. 10, 1796, 14.
28. AGN, Mexico, Indiferente de Guerra, Caja 2992, Exp. 38, 1797, 1–31.
29. AGN, Mexico, Indiferente de Guerra, Caja 2992, Exp. 38, 1797, 2.
30. See Lipsett-Rivera, *Origins of Macho*, 143–71; Germeten, *Violent Delights, Violent Ends*, 54–69.
31. AGN, Mexico, Indiferente de Guerra, Caja 2992, Exp. 38, 1797, 24.
32. AGN, Mexico, Indiferente de Guerra, Caja 2992, Exp. 38, 1797, 24–26.
33. AGN, Mexico, Indiferente de Guerra, Caja 2992, Exp. 38, 1797, 6–7.
34. AGN, Mexico, Indiferente de Guerra, Caja 2992, Exp. 38, 1797, 9–11.
35. AGN, Mexico, Indiferente de Guerra, Caja 2992, Exp. 38, 1797, 7, 10.
36. AGN, Mexico, Indiferente de Guerra, Caja 2992, Exp. 38, 1797, 19–22.
37. AGN, Mexico, Indiferente de Guerra, Caja 2992, Exp. 38, 1797, 31.
38. The contemporary name for these reports is *La parte que han dado los guardas del alumbrado de lo acaecido en esta última noche*, or, roughly, "The involvement of the light guards in what happened last night."
39. AGN, Mexico, Indiferente Virreinal, Caja, 4536, Exp. 16, 1800.
40. AGN, Mexico, Indiferente Virreinal, Caja 4536, Exp. 16, 1800, 14.
41. AGN, Mexico, Indiferente Virreinal, Caja 4536, Exp. 16, 1800, 14.

42. AGN, Mexico, Indiferente Virreinal, Caja 4536, Exp. 16, 1800, 8–14.
43. AGN, Mexico, Indiferente Virreinal, Caja 4536, Exp. 16, 1800, 17.
44. AGN, Mexico, Indiferente Virreinal, Caja 4536, Exp. 16, 1800, 4–5.
45. AGN, Mexico, Indiferente Virreinal, Caja 4536, Exp. 16, 1800, 22.
46. AGN, Mexico, Real Audiencia Judicial, vol. 17, Exp. 15, 1801–1802.
47. AGN, Mexico, Real Audiencia Judicial, vol. 17, Exp. 15, 1801, 208–9, 212, 219.
48. AGN, Mexico, Real Audiencia Judicial, vol. 17, Exp. 15, 1801, 208.
49. AGN, Mexico, Real Audiencia Judicial, vol. 17, Exp. 15, 1801, 216, 219, 224.
50. All of the 1822 nightly reports can be found in AGN, Mexico, Gobernación sin Sección, Caja 61, Exp. 13, 1822.
51. AGN, Mexico, Gobernación sin Sección, Caja 61, Exp. 13, April 6, 1822.
52. AGN, Mexico, Indifente de Guerra, Caja 3292, Exp. 8, 1803, 1.
53. AGN, Mexico, Indifente de Guerra, Caja 3292, Exp. 8, 1803, 1–11.
54. See chapter 6 for more on the topic of lantern smashing.
55. AGN, Mexico, Criminal, Caja 164, Exp 48, 1804, 10. For more on this location as a site of protest, see conclusion and Arrom, "Politics in Mexico City," 245–56.
56. Lipsett-Rivera, *Gender and Negotiation*, 157, 235, 240–41.
57. Taylor, *Drinking, Homicide, and Rebellion*, 113–51.
58. Tutino, *Mexico City, 1808*, 238.
59. Noll, *Life and Times of Miguel Hidalgo y Costilla*, 85–89, 92–95, 104–6.
60. Van Young, *The Other Rebellion*, 33, 292, 332; Rodríguez O., *We Are Now the True Spaniards*, 135–36.
61. AGN, Mexico, Archivo Histórico de la Hacienda, vol. 1044, Exp. 10, 1812.
62. McAlister, *Fuero Militar*, 6–15, 22–28.
63. AGN, Mexico, Archivo Histórico de la Hacienda, vol. 1044, Exp. 10, 1812, 3.
64. Nacif Mina, *Policía mexicana*, 84–85, 89.
65. Warren, *Vagrants and Citizens*, 24–30; Nacif Mina, *La policía*, 29–30.
66. Van Young, *The Other Rebellion*, 226–27, 326–28.
67. Lozano Armendares, *La criminalidad*, 36–39.
68. Anna, *Fall of Royal Government*, 83, 126–27.
69. Van Young, *The Other Rebellion*, 39, 107–56.
70. Warren, *Vagrants and Citizens*, 30–35.
71. AGN, Mexico, Intendencias, Caja 1325, Exp. 10, 1813, 3.
72. AGN, Mexico, Ramo de Policía y Empedrados, Caja 1954, Exp. 14, 1814, 5; idem, Caja 5478, Exp. 9, 1815, 14.
73. Yáñez Romero, *Policía mexicana*, 92–93; Nacif Mina, *Policía en la historia*, 31–34.
74. AGN, Mexico, Policía y Empedrados, Caja 3326, Exp. 53, 1815, 1–5.
75. AGN, Mexico, Indiferente Virreinal, Caja 4973, Exp. 39, 1815.
76. AGN, Mexico, Indiferente Virreinal, Caja 6603, Exp. 13, 1815, 2–6.

77. AGN, Mexico, Policía y Empedrados, Caja 4198, Exp. 4, 1818, 5–8.
78. AGN, Mexico, Indiferente Virreinal, Caja 5443, Exp. 38, 1819.
79. AGN, Mexico, Indiferente Virreinal, Criminal, Caja 924, Exp. 11, 1821, 56–57.
80. AGN, Mexico, Indiferente Virreinal, Criminal, Caja 924, Exp. 11, 1821, 40.
81. AGN, Mexico, Indiferente Virreinal, Criminal, Caja 924, Exp. 11, 1821, 12, 55.
82. AGN, Mexico, Indiferente Virreinal, Criminal, Caja 924, Exp. 11, 1821, 18.
83. AGN, Mexico, Indiferente Virreinal, Criminal, Caja 924, Exp. 11, 1821, 43.
84. AGN, Mexico, Indiferente Virreinal, Criminal, Caja 924, Exp. 11, 1821, 25.
85. AGN, Mexico, Indiferente Virreinal, Criminal, Caja 924, Exp. 11, 1821, 43–45.
86. AGN, Mexico, Indiferente Virreinal, Criminal, Caja 924, Exp. 11, 1821, 47.
87. AGN, Mexico, Indiferente Virreinal, Criminal, Caja 924, Exp. 11, 1821, 49.
88. AGN, Mexico, Indiferente Virreinal, Criminal, Caja 924, Exp. 11, 1821, 58.
89. AGN, Mexico, Indiferente Virreinal, Criminal, Caja 924, Exp. 11, 1821, 59.
90. Mendivil was involved in fighting against Mexican insurgents in 1810. See Blanco White, *El español*, 391–95.
91. AGN, Mexico, Indiferente Virreinal, Criminal, Caja 924, Exp. 11, 1821, 40.
92. AGN, Mexico, Indiferente Virreinal, Criminal, Caja 924, Exp. 11, 1821, 64.
93. AGN, Mexico, Indiferente Virreinal, Criminal, Caja 924, Exp. 11, 1821, 66–67.
94. AGN, Mexico, Indiferente Virreinal, Criminal, Caja 924, Exp. 11, 1821, 76.
95. AGN, Mexico, Indiferente Virreinal, Criminal, Caja 924, Exp. 11, 1821, 70.
96. AGN, Mexico, Indiferente Virreinal, Criminal, Caja 924, Exp. 11, 1821, 67–68.
97. AGN, Mexico, Indiferente Virreinal, Criminal, Caja 924, Exp. 11, 1821, 75–77.
98. AGN, Mexico, Indiferente Virreinal, Criminal, Caja 924, Exp. 11, 1821, 82.
99. AGN, Mexico, Indiferente Virreinal, Criminal, Caja 924, Exp. 11, 1821, 82–83.
100. AGN, Mexico, Indiferente Virreinal, Criminal, Caja 924, Exp. 11, 1821, 91. For more information on viceregal cafés, see Clementina Díaz de Ovando, "Los cafes del siglo XIX," 15–36.
101. AGN, Mexico, Indiferente Virreinal, Criminal, Caja 924, Exp. 11, 1821, 95–97.
102. AGN, Mexico, Indiferente Virreinal, Criminal, Caja 924, Exp. 11, 1821, 110–13.
103. Noll, *Life and Times of Miguel Hidalgo y Costilla*, 174–77.
104. Robertson, *Iturbide of Mexico*, 127–28, 130–31.
105. AGN, Mexico, Criminal 37, Contenedor 245, vol. 531, Exp. 9, 1821. See also table 6.
106. AGN, Mexico, Gobernación sin Sección, Caja 61, Exp. 13, 1822, 5, 42, 95–96, 106.
107. AGN, Mexico, Gobernación sin Sección, Caja 61, Exp. 13, April 9, 1822, 76.
108. McAlister, *Fuero Militar*, 15.

CONCLUSION

1. Kuethe and Andrien, *Spanish Atlantic World*, 12–18, quote on 13.

AFTERWORD

1. Fernández de Lizardi, *El periquillo sarniento*, 77; see also Fernández de Lizardi, *Mangy Parrot*, 185.
2. Sanders, *Vanguard of the Atlantic World*.
3. This motivation for modernizing law enforcement connects New Spain and Mexico to cities as distant as Berlin and New York. See Liang, *Berlin Police Force*, 94.
4. Nacif Mina, *La policía en la historia*, 35–38.
5. Yáñez Romero, *Policía mexicana*, 99–100.
6. Noll, *Life and Times of Miguel Hidalgo y Costilla*, 180; Anna, *Forging Mexico*, 96–97. Iturbide fled to Italy, then returned to Mexico in 1824, only to face execution shortly after. Meanwhile, a group of Mexican elites searched for a European prince to replace him. See Shawcross, *France, Mexico and Informal Empire*, 82–89.
7. Warren, *Vagrants and Citizens*, 63–68.
8. Shawcross, *France, Mexico and Informal Empire*, 6.
9. Nacif Mina, *La policía*, 38–40.
10. Scholarship on the history of police in the national era is superb and plentiful. For information about the Mexican police after 1830, see Nacif Mina, *La policía en la historia*; Yáñez Romero, *Policía mexicana*; Vanderwood, *Disorder and Progress*; Piccato, *City of Suspects*; and Piccato, *A History of Infamy*.
11. For a complete list of all fifty articles, see Nacif Mina, *La policía*, 41–49.
12. Styles, "Emergence of the Police," 18; Denys, "Development of Police Forces," 336; Shpayer-Makov, "Acquiring a New Masculine Image," 142; Johnson, *Policing the Urban Underworld*, 136.
13. Nacif Mina, *La policía en la historia*, 52–53.
14. Miller, *Cops and Bobbies*, 33.
15. Shaw, "Poverty and Politics," 295–310.
16. Shawcross, *France, Mexico and Informal Empire*, 90.
17. Yáñez Romero, *Policía mexicana*, 104–8.
18. Sims, *Expulsion of Mexico's Spaniards*, 42–64.
19. Sims, *Expulsion of Mexico's Spaniards*, 51; Arrom, "Politics in Mexico City," 254.
20. Arrom, "Politics in Mexico City," 245–68.
21. Sims, *Expulsion of Mexico's Spaniards*, 76–117.
22. Arrom, "Politics in Mexico City," 267–68.
23. Guerrero, "Mexico's First Black Indian President," died by firing squad in early 1831. Vincent, *Legacy of Vicente Guerrero*.
24. For more travelers' accounts, see Buchenau, *Mexico Otherwise*.

25. See Lizardi, *Mangy Parrot*, preface, xxxvi–xxxvii, for a concise biography of Lizardi.
26. For a somewhat recent fictional mishmash, which confuses the era of privately paid lighting with the creation of the serenos and includes some gratuitous and classic stereotyping of Mexican drinking habits, see Gleason and Podrug, *Aztec Rage*, 86, 361.
27. For this discussion I use both the 1842 Galván edition (pages 74–92) and the Frye translation (pages 183–94).
28. While Linati's image of the night watchman with his pike and dog is very famous, the accompanying text is quite interesting on its own. See chapter 3 for more on Linati's descriptions. See also Moriuchi, *Mexican Costumbrismo*, 33–39. Moriuchi uses art to discuss travelers' perspectives on Mexico in this era.
29. Stuart-Wortley, *Travels in the United States*, 168, 225.
30. Carranza-Castellanos, *Crónica del alumbrado*, 33–37.
31. Ferry, *Vagabond Life in Mexico*, 28–30.
32. Anonymous, *London Quarterly Review* 7 (October 1856–January 1857): 354.
33. Walling, *Recollections*, 194–97, quote on 194.
34. Mexico City had 230,000 residents in 1877, and just under half a million in 1910. Garza, *Imagined Underworld*, 14.
35. Carranza-Castellanos, *Crónica del alumbrado*, 37.
36. Hamilton, *Border States of Mexico*, xi.
37. Annetta Halliday-Antona, "Mexican Customs," *Frank Leslie's Popular Monthly* 44 (July–December 1897): 578.
38. According to Nielsen ratings, the most popular television shows thus far in the twenty-first century prominently include police procedurals and crime drama. See Joal Ryan, "Most Popular TV Shows of All Time, Ranked," accessed July 23, 2020, https://www.tvguide.com/galleries/most-popular-tv-shows-of-all-time-ranked/.
39. Gaspey, *Richmond*, 87–89.
40. Emsley, *Theories and Origins*, xi–xiii.
41. Savage, *Police Records and Recollections*; Walling, *Recollections*.
42. Gaspey, *Richmond*, 89.
43. Hugo, *Les Miserables*.
44. Shpayer-Makov, "Revisiting the Detective Figure," 165–93.
45. Barrie and Broomhall, *History of Police*.
46. Vanderwood, *Disorder and Progress*, 54.
47. Vanderwood, *Disorder and Progress*, 54–55, 63, 67, 132–33.

48. Garza, *Imagined Underworld*, 8.
49. Piccato, *History of Infamy*. Whether this antagonism can be traced to the lantern guards or the mid-nineteenth century *jefes políticos* is open to debate. On the developing corruption of rural and smaller-town justice in the nineteenth century, see Schaefer, *Liberalism as Utopia*.

BIBLIOGRAPHY

ARCHIVAL SOURCES

Archivo General de la Nación, México (AGN)
Ayuntamiento
Bandos
Cárceles y Presidios
Corregidores Procesos Civiles
Correspondencia de Diversas Autoridades
Criminal
Gobernación sin Sección
Independiente Justicia
Indiferente de Guerra
Indiferente Virreinal
Libros de Reos
Ramo de Policía y Empedrados
Real Audiencia
Real Hacienda

PUBLISHED WORKS

Aguirre, Carlos A., and Robert Buffington, eds. *Reconstructing Criminality in Latin America*. Wilmington: Scholarly Resources, 2000.

Alameddine, Rabih. *An Unnecessary Woman*. New York: Grove Press, 2014.

Alonso, Fabián, María E. Barral, Raúl O. Fradkin, and Gladys Perri. "Los vagos de la campana bonaerense: La construcción histórica de una figura delictiva (1730–1830)." *Prohistoria* 5, no. 5 (2001): 171–202.

Althouse, Aaron P. "Drunkenness and Interpersonal Violence in Colonial Michoacán." In Pierce and Toxqui, *Alcohol in Latin America*, 67–86.

Álvarez, Arturo Ordaz. "El estado de policía en la Nueva España: De la reforma borbónica y el régimen de intendencias." In *Arte y sociedad en la Nueva España*, edited by Arturo Vergara Hernández, 109–44. Hidalgo: Universidad Autónoma del Estado de Hidalgo, 2013.

BIBLIOGRAPHY

Andersson, Peter K. *Streetlife in Late Victorian London: The Constable and the Crowd.* New York: Palgrave Macmillan, 2013.

Andrew, Donna T. *Philanthropy and Police: London Charity in the Eighteenth Century.* Princeton: Princeton University Press, 2014.

Anna, Timothy E. *The Fall of the Royal Government in Mexico City.* Lincoln: University of Nebraska Press, 1978.

———. *Forging Mexico, 1821–1835.* Lincoln: University of Nebraska Press, 1998.

———. *The Mexican Empire of Iturbide.* Lincoln: University of Nebraska Press, 1990.

Apice. "Epilepsia: Mito o realidad, breve historia de la epilepsia." Accessed 20 April 2020. https://www.apiceepilepsia.org/epilepsia-y-sociedad/breve-historia-de-la-epilepsia/.

Archer, Christon I. *The Army in Bourbon Mexico, 1760–1810.* Albuquerque: University of New Mexico Press, 1977.

Arrom, Silvia M. *Containing the Poor: The Mexico City Poor House, 1774–1871.* Durham: Duke University Press, 2000.

———. "Politics in Mexico City: The Parián Riot, 1828." *Hispanic American Historical Review* 68, no. 2 (1988): 246–68.

———. *The Women of Mexico City, 1790–1857.* Stanford: Stanford University Press, 1985.

Ávila González, Jesús Salvador. "Voces y ladridos: Ensayo sobre los perros de la Ciudad de México, siglos XVIII y XIX." PhD diss., Universidad Iberoamericana, 2007.

Baldwin, Peter C. *In the Watches of the Night Life in the Nocturnal City, 1820–1930.* Chicago: University of Chicago Press, 2012.

Banton, Michael. *The Policeman in the Community.* New York: Basic Books, 1964.

Barbier, Jacques A. "The Culmination of the Bourbon Reforms, 1787–1792." *Hispanic American Historical Review* 57, no. 1 (1977): 51–68.

Barrie, David G., and Susan Broomhall, eds. *A History of Police and Masculinities, 1700–2010.* London: Routledge, 2012.

Başaran, Betül. *Selim III, Social Control and Policing in Istanbul at the End of the Eighteenth Century: Between Crisis and Order.* Leiden: Brill, 2014.

Bayley, David H. "The Police and Political Development in Europe." In Emsley, *Theories and Origins*, 47–102.

Beal, Sophia. "The Substance of Light: Literature and Public Space in 'Belle Epoque' Rio de Janeiro (1894–1914)." *Luso-Brazilian Review* 49, no. 2 (2012): 5–27.

Beamish, Anne. "Rendering the Darkness Visible: Boston at Night." In *Cities of Light: Two Centuries of Urban Illumination*, edited by Sandy Isenstadt, Margaret Maile Petty, and Dietrich Neumann, 10–19. New York: Routledge, 2015.

Beattie, J. M. *The First English Detectives: The Bow Street Runners and the Policing of London, 1750–1840.* Oxford: Oxford University Press, 2012.

Binder, Beate. "Introduction." In Meier, Hasenöhl, Krause, and Pottharst, *Urban Lighting*, 9–12.
Blanco White, J. M. *El español*. London: R. Juigue, 1810.
Bobb, Bernard E. *The Viceregency of Antonio María Bucareli in New Spain, 1771–1779*. Austin: University of Texas Press, 1962.
Borah, Woodrow. *Justice by Insurance: The General Indian Court of Colonial Mexico and the Legal Aides of the Half-Real*. Oakland: University of California Press, 2018.
Bordua, David J., ed. *The Police: Six Sociological Essays*. New York: Wiley, 1970.
Bouman, Mark J. "The 'Good Lamp Is the Best Police' Metaphor and Ideologies of the Nineteenth-Century Urban Landscape." *American Studies* 32, no. 2 (1991): 63–78.
———. "Luxury and Control: The Urbanity of Street Lighting in Nineteenth-Century Cities." *Journal of Urban History* 14, no. 1 (1987): 7–37.
Boyer, Richard E. "Honor among Plebeians: Mala Sangre and Social Reputation." In Johnson and Lipsett-Rivera, *The Faces of Honor*, 152–78.
Boyer, Richard E., and Geoffrey Spurling, eds. *Colonial Lives: Documents on Latin American History, 1550–1850*. Oxford: Oxford University Press, 2000.
Brading, David A. "Bourbon Spain and Its American Empire." In *The Cambridge History of Latin America*, vol. 1, edited by Leslie Bethell, 389–440. Cambridge, UK: Cambridge University Press, 1984.
Brandes, Stanley. *Staying Sober in Mexico City*. Austin: University of Texas Press, 2002.
Broseta, Salvador, Carmen Corona, Manuel Chust, et al., eds. *Las ciudades y la guerra, 1750–1898*. Castelló de la Plana: Universitat Jaume I, 2002.
Brown, Jennifer M., ed. *The Future of Policing*. New York: Routledge, 2014.
Brox, Jane. "Out of the Dark: A Brief History of Artificial Light in Outdoor Spaces." In Meier, Hasenöhl, Krause, and Pottharst, *Urban Lighting*, 13–30.
Bru, Josepa, and Joan Vicente. "¿Qué produce miedo en la ciudad?" In Gutiérrez, *La ciudad y el miedo*, 15–28.
Bruman, Henry J. *Alcohol in Ancient Mexico*. Salt Lake City: University of Utah Press, 2000.
Buchenau, Jürgen. *Mexico Otherwise: Modern Mexico in the Eyes of Foreign Observers*. Albuquerque: University of New Mexico Press, 2005.
Buffington, Robert M., and William E. French. "The Culture of Modernity." In *The Oxford History of Mexico*, edited by William H. Beezley and Michael C. Meyer, 373–406. Oxford: Oxford University Press, 2010.
Burkhart, Louise M. *The Slippery Earth: Nahua-Christian Moral Dialogue in Sixteenth-Century Mexico*. Tucson: University of Arizona Press, 1989.
Burkholder, Mark A. "Honor and Honors in Colonial Spanish America." In Johnson and Lipsett-Rivera, *The Faces of Honor*, 18–44.

Büschges, Christian. "Don Manuel Valdivieso y Carrión Protests the Marriage of His Daughter to Don Teodoro Jaramillo, a Person of Lower Social Standing (Quito, 1784–1785)." In Boyer and Spurling, *Colonial Lives*, 224–35.

Calderon de la Barca, Frances E. *Life in Mexico during a Residence of Two Years in That Country*. London: Chapman and Hall, 1843.

Calhoun, Frederick S. *The Lawmen United States Marshals and Their Deputies, 1789–1989*. Washington DC: Smithsonian Institution Press, 1990.

Cameron, Lain A. "The Police of Eighteenth-Century France." *European History Quarterly* 7, no. 1 (1977): 47–75.

Campos, Isaac. *Home Grown: Marijuana and the Origins of Mexico's War on Drugs*. Chapel Hill: University of North Carolina Press, 2012.

Candiani, Vera S. *Dreaming of Dry Land: Environmental Transformation in Colonial Mexico City*. Stanford: Stanford University Press, 2014.

Canete, J. Sillero F. de. "La homeopatía en el siglo XIX." *Seminario médico* 56, no. 1 (2004): 65–80.

Cañizares-Esguerra, Jorge. *Puritan Conquistadors: Iberianizing the Atlantic, 1550–1700*. Stanford: Stanford University Press, 2006.

Carranza-Castellanos, Emilio. *Crónica del alumbrado de la ciudad de México*. Mexico City: Litografía y Diseño, 1984.

Carrera, Magali M. *Imagining Identity in New Spain: Race, Lineage, and the Colonial Body in Portraiture and Casta Paintings*. Austin: University of Texas Press, 2003.

Carrillo, Ana Maria. "La profesión médica ante el alcoholismo en el México moderno." *Cuicuilco* 9, no. 26 (2002): 295–314.

Chadwick, Bruce. *Law & Disorder: The Chaotic Birth of the NYPD*. New York: Thomas Dunne Books, 2017.

Challú, Amílcar E., and Aurora Gómez-Galvarriato. "Mexico's Real Wages in the Age of the Great Divergence, 1730s–1930s." *Revista de historia económica* 33, no. 1 (2015): 83–122.

Chesnais, J. C. "Population, Urbanization, and Migration." In Vishnevsky, *Population and Development Challenges and Opportunities*, 190–201.

Chong Ho Shon, Phillip. "Bringing the Spoken Words Back In: Conversationalizing (Postmodernizing) Police-Citizen Encounter Research." *Critical Criminology* 11 (2002): 151–72.

Christie, Nils. *Crime Control as Industry: Toward Gulags, Western Style*. London: Routledge, 1993.

Cicchini, Marco. "A New 'Inquisition'? Police Reform, Urban Transparency and House Numbering in Eighteenth-Century Geneva." *Urban History* 39, no. 4 (2012): 614–23.

BIBLIOGRAPHY

Clendinnen, Inga. *Aztecs: An Interpretation*. Cambridge, UK: Cambridge University Press, 1991.

Cobb, Richard C. *The Police and the People: French Popular Unrest, 1789–1820*. London: Oxford University Press, 1972.

Connell, William F. "'Because I Was Drunk and the Devil Had Tricked Me': Pulque, Pulquerías, and Violence in the Mexico City Uprising of 1692." *Colonial Latin American Historical Review* 14, no. 4 (2005): 369–401.

Cooper, Donald. *Epidemic Disease in Mexico City 1761–1813: An Administrative, Social, and Medical Study*. Austin: University of Texas Press, 1965.

Cope, R. Douglas. *The Limits of Racial Domination: Plebeian Society in Colonial Mexico City, 1660–1720*. Madison: University of Wisconsin Press, 1994.

Cordovil Cordeiro, Bruno. "De-electrifying the History of Street Lighting: Energies in Use in Town and Country (Portugal, 1780s–1930s)." In Rüdiger, *The Culture of Energy*, 30–81.

Costello, Augustine E. *Our Police Protectors. History of the New York Police from the Earliest Period to the Present Time*. New York: C. F. Roper, 1885.

Cox, David J. *A Certain Share of Low Cunning: A History of the Bow Street Runners, 1792–1839*. New York: Routledge, 2010.

Crank, John P. "Watchman and Community: Myth and Institutionalization in Policing." *Law & Society Review* 28, no. 2 (1994): 325–51.

Cresswell, Tim. "Night Discourse: Producing/Consuming Meaning on the Street." In *Images of the Street: Planning, Identity and Control in Public Space*, edited by Nicholas R. Fyfe, 268–79. New York: Routledge. 1998.

Critchley, T. A., and P. D. James. *The Maul and the Pear Tree: The Ratcliffe Highway Murders, 1811*. London: Constable, 1971.

Crowther, Chris, and Jo Campling. *Policing Urban Poverty*. New York: St. Martin's Press, 2000.

Curcio-Nagy, Linda A. *The Great Festivals of Colonial Mexico City: Performing Power and Identity*. Albuquerque: University of New Mexico Press.

Curto, Davide del, and Angelo Landi. "Gas-Light in Italy between 1700s and 1800s: A History of Lighting." In Rüdiger, *The Culture of Energy*, 2–29.

Darnton, Robert. *Poetry and the Police: Communication Networks in Eighteenth-century Paris*. Cambridge MA: Belknap Press of Harvard University Press, 2010.

Dávalos, Marcela, Regina Hernández Franyuti, and Diego Pulido Esteva, eds. *Orden, policía, y seguridad: Historia de las ciudades*. Mexico City: Instituto Nacional de Antropología e Historia, 2018.

Davis, Jennifer. "A Poor Man's System of Justice: The London Police Courts in the Second Half of the Nineteenth Century." *Historical Journal* 27, no. 2 (1984): 309–35.

De Lint, Willem. "Nineteenth Century Disciplinary Reform and the Prohibition against Talking Policemen." *Policing and Society* 9, no. 1 (1999): 33–58.

Deans-Smith, Susan. *Bureaucrats, Planters, and Workers: The Making of the Tobacco Monopoly in Bourbon Mexico*. Austin: University of Texas Press, 1992.

Denys, Catherine. "The Development of Police Forces in Urban Europe in the Eighteenth Century." *Journal of Urban History* 36, no. 3 (2010): 332–44.

Díaz y Ovando, Clementina. "Los cafes del siglo XIX en México." *Artes de México* 192 (1976–1977): 15–36.

Diggins, Milt. *Stealing Freedom along the Mason-Dixon Line: Thomas McCreary, the Notorious Slave Catcher from Maryland*. Baltimore: Maryland Historical Society, 2015.

Dodsworth, F. M. "The Idea of Police in Eighteenth-Century England: Discipline, Reformation, Superintendence, c. 1780–1800." *Journal of the History of Ideas* 69, no. 4 (2008): 583–604.

———. "Men on a Mission: Masculinity, Violence and the Self-Presentation of policemen in England, c. 1870–1914." In Barrie and Broomhall, *A History of Police and Masculinities*, 123–40.

Domínguez, Carmen Blázquez. "Comerciantes y desarrollo urbano: La ciudad y puerto de Veracruz en la segunda mitad del siglo XVIII." *Tiempos de América* 5 (2000): 21–36.

Domínguez, Jorge I. "International War and Government Militarization: The Military—A Case Study." In Rodríguez, *Rank and Privilege*, 1–10.

Doyle, Peter. "Public Eye, Private Eye: Sydney Police Mug Shots, 1912–1930." *Scan Journal* 2, no. 3 (2005): 1–31.

Dunham, Roger G., and Geoffrey P. Alpert, eds. *Critical Issues in Policing: Contemporary Readings*, 7th ed. Prospect Heights: Waveland Press, 2015.

Dyonet, Nicole. "Reforming the Police. Police Memoirs in Eighteenth Century Europe." *Revue Historique* 655 (2010): 728–30.

Eire, Carlos M. N. *From Madrid to Purgatory: The Art and Craft of Dying in Sixteenth-Century Spain*. Cambridge, UK: Cambridge University Press, 1995.

Ekelund, Robert B., Jr., Donald R. Street, and Audrey B. Davidson. "Marriage, Divorce, and Prostitution: Economic Sociology in Medieval England and Enlightenment Spain." *European Journal of the History of Economic Thought* 3, no. 2 (1996): 183–99.

Elliott, J. H. *Spain and Its World, 1500–1700: Selected Essays*. New Haven: Yale University Press, 1989.

Emsley, Clive. "Detection and Prevention: The Old English Police and the New 1750–1900." *Historical Social Research/Historische Sozialforschung* 37 (1986): 69–88.

———. *Policing and Its Context, 1750–1870*. London: Macmillan, 1983.

Emsley, Clive, ed. *Theories and Origins of the Modern Police*. Farnham: Ashgate, 2011.

Estrada, José Wilson Marquéz. "Los dientes del estado. Control criminal y práctica judicial en los albores de la Republica Neogranadina, 1810–1840." *El taller de la historia* 5, no. 5 (2014): 213–44.

Evans, Eric J. *Sir Robert Peel: Statesmanship, Power, and Party*. 2nd ed. New York: Routledge, 2006.

Fallaw, Ben, and Terry Rugeley, eds. *Forced Marches: Soldiers and Military Caciques in Modern Mexico*. Tucson: University of Arizona Press, 2012.

Fernándes, Luís Fiães. "The Early Centuries of the Portuguese Police System: From the Quadrilheiros to the General Intendancy of Police of the Court and of the Kingdom." *Policing and Society* 22, no. 4 (2012): 448–59.

Fernández de Lizardi, José Joaquín. *El periquillo sarniento*. México: Librería de Galván, 1842.

———. *The Mangy Parrot: The Life and Times of Periquillo Sarniento*. Translated by David Frye. Indianapolis: Hackett, 2004.

Fernández Hidalgo, Carmen, and Mariano García Ruipérez. "Las luces en el 'siglo de las luces'. El alumbrado público en España a finales del antiguo régimen." *Hispania* 47, no. 166 (1987): 583–628.

Fernández-Paradas, Mercedes. *La industria de gas de Cádiz*. Barelona: Fundación Gas Natural Fenosa, 2015.

Ferry, Gabriel. *Vagabond Life in Mexico*. New York: Harper and Brothers, 1856.

Fiães Fernandes, Luís. "The Early Centuries of the Portuguese Police System: From the *Quadrilheiros* to the General Intendancy of Police of the Court and of the Kingdom." *Policing and Society* 22, no. 4 (2012): 448–59.

Fonseca, Fabián de, and Carlos de Urrutia. *Historia general de Real Hacienda*. Vol. 5. Mexico City: Imprenta de Vicente García Torres, 1852.

Font, Pablo Giménez. "El miedo a la ciudad oscura. Los primeros proyectos de alumbrado público en las ciudades valencianas y catalanas." In Gutiérrez, *La ciudad y el miedo*, 71–82.

Friedman, Lawrence M. *Crime and Punishment in American History*. New York: Basic Books, 1993.

Fyson, Donald William. *Magistrates, Police and People: Everyday Criminal Justice in Quebec and Lower Canada*. Toronto: Osgoode Society for Canadian Legal History, University of Toronto Press, 2006.

Gaines, Larry K., Victor E. Kappeler, and Joseph B. Vaughn. *Policing in America*. 2nd ed. Cincinnati: Anderson, 1997.

García, Gilberto Enrique Parada. "Delincuentes, policías, y justicias. América Latina, siglos XIX y XX por Daniel Palma Alvarado." *Anuario colombiano de historia social y de la cultura* 46, no. 1 (2019): 345–48.

Garnham, N. "Police and Public Order in Eighteenth-Century Dublin." *Proceedings of the British Academy* 107 (2001): 81–91.

Garrioch, David. "The People of Paris and Their Police in the Eighteenth Century: Reflections on the Introduction of a 'Modern' Police Force." *European History Quarterly* 24, no. 4 (1994): 511–35.

Garza, James Alex. *The Imagined Underworld: Sex, Crime, and Vice in Porfirian Mexico City.* Lincoln: University of Nebraska Press, 2008.

Gash, Norman. *Sir Robert Peel: The Life of Robert Peel after 1830.* 2nd ed. London: Faber and Faber, 2011.

Gaspey, Thomas. *Richmond: Or, Scenes in the Life of a Bow Street Officer Drawn Up from His Private Memoranda.* 3 vols. London: Henry Colburn, 1845.

Germeten, Nicole von. *Black Blood Brothers: Social Mobility for Afro-Mexicans.* Gainesville: University Press of Florida, 2006.

———. "Police Voyeurism in Enlightenment Mexico City." In Leahy and Jones, *Pornographic Sensibilities*, 248–63.

———. *Profit and Passion: Transactional Sex in Colonial Mexico.* Berkeley: University of California Press, 2018.

———. *Violent Delights, Violent Ends: Sex, Race, and Honor in Colonial Cartagena de Indias.* Albuquerque: University of New Mexico Press, 2013.

Gibson, Charles. *The Aztecs under Spanish Rule: A History of the Indians of the Valley of Central Mexico, 1519–1810.* Stanford: Stanford University Press, 1964.

Gilmore, Ruth Wilson. *Golden Gulag: Prisons, Surplus, Crisis, and Opposition in Globalizing California.* Berkeley: University of California Press, 2007.

Ginsberg, Stephen F. "The Police and Fire Protection in New York City: 1800–1850." *New York History* 52, no. 2 (1971): 133–50.

Glasco, Sharon Bailey. "A City in Disarray: Public Health, City Planning, and the Politics of Power in Late Colonial Mexico City." PhD diss., University of Arizona, 2002.

———. *Constructing Mexico City: Colonial Conflicts over Culture, Space, and Authority.* New York: Palgrave Macmillan, 2010.

Gleason, Robert, and Junius Podrug. *Aztec Rage.* New York: Tom Doherty Associates. 2006.

González, Gisela Moncada. "La fiscalidad en el Ayuntamiento de la Ciudad de México durante la Guerra de Independencia, 1810–1821." *Jahrbuch für Geschichte Lateinamerikas—Anuario de historia de América Latina* 48, no. 1 (2011): 131–50.

Gortari Rabiela, Hira de. "La ciudad de México de finales del siglo XVIII: Un diagnóstico desde la 'ciencia de la policía.'" *Historia contemporánea* 24 (2002): 115–35.

Gottschalk, Marie. *Caught: The Prison State and the Lockdown of American Politics.* Princeton: Princeton University Press, 2016.

Gutiérrez, Obdúlia, ed. *La ciudad y el miedo: VII coloquio de geografía urbana.* Girona: Universitat de Girona, 2005.

Hadden, Sally E. *Slave Patrols: Law and Violence in Virginia and the Carolinas.* Cambridge: Harvard University Press, 2001.

Hale, Donna. "Out of the Past . . . A New Police: Applied History and Police History." *Police Studies* 8, no. 4 (1985): 214–19.

Hamilton, Leonidas de Cenci. *Border States of Mexico: Sonora, Sinaloa, Chihuahua, and Durango.* New York: 1883.

Hamman, Amy C. "Eyeing Alameda Park: Topographies of Culture, Class, and Cleanliness in Bourbon Mexico City, 1700–1800." PhD diss., University of Arizona, 2015.

Harrison, Nikki. "Nuns and Prostitutes in Enlightenment Spain." *British Journal for Eighteenth-century Studies* 9, no. 1 (1986): 53–60.

Haslip-Viera, Gabriel. *Crime and Punishment in Late Colonial Mexico City, 1692–1810.* Albuquerque: University of New Mexico Press, 1999.

Hayes, Melissa A. "Sex in the Witness Stand: Erotic Sensationalism, Voyeurism, Sexual Boasting, and Bawdy Humor in Nineteenth-Century Illinois Courts." *Law and History Review* 32, no. 1 (2014): 149–202.

Henderson, Tony. *Disorderly Women in Eighteenth-Century London: Prostitution and Control in the Metropolis, 1730–1830.* London: Longman, 1999.

Hernández, Arturo Vergara, ed. *Arte y sociedad en la Nueva España.* Hidalgo: Universidad Autónoma del Estado de Hidalgo, 2013.

Hernández-Franyuti, Regina. "Historia y significados de la palabra policía en el quehacer político de la ciudad de México. Siglos XVI–XIX." *Ulúa* 3, no. 5 (2005): 9–34.

Herr, Richard. *The Eighteenth-Century Revolution in Spain.* Princeton: Princeton University Press, 1958.

Hidalgo, Jesús Requena. "Inmigración, ciudad, y policía." *Scripta nova: Revista electrónica de geografía y ciencias sociales* 5 (2001). http://www.ub.edu/geocrit/sn-94-35.htm.

Hindus, Michael Stephen. *Prison and Plantation: Crime, Justice, and Authority in Massachusetts and South Carolina, 1767–1878.* Chapel Hill: University of North Carolina Press, 1980.

Holloway, Thomas H. *Policing Rio de Janeiro: Repression and Resistance in a 19th-Century City.* Stanford: Stanford University Press, 1993.

Hugo, Victor. *Les Misérables.* Paris: Lacroix, Verboeckhoven, 1862.

Hulst, Merlijn van. "Storytelling at the Police Station: The Canteen Culture Revisited." *British Journal of Criminology, Delinquency and Deviant Social Behaviour* 53, no. 4 (2013): 624–42.

Isenstadt, Sandy, Margarete Maile Petty, and Dietrich Neumann, eds. *Cities of Light: Two Centuries of Urban Illumination*. New York: Routledge, 2015.

Jackson, Robert H. *Conflict and Conversion in Sixteenth-Century Central Mexico: The Augustinian War on and beyond the Chichimeca Frontier*. Leiden: Brill, 2013.

Jacob, Herbert, ed. *The Potential for Reform of Criminal Justice*. Beverley Hills: Sage Publications, 1974.

Jaffary, Nora E. *Reproduction and Its Discontents: Childbirth and Contraception from 1750–1905*. Chapel Hill: University of North Carolina Press, 2016.

Jennings, Paul. "Policing Public Houses in Victorian England." *Law, Crime, and History* 3, no. 1 (2013): 52–75.

Johns, Michael. *The City of Mexico in the Age of Díaz*. Austin: University of Texas Press, 1997.

Johnson, David R. *Policing the Urban Underworld: The Impact of Crime on the Development of the American Police, 1800–1887*. Philadelphia: Temple University Press, 1979.

Johnson, Lyman L., and Sonya Lipsett-Rivera, eds. *The Faces of Honor: Sex, Shame, and Violence in Colonial Latin America*. Albuquerque: University of New Mexico Press, 1998.

Juárez Flores, José Juan. "Alumbrado público en Puebla y Tlaxcala y deterioro ambiental en los bosques de La Malintzi, 1820–1870." *Historia Crítica* 30 (2005): 13–38.

Khan, Ummni. "Having Your Porn and Condemning It Too: A Case Study of a 'Kiddie Porn' Expose." *Law, Culture, and the Humanities* 5, no. 3 (2009): 391–424.

Kicza, John E. "The Pulque Trade of Late Colonial Mexico City." *Americas* 37, no. 2 (1980): 193–221.

Klein, Herbert S. *The American Finances of the Spanish Empire: Royal Income and Expenditures in Colonial Mexico, Peru, and Bolivia, 1680–1809*. Albuquerque: University of New Mexico Press, 1998.

———. *A Population History of the United States*. 2nd ed. Cambridge, UK: Cambridge University Press, 2012.

Koslofsky, Craig. *Evening's Empire: A History of the Night in Early Modern Europe*. Cambridge, UK: Cambridge University Press, 2011.

Kotkas, Toomas. *Royal Police Ordinances in Early Modern Sweden: The Emergence of Voluntaristic Understanding of Law*. Leiden: Brill, 2013.

Kuethe, Allan J., and Kenneth J. Andrien. *The Spanish Atlantic World in the Eighteenth Century: War and the Bourbon Reforms, 1713–1796*. Cambridge, UK: Cambridge University Press, 2014.

Kushner, Nina. *Erotic Exchanges: The World of Elite Prostitution in Eighteenth-Century Paris*. Ithaca: Cornell University Press, 2013.

Lane, Roger. "Introduction." In *Police Records and Recollections, or Boston by Daylight and Gaslight: For Two Hundred and Forty Years,* by Edward H. Savage. Boston: J. P. Dale, 1971.

———. "Urban Police and Crime in Nineteenth-Century America." *Crime and Justice* 15 (1992): 1–50.

Larkin, Brian. *The Very Nature of God: Baroque Catholicism and Religious Reform in Bourbon Mexico City.* Albuquerque: University of New Mexico Press, 2010.

Lawrence, Paul, Francis Dodsworth, R. M. Morris, Rosaline Crone, Janet Clark, and Haia Shpayer Makov, eds. *The Making of the Modern Police, 1780–1914.* 6 vols. London: Pickering & Chatto, 2014.

Leahy, Chad, and Nicholas R. Jones, eds. *Pornographic Sensibilities: Imagining Sex and the Visceral in Premodern and Early Modern Spanish Cultural Production.* New York: Routledge, 2021.

Lechner, Juan. "El concepto de 'policía' y su presencia en la obra de los primeros historiadores de Indias." *Revista de Indias* 41 (1981): 395–409.

LeMay, Michael C. "Mushrooming Cities: Immigration and the Beginnings of Urbanization, 1790–1865." In *Transforming America: Perspectives on U.S. Immigration,* 47–72. Santa Barbara: Praeger, 2013.

Leonard, Irving A. *Baroque Times in Old Mexico: Seventeenth-Century Persons, Places, and Practices.* Ann Arbor: University of Michigan Press, 1959.

———. "The Theater Season of 1791–1792 in Mexico City." *Hispanic American Historical Review* 31, no. 2 (1951): 349–64.

Liang, His-Huey. *The Berlin Police Force in the Weimar Republic.* Berkeley: University of California Press, 1970.

Linati, Claudio. *Trajes civiles, militares, y religiosos de México (1828).* Translated by Justino Fernández. Mexico City: Imprenta Universitaria, 1956.

Lipsett-Riviera, Sonya. *Gender and the Negotiation of Daily Life in Mexico, 1750–1856.* Lincoln: University of Nebraska Press, 2012.

———. *The Origins of Macho: Men and Masculinity in Colonial Mexico.* Albuquerque: University of New Mexico Press, 2019.

———. "Scandal at the Church: José de Alfaro Accuses Doña Teresa Bravo and Others of Insulting and Beating His Castiza Wife, Josefa Cadena (Mexico, 1782)." In Boyer and Spurling, *Colonial Lives,* 216–23.

Lira, J. "Apuntes sobre la farmacopea tradicional andina." *Bulletin de l'Institut Français d'Études Andines* 19, no. 1–2 (1980): 125–54.

Loftus, Bethan, Benjamin Goold, and Shane Mac Giollabhui. "From a Visible Spectacle to an Invisible Presence: The Working Culture of Covert Policing."

British Journal of Criminology, Delinquency and Deviant Social Behaviour 56, no. 4 (2016): 626–45.

Lozano Armendares, Teresa. *La criminalidad en la Ciudad de México, 1800–1821.* Mexico City: Universidad Nacional Autónoma de México, 1987.

Lubet, Steven. *Fugitive Justice Runaways, Rescuers, and Slavery on Trial.* Cambridge MA: Belknap Press of Harvard University Press, 2010.

Lynch, John. *Bourbon Spain 1700–1808.* Oxford: Basil Blackwell, 1989.

MacLachlan, Colin. *Criminal Justice in Eighteenth-Century Mexico: A Study of the Tribunal of the Acordada.* Berkeley: University of California Press, 1974.

———. *Spain's Empire in the New World: The Role of Ideas in Institutional and Social Change.* Berkeley: University of California Press, 1988.

Maguire, Brendan. "The Police in the 1800s: A Three City Analysis." *Journal of Crime and Justice* 13, no. 1 (1990): 103–32.

Maher, Timothy M. "Police Sexual Misconduct: Officers' Perceptions of Its Extent and Causality." *Criminal Justice Review* 28, no. 2 (2003): 355–81.

Malka, Adam. *The Men of Mobtown: Policing Baltimore in the Age of Slavery and Emancipation.* Chapel Hill: University of North Carolina Press, 2018.

Manion, Jen. *Liberty's Prisoners: Carceral Culture in Early America.* Philadelphia: University of Pennsylvania Press, 2015.

Manning, Peter K. "Policing: Privatizing and Changes in the Policing Web." In Brown, *The Future of Policing*, 23–39.

Manning, Peter K., and A. J. P. Butler. "Perceptions of Police Authority." *Police Journal* 55, no. 4 (1982): 333–44.

Manning, Peter K., and John Van Maanen. *Policing: A View from the Street.* Santa Monica: Goodyear, 1978.

Martínez, María Elena. *Genealogical Fictions: Limpieza de Sangre, Religion, and Gender in Colonial Mexico.* Stanford: Stanford University Press, 2008.

Martínez-López, Alberte. "Capital extranjero y energía: Madrileña de gas, 1846–1935." *Investigaciones de historia económica* 16 (2020): 1–11.

Martínez Ruiz, Enrique. *La seguridad publica en el Madrid de la ilustración.* Madrid: Ministerio del Interior, Secretaría General Técnica, 1988.

———. *Policía y proscritos: Estado militarismo y seguridad en la España borbónica (1700–1870).* Madrid: Actas, 2014.

Martland, Samuel J. "Progress Illuminating the World: Street Lighting in Santiago, Valparaiso and La Plata, 1840–90." *Urban History* 29, no. 2 (2002): 223–38.

McAlister, Lyle N. *The Fuero Militar in New Spain, 1764–1800.* Gainesville: University Press of Florida. 1957.

———. "The Reorganization of the Army of New Spain, 1763–1766." *Hispanic American Historical Review* 33, no. 1 (1953): 1–32.

McCormack, Matthew. "'A Species of Civil Soldier': Masculinity, Policing, and the Military in 1780s England." In *A History of Police and Masculinities, 1700–2010*, edited by David G. Barrie and Susan Broomhall, 55–71. New York: Routledge, 2011.

McGrath, Roberta. "Medical Police." *Ten* 8, no. 14 (1984): 13–18.

Mehl, Eva Maria. "Mexican Recruits and Vagrants in Late Eighteenth-Century Philippines: Empire, Social Order, and Bourbon Reforms in the Spanish Pacific World." *Hispanic American Historical Review* 94, no. 4 (2014): 547–79.

Meier, Josiane, Ute Hasenöhrl, Katharina Krause, and Merle Pottharst, eds. *Urban Lighting, Light Pollution, and Society*. New York: Routledge, 2015.

Meijide Pardo, María Luisa. "Mendicidad, vagancia, y prostitución en la España de siglo XVIII: La casa galera y los departamentos de corrección para mujeres." PhD diss., Universidad Complutense de Madrid, 1992.

Merrick, Jeffrey. "Sodomites and Police in Paris, 1715." *Journal of Homosexuality* 42, no. 3 (2002): 103–28.

Metzl, Jonathan. "From Scopophilia to Survivor: A Brief History of Voyeurism." *Textual Practice* 18, no. 3 (2004): 415–34.

Miller, Wilbur R. *Cops and Bobbies: Police Authority in New York and London, 1830–1870*. Chicago: University of Chicago Press, 1977.

———. "Police Authority in London and New York City 1830–1870." *Journal of Social History* 8, no. 2 (1975): 81–101.

Monkkonen, Eric H. "History of Urban Police." *Crime and Justice* 15 (1992): 547–80.

Moriuchi, Mey-Yen. *Mexican Costumbrismo: Race, Society, and Identity in Nineteenth-Century Art*. University Park: Pennsylvania State University Press, 2018.

Multhauf, Lettie S. "The Light of Lamp-Lanterns: Street Lighting in 17th-Century Amsterdam." *Technology and Culture* 26, no. 2 (1985): 236–52.

Munck, Thomas. "Keeping the Peace: 'Good Police' and Civic Order in 18th-Century Copenhagen." *Scandinavian Journal of History* 32, no. 1 (2007): 38–62.

Mundy, Barbara E. *The Death of Aztec Tenochtitlan, the Life of Mexico City*. Austin: University of Texas Press, 2015.

Muñon Chimalpahin Quauhtlehuanitzin, Don Domingo de San Antón. *Annals of His Time*. Edited and translated by James Lockhart, Susan Schroeder, and Doris Namala. Stanford: Stanford University Press, 2006.

Nacif Mina, Jorge. *La policía en la historia de la Ciudad de México*. Mexico City: Secretaría General de Desarrollo Social, 1986.

Nebrija, Antonio. *Vocabulario español-latino*. Salamanca: Juan de Porras, 1495.

Neufeld, Stephen. "Behaving Badly in Mexico City: Discipline and Identity in the Presidential Guards, 1900–1911." In *Forced Marches: Soldiers and Military Caciques in Modern Mexico*, edited by Ben Fallaw and Terry Rugeley, 81–109. Tucson: University of Arizona Press, 2012.

Noll, Arthur Howard. *The Life and Times of Miguel Hidalgo y Costilla*. Chicago: A. C. McClurg, 1910.

Oberto, Arnaud Exbalin. "Alumbrado y seguridad en la ciudad de México (1760–1810)." *Antropología, Revista interdisciplinaria del inah* 54, no. 4 (2019): 43–54.

———. "Los alcaldes de barrio: Panorama de los agentes del orden público en la ciudad de México a finales del siglo XVIII." *Antropología* 94 (2012): 49–59.

———. "Perros asesinos y matanzas de perros en la Ciudad de México (siglos xxi–xviii)." *Relaciones* 137 (2014): 91–111.

———. "Policing, a Practical Science of Urban Management: Street Lighting in Mexico (Late Eighteenth and Early Nineteenth Centuries)." *Nuevo Mundo, Mundos Nuevos*, 2019. https://journals.openedition.org/nuevomundo/75813.

O'Callaghan, Joseph F. *A History of Medieval Spain*. Ithaca: Cornell University Press, 2013.

Ogborn, Miles. "Ordering the City: Surveillance, Public Space and the Reform of Urban Policing in England 1835–56." *Political Geography* 12, no. 6 (1993): 505–21.

Paley, Ruth. "'An Imperfect, Inadequate, and Wretched System'? Policing London before Peel." In Emsley, *Theories and Origins*, 413–48.

Palma Alvarado, Daniel, ed. *Delincuentes, policías, y justicias: América Latina siglos XIX y XX*. Santiago de Chile: Ediciones Universidad Alberto Hurtado, 2015.

———. "Los cuerpos de serenos y el origen de las modernas funciones policiales en Chile (siglo xix)." *Historia* 49, no. 2 (2016): 509–45.

Payno, Manuel. *The Bandits of Río Frío: A Naturalistic and Humorous Novel of Customs, Crimes, and Horrors*. Translated by Alan Fluckey. Tucson: Wheatmark, 2007.

Pérez, Maria de la Paz Solano. "The Early Path, from the Sacred to the Profane in Fermented Beverages in New Galicia, New Spain (Mexico), Seventeenth to Eighteenth Century." *Crossroads* 14 (2016): 219–56.

Piccato, Pablo. *City of Suspects: Crime in Mexico City, 1900–1931*. Durham: Duke University Press, 2001.

———. *A History of Infamy: Crime, Truth and Justice in Mexico*. Berkeley: University of California Press, 2017.

Pierce, Gretchen. "Parades, Epistles, and Prohibitive Legislation: Mexico's National Anti-Alcohol Campaign and the Process of State-Building, 1934–1940." *Social History of Alcohol and Drugs* 23, no. 2 (2009): 151–80.

Pierce, Gretchen, and Áurea Toxqui, eds. *Alcohol in Latin America: A Social and Cultural History*. Tucson: University of Arizona Press, 2014.

Pilcher, Jeffrey. *¡Que Vivan los Tamales! Food and the Making of Mexican Identity*. Albuquerque: University of New Mexico Press, 1998.

Pluskota, Marion. *Prostitution and Social Control in Eighteenth-Century Ports*. New York: Routledge, 2016.

Poinsett, Joel Roberts. *Notes on Mexico Made in the Autumn of 1822*. Philadelphia: H. C. Carey and L. Lea, 1824.

Potter, Gary. *The History of Policing in the United States*. EKU Online, 2013. www.plsonline.eku.edu/sites/plsonline.eku.edu/files/the-history-of-policing-in-us.pdf.

Pottharst, Merle, and Florian Wukovitsch. "The Economics of Night-Time Illumination." In Meier, Hasenöhl, Krause, and Pottharst, *Urban Lighting*, 203–23.

Priestly, Herbert Ingram. *José de Gálvez: Visitor General of New Spain (1765–1771)*. Berkeley: University of California Press, 1916.

Proctor, Frank "Trey," III. *Damned Notions of Liberty: Slavery, Culture, and Power in Colonial Mexico, 1640–1769*. Albuquerque: University of New Mexico Press, 2010.

Pulido Esteva, Diego. "Gendarmes, inspectores y comisarios: historia del sistema policial en la ciudad de México, 1870–1930." *Ler Historia* 70 (2017): 37–58.

———. "Policía: Del buen gobierno a la seguridad, 1750–1850." *Historia Mexicana* 60, no. 3 (2011): 1595–642.

———. "Trabajo, clase, y prácticas policiales en las comisarías de la Ciudad de México, 1870–1920." *Historia mexicana* 68, no. 2 (2018): 667–712.

Ramos, Ma. Bianca, and Sonia Flores. "El tratamiento del alcoholismo en México en el siglo XIX." *Salud mental* 22, no. 1 (1999): 11–16.

Rappaport, Joanne. *The Disappearing Mestizo: Configuring Difference in the Colonial New Kingdom of Granada*. Durham: Duke University Press, 2014.

Raspa, Darren. *Bloody Bay: Grassroots Policing in Nineteenth-Century San Francisco*. Lincoln: University of Nebraska Press, 2000.

Reiss, Albert J., Jr., and David J. Bordua. "Environment and Organization: A Perspective on the Police." In Bordua, *The Police*, 25–55.

Reith, Charles. "Preventive Principle of Police." In *Theories and Origins of the Modern Police*, edited by Clive Emsley, 3–6. Farnham: Ashgate, 2011.

Rey, Michel. "Police and Sodomy in Eighteenth-Century Paris: From Sin to Disorder." *Journal of Homosexuality* 16, no. 1–2 (1989): 129–46.

Reynolds, Elaine A. *Before the Bobbies: The Night Watch and Police Reform in Metropolitan London, 1720–1830*. Stanford: Stanford University Press, 1998.

Risjord, Norman K. *Chesapeake Politics, 1781–1800*. New York: Columbia University Press, 1978.

Robertson, William Spence. *Iturbide de México*. New York: Greenwood Press, 1968.

Robinson, Cyril D. "Ideology as History: A Look at the Way Some English Police Historians Look at the Police." In *Theories and Origins of the Modern Police*, edited by Clive Emsley, 7–22. Farnham: Ashgate, 2011.

Rodríguez, Linda Alexander, ed. *Rank and Privilege: The Military and Society in Latin America*. Wilmington: SR Books, 1994.

Rodríguez O., Jaime E. *"We Are Now the True Spaniards": Sovereignty, Revolution, Independence, and the Emergence of the Federal Republic of Mexico, 1808–1824*. Stanford: Stanford University Press, 2012.

Romay, Francisco L. *Los serenos de Buenos Aires (policía nocturna)*. Buenos Aires: Editorial Policial, 1947.

Ross, Jeffrey Ian. "Varieties of Prison Voyeurism: An Analytic/Interpretive Framework." *Prison Journal* 95, no. 3 (2015): 397–417.

Rüdiger, Mogens, ed. *The Culture of Energy*. Newcastle: Cambridge Scholars, 2008.

Russell Wood, A. J. R. "Black and Mulatto Brotherhoods in Colonial Brazil: A Study in Collective Behavior." *Hispanic American Historical Review* 54, no. 4 (1974): 567–602.

Sanchez-Archilla Bernal, Jose. "Fondos del archivo general de la nación de la Ciudad de México: Los 'libros de reos' y las 'cuerdas de reos' como fuentes para el estudio de la criminalidad en la Nueva España a fines del periodo colonial." *Clio & Crimen* 10 (2013): 155–75.

———. *Jueces, criminalidad, y control social en la Ciudad de México a finales del siglo XVII*. Madrid: Dukinson, 2016.

———. "La administración de justicia inferior en la Ciudad de México a finales de la época colonial: la punición de la embriaguez en los Libros de Reos (1794–1798)." *Cuadernos de historia del derecho* 7 (2000): 309–456.

———. "La delincuencia femenina en la Ciudad de México a finales del siglo XVIII." *Cuadernos de Historia del Derecho* 20 (2013): 89–154.

Sánchez de Tagle, Esteban. "La remodelación urbana de la Ciudad de México en el siglo xviii: Una crítica de los supuestos." *Tiempos de America* 5–6 (2000): 9–19.

Sanders, James E. *The Vanguard of the Atlantic World: Creating Modernity, Nation, and Democracy in Nineteenth-Century Latin America*. Durham: Duke University Press, 2014.

Sanz de la Higuera, Francisco José. "La iluminación doméstica en el Burgos del siglo XVIII." *Arte y sociedad, revista investigación* 5 (2013): 1–36.

Sarrelangue, Delfina López. "La policía de la Ciudad de México en 1788." *Revista de Indias* 32 (1972): 227–40.

Savage, Edward H. *Police Records and Recollections, Or, Boston by Daylight and Gaslight: For Two Hundred and Forty Years*. Boston: J. P. Dale, 1873.

Scardaville, Michael C. "Alcohol Abuse and Tavern Reform in Late Colonial Mexico City." *Hispanic American Historical Review* 60, no. 4 (1980): 643–71.

———. "Crime and the Urban Poor: Mexico City in the Late Colonial Period." PhD diss., University of Florida, 1977.

———. "(Hapsburg) Law and (Bourbon) Order: State Authority, Popular Unrest, and the Criminal Justice System in Bourbon Mexico City." *Americas* 50, no. 4 (1994): 501–25.

———. "Justice by Paperwork: A Day in the Life of a Court Scribe in Bourbon Mexico City." *Journal of Social History* 36, no. 4 (2003): 979–1007.

Schaefer, Timo H. *Liberalism as Utopia: The Rise and Fall of Legal Rule in Post-Colonial Mexico, 1820–1900*. Cambridge, UK: Cambridge University Press, 2019.

Schendel, Gordon, José Álvarez Amézquita, and Miguel E. Bustamante. *Medicine in Mexico: From Aztec Herbs to Betatrons*. Austin: University of Texas Press, 1968.

Schivelbusch, Wolfgang. *Disenchanted Night: The Industrialization of Light in the Nineteenth Century*. Translated by Angela Davies. Berkeley: University of California Press, 1995.

Schwaller, Robert C. *Géneros de Gente in Early Colonial Mexico: Defining Racial Difference*. Norman: University of Oklahoma Press, 2016.

Seed, Patricia. *To Love, Honor, and Obey in Colonial Mexico: Conflicts over Marriage Choice, 1574–1821*. Stanford: Stanford University Press, 1988.

Seijas, Tatiana. *Asian Slaves in Colonial Mexico: From Chinos to Indians*. Cambridge, UK: Cambridge University Press, 2014.

Sellers-Garcia, Sylvia. "Walking while Indian, Walking while Black: Policing in a Colonial City." *American Historical Review* 126, no. 2 (2021): 455–80.

Senosiain, Lillian Briseño. *La noche develada: La Ciudad de México en el siglo XIX*. Santander: Ediciones Universedad Cantabria, 2017.

Serulnikov, Sergio. "Customs and Rules: Bourbon Rationalizing Projects and Social Conflicts in Northern Potosí during the 1770s." *Colonial Latin America Review* 8, no. 2 (1999): 245–74.

Shaw, Frederick John. "Poverty and Politics in Mexico City, 1824–1854." PhD diss., University of Florida, 1975.

Shawcross, Edward. *France, Mexico, and Informal Empire in Latin America, 1820–1867: Equilibrium in the New World*. Cham: Palgrave Macmillan, 2018.

Shelden, Randall G. *Controlling the Dangerous Classes: A Critical Introduction to the History of Criminal Justice*. Boston: Allyn and Bacon, 2001.

Shpayer-Makov, Haia. "Revisiting the Detective Figure in Late Victorian and Edwardian Fiction: A View from the Perspective of Police History." *Law, Crime and History* 1, no. 2 (2011): 165–93.

———. "Shedding the Uniform and Acquiring a New Masculine Image: The Case of the Late-Victorian and Edwardian English Police Detective." In Barrie and Broomhall, *A History of Police and Masculinities*, 141–62.

Sierra Silva, Pablo Miguel. *Urban Slavery in Colonial Mexico: Puebla de Los Ángeles, 1531–1706*. Cambridge, UK: Cambridge University Press, 2018.

Sigal, Pete. *The Flower and the Scorpion: Sexuality and Ritual in Early Nahua Culture*. Durham: Duke University Press, 2011.

Silver, Allan. "The Demand for Order in Civil Society: A Review of Some Themes in the History of Urban Crime, Police, and Riot." In Emsley, *Theories and Origins*, 23–46.

Simón Palmer, María del Carmen. "Faroleros y serenos (notas para su historia)." *Anales de Instituto de Estudios Madrileños* 12 (1976): 183–204.

———. "Los serenos, faroleros en sus primeros tiempos." *Villa de Madrid: Revista del excmo. ayuntamiento* 38 (1973): 62–66.

Sims, Harold Dana. *The Expulsion of Mexico's Spaniards, 1821–1836*. Pittsburgh: University of Pennsylvania Press, 1990.

Sluhovsky, Moshe. "History and Voyeurism: From Marguerite de Valois to *La Reine Margot*." *Rethinking History* 4, no. 2 (2000): 193–210.

Smith, Phillip Thurmond. "Scotland Yard and Public Order in Early 19th-Century London." *Criminal Justice Review* 13, no. 2 (1988): 41–49.

Smith, Robert S. "A Research Report on Consulado History." *Journal of Inter-American Studies* 3, no. 1 (1961): 41–52.

Sousa, Lisa. "The Devil and Deviance in Native Criminal Narratives from Early Mexico." *Americas* 59, no. 2 (2002): 161–79.

Stein, Barbara H., and Stanley J. Stein. *Crisis in an Atlantic Empire: Spain and New Spain, 1808–1810*. Baltimore: Johns Hopkins University Press, 2014.

Steinberg, Allen. *The Transformation of Criminal Justice, Philadelphia, 1800–1880*. Chapel Hill: University of North Carolina Press, 1989.

Stern, Steve. *The Secret History of Gender: Women, Men, and Power in Late Colonial Mexico*. Chapel Hill: University of North Carolina Press, 1995.

Stevens, Donald Fithian. *Mexico in the Time of Cholera*. Albuquerque: University of New Mexico Press, 2019.

Stuart-Wortley, Lady Emmeline. *Travels in the United States during 1849–1850*. Paris: A&W Galignani, 1851.

Styles, John. "The Emergence of the Police—Explaining Police Reform in Eighteenth and Nineteenth Century England." *British Journal of Criminology* 27, no. 1 (1987): 15–22.

Tamang, J. P., W. H. Holzapfel, D. H. Shin, and G. E. Felis. "Editorial: Microbiology of Ethnic Fermented Foods and Alcoholic Beverages of the World." *Frontiers in Microbiology* (2017): 1–2.

Taylor, William B. *Drinking, Homicide, and Rebellion in Colonial Mexican Villages*. Stanford: Stanford University Press, 1979.

———. *Magistrates of the Sacred: Priests and Parishioners in Eighteenth-Century Mexico*. Stanford: Stanford University Press, 1996.

Terreros y Pando, Esteban. *Diccionario castellano con las voces de ciencias y artes y sus correspondientes en las tres lenguas francesa, latina, e italiana*, vol. 2. Madrid: Viuda de Ibarra, 1786.

———. *Diccionario castellano con las voces de ciencias y artes y sus correspondientes en las tres lenguas francesa, latina, e italiana*, vol. 3. Madrid: Viuda de Ibarra, 1788.

Thale, Christopher. "Assigned to Patrol: Neighborhoods, Police, and Changing Deployment Practices in New York City before 1930." *Journal of Social History* 37, no. 4 (2004): 1037–64.

Tomlins, Christopher L. "Law, Police, and the Pursuit of Happiness in the New American Republic." *Studies in American Political Development* 4 (1990): 3–34.

Toner, Deborah. "Everything in Its Right Place? Drinking Places and Social Spaces in Mexico City, c. 1780–1900." *Social History of Alcohol and Drugs* 25, no. 1–2 (2011): 26–48.

Torales Pacheco, Josefina María Cristina. "Ilustrados en la Nueva España: Los socios de la Real Sociedad Bascongada de los Amigos del País." PhD diss., Universidad Iberoamericana, 2001.

Toulalan, Sarah. "'Private Rooms and Back Doors in Abundance': The Illusion of Privacy in Pornography in Seventeenth-Century England." *Women's History Review* 10, no. 4 (2001): 701–20.

Toxqui Garay, María Aurea. "'El Recreo de los Amigos': Mexico City's Pulquerías during the Liberal Republic (1856–1911)." PhD diss., University of Arizona, 2008.

Turrado Vidal, Martín. *La policía en la historia contemporánea de España (1766–1986)*. Madrid: Ministerio de Justicia e Interior, 1995.

Tutino, John. *Making a New World: Founding Capitalism in the Bajío and Spanish North America*. Durham: Duke University Press, 2011.

———. *Mexico City, 1808: Power, Sovereignty, and Silver in an Age of War and Revolution*. Albuquerque: University of New Mexico Press, 2018.

Twinam, Ann. *Purchasing Whiteness: Pardos, Mulattos, and the Quest for Social Mobility in the Spanish Indies*. Stanford: Stanford University Press, 2015.

Uchida, Craig D. "Development of the American Police: An Historical Overview." In Dunham and Alpert, *Critical Issues in Policing*, 11–30.

Uribe-Uran, Victor M. "Colonial Baracunatanas and Their Nasty Men: Spousal Homicides and the Law in Late Colonial New Granada." *Journal of Social History* 35, no. 1 (2001): 43–72.

———. *Fatal Love: Spousal Killers, Law, and Punishment in the Late Colonial Spanish Atlantic*. Stanford: Stanford University Press, 2015.

Valdés, Alfonso de. *Diálogo de Mercurio y Carón: En que allende de muchas cosas graciosas*. Nebrija, 1530. https://biblioteca.org.ar/libros/749.pdf. Accessed November 18, 2019.

Valdés, Dennis Nodin. "The Decline of the 'Sociedad de Castas' in Mexico City." PhD diss., University of Michigan, 1978.

Valdés, Manuel Antonio. *Gacetas de México: Compendio de noticias de Nueva España*, vol. 4. Mexico City: Don Felipe de Zúñiga y Ontiveros, 1971.

Valente, Joseph. "The Novel and the Police (Gazette)." *Novel: A Forum on Fiction* 29, no. 1 (1995): 8–18.

Van Maanen, John. "Working the Street: A Developmental View of Police Behavior." In Jacob, *The Potential for Reform*, 83–130.

Van Young, Eric. *The Other Rebellion: Popular Violence, Ideology, and the Mexican Struggle for Independence, 1810–1821*. Stanford: Stanford University Press, 2001.

Vanderwood, Paul J. *Disorder and Progress: Bandits, Police, and Mexican Development*. Wilmington: Scholarly Resources, 1992.

Vila, Bryan, and Cynthia Morris. *The Role of Police in American Society: A Documented History*. Westport: Greenwood Press. 1999.

Vincent, Theodore. *The Legacy of Vicente Guerrero: Mexico's First Black Indian President*. Gainesville: University Press of Florida, 2001.

Vinson, Ben, III. *Bearing Arms for His Majesty: The Free-Colored Militia in Colonial Mexico*. Stanford: Stanford University Press, 2001.

———. "Free Colored Voices: Issues of Representation and Racial Identity in the Colonial Mexican Militia." *Journal of Negro History* 80, no. 4 (1995): 170–82.

Viqueira Albán, Juan Pedro. *Propriety and Permissiveness in Bourbon Mexico*. Translated by Sonya Lipsett-Rivera and Sergio Rivera Ayala. Lanham: SR Books, 2004.

Vishnevsky, Anatoly G., ed. *Population and Development Challenges and Opportunities: Encyclopedia of Life Support Systems*. Oxford: Eolss, 2009.

Voekel, Pamela. *Alone before God: The Religious Origins of Modernity in Mexico*. Durham: Duke University Press, 2002.

———. "Peeing on the Palace: Bodily Resistance to Bourbon Reforms in Mexico City." *Journal of Historical Sociology* 5, no. 2 (1992): 183–208.

Von Hoffman, Alexander. "An Officer of the Neighborhood: A Boston Patrolman on the Beat in 1895." *Journal of Social History* 26, no. 2 (1992): 309–30.

Wadman, Robert C., and William Thomas Allison. *To Protect and Serve: A History of Police in America*. Upper Saddle River NJ: Prentice Hall, 2004.

Walling, George W. *Recollections of a New York Chief of Police*. New York: Caxton Book Concern, 1887.

Walsh, Casey. *Virtuous Waters: Mineral Springs, Bathing, and Infrastructure in Mexico*. Berkeley: University of California Press, 2018.

Warren, Richard A. *Vagrants and Citizens: Politics and the Masses in Mexico City from Colony to Republic*. Wilmington: Scholarly Resources, 2001.

Williams, Alan. "The Police and the Administration of Eighteenth-Century Paris." *Journal of Urban History* 4, no. 2 (1978): 157–82.

Williams, Chris A. *Police Control Systems in Britain, 1775–1975: From Parish Constable to National Computer.* Manchester: Manchester University Press, 2014.

Williams, Kristian. *Our Enemies in Blue Police and Power in America*, 3rd ed. Oakland: AK Press, 2013.

Williams, Robert. "Night Spaces: Darkness, Deterritorialization, and Social Control." *Space and Culture* 11, no. 4 (2008): 514–32.

Yáñez Romero, José Arturo. *Policía mexicana: Cultura política, (in)seguridad, y orden público en el gobierno del Distrito Federal, 1821–1876.* Mexico City: Universidad Autónoma Nacional de México, 1999.

Zakaib, Susan. "Performing Reform: The Bourbon Quest for Refinement, Decency and Good Taste at Mexico City's Royal Theater, 1752–1821." ILASSA Conference Paper, 2010, 1–39.

INDEX

Page numbers in italics refer to figures and tables.

Acordada (Mexico City court), 4, 255
Alameda park, 15, 112, 116
alcalde (neighborhood official), 1–5, 22, 76, 80–85, 104, 197, 222, 230, 236
alcohol consumption: arrest statistics for, 16–19, 64, 113–20, 130–32; deaths from, 100–101, 150; denial of, 153; and elderly, 112–13, 149; geography of, 134–43; historiography of, 127–28; hospitalization for, 117–19; and Indigenous people, *113*, 128–29, 143–48; judicial response to, 115, 119, 149–50; leading to unconsciousness, 151–53; by night watchmen, 160–64; and nudity, 152–53; records of, 119, 128–29; remedies for, 119–21; timing of, *132*; and violence, 100, 131; and women, 100–101, 114–15, 117–19, 121, 171–73; words for, 149–51. See also *pulque* and *pulquerías*
audiencia (high court), 3–4, 42–48, 79

Bernal, José Manuel (corporal of the guard): biography of, 8–11, 14–19, 246–50; and camaraderie with other guards, 84; and conflicts with judiciary, 1–3; and conflicts with military, 5–6, 222, 225–28; patrol area of, 64, 147; reputation of, 80–82
Bonavía, Bernardo, *corregidor*, 49, 53, 89, 120, 174, 218
Bourbon dynasty, 6
Bourbon Reforms: and Catholic Church, 32, 62–63, 95–96; as civilizers, 119, 148, 250, 253; historiography of, 20–22, 245–46; and imperial finances, 12; and urban poor, 86, 110, 128. See also street lighting
Bucareli, Antonio María de, viceroy, 36–37, 40, 66, 246

cabos (corporals of the guard), 16–17, 67, 73–74, 165
Catholic Church: and fires, 104; and public health, 86; and public illumination, 31–33; and rituals at death, 98–99; sacraments of, 68–69. See also church buildings; priests
Chimalpahin, don Domingo de, 31
church buildings, 107, 109, 112, 131–34, 140, 229
Cobb, R. C., 19, 245

INDEX

Cope, Douglas, 145
corregidor (municipal government official), 3–4, 76, 87, 182–83, 199, 204. *See also* Bonavía, Bernardo, *corregidor*
crime: in literature, 259–62; and poor residents, 9, 20, 23–24, 26–27, 47–48, 145–48, 207; and property, 102–3, 234; and street lighting, 33, 35–40, 52–53, 189. *See also* night watchmen; safety; security
Cruillas, Marquis de, viceroy, 35–35, 246

Dongo, Joaquín de, 52, 84, 247
drinking. *See* alcohol consumption

Enlightenment, 10, 23, 33–34, 86

French Revolution, 6, 21–22, 26
fuero militar. *See* military and militia

Gálvez, Bernardo de, viceroy, 46–47
Gálvez, José de, 36
Gálvez, Matías de, viceroy, 41–43
Garibay, Pedro de, viceroy, 56–58
Gibson, Charles, 127
guarda faroleros (lantern guards). *See* night watchmen
guarda mayor (head guard): complaints against, 57–59, 241; disciplining night watchmen, 157–65; duties of, 50, 53, 59, 74–76, 89, 94; names of, 75; reports by, 19, 67, 81, 85, 88, 98, 102–4, 129, 189; salary of, 24, 51, 97
Guerrero, Vicente, 242, 255–56

Hidalgo, Miguel de, 22, 214, 230, 232
honor, 9, 68, 80–82, 168, 196–98, 204, 222–28

Indigenous peoples: attacking guards, 84, 197–200; and drinking, 12, 117, 126–29, 134–35, 143–49; and lantern smashing, 191–92, 249; as legal minors, 106; as night watchmen, 72, 236–37; protests by, 22–23; resisting arrest, 167–72, 207–10; as urban plebians, 13, 51, 69, 107–9. *See also* Tenochtitlán
insurgency, 56, 84, 180, 194, 214; and attacks on night watchmen, 102, 196, 230–43; and security, 8; and violence in Mexico City, 118, 252–53
Iturbide, Agustín de, 19, 74, 88, 242, 252–53
Iturrigaray, José de, viceroy, 56–58, 97, 202, 229

Libros de Reos (court dockets): archiving intoxication, 119, 127–29, 134–37, 143, 149–52; and biographies of guards, 67–68, 70–71, 147; guards as first responders in, 102, 106, 110–11, 116–17; guards as offenders in, 74–75, 161, 170; guards as victims in, 190–91, 202, 206, 208; military men in, 218–20, 220, 231; statistical analysis of, 16–19
Linati, Claudio, 61–63, 77–78, 86, 99, 258
Lipsett-Rivera, Sonya, 200
Lizardi, José Joaquín Fernández de, 251, 257–58

masculinity and *machismo*, 2, 82, 106, 157, 196, 262
Mexico City: and animal control, 8, 254; beautification projects in, 7–8, 30, 33, 37, 40–41, 129, 219, 253; bodily functions on streets of, 13, 129–30; carriages in, 5, 12, 18, 33, 57, 243, 253; and elections, 234, 255; and insurgency, 102, 118, 214, 230–36, 249, 252–53, 257; mail in, 95, 282n6;

Masonic lodges in, 255; militarization of, 205, 215, 230–36, 254; parks of, 112, 116; poor house in, 112–13; population of, 8–15, 21, 39–40, 70–72; post-insurgency riots in, 255–56; and reforms in 1820s, 252–55; stray dogs in, 49, 63, 86–90, 197–98, 235, 281n98; street addresses in, 8, 59; street grid (*traza*) of, 15; vagrancy in, 86–87, 107–8, 145. *See also* street lighting

midwives, 54, 63, 93–96, 105, 118

military and militia: and conflict with night watchmen, 89–90, 201–2, 216–43, *231*; in early independence era, 252–55; increases in, 21–22, 214–15; during insurgency, 230–36; judicial privileges of, 97, 206, 214–16; murdering night watchmen, 236–42; as night watchmen, 173–75; *pardo*, 45–46; and sexual offenses, 107, 119, 181–82, 220, *231*

Montserrat, Joaquín de, Marquis de Cruillas, viceroy, 35–36, 246

night: attempts to conquer, 29–30; dangerous, 33, 36–40, 48, 52; and moonlight, 49, 57; as a plebeian space, 124–25, 129. *See also pulque* and *pulquerías*; street lighting

night watchmen: absenteeism of, 157–60; as accomplices to offenses, 173–75; age of, 68–70; anonymous, 13–19; birthplaces of, 69–72; calling the time and weather, 77–78, 80; clothing of, 86, 186, 194; collective biography of, 72–73; and conflicts with *alcaldes*, 3, 8, 24–25, 80–81, 165; and conflicts with priests, 99–100; and discipline issues on duty, 155–64; and enslaved individuals, 110–11; and epileptics, *113*, 113–16; equipment of, 78–85, 205–6; foreigners' accounts of, 258–60; foundation of, 49–54, 94–95; group identity of, 62, 66, 79–85; guarding property, 102–3; and honor, 9, 68, 80–82, 106, 156, 196–98, 204, 222–23; and illiteracy, 67, 72–73, 238; impersonating superior, 176–82; and interactions with children, 105–12; ladders of, 5–6, 43–44, 50–51, 173–75; marital status of, 68; as martyrs, 97; name origins of, 77–78; in novels, 257–58; as plebeians, 10, 68–69, 82, 90; race labels of, 10, 68, 71–72; ranks of, 73–76; as representatives of the state, 5–7, 9, 23; resistance to, 204–9; salary of, 50–52; and sex on the job, 165–68; and sexual assault, 167, 178–83; sleeping on the job, 164–65; stealing from civilians, 171–72, 201–2; taking bribes, 170–74; and thefts of equipment, 17, 175, 194; as violent, 165, 190, 200–201, 217–18; weapons of, 84–85, 223–24; weather and time reporting, 77–78; whistles of, 78–82, 237–38. *See also Libros de Reos* (court dockets); *pulque* and *pulquerías*

Parián market, 229, 255–56

police: and Bow Street Runners, 25, 260–62; definition of modern, 22–27; and guns, 206; history in France of, 6, 19–20, 23–24, 26–27, 94, 205; history in London of, 23–25, 53, 204–5, 254, 259; history in Spain of, 4; idealized, 62–63, 96; in literary sources, 82, 260–63; in Madrid, 8, 21–22, 77–79, 84, 233; and masculinity, 82; in the Mexican Republic, 73, 163, 254–60; origins of word, 7; uniforms

INDEX

police (*cont.*)
of, 23–25, 77, 90–91, 254, 261–63; in the United States, 122, 206. *See also* night watchmen
policía (good government), 5–8, 21–22, 46, 52, 63, 232–33, 253
priests, 17, 54, 56, 63, 93–96, 98–101, 118, 145. *See also* Catholic Church
pulque and *pulquerías*, 130–33; arrests in, 107, 115, 173, 225; attempts to reform, 126, 154, 249; geography of, 43, 123–24, 134–43, 147–48; historiography of, 127, 144–45; and night watchmen, 162–64, 181, 248. *See also* alcohol consumption

race labels: for arrested children, 107–8; and arrests for drunkenness, 146–48; and attacks on guards, 199; and lantern smashing, 190–91; among night watchmen, 71–72
Revillagigedo, Juan Vicente de Güemes, viceroy: and animal control, 87–89; and fire prevention, 104; and founding night watchmen, 66, 73–75, 80, 93, 186–87; and judicial reform, 4–5, 247; organizing street lighting, 49–55; preventing robberies, 102
rurales, 262–63

safety: and night watchmen, 236, 256, 259; and plebians, 12, 33–34, 47; and street lighting, 52, 75
Scardaville, Michael, 125–29, 145–46, 269n74, 270n79
Schivelbusch, Wolfgang, 29, 189, 192
security, 47–54, 255–56. *See also* safety
serenos. *See* night watchmen
sex workers, 83, 107, 176–83, 219–20, 284n51, 292n3

slavery, x, 110–11, 144
Spain: court system of, 3–4; government of, 9–10. *See also* Bourbon reforms; *policía* (good government)
street lighting: complaints about, 44–47, 57; conflicts caused by, 44–47; costs of, 43–44, 49, 53; and crime prevention, 33–34, 39–40, 47–48, 52; design of, *38*, 43; and extent of illumination, 54–55, 57; and fuel shortages, 57–58; and gas, 124, 192, 258; history in Europe of, 34–35; in imitation of Europe, 36–41, 47; and law enforcement, 49–50, 52; and oil source, 40, 58; petitions about, 36–40; privately funded, 35–36, 43, 48; punishment for smashing, 49–51; refusal to pay for, 44–46; regulations of, 50; and smashing lanterns, 188–96, 210–11, 229–30, 234, 242–43, 296n19; and social class, 44–46, 51–52; and stealing lanterns, 50, 79, 171, 173; taxation for, 51–52; technology of, 55; as urban beautification, 37, 40, 49; and viceroys, 35–36, 40–42, 49–54, 57
surgeons, 95, 105, 117, 120–22, 169–70, 236–37

Taylor, William B., 127, 146
Tenochtitlán, 15; governance of, 7; lighting of, 32, 260; population of, 11
tobacco factory workers, 22, 187

Vanderwood, Paul, 73, 163
Venegas, Francisco de, viceroy, 56, 59, 161, 230, 232–33
vinaterías, 100–101, 185–86, 199, 208–9, 225–27

women: and arrests for sex-related offenses, 166–67, 180–83, 219, 235; asking for help from night watchmen, 63, 105; and conflicts with night watchmen, 186, 190, 198–99, 201–2, 206–9; lantern smashing, 190–91; and punishments for public intoxication, 149–53; resisting arrest, 112; and violence, 118–19, 169–70; as workers, 22, 130

IN THE CONFLUENCIAS SERIES:

The Enlightened Patrolman: Early Law Enforcement in Mexico City
By Nicole von Germeten

Strength from the Waters: A History of Indigenous Mobilization in Northwest Mexico
By James V. Mestaz

To order or obtain more information on these or other University of Nebraska Press titles, visit nebraskapress.unl.edu.

www.ingramcontent.com/pod-product-compliance
Lightning Source LLC
Chambersburg PA
CBHW031851220426
43663CB00006B/575